Creativity

Creativity: An Introduction is a systematic and straightforward introduction to the interdisciplinary study of creativity. Each chapter is written by one or more of the world's experts and features the latest research developments, alongside foundational knowledge. Each chapter also includes an introduction, key terms, and critical thought questions to promote active learning. Topics and authors have been selected to represent a comprehensive and balanced overview. Any reader will come away with a deeper understanding of how creativity is studied – and how they can improve their own creativity.

James C. Kaufman is Professor of Educational Psychology at the University of Connecticut. He is the author/editor of more than forty-five books, including *Creativity 101* (2nd Edition, 2016). Kaufman has also published books with his wife, Allison, on animal creativity and pseudoscience and a book about terrible baseball pitchers with his father, Alan. He has published more than 400 papers and won many awards, including from Mensa, APA, and NAGC. Kaufman has tested Dr. Sanjay Gupta's creativity on CNN, appeared in the hit Australia show *Redesign Your Brain*, and narrated the comic book documentary *Independents*. His musical *Discovering Magenta* played NYC.

Robert J. Sternberg is Professor of Human Development at Cornell University and Honorary Professor of Psychology at the University of Heidelberg, Germany. He is a past winner of the Grawemeyer Award in Psychology and the William James and James McKeen Cattell Awards of the Association for Psychological Science. His PhD is from Stanford University and he has been awarded thirteen honorary doctorates. He is a member of the National Academy of Education and the American Academy of Arts and Sciences. He is past president of the American Psychological Association. His work has been cited more than 190,000 times in the scholarly literature.

Creativity

An Introduction

Edited by

James C. Kaufman
University of Connecticut

Robert J. Sternberg
Cornell University

CAMBRIDGE
UNIVERSITY PRESS

CAMBRIDGE
UNIVERSITY PRESS

University Printing House, Cambridge CB2 8BS, United Kingdom

One Liberty Plaza, 20th Floor, New York, NY 10006, USA

477 Williamstown Road, Port Melbourne, VIC 3207, Australia

314–321, 3rd Floor, Plot 3, Splendor Forum, Jasola District Centre, New Delhi – 110025, India

79 Anson Road, #06-04/06, Singapore 079906

Cambridge University Press is part of the University of Cambridge.

It furthers the University's mission by disseminating knowledge in the pursuit of education, learning, and research at the highest international levels of excellence.

www.cambridge.org
Information on this title: www.cambridge.org/9781108489379
DOI: 10.1017/9781108776721

First published 2021

Printed in the United Kingdom by TJ Books Ltd, Padstow Cornwall, 2021

A catalogue record for this publication is available from the British Library.

Library of Congress Cataloging-in-Publication Data
Names: Kaufman, James C., editor. | Sternberg, Robert J., editor.
Title: Creativity : an introduction / edited by James C. Kaufman, Robert J. Sternberg.
Other titles: Creativity (Cambridge University Press)
Description: Cambridge, United Kingdom ; New York, NY : Cambridge University Press, 2021. | Includes
  bibliographical references and index.
Identifiers: LCCN 2020030217 (print) | LCCN 2020030218 (ebook) | ISBN 9781108489379 (hardback) |
  ISBN 9781108702379 (paperback) | ISBN 9781108776721 (epub)
Subjects: LCSH: Creative ability.
Classification: LCC BF408 .C75465 2021 (print) | LCC BF408 (ebook) | DDC 153.3/5–dc23
LC record available at https://lccn.loc.gov/2020030217
LC ebook record available at https://lccn.loc.gov/2020030218

ISBN 978-1-108-48937-9 Hardback
ISBN 978-1-108-70237-9 Paperback

Contents

Figures and Tables

FIGURES

TABLES

Contributors

Selcuk Acar
State University of New York College at Buffalo

Ronald A. Beghetto
Arizona State University

Ana Camargo
University of Paris

Shelley Carson
Harvard University

Herie de Vries
Yale University

Gregory Feist
San Jose State University

Marie Forgeard
William James College

Vlad P. Glăveanu
Webster University, Geneva and University of Bergen

Mavis W. J. He
The Education University of Hong Kong

Beth A. Hennessey
Wellesley College

Jessica Hoffmann
Yale Center for Emotional Intelligence, Yale University

Anna N. N. Hui
City University of Hong Kong

Zorana Ivcevic
Yale Center for Emotional Intelligence, Yale University

James C. Kaufman
University of Connecticut

Yuliya Kolomyts
University of Alabama

Todd Lubart
University of Paris

Matthew C. Makel
Talent Identification Program, Duke University

Kevin S. Mitchell
University of Nebraska at Omaha

Jonathan A. Plucker
Center for Talented Youth and School of Education, Johns Hopkins University

Meihua Qian
College of Education, Clemson University

Roni Reiter-Palmon
University of Nebraska at Omaha

Anne M. Roberts
University of Connecticut

Ryan P. Royston
University of Nebraska at Omaha

Mark A. Runco
Southern Oregon University

Dean Keith Simonton
University of California–Davis

Robert J. Sternberg
Cornell University

Martin Storme
University of Paris

Oshin Vartanian
University of Toronto

Thomas B. Ward
University of Alabama

Ellen Yang
William James College

Preface

The editors of this textbook both teach courses on creativity. There is no lack of potential textbooks for our courses, including books we have written or edited. But both of us have experienced some frustration in trying to find a textbook that fits our courses. Either the books are too long or too short, too low-level or too high-level, or just do not teach the topics we want to teach. And that is why we decided to create this textbook.

This textbook is the second in a series. The first was *Human Intelligence: An Introduction*, also published by Cambridge University Press. The third, still in preparation, will be *Wisdom: An Introduction* and will be published by Cambridge University Press as well.

Diverse people inside and outside academia are increasingly recognizing the importance of creativity. They perhaps have been slow to do so because our educational system is so driven by conventional teaching and standardized tests, neither of which particularly emphasizes creativity. But all the major contemporary engines of economic and social development gain their edge through creativity. At some level, this always has been true. But it is even more compelling in an era when knowledge and innovation leap forward at breathtaking speed.

In art, literature, music, science, and virtually every field of endeavor, the skills that lead to lasting recognition are not exactly those taught in conventional schooling or measured on standardized tests. Perhaps first among all these skills is creativity. The greats in any field – people like Scott Joplin, Charles Darwin, Marie Curie, Albert Einstein, Frida Kahlo, and Maya Angelou – are remembered for their creative contributions, not for their school grades or IQ scores.

For this textbook, we chose authors who we believed combined three characteristics. First, they are experts in their respective fields and thus bring to the task of writing chapters a diversity of perspectives and viewpoints that one would not obtain in a textbook written by just one author. Second, they are individuals in whom we had confidence regarding their ability to write at a level that would be accessible and interesting to students of creativity – both undergraduate and graduate. Third, we chose individuals who we were confident would not use their chapters to grind their own idiosyncratic point of view regarding creativity. All of us scholars in the field have such viewpoints. But a textbook is not a place to argue for just a single viewpoint. The authors have done a commendable job, we believe, of fairly representing the field as it exists today in the second decade of the millennium.

We have chosen topics that we believe represent the most important areas of theory, research, and practice in the field of creativity as it exists today. Because this is a textbook, we have had to limit the number of chapters to one that reasonably could be covered in a one-semester course on creativity. We believe you will find that virtually every important topic in creativity today is represented in our textbook.

Our textbook is written for both upper-level undergraduate and graduate-level courses on creativity. We, the editors, teach courses on creativity at both levels, and we strove to develop a textbook that could be used at both levels, as well as at schools that have students of different interests, educational experiences, and backgrounds.

Some users might wonder, why an edited textbook? We believe there are several advantages to an edited as opposed to written textbook:

- Expertise: The field of creativity has blossomed since the twentieth century and requires far more knowledge and expertise than in the past. We have chosen authors who are specialists in their particular topic within the field of creativity, so we believe we have selected those individuals who are best qualified to tackle each topic.
- Timeliness: Having an edited textbook enabled us to finish the textbook somewhat more quickly than would be the case for a single-authored book, so that readers get material that is up to date rather than written some time ago. With single-authored texts, the chapters written early are often out of date by the time the author gets to the later chapters. This is especially important in a rapidly advancing field such as that of creativity.
- Diversity: Our authors represent a welcome diversity of national origins, ethnicity, research methods, and points of view, so they are able to provide a variety of perspectives on the field that would not be possible in an authored book.

We believe our textbook is unique. It has, we suggest, the following distinctive features:

- The most distinguished group of authors one can find in the contemporary field of creativity
- The most comprehensive coverage of topics to be found in any textbook
- Absence of a single ideology or strong point of view that might discourage use of the book by those who take a different point of view
- Pedagogical features that are second to none
- Completely up-to-date coverage in a field where some of the other textbooks are becoming out of date

The textbook has a number of pedagogical features that we believe will be useful to students. The pedagogical features for each chapter include:

a. **Chapter introduction** that highlights the main conceptual issues dealt with in the chapter
b. **Chapter summary** that summarizes the main points in the chapter
c. **Bolded key terms** that are defined where they are first used
d. **Glossary** that separately defines the key terms for easy reference
e. **Five or more critical/creative thinking questions** for those students who wish to reflect more deeply on the material in the chapter
f. **My/Our Research Contribution** box that highlights in roughly 250 words what the authors see(s) as the main research contribution to the field presented in the chapter
g. **Figures and tables** that illustrate the main ideas in the textbook

We hope you find the textbook useful and fun to read. And we hope the book gives you new insights into the nature of human creativity.

We are grateful to our editors at Cambridge University Press, Stephen Acerra and David Repetto, for making the book possible, to Emily Watton for her careful editing of each chapter of the book, and to Trent Hancock for copyediting the final manuscript. Thanks also to Dr. Sareh Karami for her helpful suggestions.

1 Creativity
A Historical Perspective
VLAD P. GLĂVEANU AND JAMES C. KAUFMAN

INTRODUCTION

We are all creative, at least potentially. To create means to bring new and useful ideas or things into existence. Being creative is not a luxury but a necessity in today's changing world. Creativity is the key to success in almost all areas of life, personal and professional. Creativity can and should be educated. You can never have enough of it in most civilized societies.

The statements above will probably sound familiar to you. They reflect contemporary views of creativity that are often found within scientific research, societal debates, and policy documents. They all express the generally shared belief (at least in the West) that creativity is universal, important, and that it defines who we are as human beings and as societies. When considering these statements from a historical perspective though, we might be struck to discover that they represent an exception, rather than the norm, both in the past and nowadays. Indeed, it is not only the case that our ancestors lived, prospered, and created, for centuries, without the word "creativity," but also that the phenomena we designate with this term today have often been – and in many ways continue to be – seen as strange, undesirable, and even dangerous.

Creativity: A Historical Perspective

A deeper understanding of **history** reveals the fact that creativity is a modern concept and a modern value (Weiner, 2000; Mason, 2003; Reckwitz, 2017). It both grows out of and reinforces our general belief in the power of individuality and our capacity to create new things and ideas (Negus and Pickering, 2004). But this contemporary interest in and admiration for creativity needs to be understood in its social, scientific, technological, economic, and political context. In other words, it needs to be understood historically. What history teaches us is the fact that, just like our societies are in a constant state of transformation, so too is our conception of creativity and creative people.

Indeed, it is impossible to study the history of creativity outside of the history of civilization and ideas. If creativity is a "child" of the current era, its older incarnations – genius, talent, invention, discovery, or imagination – were also understood differently than today (for a discussion of imagination see Glăveanu, 2017a). These meanings connected to the social, political, and economic conditions at the time, which makes writing about history, particularly the history of ideas, a challenging task. Such attempts are always vulnerable to the dangers of presentism (interpreting the past through the lenses of the present). For example, from the standpoint of the present, medieval societies seem excessively traditional, closed, and stable; in other words, they would not be considered nurturing of creativity. Yet many of the cathedrals, icons, and jewels we admire today in cities and museums originated during those times (see Davids and De Munck, 2016). Are these not examples of creativity? They are, of course, but such "creativity" was not labeled or understood in the same manner as today. It was highly unlikely, for instance, for the creators of these historical artifacts to be considered the actual "authors" of their productions.

These inconsistencies make any historical account necessarily selective and incomplete. This chapter will be no different, as we aim to take a historical perspective on creativity without exhausting the richness of the events, people, and ideas that contributed to its development (if you are interested to know more about this topic do consult Weiner, 2000; Mason, 2003; and Pope, 2005). Importantly, we start from the premise that there is no single, unitary, and final history of creativity to be told. Instead, there are multiple "histories" of creativity with their own angles and perspectives; each one would tell its own narrative. In this chapter, we will thus focus on the historical development of key debates that resonate up to the present day within creativity research. But, first, why does this all matter?

Why History Matters

A great example of why history matters is offered by the word "creativity" itself. The etymological roots of the term take us back to the Latin verb *creare*, which meant bringing something forth – making or producing something. However, this notion was not applied to human creativity for several centuries. Instead, the idea of "creation" was associated with God and the generative powers of nature. As such, the earliest thirteenth-century uses of "create" were in the passive past participle (was created). It is only in the fifteenth century that the present tense (to create) and present participle (creating) of the verb began to be used (Pope, 2005). Thus, creativity was associated with the divine as opposed to the human for hundreds of years. This conception was first challenged in the **Renaissance** and replaced more or less completely during the **Enlightenment**.

The word "creativity" came into being, or at least was first documented, in 1875 in Adolfus William Ward's *History of Dramatic English Literature*, in reference to Shakespeare's "poetic creativity" (see Weiner, 2000, p. 89). The use of this word marked a radical change in our understanding of creating: from something that already happened and was out of reach to an ongoing process and, finally, a more generalizable trait or phenomenon. The word "creativity" was not very popular at first. It took over fifty years and such significant societal transformations, as World War II, for it to enter standard dictionaries and infiltrate languages other than English.

This brief story of the word "creativity" teaches us several things. First, the history of a phenomenon does not start with the moment it is named; it can (and should) be traced back to other times, words, and belief systems. Second, although we retroactively apply the word "creativity" to great works of the past, the creators of that time and their audiences would likely not understand this concept (Hanchett Hanson, 2015). Third, current studies of creativity should consider the field's proper historical context, as the "hallmark of our modern, secular, democratic, capitalistic society" (Weiner, 2000, p. 1) without, of course, being limited to such societies.

In summary, there are at least three reasons why history matters, briefly summarized below:

1. A historical approach to creativity helps us put things "in perspective" and understand the roots of both old and new debates.
2. This historical study is not only about the past; it is just as relevant to the present and the future. Knowing history allows one to see where a field is and where it is going.
3. History is said to have a tendency to repeat itself. Given the current rate at which the field of creativity research is expanding, a historical perspective can help us detect the difference between old wine being sold in new bottles from actual advances in scholarship.

The Main Historical Narrative

We do have a main narrative about the historical evolution of the idea of creativity. This narrative is rather straightforward (see Dacey, 1999; Kearney, 2009). From **Antiquity** (when the first written histories emerge) to the **Middle Ages** (from the fifth century until Columbus's voyage in 1492) to the Renaissance (a European movement between the fourteenth and seventeenth centuries), creative acts were believed to be the outcome of divine inspiration. The Renaissance marked the beginning of the long "transition" from God to human beings. This movement culminated during the Enlightenment and Romanticism in the image of the genius. After World War II, the scientific study of creativity intensified, eventually leading to a better balance between individualistic and social approaches to this phenomenon. The history of creativity thus reflects a long search for suitable explanations for how and why we create. Initially, the answers pointed outside of the person, to God or gods; gradually, the focus became more and more internal (within the abilities and characteristics of the person). In today's global age of connectivity and communication, there may be another great shift slowly underway in how we understand creativity. What are the big landmarks of this long and complex history?

Prehistory

There is little we know about the nature, value, and meaning of creative acts during prehistoric times. What is certain is a fundamental contradiction: Despite a general view of societies at the time as being primitive, static, and averse to change, some of the most important creations and inventions in the history of humanity date from that period. These include the domestication of animals, the invention of the alphabet, the creation of cities, and art that lasts to this day. Importantly, it is clear that people at the time saw some creations as valuable enough to be kept and transmitted. It is harder to discern how these achievements were thought about or how creators themselves were treated by others. Most probably, given the first records we have, the very first acts of creativity were seen as divine manifestations. This conception is well established in the Hebrew Bible, which starts with an account of how God created heaven and Earth out of nothing (ex nihilo), demonstrating what certainly would be viewed as a supreme and unparalleled creative power. Since people were made in the image of God, they could participate in His creativity by following the commandment to be fruitful and multiply. Human creativity was, in this sense, derivative and limited to strictly following God's instructions (Weiner, 2000, p. 26).

Antiquity

Interestingly, the early Greeks, who are credited with some of the greatest creative feats during **Antiquity**, were reserved when it came to human creativity. Consider the legend of Prometheus. He steals fire to give to humankind and, according to some versions, also teaches people the basic concepts of the arts and sciences. His daring, benevolence, and ingenuity are not celebrated; instead, he is eternally punished by the gods for his disobedience. Prometheus's fate warns of the danger and potential ramifications of being too "creative" and disturbing the universal order. Greek tragedies often emphasized the same message and warned their audience not to take risks or offend the gods. In exchange, the gods were able to inspire people. Homer, for instance, attributed his poetry to the divine, and Plato often pointed to the Muses. In the end, a great ambivalence toward creativity emerges from ancient times: worshipped and dangerous, moral and immoral, harmonious but also possibly disastrous (Mason, 2003).

The Middle Ages

This legacy was carried over to the **Middle Ages** when, at least in Western Europe, it was widely believed that human beings could not truly create; this ability was a prerogative of God alone. And yet, paradoxically, the Church was often a patron of what are today considered to be great creative achievements in sculpture, painting, metalwork, and architecture. The purpose of most of these was the glorification of God and any signs of individuality and authorship were discouraged. Such practices were in place to reflect the collaborative nature of the work, which was often performed in guilds by communities of craftsmen or artisans. In the end, medieval societies were not static but rather in a state of constant transformation, as can be seen by the rapid expansion of cities, technology, and trade.

The Renaissance

The heights of this cultural progress were reached during the Renaissance, the first historical era to celebrate the creative ideal and relocate it from God to men (unfortunately, women remained largely excluded). The spirit of this time blurred the line between the human and the divine. Several key inventions, such as the printing press, led to an unprecedented ability to transmit ideas and gain new knowledge. It was also a time of invention and exploration (for example, the discovery of the New World), of ingenuity and trade (anticipating the birth of capitalism), and one that encouraged individual thinking and hard work (through the Protestant Reformation). The Renaissance made it possible for creators to be acknowledged and paid for their services. As such, it cultivated creative productions in the arts and beyond. Unsurprisingly, some of the greatest creators at the time, such as Leonardo da Vinci, were polymathic geniuses. A new conception of genius, as we will see later, had its roots in this period.

The Enlightenment and Romanticism

The Enlightenment radically changed the landscape for creativity. A new belief in the power of human reason and capacity to change the world offered the foundation for a much more individual notion of creativity. The idea of progress, in particular, scientific progress, became very popular, and this fueled the Industrial Revolution and the major technological and societal breakthroughs that accompanied it. At the same time, the accumulation of wealth, even if acquired through the exploitation of others or of natural resources, came to be seen as a virtue. The ideology of individualism gained currency. Problem solving became a paradigmatic way of expressing one's creativity; the authority of the Bible and its views of creation were fundamentally challenged (Dacey, 1999). However, the celebration of reason, order, and progress left many people at the time unsatisfied. This discontent gave birth to the current of Romanticism, arguably one of the eras that had the deepest impact on modern conceptions of creativity. In contrast to the rational "light" of the Enlightenment, Romanticism emphasized torment, unhinged fantasy, and disorder (Negus and Pickering, 2004). It also established the genius as a natural category that was soon pathologized (think about the mad genius).

Contemporary Approaches

Contemporary culture is much more skeptical about glorified images of the genius. In fact, in an age of mechanical reproduction, the expression of creativity can be more associated with the mixing and remixing of existing cultural elements. The relatively easy access to culture led to a much wider "democratization" of creativity than at any other time in history. The distinction between "low" and "high" culture became blurred. Multiculturalism brought us much closer in contact with others and otherness (not necessarily turning us into more tolerant or inclusive beings and societies, however, as many events of the early twenty-first century illustrate). Speed, connectivity, and traveling define this day and age and require new, more distributed and participatory ways of conceptualizing creativity (Glăveanu, 2014; Clapp, 2016). "The Internet has reinforced the contemporary idea of creativity coming from anyone, anywhere, at any time" (Weiner, 2000, p. 107). At the same time, it has legitimized the phenomenon of ephemeral popularity or instant fame, as audiences themselves became global and, to a large extent, anonymous. Creative work is recognized today as very often being collaborative, not always out of preference but necessity. Consider, for example, the many different ways that the average person may be creative in day-to-day life, such as adding a witty comment to a Facebook post, creating a variant on an existing meme, or posting an original photo on Instagram. These creative acts (most equivalent to mini-c, or personal creativity that may not be valued by others; Beghetto and Kaufman, 2009; 2014) build off of existing cultural expressions and shared language.

Before ending this brief, chronological presentation of the "main narrative," it is important to stress that this history is fundamentally Western and, to a large extent, European and American. The West gave birth to the word "creativity" (a word of Latin origin), shaped our understanding of this phenomenon in its image, and "exported" it to other cultural spaces around the world. Unfortunately, in constructing themselves as "inventors" of creativity and its special heirs, Western societies deliberately depicted other people and other cultures as non-creative, traditional, or stuck in time. If creativity is a modern value, as we noted at the start, it is also a sign of power to be able to decide who and what is "creative." Eastern conceptions of creativity date back to Confucius (Niu, 2012) and often emphasize different components, such as harmony, societal benefit, and incremental or adaptive advances (Niu and Kaufman, 2012). Such a focus, although acknowledged in Western studies, is less often part of the dialogue about creativity. It is also important to note that the perspectives and accomplishments of female creators have often been minimized in traditional past approaches (Helson, 1990); we hope that, in moving forward, the narrative of creativity will continue to expand and include a much more diverse array of voices.

Histories of Creativity

Historical narratives about creativity are neither unitary not singular. In fact, there are many other "stories" that could be told about the ways in which past ideas and practices feed into today's conceptions. A careful study of different historical strands could shed new light on the many debates embedded within creativity research (see Glăveanu, 2013, 2016). Among them, three oppositions stand out due to their implications for how we define, measure, and enhance creativity. These concern the following aspects:

1. Creative people: **Individual** and/or **Social**?
2. Creative artifacts: **Novelty** and/or **Value**?
3. Creative process: **Ideas** and/or **Action**?

Although they constitute points of tension in the field today, each one of these pairs has their own histories, which often intersect. We will consider each in turn, pointing to the continuities (and discontinuities) between past and present thoughts on these issues. Our Conclusion will look toward the future.

Individual and/or Social

The question of whether creativity comes from within or from beyond the person is as old as the history of human civilization. Scientific research into the creative process, done soon after World War II, is based on the assumption that creativity emerges from within the individual, more specifically, from a dynamic interaction between cognition, affect, and purpose (see Gruber, 1988). This dynamic is shaped by the environment, particularly social relations, but creativity fundamentally remains an individual property or trait. And yet, as argued before, this widespread belief would have made little sense a few centuries ago. Indeed, as mentioned earlier, the first conceptions of creativity viewed it as originating completely from outside of the person, within the realm of the divine.

How did we come to prioritize the individual over his or her environment? The history of thinking about creativity can be largely seen as one of gradual individualization, starting from the Renaissance, accelerating during the Enlightenment and the Romantic period, and peaking within the neoliberal, consumerist societies of today. This process has been marked, in recent centuries, by macro-social changes (e.g., the emergence of an individual rights doctrine enforced during the American and French Revolutions), and the gradual establishment of individual recognition practices (e.g., granting copyright as a personal economic incentive to create). This individualization is matched, in recent decades, by a certain degree of "democratization" of creative potential. We have evolved from a world in which only God creates to one that glorified creative geniuses to our current common belief that everyone has the potential to be creative in some way (Weiner, 2000, p. 257).

These debates about whether or not human beings create and, if they do, whether all or only a few are destined to be creative, are crystallized in the history of genius. This notion of genius, used today to designate eminent forms of creativity (or intelligence or leadership; see Simonton, 2009), represented for centuries a way of speaking about creativity before the term was invented. Geniuses were historically revered due to their evidenced capacity to almost singlehandedly revolutionize society and transform culture. From the eighteenth century onwards, geniuses became associated with "individuality, insight, outstanding ability and, in particular, fertility" of the mind (Mason, 2003, p. 111). Just as with creativity, this (radical) individualization was, however, a historical invention.

The roots of genius are in the Latin word, *genio*, which translates to creator or begetter. Interestingly, though, the creator was not a person but rather a guardian spirit (*daimon*) assigned to the person and meant to govern his fortunes and protect the family home (Negus and Pickeri 2004). Thus, genius was initially connected to individuals and families but did not belong to the individual. The internalization of this notion was gradual and aided in the seventeenth century by the linguistic proximity between *genio* and *ingenium* or innate talent

(Negus and Pickering, 2004). Indeed, by the nineteenth century, especially through the work of Francis Galton (1874), genius became a hereditary category (nature) and the role of the environment (nurture) was minimized. Not all scholars at the time agreed with this assessment; William James was one of the first scientists to argue for an interaction between genetic heredity and environment in the makeup of geniuses (Dacey, 1999). Calls to consider genius in more social terms and as an ideological belief (used to promote an elitist view of certain people or groups within society) continue to this day (Negus and Pickering, 2004).

Another factor pointing toward the internalization of genius has historically been the close connection between this phenomenon and madness. Mental illness was often used to account for the creative achievements of great artists, musicians, and writers, primarily by nineteenth-century authors such as Augustin Morel, Cesare Lombroso, and Max Nordau (G. Becker, 2014). Once more, the history of these associations is much older since, as Eysenck (1995) noted, there was no distinction made in Latin between madness and inspiration, which was often seen as a form of demonic possession. Romantics associated the individual genius with mental illness to such an extent that some Romantic poets and artists were known to embrace madness in part because they felt compelled to do it (Sawyer, 2012); how else could they demonstrate their creativity? G. Becker (2014) also attributed the image of the mad genius to Romanticism. He argued that the connection between creativity and mental illness is not entirely fabricated and that a good amount of current research today connects genius with manic-depressive symptoms or mood disorders. Although we acknowledge some studies supporting the mad-genius stereotype (Simonton, 2014a, 2014b), much past research has been strongly challenged (Schlesinger, 2009, 2012). The general consensus is that the connection between creativity and mental illness is slight at best and much more nuanced and context-dependent than previously assumed (Kaufman, 2016b).

The decade of the 1950s proposed a much broader conception of creativity as a widespread process and a personal trait that can and should be educated. Guilford's (1950) APA address emerged at a time in which the scientific climate in the United States were ripe for studies of little-c or mundane creativity (Kaufman and Beghetto, 2009) and creative potential. Meanwhile, the sociopolitical climate in the United States, with the Cold War and competition with the Russians to explore space, led to an emphasis on giftedness and creativity in the educational system (Cropley, 2015). As creativity became more egalitarian and moved away from belonging only to the elite, the association with mental illness became weaker (Silvia and Kaufman, 2010; Kaufman, 2014). Further, more attention was paid to possible positive mental-health benefits of creativity (Barron, 1963). Creativity grew to be celebrated not only as an individual quality but also as a personal responsibility, particularly in the West. People were implicitly expected to cultivate their creative potential, to live a successful life and contribute to society. This discourse fits the broader cultural landscape in America, defined by the values of individualism, industriousness, and the image of the self-made man.

However, this democratization of creativity did not take into account the role of the social environment except as something to be confronted and defied (see Sternberg, 2018, for more on creativity as defiance). It was not until the 1980s that more systemic or distributed conceptions of creativity began to flourish (e.g., Csikszentmihalyi, 1988). Today's interconnected world offers a new opportunity to address this dichotomy and "socialize" not only our practices of creativity but also our theories of it.

Novelty and/or Value

After 1950, creativity grew as a topic for academic study. It has been explicitly defined more or less consistently in terms of two components: novelty/originality and value/appropriateness (see Runco and Jaeger, 2012). These two dimensions are considered equally important by researchers although, in practice, there is a tendency (at least within Western societies) for novelty/originality to be the object of more research studies (Kaufman, 2016a) and to be more closely aligned with lay beliefs (Sternberg, 1985) than value/appropriateness. Of course, this will depend on the domain in which creativity is expressed.

The arts and the sciences, for example, are two broad domains of creativity that offer distinct views of the creative process and its products. Consider the arts – they are based on divergence and self-expression, highly likely to produce novelty, and can be messy and unpredictable. The sciences are more likely to gravitate toward convergence and effective problem-solving, potentially practical outcomes, functionality, and orderliness (Kaufman and Baer, 2002; Cropley and Cropley, 2010). The historical debate between Romanticism and the Enlightenment continues to play out in our understanding of artistic and scientific creativity.

If we move further back in time, we can notice that the first question that animated this debate was whether creating anything new was even possible. As mentioned earlier, the dominant conception during Antiquity and the Middle Ages was that God (or the gods) is the true source of novelty and that human activity is merely a reproduction of His creation. For Aristotle, arts and crafts were essentially imitative; his teacher, Plato, went even further by postulating that art is a copy of a copy since it tries to imitate nature, which already imitates eternal ideas (Weiner, 2000). These views make the biblical feat of God, of creating the world out of nothingness, even more extraordinary. In contrast, human activity was reduced to a derivative form. There is "nothing new under the sun" (1:9), claims the author of Ecclesiastes, and striving to produce novelties only reveals our "vanity."

In contrast, today "making the new is our culture's agenda" (Weiner, 2000, p. 98). So, how exactly did we get from believing novelty is impossible to placing it as the cornerstone of our societies in many domains? The key to understanding this evolution resides in the notion of self-expression and its glorification during the Romantic period (Negus and Pickering, 2004). Romanticism exulted the human capacity to imagine and, above all, the possibility of a creative – not only reproductive – imagination (Glăveanu, 2017a). Self-expression was infused by both imagination and affect and was considered essential for creativity in the arts. Later on, at the dawn of Modernism, this focus on self-expression gave way to novelty; for example, Impressionist painters started being concerned with the novel aspects of their work and with visibly breaking with the old traditions of the Academy.

More contemporary echoes of these concerns can be found in the work of Maslow (1943) and his ideas about self-actualization. The actualized self experiences life fully, spontaneously, and independently of others' opinions and views. It is, ultimately, a person who embraces novelty, lives a psychologically healthy life, and is capable of acting creatively in relation to both self and others.

More contemporary associations with creative value move us away from the sphere of individual well-being and health and toward capitalist concerns for production and consumption. Much of creativity's current popularity is its perceived contribution mainly to the economy, including creative economy, and rapidly evolving technology. This market orientation seeks novelty inasmuch as it can attract interest and produce tangible rewards – in other words, as long as it sells. At the same time, creative contributions that are highly original run the risk of being ahead of their time and only appreciated in retrospect, whereas small incremental advances can be more profitable in the short term (Sternberg, Kaufman, and Pretz, 2001; 2003).

The increased focus on value/appropriateness is only one of many shifting perspectives on the creative product throughout history. Why do these historical considerations matter today? It is because our contemporary definition of creativity is not accidental and neither are the measures we use to evaluate creative work (see Glăveanu, 2017c). Divergent thinking is quintessentially a task aimed at revealing self-expression and spontaneity. Converging-thinking tasks (as well as related insight and problem-solving tests) take a more orderly and oftentimes logical approach. It should not surprise us, then, if the creativity we measure with one differs from the creativity we identify with the other. In the end, creativity requires both divergent and convergent processes. The key question, from a historical perspective, is which "legacy" are we actually continuing and with what consequences?

Ideas and/or Action

The biblical story of Genesis begins with God creating the world through the power of His word. This story illustrates the divine prerogative of creating something out of nothing; it also points to the importance of speech for the act of creation itself. God's word precedes His actions in His creative process. Indeed, although in a completely different context, we still uphold that creativity starts from an idea and is usually communicated through language (which can be words but also musical notes, dance moves, or numbers and symbols). The popular metaphor of the lightbulb, often associated with creativity, is based on this assumption: Creativity begins in one's mind in the form of insight. Broadly speaking, to reach creative achievement, this insight needs additional components, such as the knowledge and experience to nurture the idea and the actions needed to implement and produce the idea.

This debate between prioritizing ideas versus embodied action – between head versus hands – can be traced back to centuries-long discussions about arts and crafts. The arts have long been considered to depend on the power to generate creative ideas or perspectives (think, for example, about the cubist visions of Picasso), whereas crafts are often – incorrectly – traditionally associated with the skillful making of objects, oftentimes repetitive or unimaginative. Similar comparisons can be seen in music (the composer versus the orchestra musician) or dance (the choreographer versus ensemble member). In European cultures, the arts – particularly the fine arts – have been considered superior, whereas craft objects are seen as less worthy and certainly not very creative (Sawyer, 2012). This hierarchy, however, is a product of the past couple of centuries. It does not reflect how the relationship between art and craft has been conceived for much of Western history and it certainly doesn't do justice to the actual creativity of craftsmen, musicians, and dancers.

The story again begins in Antiquity, in the discussion about novelty and imitation referred to in the previous section. It is not only that arts and crafts were considered imitative at this time (like any other form of human creativity) but that both relied on craftsmanship or technique. The Greek word *techne*, which can be roughly translated by making or the making of things according to rules, referred to both types of activities. In other words, there was no distinction between artists and artisans, at least not in the way we make it today (Nelson, 2010). Art was not about creative ideas but "a practice that could be taught and learnt" (p. 55). It was a notion applied by the Romans to any kind of masterful activity. This meaning is rare in contemporary culture but not altogether gone (e.g., references to the art of cooking, the art of management).

Once more, the Renaissance marked a shift in this conception by considering the great artists of the time as more than craftsmen and separating artistic creativity from mere technique. It was by appealing to this superior status that artists were able to claim and receive the support of rich patrons interested in cultivating "real" creations. It is then no surprise that when the word "creative" appeared, it was first associated with the arts in the middle of the nineteenth century (Pope, 2005). The Romantic elevation of art to a superior status was done at the expense of craft activities, which became mundane and considered less (or not) creative. The distinction between "fine" and "applied," "folk" or "decorative" arts, dates from this time and continues to be popular today, despite other efforts to consider both within an integrative framework (see, for instance, the Arts and Crafts Movement). Interestingly, this distinction is being deliberately blurred today, with craftsmen aspiring to be recognized for their art and artists relinquishing their status and trying to go beyond "intentional" and "conceptual" art with the help of craft techniques (for a discussion of this process, see H. Becker, 2008).

How are these shifts reflected in creativity theory? Building on historical preference for ideation over action, the field has developed many models focused on the way in which people generate and evaluate ideas. Materiality and the body are still hard to integrate within psychology (Moro, 2015), including the psychology of creativity. However, with the resurgence of craft in popular culture – reflected, for example, in the Do It Yourself (DIY) and Makerspace movement – one can expect more interest in the future for the craft dimensions of creativity (see Glăveanu, 2017b).

My Research Contribution

Creativity As Craft – Vlad Glăveanu

One of the things I have advocated for most when it comes to creativity is the fact that to create doesn't mean only to think but to do or make things. Thinking itself is not opposed to or different from action; it represents an integral part of it. As such, getting creative ideas is integrated within wider systems of activity in which we engage with the world not only as brains but as bodies and, most of all, as social and cultural beings. I have spent five years studying this dynamic in the case of craft – in particular Easter egg decoration in Romanian communities – and what this case study has shown me is that being creative is a highly embodied and social process. This process requires learning (often in the form of apprenticeships), habits (to perfect one's abilities), community support, and cultural resources (outside of which no creativity is possible). And it also made me think that these are not only features specific to craft but a wider range of human creative activities. Being an artist, designer, or scientist, for instance, involves crafting ideas and products that relate to – build on and sometimes go against – certain traditions and communities. And they all need time and exercise. In the end, the insight or aha moment of creative thinking that we often talk about in history is integrated within long-term forms of activity that lead to mastery and masterful performances.

CONCLUSION

We started this chapter with a few arguments for why the study of history matters in creativity studies. We argued that it is of great value for contextualizing and understanding the roots of today's ideas but that it can also, paradoxically, shed light on the future. In the end, all predictions of the future are grounded in past experience (Schacter, Addis, and Buckner, 2008). So, what does the long history creativity's lineage tell us about its present state and current directions?

First, it shows how conceptions about creativity and its many facets – individual and social, based on novelty and on value, grounded in ideation and action – are intertwined with our conceptions of human beings, God, society, and culture. More than most phenomena studied within psychology, the way we define and study creativity has deep implications for how we see ourselves – as more or less agentic beings, as determined by our society and culture or actively shaping it, as different from or similar to the divine or as both at the same time. How we answer each of these questions has an impact on how we measure, nurture, and utilize creativity. Do we emphasize inspiration? Do we pay equal attention to the craft and quality of a creative product? Are creators challenging the divine order and inviting potentially negative perceptions and traits (Yahn and Kaufman, 2015), or is their creativity reflecting a deeper greatness? A careful reading of history can inform our current beliefs of creativity as well as make us aware that our thoughts and perceptions can continue to evolve and change (as they have in the past).

Second, studying the history of a field makes us more aware of our own contributions to it. Indeed, as Hanchett Hanson (2015) notes, we are actors that maintain and construct certain ideologies of creativity (understood here as systems of belief rather than biased or manipulative conceptions). How are we using this agency? What kind of agendas do we promote or continue through our work? And what kind of visions of individuals and society are associated with them? The questions we ask help to guide the field as much as the answers to these questions.

Bakhtin (1929/1973) famously wrote that the final word about reality had not been spoken and that human beings and their society are always in the making and open to change. This thought applies even more to a topic such as creativity, which is so grounded in notions of change and transformation. As the world faces unprecedented challenges – environmental, economic, social, and political – the stakes are higher than ever for creativity researchers and practitioners to understand the history of their field and to continue writing it.

Critical/Creative Thinking Questions

1. The history of creativity presented here is mostly a Western history. How might its trajectory look if we were to consider it from another perspective, such as an Eastern or Global South one? Or think about the history of creativity in your own specific country.
2. Women's creativity has been either ignored or outright oppressed for much of our history. What major historical contributions from women in history can you identify that left their mark on our understanding of creativity?
3. While the Renaissance generated the conditions for a historical shift in our view of creativity and creative people, it is arguably Romanticism that shaped our current conceptions of creativity the most. Would you agree with this statement?
4. Consider a particular creative discipline or domain that you enjoy. How has the history of creativity in that area evolved? How similar is it to the more general narrative presented here?
5. History matters for the present and for the future. What would you predict might be the next developments in our understanding of creativity based on current societal and technological transformations?

GLOSSARY

action: The coordination between psychological processes and behavioral expression that, in the case of humans, is intentional, goal-oriented, and culturally mediated.

Antiquity: The period between the emergence of recorded (written) history and the start of the Middle Ages, roughly 3000 BC to the mid-400s AD.

Enlightenment: A philosophical and intellectual movement focused on the values of reason and science that dominated Europe in the eighteenth century.

history: The set of narratives we hold about past events, typically concerning the evolution of society but also particular groups or ideas within it (for example, the history of ideas about creativity).

idea: The mental representation of objects, states, people, or events that is constructed through experience with the help of specific mental processes, for example, combination, abstraction, and generalization.

individual: The person with his or her biological and psychological makeup, from genes to mental functions such as personality and intelligence.

Middle Ages: In the history of Europe, it is a period that lasted roughly between the mid-400s to 1492 (marking Columbus's first voyage to the Americas), described by a feudal organization of society and the dominance of religious thought.

novelty: The property of ideas or things being different from what existed before.

Renaissance: A cultural, intellectual, and artistic movement in Europe between the fourteenth and seventeenth centuries considered as a rebirth and reevaluation of ideals from Antiquity.

social: The sphere of interpersonal and intergroup processes including phenomena such as communication, social influence, and groupwork.

value: The quality of ideas or things that makes them useful for solving a problem or appropriate for a specific task.

REFERENCES

Bakhtin, M. (1973). *Problems of Dostoevsky's Poetics*, 2nd ed. R. W. Rotsel (Trans.). Ann Arbor: Ardis. (Original work published 1929)

Barron, F. (1963). *Creativity and Psychological Health*. Princeton: D. Van Nostrand Company.

Becker, G. (2014). A Socio-Historical Overview of the Creativity – Pathology Connection: From Antiquity to Contemporary Times. In J. C. Kaufman (Ed.), *Creativity and Mental Illness* (pp. 3–24). New York: Cambridge University Press.

Becker, H. S. (2008). *Art Worlds: Updated and Expanded*. Berkeley: University of California Press.

Beghetto, R. A., and Kaufman, J. C. (2009). Intellectual Estuaries: Connecting Learning and Creativity in Programs of Advanced Academics. *Journal of Advanced Academics, 20*, 296–324.

(2014). Classroom Contexts for Creativity. *High Ability Studies, 25*, 53–69.

Clapp, E. P. (2016). *Participatory Creativity: Introducing Access and Equity to the Creative Classroom*. London: Routledge.

Cropley, D. H. (2015). *Creativity in Engineering: Novel Solutions to Complex Problems*. San Diego: Academic Press.

Cropley, D. H., and Cropley, A. J. (2010). Functional Creativity: "Products" and the Generation of Effective Novelty. In J. C. Kaufman and R. J. Sternberg (Eds.), *The Cambridge Handbook of Creativity* (pp. 301–317). New York: Cambridge University Press.

Csikszentmihalyi, M. (1988). Society, Culture, and Person: A Systems View of Creativity. In R. Sternberg (Ed.), *The Nature of Creativity: Contemporary Psychological Perspectives* (pp. 325–339). Cambridge: Cambridge University Press.

Dacey, J. (1999). Concepts of Creativity: A History. In M. Runco and S. Pritzker (Eds.), *Encyclopaedia of Creativity*, vol. 1 (pp. 309–322). San Diego: Academic Press.

Davids, K., and De Munck, B. (Eds.) (2016). *Innovation and Creativity in Late Medieval and Early Modern European Cities*. London: Routledge.

Galton, F. (1874). *English Men of Science: Their Nature and Nurture*. London: Macmillan.

Glăveanu, V. P. (2013). From Dichotomous to Relational Thinking in the Psychology of Creativity: A Review of Great Debates. *Creativity and Leisure: An Intercultural and Cross-Disciplinary Journal, 1*(2), 83–96.

(2014). *Distributed Creativity: Thinking outside the Box of the Creative Individual*. Cham: Springer.

(2016). The Psychology of Creating: A cultural-Developmental Approach to Key Dichotomies within Creativity Studies. In V. P. Glăveanu (Ed.), *The Palgrave Handbook of Creativity and Culture Research* (pp. 205–224). London: Palgrave.

(2017a). From Fantasy and Imagination to Creativity: Towards Both a "Psychology with Soul" and a "Psychology with Others". In B. Wagoner, I. Bresco, and S. H. Awad (Eds.), *The Psychology of Imagination: History, Theory and New Research Horizons* (pp. 175–189). Charlotte: Information Age.

(2017b). Creativity in Craft. In J. C. Kaufman, V. P. Glăveanu, and J. Baer (Eds.), *The Cambridge Handbook of Creativity in Different Domains* (pp. 616–634). Cambridge: Cambridge University Press.

(2017c). Creativity in Perspective: A Sociocultural and Critical Account. *Journal of Constructivist Psychology, 31*, 118–129.

Gruber, H. E. (1988). The Evolving Systems Approach to Creative Work. *Creativity Research Journal, 1*, 27–51.

Guilford, J. P. (1950). Creativity. *American Psychologist, 5*, 444–454.

Hanchett Hanson, M. (2015). *Worldmaking: Psychology and the Ideology of Creativity*. London: Palgrave Macmillan.

Helson, R. (1990). Creativity in Women: Outer and Inner Views over Time. In M. A. Runco and R. S. Albert (Eds.), *Theories of Creativity* (pp. 46–58). Newbury Park: Sage.

Kaufman, J. C. (Ed.) (2014). *Creativity and Mental Illness*. New York: Cambridge University Press.

(2016a). *Creativity 101*, 2nd ed. New York: Springer.

(2016b). Creativity and Mental Illness: So Many Studies, So Many Wrong Conclusions. In J. A. Plucker (Ed.), *Creativity and innovation: Theory, Research, and Practice* (pp. 199–204). Waco: Prufrock Press.

Kaufman, J. C., and Baer, J. (2002). Could Steven Spielberg Manage the Yankees?: Creative Thinking in Different Domains. *Korean Journal of Thinking and Problem Solving, 12*, 5–15.

Kaufman, J. C., and Beghetto, R. A. (2009). Beyond Big and Little: The Four C Model of Creativity. *Review of General Psychology, 13*, 1–12.

Kearney, K. (2009). History of Creativity. In B. Kerr (Ed.), *Encyclopedia of Giftedness, Creativity, and Talent* (pp. 425–427). Thousand Oaks: Sage.

Maslow, A. H. (1943). A Theory of Human Motivation. *Psychological Review, 50*(4), 370.

Mason, J. H. (2003). *The Value of Creativity: The Origins and Emergence of a Modern Belief*. Hampshire: Ashgate.

Moro, C. (2015). Material Culture: Still "Terra Incognita" for Psychology Today? *Europe's Journal of Psychology, 11*(2), 172–176.

Negus, K., and Pickering, M. (2004). *Creativity, Communication and Cultural Value*. London: Sage.

Niu, W. (2012). Confucian Ideology and Creativity. *The Journal of Creative Behavior, 46*, 274–284.

Niu, W., and Kaufman, J. C. (2013). Creativity of Chinese and American People: A Synthetic Analysis. *Journal of Creative Behavior, 47*, 77–87.

Pope, R. (2005). *Creativity: Theory, History, Practice*. London: Routledge.

Reckwitz, A. (2017). *The Invention of Creativity: Modern Society and the Culture of the New*. Cambridge: Polity.

Runco, M. A., and Jaeger, G. J. (2012). The Standard Definition of Creativity. *Creativity Research Journal*, *24*(1), 92–96.

Sawyer, K. (2012). *Explaining Creativity: The Science of Human Innovation*, 2nd ed. Oxford: Oxford University Press.

Schacter, D. L., Addis, D. R., and Buckner, R. L. (2008). Episodic Simulation of Future Events. *Annals of the New York Academy of Sciences*, *1124*(1), 39–60.

Schlesinger, J. (2009). Creative Mythconceptions: A Closer Look at the Evidence for "Mad Genius" Hypothesis. *Psychology of Aesthetics, Creativity, and the Arts*, *3*, 62–72.

(2012). *The Insanity Hoax: Exposing the Myth of the Mad Genius*. New York: Shrinktunes Media.

Silvia, P. J., and Kaufman, J. C. (2010). Creativity and Mental Illness. In J. C. Kaufman and R. J. Sternberg (Eds.), *The Cambridge Handbook of Creativity* (pp. 381–394). New York: Cambridge University Press.

Simonton, D. K. (2009). *Genius 101*. New York: Springer.

(2014a). The Mad-Genius Paradox: Can Creative People Be More Mentally Healthy but Highly Creative People More Mentally Ill? *Perspectives on Psychological Science*, *9*, 470–480.

(2014b). More Method in the Mad-Genius Controversy: A Historiometric Study of 204 Historic Creators. *Psychology of Aesthetics, Creativity, and the Arts*, *8*, 53–61.

Sternberg, R. J. (1985). Implicit Theories of Intelligence, Creativity, and Wisdom. *Journal of Personality and Social Psychology*, *49*, 607–627.

(2018). A Triangular Theory of Creativity. *Psychology of Aesthetics, Creativity, and the Arts*, *12*, 50–67.

Sternberg, R. J., Kaufman, J. C., and Pretz, J. E. (2001). The Propulsion Model of Creative Contributions Applied to the Arts and Letters. *Journal of Creative Behavior*, *35*, 75–101.

Sternberg, R. J., Pretz, J. E., and Kaufman, J. C. (2003). Types of Innovations. In L. Shavinina (Ed.), *The International Handbook of Innovation* (pp. 158–169). Mahwah: Lawrence Erlbaum.

Weiner, R. P. (2000). *Creativity and Beyond: Cultures, Values, and Change*. New York: State University of New York Press.

Yahn, L., and Kaufman, J. C. (2016). Asking the Wrong Question: Why Shouldn't People Dislike Creativity? In D. Ambrose and R. J. Sternberg (Eds.), *Creative Intelligence in the 21st Century* (pp. 75–88). Rotterdam: Sense Publishers.

2 An Overview of Creativity Theories

JAMES C. KAUFMAN AND VLAD P. GLĂVEANU

INTRODUCTION

Creativity is a vast topic that can encompass so many different things. When we talk about creativity, we could be talking about a sudden moment of insight, a beautiful painting, Beyoncé, an improv group working together, a new printer that uses less ink, a child learning to tell a story, or a scientific equation. If we want to sort out how we can even try to study such a multifaceted concept, we need different theories that can propose how we can think about creativity, what are the necessary ingredients to be creative, how we can encourage ourselves or others to be creative, and so many other possible questions.

A strong creativity theory can break down complicated or massive ideas into smaller units that can be studied. A good theory can offer compelling reasons for why some constructs might be associated with other ones. Theories can pose questions and make predictions that can be tested. Creativity scholars propose theories to try to explain, connect, or unpack creativity and to inspire future research. In this chapter, we will highlight some important theories.

Before diving into creativity theory, we should start with a basic definition. Although you may hear people say that no one can agree on what creativity is, that is not true for creativity researchers. There is strong consensus about how to define creativity, with two traditional components (Guilford, 1950; Barron, 1955; Hennessey and Amabile, 2010; Simonton, 2012). First, creativity is something that is new and original. Second, creativity is task-appropriate; in other words, it meets the basic requirements of whatever it is attempting to do. A task can be as small as doodling for amusement's sake or as big as designing a space shuttle; the basic requirements for each are radically different. There are many possible additional components to this definition, such as high quality (Sternberg, 1999a), surprise (Boden, 2004), aesthetics, authenticity (Kharkhurin, 2014), and the creation of a product (Plucker, Beghetto, and Dow, 2004).

Going beyond a basic definition, however, it gets more complicated. Creativity can mean so many different things that simply cataloging the most-cited theories would be as coherent as learning modern cinema by seeing a minute-long clip of every Oscar-winning movie. We will therefore aim to highlight key theories based on the questions they ask.

Here are our interpretations of how creativity theories answer different core questions, from the underlying structure of creativity, its prerequisites, and drivers to how we create alone and together and what makes creative works last.

What Is the Underlying Structure of Creativity?

Some theories aim to uncover the underlying structure of creativity. Even within these parameters, there are diverse approaches. Is it how creativity is studied or conceptualized? Perhaps it is how creativity evolves within a person or how the domains of creativity align together.

One of the foundations of creativity research is the Four P framework proposed by Rhodes (1961), who reviewed the existing literature to see how creativity was being studied. He synthesized everything into four primary categories, which are known as the **Four P's**: Person, Product, Process, and Press (i.e., environment). The Four P's represent four possible questions: What type of person is creative? What is considered to be creative? How do we create? How does the environment shape creativity? The Four P's are focused on the way that an individual creates.

More recently, Glăveanu (2013) updated this basic vocabulary by proposing a Five A framework including Actors, Audiences, Actions, Artifacts, and Affordances (or material resources). This framework not only recognizes the "double" nature of the environment (both social and material) but raises new questions about the interrelation between different elements of creativity: How do actors relate to their audiences in creativity? How does creative action make use of sociocultural and material **affordances**? And do creative actors use existing artifacts in producing new ones? The **Five A's** are focused on how individuals interact together.

If the Four P's and the Five A's are theories that explore the underlying structure of how creativity is operationalized, the Four C's is a developmental trajectory that is more focused on the individual. It is an expansion of the distinction between **little-c** (everyday creativity) and **Big-C** (eminent creativity). The first stage is **mini-c** (Beghetto and Kaufman, 2007), which is creativity that is personally meaningful and new to the creator, even if not to others. Mini-c can evolve into little-c with appropriate feedback and guidance, to the point that something is recognized as being creative by other people. Years of deliberate practice, training, and growth are required to improve one's creativity to the point that she or he is considered a true creative professional or expert; this stage is called **Pro-c** (Kaufman and Beghetto, 2009). Finally, if someone's creativity is so genius that it continues to be a legacy for years after his or her death, then it can be considered Big-C. One of the key elements of the Four C's is recognizing that, although there are certainly differences between a child writing a first story, a published author, and Toni Morrison, all levels of creativity "count" and have value.

The structural models presented in this section reflect the field and encompass many of its core issues. They offer useful lenses through which to study concrete acts of creativity. However, if the Four P's/Five A's or the Four C's can be applied to any situation, we still need to reflect on what is required for creative action to actually take place.

What Is Needed to Be Creative?

Another category of theories thus focuses on the ingredients necessary for creativity. What attributes, abilities, and circumstances must unite for creativity to emerge? These are sometimes called componential approaches, and, indeed, one of the leading ones is the **componential model of creativity** (Amabile, 1983, 1996). In the original model, Amabile proposed that three interconnected variables were the key to individual creativity (and organizational creativity; Amabile, 1988). The first was domain-relevant skills, which are technical skills and talents and specific knowledge. Creativity-relevant processes are broader, such as being tolerant of ambiguity and willing to take appropriate risks. Finally, she included intrinsic motivation, taking part in an activity because it is enjoyable or meaningful. Extrinsic motivation, in contrast, is when someone is driven by an external reason, such as money, grades, or praise. A creative writer, for example, might have domain-relevant skills such as being able to construct a narrative and use beautiful language, creativity-relevant processes such as being curious about the world and wanting to understand other people, and intrinsic motivation in that she enjoys telling stories and finds the act of creative writing fun and valuable.

Four additional pieces have been added for the revised model (Amabile and Pratt, 2016). Intrinsic motivation is now paired with synergistic extrinsic motivation, which occurs when external motivators are present yet either add to or are consistent with a person's knowledge, competence, values, and engagement (Deci and Ryan, 1985). Work orientation (which can include, among other things, seeing work as a job, a career, a calling, or a passion; Pratt, Pradies, and Lepisto, 2013) can impact one's motivation. Affect (specifically positive affect) plays a role as a creativity-related process and can enhance motivation. Finding meaning in one's work can increase both motivation and affect.

Also noteworthy is the **investment theory of creativity** (Sternberg and Lubart, 1995), which uses a central analogy of a creative person being comparable to a financial investor. To be creative, one needs to buy low and sell high in the world of ideas. Thus, the successful creator can recognize undervalued ideas, convince others of their worth, and then move on to the next project. Sternberg and Lubart propose six different components that need to be consistent with creative values: motivation, intelligence, knowledge, personality, thinking styles, and environment. So, for example, an ideal pattern for a creative person might be someone who is intrinsically motivated, has relevant cognitive strengths and appropriate domain knowledge, is open to experiences (e.g., Feist, 1998), has a legislative (creative and self-directed) thinking style (Sternberg, 1999b), and develops within a nurturing (or at least tolerant) environment.

Part of being a successful creator according to this theory is the willingness to defy the crowd. Sternberg (2018) expanded and developed this concept in his **triangular theory of creativity**. In this theory, he posits that creative people need to not only defy the crowd (such as other people) but also be able to defy their own beliefs and values and to defy the current Zeitgeist (the existing shared presuppositions of a domain).

One commonality in both Amabile's and Sternberg's evolving theoretical models is that motivation is essential. Amabile places motivation at the heart of her model, and Sternberg's idea of defiance requires a strong drive and will. What makes people feel that need to be creative?

What Drives People to Be Creative?

The desire to create goes beyond creativity research; it is a core human need (Lifton, 2011). Yet what are the mechanisms behind this need? Given the many obstacles and challenges that face those who create (Sternberg and Kaufman, 2018), not to mention basic inertia and the many other demands for one's time, why do people continually make the choice for creativity?

Gruber's (1988; Gruber and Wallace, 1999) **evolving systems approach** conceptualized creativity as a need to answer questions that triggered the creator's curiosity. This approach looks at creative work over time and considers the dynamic between knowledge, affect, and purpose in creativity. It aims to understand what exactly makes creators passionate about what they do.

One articulation of this passion is Csikszentmihalyi's (1996) optimal experience, better known as **flow**. When people are intensely engaged in a favorite (yet still challenging) activity, they may enter an exhilarating, pleasurable moment of complete absorption. This sensation, called flow, is rewarding by itself; as a result, people may be creative simply to experience these feelings without worrying as much about a specific end goal or external reason.

A different motivational theory is the **matrix model** (Unsworth, 2001), from industrial/ organizational psychology. This model focuses on the reason (or motivation) and context (the type of problem to be solved). A reason can be intrinsic (driven by enjoyment) or extrinsic (driven by rewards) and a problem can be open or closed. The corresponding matrix suggests four types of creativity. Responsive creativity (extrinsic, closed) involves doing a specific task for an extrinsic reason. Expected creativity (extrinsic, open) is being asked to be creative; there is more freedom, but the impetus is still someone else. Contributory creativity (intrinsic, closed) is being engaged and interested but focused on a specific, often more narrow problem. Finally, proactive creativity is creating for your own reasons and to your own specifications (and is likely the most comparable to most conceptions of creativity).

A common theme of these theories is that our reason for being creative is important, and this reason intersects with the specific situation (such as the desired audience or the context of the problem). Although having an internal, personal reason for creating is usually associated with better outcomes, it is not so simple (see Chapter 10 in this volume, for a thorough discussion). In many ways, motivation is the spark that enables creative action. Once this action is underway, however, the focus shifts to the actual process of being creative.

How Do We Create?

Once someone has the needed components and has the drive to be creative, what is the actual process like? Some of the earliest theoretical work in creativity scholarship has tried to answer this question. Wallas (1926), in his book *The Art of Thought*, tackled these ideas with a model of the cognitive creative process that is still used today. Wallas's first stage was preparation, in which the problem solver begins to study and gather knowledge. Next comes incubation, in which the mind keeps thinking about the question even if the person is doing other tasks. This stage may be brief or last a long time. His third stage, intimation, is often dropped from modern perspectives on his work; it is the moment of realizing a breakthrough is imminent. In the illumination phase, the person has the "aha" moment – the awaited insight in which the solution appears. Finally, the verification phase is when the idea is tested, expanded, and implemented.

Wallas proposed a stage or phase model of creativity. However, in time, and especially following the cognitive revolution, a new interest developed for mental processes underpinning the entire creativity cycle (see Lubart, 2001). An example of an early and influential model in this regard is Guilford's (1950, 1967) structure of intellect model. Although primarily an intelligence theory, creativity figured prominently; it was not until Sternberg's (1985) Triarchic theory and modified theory of successful intelligence (Sternberg, 1996) that another intelligence framework so heavily featured creativity (Kaufman and Plucker, 2011). Two of Guilford's proposed thought processes were divergent and convergent thinking. **Divergent thinking** is the ability to think of as many different possible solutions to an open-ended question or problem, whereas **convergent thinking** is choosing which idea or answer is most worth pursuing. These two thinking processes are sometimes called idea generation and idea evaluation. The concept of divergent thinking is the central conceit behind most creativity tests, such as the Torrance Tests of Creative Thinking (Torrance, 1974, 2008).

Some current conceptions of the creative process have roots in Wallas's and Guilford's scholarship. There are many different models of creative problem solving, such that examining each one in detail is beyond the scope of this chapter. (Sawyer, 2012, presents an excellent synthesis.) These stages have also been linked to how people appreciate creative work. Many of these models include variants of preparation, idea generation, idea evaluation, and validation. Perhaps the most notable addition has been problem construction (Mumford et al., 1991; Reiter-Palmon and Robinson, 2009). This early stage (often the first step to be taken) requires one to understand and identify the exact problem that needs to be solved; it can extend to deciding which problem one wants to pursue in the first place (Zuckerman, 1978). In exercises or tests, the problem is often presented explicitly; in life, the nature of the problem is not always clear. If you are losing money each month, for example, you might perceive the problem to be either not having enough income or having too many expenses. Your understanding of the problem would greatly influence your selection of solutions.

Some models of the creative process take a deeper look at specific components. The Geneplore (Generate-Explore) model (Finke, Ward, and Smith, 1992) is an expansion of Guilford's original concept of idea generation and evaluation. In the first generative phase, the problem solver develops mental representations of possible solutions, called preinventive structures. In the second, explorative phase, these different preinventive structures are evaluated for how well they would fit within the constraints of the desired goal. Several different cycles may occur before a workable and creative solution is found.

Another prominent theory of the creative process is Mednick's (1962) **associative theory**, which emphasizes the ability to make connections between remote concepts or ideas. When presented with a word, according to this theory, a more creative person could generate related words that would be less commonly associated. For example, the word "milk" might inspire most people to say "cow" or "white," but more remote associations might include "mustache" (as in a milk mustache) or "Jersey" (a breed of cow). Notice, however, that this ability is heavily reliant on knowledge, intelligence, and culture (Kaufman, 2016).

The models of the creative process presented in this section call our attention to a wide range of phases and processes within and across them. Despite this variety, they nonetheless all focus exclusively on the individual creator. However, in real life (particularly as technology continues to advance), we are more likely to create in implicit and explicit collaboration with other people. Such scenarios mean that modern creators are likely to also consider and integrate other people's ideas and perspectives (Barron, 1999). How can we understand the mechanisms and implications of such collaborative creativity?

How Do We Create Together?

There are at least two ways to conceptualize this question. The first way focuses our attention on the creative outcomes of groups. Such work, often in laboratory settings, strives to understand what dynamics enable successful groups and how creativity differs between teams and individuals. The second way considers the interaction and communication processes that occur within real-life collaborators or teams. The former is well represented by the literature on group creativity, whereas the latter is addressed by studies of collaborative creativity (Glăveanu, 2011).

The literature on collaborative creativity sheds new light on this by drawing on sociocultural scholarship, dating back to Lev Vygotsky (1978). Vygotsky suggested that children, as they grow, internalize knowledge and acquire skills in interaction with others. Moreover, through this interaction, they are capable of performing tasks they could not do alone. He called this idea of not merely studying what children can achieve but also what they are capable of doing with others (which also includes mentorship or teaching) the **zone of proximal development**. John-Steiner (1992) studied this potential of social interaction to foster learning and creativity in relation to real-life, long-term collaborations. She found that productive collaborations are characterized by tensions, complementarity, and emergence. The complementarity of knowledge and skills can lead to disagreements between collaborators, but it is precisely through such disagreements that new ideas can emerge.

But what exactly do we learn when we collaborate with other people that is useful for the creative process? Glăveanu (2015b) recently proposed that we get to understand their perspective on the situation or the problem at hand. In his perspectival model, creativity is conceptualized in terms of dialogues between different perspectives and the capacity to reflect on one's view from the standpoint of another person. These processes – perspective-taking and reflexivity – are cultivated within social interactions and, when fostered within groups, they can make the difference between low and high productivity.

There are other factors that play a crucial role when creating together with other people. The motivated information processing in groups model (De Dreu et al., 2011) sees group creativity and innovation as a function of both epistemic motivation (the degree to which group members seek to systematically process and disseminate information) and prosocial motivation (whether group members seek a collective gain rather than a personal one). Different conditions are considered to play a part in this dynamic, including time constraints, openness to experience, and the existence of a shared identity.

Another important work-related factor is climate. Karwowski (2011; Karwowski and Lebuda, 2013) proposes three primary factors that contribute to a creative climate: how well the group coheres on the approach to the task, how well the group interacts interpersonally, and some dynamic elements that balance group members' need for stability and desire to take risks. Finally, there are elements of the context that go beyond team or organizational climate and relate to the general culture within which people create. There are marked differences, for example, between Western forms of creativity, which emphasize individuality, risk taking, and the separation between the new and the old, and Eastern conceptions, highlighting the need for continuity, adaptation, and renewal of traditions (Niu and Kaufman, 2013). These larger elements shape both individual and social forms of creativity and raise the final question: What makes certain creative outputs endure whereas others – in fact, most others – are either not recognized or ultimately forgotten?

What Makes Creative Work Endure?

Thinking back to the Four-C model, what is that quality that separates Pro-c from Big-C? Which creative works last generations, and which fade away? One influential approach is Csikszentmihalyi's (1999) **systems model**, which looks at the relationship between the person, field, and domain. The person is the creator and his or her creative work remains constant. The collected contributions of a Mark Twain or Louis Armstrong do not change; it is current perceptions of their work that evolve over time. The field represents the people who are in positions of authority to promote, evaluate, or recognize creativity. The field might include critic groups, associations that bestow awards, tenure committees, publishers, or mentors. The domain is the area of the study and the consumers or practitioners in that area.

These three components interact and the field and domain can change over generations. A singer (the creator) may become a star or remain unknown, in part depending on whether the field recognizes his or her creativity. Members of the field, in this case, may include studio executives, concert bookers, disc jockeys, music critics, currently well-known singers, or many others. Sometimes the field can value a creator but the domain does not expand to include the creator's work; think of the singers who are heavily promoted but whose music does not become a key component of the domain. With current technology and social media, creators have an easier time reaching the audiences who partake in a domain without getting the approval of the field (Gangadharbatla, 2010). Singers can now market themselves on social media, sell their music on digital platforms, and reach a much larger audience than would have been possible even a few decades ago. As time passes, so can the field and domain change. Creative work can stay meaningful and influential, or it can be forgotten. For many reasons, from sociocultural movements to shifting values, some creators (such as Mozart or Shakespeare) continue to be promoted by the field and considered to be a key part of the domain for centuries. Occasionally, creators may be ignored in their own lifetimes but recognized posthumously. More commonly, once-acclaimed creators end up as minor footnotes, dubbed irrelevant by the field and forgotten by the corpus of the domain.

Another way of considering which creative contributions last is to analyze different products as to how they change their domain. The **propulsion model of creativity** (Sternberg, 1999a; Sternberg, Kaufman, and Pretz, 2001) outlines eight different types of creative contributions that are categorized by how they propel the domain forward. Four types maintain the existing paradigm. Perhaps the most straightforward are conceptual replications, which simply reproduce or reinforce past creative work. Redefinitions stay within the same domain but have a new angle or perspective. Forward incrementations push things slightly forward on a small scale. Advance forward incrementations go further to advance things, to the point of sometimes being too far ahead of their time to be appreciated.

The remaining four types are ways of either rejecting or replacing the existing paradigm. Redirections try to alter the direction a domain is moving. Reconstructions/Redirections not only want to alter the direction but to go back to a past period of time and ignore recent developments. Integrations aim to merge two different areas together to synthesize into a new domain. Finally, Reinitiations want to dramatically alter and reinvent a domain, virtually creating their own starting point and end goal. People who try to reinitiate a field are likely those who (in Sternberg's triangular theory) are willing to defy the crowd, themselves, and the Zeitgeist.

The core distinction between those who want to create within a paradigm versus those who want to change a paradigm is represented in many other related theories.

CONCLUSION

Certainly, the future will bring additional theoretical development (and empirical work) that continues to explore, expand, and attempt to answer these questions. An interesting thought to also consider is, which new questions will be asked? How can we anticipate what we do not know? One of our ongoing projects (e.g., Kaufman and Glăveanu, 2020) is to align creativity theory in a matrix of the Five A's and the Four C's to see which areas are amply represented and which ones are rife for further exploration.

There are several possible questions that could be addressed by theory. There has been extensive thought given to the personal requirements for creativity (such as the

Componential and Investment Theories). In contrast, consider the question, *What are the resources and support systems needed to be creative?* Instead of personal attributes, what affordances (action possibilities) of material objects are needed? How can mentors, access to materials, social networks, and new technologies help nurture someone's creativity? There have been empirical studies on these issues (Eubanks et al., 2016; McKay, Grygiel, and Karwowski, 2017), but there is room for theories that connect existing research and suggest new directions.

Another possible question is *How does a novice become a creative expert?* There are several concepts from the expertise literature, such as the importance of deliberate practice over many years, which can and has been applied to creativity (e.g., Ericsson, Roring, and Nandagopal, 2007). But creativity has its own nuances. This transition is part of the Four C model (Kaufman and Beghetto, 2009); one way that creators can advance from little-c to Pro-c is by increasing their creative metacognition (Kaufman and Beghetto, 2013; Kaufman, Beghetto, and Watson, 2016). Creative metacognition is composed of two components: understanding your creative strengths and weaknesses and being able to determine the best times to share your creative ideas. There remains much more theoretical work that could be done to outline the different pathways that one can take toward professional-level creativity.

Last but not least, there is a pressing need to raise the question of *How can creativity contribute to positive societal change?* Over time, our ideas of what domains are creative have grown from the arts and sciences to include business, education, everyday life, and many other domains (Kaufman, Glăveanu, and Baer, 2017). What would it mean to consider society as its own domain? What is the relation between creativity and social change? How can it help us, individually and as groups, address collective challenges such as climate change, immigration, and the need to build more open and inclusive societies (Glăveanu, 2015c)? How can creativity be used to foster social justice and equity (Kaufman, 2010; Luria, O'Brien, and Kaufman, 2016)? How can we ensure that future generations are able to use their creativity (and intelligence) to make wise, benevolent decisions (Sternberg, 2016)? Answering these questions will require us to adopt a more systemic, distributed, and participative model of creativity and to reflect more consistently on the ethical dimensions of both creating within society and engaging in creativity research.

There is no (successful or widely accepted) grand theory of creativity that takes into account every possible question, variable, or approach (Baer, 2011). Nor, truly, is there any particular need for one. Creativity is so complex and multifaceted that any theory that tried to explain everything would be unwieldly to the point of being incomprehensible. What we do hope, however, is that creativity theorists will think carefully about what underlying question they are trying to address. A good theory tells a story that is consistent with existing empirical research and suggests interesting questions that can be tested. A good theory will make the often contradictory scholarship easier to understand, instead of further muddying the waters. We hope to be able to include new such theories in future editions of this book.

Our Research Contribution

Some of our past research contributions can be seen in this chapter; each of us has coauthored some of the theories discussed here. We would like to briefly discuss how and why we collaborate, even though our initial passions for creativity research were quite different. Kaufman has always been interested in what are called individual differences – what makes us stand out. All of us have different personalities, interests, values, strengths, and weaknesses. What are the best combinations that can help people be creative (and in which ways)? What are aspects of ourselves that we can train or modify if we want to be more creative? Glăveanu focuses on the role of other people and of culture in a person's creative expression. Instead of seeing the input of others as important either before or after someone creates something, he argues that, in fact, the creative process itself is based on combining one's ideas with the views of others within concrete social and material settings. Questions of interest here are: How do acts of collaboration contribute to individual and group creativity? And how does perspective-taking contribute to the creative process in domains as different as the arts, sciences, and business?

Critical/Creative Thinking Questions

1. Why do we need theory in the study of creativity? Think about two theories presented in this chapter and consider their practical applications.
2. Take any two theories or models of creativity presented in this chapter and try to integrate them. What would their combination look like? Might it lead us to a new, possibly useful theoretical framework?
3. We have grouped the presentation of theories here based on six fundamental questions. Can you think of another question about creativity that is important and could be added to the six? Are any theories included here addressing it already?
4. Do theories about how we create as individuals help us also understand how we create together? In what ways? What might be their limitations?
5. Considering the different theories covered in this chapter, which one(s) do you think apply best to how you create? Which one(s) describe best your experience and why?

GLOSSARY

affordances: Social and material resources that make certain actions possible.

associative theory: Conceptualizing creativity as the ability to make connections between remote concepts.

Big-C: Eminent creativity.

componential model of creativity: A model highlighting the interrelationship of domain-relevant skills, creativity-relevant processes, and motivation.

convergent thinking: Choosing the best out of many ideas to pursue.

divergent thinking: The ability to think of as many different possible solutions to an open-ended question.

evolving systems approach: Theory that looks at creativity as the need to answer questions.

Five A's: A view of creativity as a dynamic system that includes five categories: Actors, Audiences, Actions, Artifacts, and Affordances.

flow: A pleasurable sensation that can occur when one is intensely engaged in a favorable yet challenging activity.

Four C's: A developmental trajectory of creativity that goes from personal creativity to genius.

Four P's: A synthesis of how creativity is studied that includes four categories: Person, Process, Product, and Press

investment theory of creativity: A theory that says creators must buy low and sell high with creative ideas.

little-c: Everyday creativity.

matrix model: A model that considers the reason for solving a problem and the context of the problem.

mini-c: Personally meaningful creativity that others may not appreciate.

problem construction: Understanding and identifying the exact problem that needs to be solved.

propulsion model of creativity: Eight different categories of creative contributions that focus on how the works propel the domain.

Pro-c: Professional, expert-level creativity.

systems model: The intersection of the creative person, field, and domain.

triangular theory of creativity: Great creators must defy the crowd, the Zeitgeist, and themselves.

zone of proximal development: What children can achieve not only by themselves but also with collaboration, mentorship, or teaching.

REFERENCES

Amabile, T. M. (1983). The Social Psychology of Creativity: A Componential Conceptualization. *Journal of Personality and Social Psychology*, *45*, 357–376.

(1988). A Model of Creativity and Innovation in Organizations. In B. S. Cummings (Ed.), *Research in Organizational Behavior* (pp. 123–167). Greenwich: JAI Press.

(1996). *Creativity in Context: Update to "The Social Psychology of Creativity"*. Boulder: Westview Press.

Amabile, T. M., and Pratt, M. G. (2016). The Dynamic Componential Model of Creativity and Innovation in Organizations: Making Progress, Making Meaning. *Research in Organizational Behavior*, *36*, 157–183.

Baer, J. (2011). Why Grand Theories of Creativity Distort, Distract, and Disappoint. *International Journal of Creativity and Problem Solving*, *21*, 73–100.

Barron, F. (1955). The Disposition Toward Originality. *Journal of Abnormal and Social Psychology*, *51*, 478–485.

(1999). All Creation Is a Collaboration. In A. Montuori and R. Purser (Eds.), *Social Creativity*, vol. I (pp. 49–59). Cresskill: Hampton Press.

Beghetto, R. A., and Kaufman, J. C. (2007). Toward a Broader Conception of Creativity: A Case for "mini-c" Creativity. *Psychology of Aesthetics, Creativity, and the Arts*, 1, 13–79.

(2013). Fundamentals of Creativity. *Educational Leadership*, 70, 10–15.

Boden, M. A. (2004). *The Creative Mind: Myths and Mechanisms*. London: Routledge.

Campbell, D. T. (1960). Blind Variation and Selective Retentions in Creative Thought As in Other Knowledge Processes. *Psychological Review*, 67, 380–400.

Cropley, A. J., and Cropley, D. (2009). *Fostering Creativity: A Diagnostic Approach for Higher Education and Organizations*. Cresskill: Hampton Press.

Csikszentmihalyi, M. (1996). *Creativity: Flow and the Psychology of Discovery and Invention*. New York: HarperCollins.

(1999). Implications of a Systems Perspective for the Study of Creativity. In R. J. Sternberg (Ed.), *Handbook of Creativity* (pp. 313–335). Cambridge: Cambridge University Press.

De Dreu, C. K., Nijstad, B. A., Bechtoldt, M. N., and Baas, M. (2011). Group Creativity and Innovation: A Motivated Information Processing Perspective. *Psychology of Aesthetics, Creativity, and the Arts*, 5, 81–89.

Deci, E., and Ryan, R. (1985). The General Causality Orientations Scale: Self- Determination in Personality. *Journal of Research in Personality*, 19, 109–134.

Ericsson, K. A., Roring, R. W., and Nandagopal, K. (2007). Giftedness and Evidence for Reproducibly Superior Performance: An Account Based on the Expert-Performance Framework. *High Ability Studies*, 18, 3–56.

Eubanks, D. L., Palanski, M. E., Swart, J., Hammond, M. M., and Oguntebi, J. (2016). Creativity in Early and Established Career: Insights into Multi-Level Drivers from Nobel Prize Winners. *The Journal of Creative Behavior*, 50, 229–251.

Feist, G. J. (1998). A Meta-Analysis of Personality in Scientific and Artistic Creativity. *Personality and Social Psychology Review*, 2, 290–309.

Finke, R. A., Ward, T. B., and Smith, S. M. (1992). *Creative Cognition: Theory, Research, and Applications*. Cambridge, MA: MIT Press.

Gangadharbatla, H. (2010). Technology Component: A Modified Systems Approach to Creative Thought. *Creativity Research Journal*, 22, 219–227.

Glăveanu, V. P. (2011). How Are We Creative Together? Comparing Sociocognitive and Sociocultural Answers. *Theory and Psychology*, 21, 473–492.

(2013). Rewriting the Language of Creativity: The Five A's Framework. *Review of General Psychology*, 17, 69–81.

(2015a). Theory and Context / Theory in Context: Towards an Expanded View of the Creativity Field. *Creativity: Theories – Research – Applications*, 1, 268–280.

(2015b). Creativity As a Sociocultural Act. *Journal of Creative Behavior*, 49, 165–180.

(2015c). Developing Society: Reflections on the Notion of Societal Creativity. In A.-G. Tan and C. Perleth (Eds.), *Creativity, Culture, and Development* (pp. 183–200). Singapore: Springer.

Glăveanu, V. P., and Kaufman, J. C. (2020). The Creativity Matrix: Spotlights and Blind Spots in Our Understanding of the Phenomenon. *Journal of Creative Behavior*. doi.org/10.1002/jocb.417.

Gruber, H. E. (1988). The Evolving Systems Approach to Creative Work. *Creativity Research Journal*, 1, 27–51.

Gruber, H. E., and Wallace, D. (1999). The Case Study Method and Evolving Systems Approach for Understanding Unique Creative People at Work. In R. J. Sternberg (Ed.), *Handbook of Creativity* (pp. 93–115). New York: Cambridge University Press.

Guilford, J. P. (1950). Creativity. *American Psychologist, 5,* 444–454.

(1967). *The Nature of Human Intelligence.* New York: McGraw-Hill.

Hennessey, B. A., and Amabile, T. M. (2010). Creativity. *Annual Review of Psychology, 61,* 569–598.

John-Steiner, V. (1992). Creative Lives, Creative Tensions. *Creativity Research Journal, 5,* 99–108.

Karwowski, M. (2011). Teachers' Personality and Perception of the Climate for Creativity in a School. *International Journal of Creativity and Problem Solving, 21,* 37–52.

Karwowski, M., Kaufman, J. C., Lebuda, I., Szumski, G., and Firkowska-Mankiewicz, A. (2017). Intelligence in Childhood and Creative Achievements in Middle-Age: The Necessary Condition Approach. *Intelligence, 64,* 36–44

Karwowski, M., and Lebuda, I. (2013). Extending Climato-Economic Theory: When, How, and Why It Explains Differences in Nations' Creativity. *Behavioral and Brain Sciences, 36,* 493–494.

Kaufman, J. C. (2010). Using Creativity to Reduce Ethnic Bias in College Admissions. *Review of General Psychology, 14,* 189–203.

(2012). Counting the Muses: Development of the Kaufman-Domains of Creativity Scale (K-DOCS). *Psychology of Aesthetics, Creativity, and the Arts, 6,* 298–308.

(2016). *Creativity 101,* 2nd ed. New York: Springer.

Kaufman, J. C., and Beghetto, R. A. (2009). Beyond Big and Little: The Four C Model of Creativity. *Review of General Psychology, 13,* 1–12.

(2013). In Praise of Clark Kent: Creative Metacognition and the Importance of Teaching Kids When (Not) to Be Creative. *Roeper Review, 35,* 155–165.

Kaufman, J. C., Beghetto, R. A., and Watson, C. (2016). Creative Metacognition and Self Ratings of Creative Performance: A 4-C Perspective. *Learning and Individual Differences, 51,* 394–399.

Kaufman, J. C., and Glăveanu, V. P. (2020). Making the CASE for shadow Creativity. *Psychology of Aesthetics, Creativity, and the Arts.* doi-org.ezproxy.lib.uconn.edu/10.1037/aca0000313.

Kaufman, J. C., Glăveanu, V., and Baer, J. (Eds.) (2017). *The Cambridge Handbook of Creativity across Domains.* New York: Cambridge University Press.

Kaufman, J. C., and Plucker, J. A. (2011). Intelligence and Creativity. In R. J. Sternberg and S. B. Kaufman (Eds.), *The Cambridge Handbook of Intelligence* (pp. 771–783). New York: Cambridge University Press.

Kharkhurin, A. V. (2014). Creativity 4 in 1: Four-Criterion Construct of Creativity. *Creativity Research Journal, 26,* 338–352.

Lifton, R. J. (2011). *Witness to an Extreme Century: A Memoir.* New York: Free Press.

Lubart, T. I. (2001). Models of the Creative Process: Past, Present and Future. *Creativity Research Journal, 13,* 295–308.

Luria, S. R., O'Brien, R. L., and Kaufman, J. C. (2016). Creativity in Gifted Identification: Increasing Accuracy and Diversity. *Annals of the New York Academy of Sciences, 1377,* 44–52.

McKay, A. S., Grygiel, P., and Karwowski, M. (2017). Connected to Create: A Social Network Analysis of Friendship Ties and Creativity. *Psychology of Aesthetics, Creativity, and the Arts, 11,* 284–294.

Mednick, S. A. (1962). The Associative Basis of the Creative Process. *Psychological Review, 69,* 220–232.

Mumford, M. D., Mobley, M. I., Uhlman, C. E., Reiter-Palmon, R., and Doares, L. M. (1991). Process Analytic Models of Creative Capacities. *Creativity Research Journal, 4,* 91–122.

Niu, W., and Kaufman, J. C. (2013). Creativity of Chinese and American people: A Synthetic Analysis. *Journal of Creative Behavior, 47,* 77–87.

Plucker, J. A., Beghetto, R. A., and Dow, G. (2004). Why Isn't Creativity More Important to Educational Psychologists? Potential, Pitfalls, and Future Directions in Creativity Research. *Educational Psychologist, 39*, 83–96.

Pratt, M. G., Pradies, C., and Lepisto, D. A. (2013). Doing Well, Doing Good, and Doing With: Organizational Practices for Effectively Cultivating Meaningful Work. In B. J. Dik, Z. S. Byrne, and M. F. Steger (Eds.), *Purpose and Meaning in the Workplace* (pp. 173–196). Washington, DC: American Psychological Association.

Reiter-Palmon, R., and Robinson, E. J. (2009). Problem Identification and Construction: What Do We Know, What Is the Future? *Psychology of Aesthetics, Creativity, and the Arts, 3*, 43–47.

Rhodes, M. (1961). An Analysis of Creativity. *Phi Delta Kappan, 42*, 305–311.

Sawyer, R. K. (2012). *Explaining Creativity: The Science of Human Innovation*, 2nd ed. New York: Oxford University Press.

Simonton, D. K. (2012). Taking the US Patent Office Creativity Criteria Seriously: A Quantitative Three-Criterion Definition and Its Implications. *Creativity Research Journal, 24*, 97–106.

Snow, C. P. (1959). *The Two Cultures*. New York: Cambridge University Press.

Sternberg, R. J. (1985). *Beyond IQ: A Triarchic Theory of Human Intelligence*. New York: Cambridge University Press.

(1996). *Successful Intelligence*. New York: Simon & Schuster.

(1999a). A Propulsion Model of Types of Creative Contributions. *Review of General Psychology, 3*, 83–100.

(1999b). *Thinking Styles*. New York: Cambridge University Press.

(2016). *What Universities Can Be: A New Model for Preparing Students for Active Concerned Citizenship and Ethical Leadership*. Ithaca: Cornell University Press.

(2018). A Triangular Theory of Creativity. *Psychology of Aesthetics, Creativity, and the Arts, 12*, 50–67.

Sternberg, R. J., and Kaufman, J. C. (2018). Societal Forces That ERODE Creativity. *Teacher's College Record, 120*, 1–18.

Sternberg, R. J., Kaufman, J. C., and Pretz, J. E. (2001). The Propulsion Model of Creative Contributions Applied to the Arts and Letters. *Journal of Creative Behavior, 35*, 75–101.

Sternberg, R. J., and Lubart, T. I. (1995). *Defying the Crowd*. New York: Free Press.

Torrance, E. P. (1974). *Torrance Tests of Creative Thinking: Directions Manual and Scoring Guide, Verbal Test Booklet B*. Bensenville: Scholastic Testing Service.

(2008). *The Torrance Tests of Creative Thinking Norms-Technical Manual Figural (Streamlined) Forms A & B*. Bensenville: Scholastic Testing Service.

Unsworth, K. (2001). Unpacking Creativity. *Academy of Management Review, 26*, 289–297.

Vygotsky, L. S. (1978). *Mind in Society: The Development of Higher Psychological Processes*. Edited by M. Cole, V. John-Steiner, S. Scribner, and E. Souberman. Cambridge, MA: Harvard University Press.

Wallas, G. (1926). *The Art of Thought*. New York: Harcourt, Brace, and World.

Zuckerman, H. (1978). Theory Choice and Problem Choice in Science. *Sociological Inquiry, 48*, 65–95.

3 Creativity in Society

DEAN KEITH SIMONTON

INTRODUCTION

Creativity is most frequently viewed as an individual phenomenon. We speak of creativity as a distinguishing characteristic of persons much like some cognitive ability or personality characteristic. Not surprisingly, most creativity researchers focus on the individual as the basic unit of analysis. It is for this reason that these researchers are most likely to be found in academic departments such as psychology and education. To be sure, some investigators exhibit a stronger interest in group creativity, such as that found in research teams in industry (Paulus and Nijstad, 2019). This focus is especially commonplace among researchers in business schools. Even so, the group members in these studies seldom lose their individual identities. Indeed, it cannot be otherwise because often the interest is in group composition, such as membership diversity, which requires that the investigator still keep track of personal characteristics.

In this chapter, I wish to raise the study of creativity to a far more encompassing level – the society. Just as we can talk about creative individuals, so we can discuss creative societies. Individuals can vary in their creativity and so can societies similarly vary (Simonton, 2019). I will illustrate this point by looking at three levels of analysis: cities, nations, and civilizations. Afterwards, I will discuss how societal creativity remains compatible with individual creativity. A complete understanding of the phenomenon demands that we adopt multiple levels of analysis (see also Csikszentmihalyi, 2014).

Cities

Although all human cultures exhibit creativity in various forms – such as song, dance, ceramics, and textiles – the specific form it takes varies according to degree of **urbanization**. A culture is urbanized to the extent that its population is concentrated into cities and metropolitan areas. In the historical evolution of a given culture, temporary settlements may turn into permanent settlements, which in turn may grow in size to become villages and then cities. Empirical research then shows that (a) craft specializations do not appear until communities attain a size of roughly 100 or more occupants, (b) political or religious leaders will not hire artisans to glorify their rule until towns emerge with roughly 2,000 or more occupants, and (c) full-time sculptors, painters, architects, and engineers do not become conspicuous until cities contain roughly 10,000 or more citizens (Carneiro, 1970). Cities can then become the locus of creative achievements that would not be possible in a town or village. This connection is illustrated, for example, in Weiner's (2016) *The Geography of Genius*, in which Weiner narrates the creative explosions seen in Athens, Hangzhou, Florence, Edinburgh, Calcutta, Vienna, and Silicon Valley. In the case of Athens, its Golden Age did not burst out until it had a population of about 90,000 freeborn persons (Galton, 1869). In philosophy alone, the florescence included Socrates, Plato, and Aristotle in quick succession.

The reasons for the creative ascendency of certain cities are far too numerous to discuss in detail here. Whole chapters and books have been written about the subject (Andersson, Andersson, and Mellander, 2011; Simonton, 2011). So may it suffice to make some brief observations.

To the extent that the abilities and dispositions associated with creativity reflect a **normal distribution** in the population – the "bell curve" discussed in every introductory psychology text – then as a city grows in size it will possess an ever larger number of denizens who represent the extreme upper tail of the distribution. For example, a village of only 1,000 people can have only 10 persons in the top 1 percent in intelligence. But a city with 100,000 will have 1,000 such individuals, plus a sizable number at even more rarified percentiles. What makes this distributional effect especially critical is that creativity most often requires the convergence of several individual-difference variables, many of which are only weakly correlated, if at all (e.g., Feist, 1998). As a consequence, an even larger city would be necessary to obtain creators at the upper tail on several participatory factors. For instance, suppose that creative achievement also demands appreciable persistence and determination (Duckworth, 2016). If this motivational factor is uncorrelated with intelligence, and if an individual must be in the top 1 percent on both, then a city with a population of 100,000 will only have 10 eligible souls – only a very tiny proportion of the overall population.

Of course, these creators do not have to be native-born but instead may have arrived from elsewhere once a city becomes known for activity in a particular creative domain. Well-known examples include the numerous twentieth-century artists and writers who emigrated to Paris and later New York City (Hellmanzik, 2014). I grew up in a Californian city – Los Angeles – that often called itself the "Creative Capital of the World." In fact, a very large proportion of Angelinos are employed in the "creative industries," especially entertainment, but many of the creators and talents who fill those ranks were born elsewhere, immigrating to LA to become "rich and famous." Even if most do not make it, the talent scouts and agents have the luxury of selecting the best of the best.

Importantly, the tremendous influx does not just increase the **per capita** representation of first-rate creators. The concentration of such creative personalities facilitates the formation of social networks and other dynamic interactions that are also highly supportive of outstanding creativity (Simonton, 1984a, 1992b; Hellmanzik, 2014). For instance, creative artists can meet at sidewalk cafes, attend showings of their respective works, and form academies and conservatories for the training of the next generation of artists. Although the advent of the internet has enhanced the capacity to engage in such stimulating exchanges at a distance, it may still take some time before cities cease to have this facilitative role. Skype and FaceTime may not be enough.

Nations

In some periods of history, cities, or rather city-states, formed the primary societal unit. In the Golden Age of Greece, there was no Greek nation, just as the Italian Renaissance took place hundreds of years before a nation called Italy appeared. With the rise of nationalism, however, the city was gradually replaced by the nation as the unit of societal creativity. The very first scientist to investigate cross-national differences in creativity was Alfonse de Candolle. Candolle (1873) hypothesized that cross-national variation could be ascribed to various political, economic, educational, ideological, and geographic differences.

To conduct this inquiry, Candolle chose to concentrate on a single form of creativity, namely, exceptional scientific achievement. A key advantage of this choice is that it helps avoid potential **ethnocentrism**. The contributions of scientists are evaluated by more object-ive standards than are the contributions of artists (Simonton, 2009). Nor was this his sole methodological precaution. Because societal creativity tends to increase with population size, he decided to introduce a critical methodological control. Rather than look at a nation's total output of notable scientists, he focused on per capita output (i.e., the number of eminent scientists divided by the nation's population; cf. Lehman, 1947). But another methodological device was especially striking. To remove any residual nationalistic biases that might confound his calculation of cross-national contributions to science, he only counted scientists as eminent if they had received an international reputation, a status that could only be attained by receiving honors in a nation outside their own. Accordingly, a French scientist who had earned election to the Académie des Sciences in France but not to any foreign academy would not be considered eminent. When this precaution is combined with the control for population size, Candolle found that his own nation, France, did not perform as well as Switzerland, a much smaller country. Indeed, the per capita output of eminent Swiss scientists is about five times greater than that of eminent French scientists. Interestingly, although French-born (albeit to a Swiss father), Candolle acquired an inter-national reputation, receiving honors in both Sweden and Great Britain; he ended his career as professor at the University of Geneva in Switzerland.

By combining these corrected cross-national assessments with other characteristics of various European nations, Candolle (1873) was able to discern the conditions that support outstanding scientific creativity. For example, nations with higher activity were more prone to possess a large group of individuals who did not have to preoccupy themselves with manual labor. That is, such nations enjoy a large percentage of persons with both the leisure and the desire to engage in cultural and intellectual pursuits. This engagement was reinforced by a cultural value placed on real-world knowledge rather than spiritual concerns. In particular, the general lay public should have a favorable attitude toward science rather than being anti-scientific. One crucial manifestation of this cultural value should be the abundance of institutions conducive to scientific activity, such as observatories, laboratories, libraries, and collections. There should also be many families who have a long tradition of supporting the involvement of members in intellectual activities – a condition descriptive of Candolle's own situation.

Candolle (1873) identified other national characteristics associated with scientific achievement, such as freedom from persecution for the expression of new ideas, openness to the immigration of foreign intellects, an exceptional educational system that provides support for both students and teachers, proximity to other scientifically active nations, and a climate that is generally moderate rather than extremely cold or hot. Especially fascinating was Candolle's observation that certain languages were most conducive to scientific creativity, namely, English, French, and German. These three had become the international languages of science to such a degree that scientific contributions published in other important languages, such as Italian or Russian, would often not become fully disseminated until translated into one of these three languages. Based on demographic trends, Candolle went one step further to argue that one specific language would become the dominant language of science, namely, English. I think it ironic that Candolle's important work is often overlooked because it has never been translated from French into English!

Needless to say, research on national differences in scientific creativity has advanced considerably since Candolle's (1873) pioneering effort (Szabo, 1985). For example, although he examined how cross-national variation changed across historical time, his data did not cover a sufficient period of time to identify how the centers of scientific creativity have switched from one nation to another. For instance, a century later, Yuasa (1974) showed that science was dominated by various nations in the following order: Italy, 1540–1610; Great Britain, 1660–1730; France, 1770–1830; Germany, 1810–1920; and the United States, 1920 on. Even so, Candolle's inquiry still provides a classic illustration of how and why creativity can vary across national systems.

Civilizations

Alfred Kroeber (1944), an eminent cultural anthropologist, argued that creativity depends strongly on the societal context. To make his case, Kroeber offered two main arguments. The first concerned independent discovery and invention, the second configurations of culture growth.

Independent Discovery and Invention

Kroeber (1917) was among the first social scientists to draw major inferences about creative genius from the phenomenon of independent discovery and invention, or what the sociologist Robert Merton (1961) later called **multiples** (see also Lamb and Easton, 1984). Kroeber offered numerous classic instances, such as the creation of calculus by Newton and Leibniz, the conception of the theory of evolution by natural selection by Darwin and Wallace, and the invention of the telephone by Bell and Gray. Kroeber was particularly taken by the fact that many multiples are not just independent but also simultaneous, or nearly so. Thus, Bell and Gray both sought patent protection for their respective telephones on the *same day*! Seemingly, such events could have only one explanation: The creative products of so-called genius are actually the deterministic outcomes of the larger sociocultural milieu. At a particular moment in the history of any civilization, certain discoveries or inventions become absolutely inevitable (see also Ogburn and Thomas, 1922). Hence, if Newton had not invented calculus, Leibniz would have, and if both Newton and Leibniz had died in the crib, then somebody else, perhaps someone completely unknown to us today, might have gotten credit for the invention. The civilization is the creative agent, not the individual creator, who is a mere pawn.

Naturally, this interpretation seems to undermine the view that creativity constitutes an individual phenomenon. There seems to be no room for psychological process. However, in a series of investigations spread out over more than forty years, I have shown that the foregoing, anti-psychological viewpoint is vastly overstated (e.g., Simonton, 1979, 2010). In the first place, probabilistic models do a much better job predicting the nitty-gritty of the phenomenon (Simonton, 2010). For example, such models successfully predict that the distribution of **multiple grade** – the number of independent inventors or scientists credited with the same contribution – should be described by a **Poisson distribution**. In rough terms, the higher a multiple's grade, the lower is its likelihood. The Poisson distribution is inherently incompatible with any deterministic process because it can only be generated by a probabilistic model. In fact, the distribution applies best to low-probability events, such as the number of Prussian soldiers killed by horse kicks each year. Who would argue that these unfortunate accidents are deterministic?

In addition, the individual contributor does play a significant role. For instance, it turns out that the independent contributions grouped together as a single identified multiple are often extremely different from each other. Leibniz's calculus was not a duplicate of Newton's, with the contrasts sufficiently striking that the history of mathematics would have differed had one or the other died young. Indeed, such cross-creator contrasts become even more pronounced in artistic domains, where multiples almost never happen (Price, 1986). Beethoven's Fifth Symphony, Michelangelo's Sistine Chapel frescoes, and Cervantes' *Don Quixote* were created only once and could only be created once.

This is not to say that my research program was designed to throw out the baby with the bath water. The goal was certainly not to replace a sociocultural reductionism with a psychological reductionism. Instead, my more modest aim was to identify their relative spheres of explanation. In particular, the sociocultural system makes two main contributions. First, the system provides the necessary (but not sufficient) basis for any given discovery or invention. Galileo could not have made his astronomical discoveries had the telescope not yet been first invented (Simonton, 2012b). Second, the sociocultural conditions can determine how many creative individuals focus on a particular problem, and increasing how many creators concentrate on a given problem necessarily enhances the probability not only of a solution but also of how many come up with the same discovery or invention. To illustrate, after Galileo first shocked the world with his initial discoveries regarding lunar mountains and Jovian moons, he quickly found himself surrounded by competitors armed with newfangled telescopes, so that sunspots became a multiple discovery rather than his alone (Simonton, 2012b). Yet, it is worth noting, it was Galileo himself who altered those sociocultural conditions! If he had not been so quick to publish his initial results, he might have avoided sharing credit. Genius shapes the **Zeitgeist** – the "spirit of the times."

Configurations of Culture Growth

Over a quarter century after his 1917 observations regarding multiples, Kroeber (1944) demonstrated that creative genius tends to cluster into **configurations of culture growth**. To be specific, creative activity in civilizations tends to concentrate in "Golden Ages" interspersed with "Dark Ages," although sometimes the former period might be followed by a "Silver Age" of less pronounced creative activity (see also Spiller, 1929; Sorokin and Merton, 1935; Simonton, 2018). This clustering of creative genius has been replicated multiple times across the world's major civilizations for which there exist sufficient historical data (Simonton and Ting, 2010).

Besides providing extensive cross-civilization documentation for these configurations, Kroeber (1944) ventured to provide an explanation. Quoting an ancient Roman historian who had made the same observations with respect to Greek civilization, Kroeber argued that each generation builds upon the creative contribution of their predecessors. That cumulative effort leads to a creative peak that may endure for some generations, but then that peak is followed by decline as the initial "cultural pattern" that inspired the florescence becomes "exhausted." My 1974 doctoral dissertation was partly dedicated to converting his explanation into a testable hypothesis. In particular, Kroeber's idea was translated into the concept of **role-model availability**, that is, the number of eminent creators who are active in the same domain during a youth's childhood and adolescence (Simonton, 1984b). Specifically, the researcher begins with a large sample consisting of the thousands of eminent creators who are most representative of a given civilization (Kroeber, 1944; Galton, 1969; Murray, 2003). The civilization is then divided into consecutive generations (or twenty-year periods). Each creator is then assigned to that generation where he or she attained their creative peak (estimated at age forty). The resulting data enables the investigator to test whether the number of creators in any generation is a positive function of the number of creators in the previous generation (or previous two generations), the latter representing potential role models. Of course, for this analysis to work correctly, the creators must be separated by domain because role models are necessarily domain-specific. In any event, Kroeber's conjecture has been confirmed multiple times and not only for Western civilization (Simonton, 1975) but also for other civilizations (Murray, 2003), such as Chinese, Japanese, and Islamic (Simonton, 1988, 1992a, 2018; Simonton and Ting, 2010). Eminent creators are dependent on their immediate predecessors.

To be sure, the rise and fall of creative activity is not the sole result of such role-modeling effects. Other societal factors are involved as well, such as the prevailing political conditions (Simonton, 1975; see also Murray, 2003; Simonton and Ting, 2010). Subsequent research has scrutinized other relevant factors, such as the impact of ideology and **multiculturalism** (Simonton, 1992a, 1997b). By now it has become evident that the coming and going of Golden Ages cannot be attributed to role-model availability alone. So many diverse factors operate that it is no wonder that such great periods of creative florescence stand out in the history of civilization. Such epochal moments are rare and brief. Although Plato's famed Academy endured intermittently for centuries in an increasingly provincial Athens, it was largely staffed by philosophical epigones, such as the obscure Philo of Larissa.

Discussion

We have just seen how creativity is more than a psychological phenomenon. Besides speaking of creative individuals, it is also meaningful to speak of creative cities, nations, and civilizations. Naturally, other societal units are possible as well. For example, cross-cultural studies have been published on creativity in pre-literate societies (Martindale, 1976). Another alternative is to break a single nation down into smaller units, such as the states or even counties making up the United States (Runco, Acar, and Cayirdag, 2017). Whatever the specifics, the societal units of analysis enable creativity researchers to investigate phenomena that are impossible to study at the individual level. That much admitted, the reality of these collective entities does not compromise in any way the central role played by the individual creator's psychology. To understand why, consider the following individual-level phenomena: creative productivity, creative personality, and creative development.

Creative Productivity

Within any given cohort of creators who are active at a given time and place, there remains impressive variation in creativity that cannot possibly be explicated according to sociocultural conditions. A case in point is the existence of substantial individual differences in creative productivity (Simonton, 1991a, 1991b, 1997a). Beyond any doubt, not all creators born under identical milieus are equally productive across their lifespans. Indeed, only a small proportion of the creators will produce enough to count as genuine creative geniuses (Albert, 1975). Because the sociocultural circumstances are effectively held constant, this variation must have a personal source, such as the personality and developmental factors to be discussed shortly. Moreover, the larger the number of creative individuals who are active in a given historical time and geographical location, the more extreme is the variation in productivity exhibited by those creators (Price, 1986; Simonton, 1988). A Golden Age is like a large pyramid, with big-name creators represented by big blocks at the apex and a very large number of more obscure figures forming a sufficiently broad base of small bricks, whereas a Dark Age consists of a small pile of pebbles, the top pebble only slightly larger than the rest. Leonardo da Vinci, Michelangelo, and Raphael rubbed shoulders with numerous lesser artists who, nonetheless, collectively defined the Italian Renaissance. To drive home the point, Giorgio Vasari's 1550 *Lives of the Most Excellent Painters, Sculptors, and Architects, from Cimabue to Our Times* provides biographies – of highly variable length – for nearly 300 Italian artists. Most art lovers will likely claim familiarity with no more than two dozen at best (see Ginsburgh and Weyers, 2006).

Closely related to the preceding is another crucial fact regarding creative productivity: Besides variation across individuals, we also must recognize the importance of within-individual longitudinal changes (Jones, Reedy, and Weinberg, 2014; Kozbelt, 2014; McKay and Kaufman, 2014). Except for **one-hit wonders** whose creative productivity begins and ends with a single work (see, e.g., Kozbelt, 2008), most highly creative individuals will have their contributions distributed over the course of a long career (e.g., Simonton, 1977b). Typically, output is described by a single-peaked age curve (Simonton, 2012a). Moreover, their first high-impact product will appear in their mid to late twenties, their single best work around age forty, and their last high-impact product a little after age fifty (Raskin, 1936; Simonton, 1991a, 1991b). To be sure, the precise details of the career trajectory will vary according to several factors, such as cross-sectional variation in lifetime output, the nature of the creator's discipline, and whether the creator is an early or late bloomer (Simonton, 1997a). Yet the crucial point is that the longitudinal changes in creative output are largely driven by intrinsic factors connected with the individual's career age (Simonton, 2012a). Even if truly dramatic external factors, such as outright war, might influence the career course, these influences are usually small and transient with respect to active creators (e.g., Simonton, 1977a; Cerulo, 1984; Borowiecki, 2014). For example, Beethoven's creative peak occurred right in the middle of the Napoleonic Wars, which even saw French forces occupying Vienna, where he lived. In short, the sociocultural system often plays a minimal role in shaping a creator's career trajectory. Obviously, this statement only applies to those contexts that allow a regular creative career to unfold. Dark Ages remain dark.

Creative Personality

For the sociocultural system to dominate the individuals who make up that system, it would be expected that those individuals would display personality traits most related to conforming to social roles and cultural norms. Such persons should be highly conventional conformists whose interests and values tightly match the mainstream or majority culture. When such persons train for a specific domain, the same conforming conventionality should be apparent. Their knowledge and skills should be closely constrained to a narrowly defined domain-specific expertise.

Yet what I have just described is essentially the exact antithesis of the creative personality! Not only are highly creative people far more likely to be unconventional nonconformists who value their autonomy, but they also exhibit broad interests and experiential openness that go well beyond the demands of any domain-specific expertise (Carson, 2014; McCrae and Greenberg, 2014). In extreme instances, and especially in the arts, this disposition can even incline them toward subclinical levels of psychopathology and thus they are far more deviant from cultural norms than the average person on the street (Simonton, 2014). Moreover, the greater the creative genius, the more conspicuous is this tendency to "defy the crowd" (Sternberg and Lubart, 1995). This pronounced tendency is clearly apparent in the lives of great thinkers, for example (Simonton, 1976). Such intellects advocate extreme positions and unusual ideational combinations that are out of sync with the prevailing intellectual Zeitgeist of their day. It is only the lesser thinkers who show any willingness to conform to an already well-established school of thought rather than founding a new school entirely their own (see also Simonton, 2000b).

Creative Development

The development of highly creative persons echoes what has just been said about the personality of highly creative persons. If the sociocultural system is to so intimately shape the individual creator, making him or her but a causal epiphenomenon, then creative development must be seriously confined by that system. Creative individuals should grow up in highly conventional families, with mainstream or majority-culture parents, and have their socialization similarly constrained by the educational system, as manifested in the individual's academic performance and domain-specific training. The result is a person highly representative of both the society and the domain – the perfect embodiment of the time and place.

But, again, the opposite is the case! Instead, creative development is highly dependent on "diversifying experiences that help weaken the constraints imposed by conventional social- ization" (Simonton, 2000a, p. 153). These **diversifying experiences** can involve any combin- ation of the following: (a) parents who are different from the dominant culture with respect to ethnicity, religion, geographic origins, and/or socioeconomic background; (b) disruptive events in childhood or adolescence, such as orphanhood or economic instabilities; (c) stigmatizing features that make the young person feel different from peers, such as cognitive or physical disabilities; and (d) unusual events or encounters in education and training, such as poor performance, distinctive teachers and mentors, or changes in career goals (Damian and Simonton, 2014, 2015). Of special interest are the positive repercussions of bilingualism and multiculturalism, which, by their very nature, set the individual upon a divergent developmental path, allowing the person to see the world from at least two sociocultural perspectives rather than just one (Leung et al., 2008; Simonton, 2008). It is no accident that a significant proportion of highly creative persons are either immigrants or the children of immigrants (Damian and Simonton, 2014). Interestingly, although the original research on diversifying experiences was correlational, recent laboratory experiments have been able to simulate their impact on creativity (e.g., Ritter et al., 2012; Saad et al., 2013; Vohs, Redden, and Rahinel, 2013). Creativity is enhanced when people are jarred out of normal, everyday thinking.

CONCLUSION

Considerably more empirical inquiry is necessary before we can fully comprehend creativity at the societal level. Unhappily, current trends in psychology and other relevant domains are not moving in the right direction for such investigations to continue. Most notably, psychol- ogy's present infatuation with the neurosciences has pulled the discipline further away from studying the larger sociocultural forces that have such a critical place in creativity. I would hope that research becomes more balanced in the near future. In the meantime, it has at least been established that creativity manifests itself in larger units than just persons: namely, cities, nations, and civilizations. The latter phenomena do not invalidate personal creativity as a psychological phenomenon but rather demonstrate creativity's supreme importance beyond the individual creator. Creativity has a major role in society.

My Research Contribution

Although I have published creativity research using standard methods, such as laboratory experiments, mathematical models, and computer simulations, the vast majority of my empirical publications use historiometric methods. These methods apply quantitative measurements and analyses to biographical and historical data regarding eminent creators and leaders. The very first example of this application was my 1974 Harvard doctoral dissertation in which I examined how more than 5,000 creators in Western civilization were distributed across 127 generations from antiquity to modern times. Besides estimating the effect of role-model availability, I also assessed the influence of several political events, such as war and civil disturbances. Later, the same strategy was used to scrutinize the fluctuations of historic figures in Islamic, Chinese, and Japanese civilizations, yielding a series of studies published between 1975 and 2018. Even so, I have conducted an even larger number of historiometric inquiries in which the individual creator provides the basic unit of analysis. I have even combined generational and individual units to produce investigations in which individual creative geniuses are examined within their sociocultural context.

Critical/Creative Thinking Questions

1. When researchers study creativity at the individual level, they are often interested in learning how to make people more creative. Workshops even try to apply research findings to enhance personal creativity. Yet how useful is knowledge about creativity taking place at the level of cities, nations, or civilizations? Can we intervene to produce Golden Ages or prevent Dark Ages?

2. Correlations between variables at the societal level do not have to correspond to parallel correlations at the individual level. For example, in the United States, being able to read and write in English is positively correlated with a person's income, but the wealthiest states tend to have a higher proportion of citizens who do not have English-language literacy. The reason for this apparent discrepancy is that the richer states attract more immigrants from countries where English is not the first language. Yet a recent study

showed that those states that tended to vote for conservative political candidates exhibit lower creativity as measured by output of patents (Runco, Acar, and Cayirdag, 2017). Is it safe to conclude that at the individual level conservative political attitudes are also negatively correlated with creativity? If so, why? If not, why not?

3. We have seen that creativity tends to come and go in various times and places. Yet people located at a particular time and place don't always know whether they are living in a Dark Age or Golden Age. For example, with the exception of architecture and mosaics, Byzantine civilization is usually seen today as far less creative than Athens during its Golden Age. Yet the Byzantines did not necessarily see it that way, viewing their Christian civilization as a vast advance over the pagan Greeks. What do you think about our current modern civilization? Are we in a Golden Age? How would you know?

4. This chapter concentrated on output quantity rather than the nature of that output. Yet it is clear that the society has some say in the form and content of the products conceived by its creators. Chinese paintings look very different from European paintings, just as Islamic architecture is distinguishable from Japanese architecture. What kinds of societal factors do you think are responsible for these creative contrasts?

5. Can you come up with your own hypothesis that can only be tested using societal level data? Such as cities, nations, or civilizations? Why can't the hypothesis be tested solely at the individual level, like psychologists normally do?

GLOSSARY

configurations of culture growth: Kroeber's (1944) concept that civilizations start with a given "cultural pattern" that is then developed over time until the pattern is "exhausted."

diversifying experiences: Events and circumstances in childhood and adolescence that set a young person on an unconventional and divergent developmental trajectory.

ethnocentrism: The inclination to judge other cultures according to values and standards characteristic of one's own particular culture.

multiculturalism: When a given individual or society is described by a diversity of cultures that are interconnected rather than segregated.

multiples: Discoveries or inventions that are independently and sometimes simultaneously conceived by two or more creators.

multiple grade: The number of creators credited with the same independent discovery or invention.

normal distribution: The well-known symmetrical "bell shaped" curve describing how people vary on many physical and psychological traits, such as height and intelligence; most people fall in the middle, near the average or mean, whereas people either extremely low or extremely high are far less common, forming the "tails" of the distribution.

one-hit wonders: Creators who are known for only a single creative contribution, whether or not they might have produced many more attempts.

per capita: A routine calculation that corrects for population size, such as counting the number of Nobel laureates born in each nation and then dividing by the size of each nation's population.

Poisson distribution: Quite unlike the "bell shaped" curve, this distribution is not symmetrical but instead has a tail on the right much longer than the tail on the left and may not have a left tail at all;

it tends to describe the distribution of low-probability events in which the highest probability is that the event will not occur at all.

probabilistic models: Models that account for a phenomenon only by incorporating an essential random or chance component. A primary characteristic of such models is that instead of predicting a specific value, their predictions produce probability distributions. For example, the normal distribution is generated by a probabilistic model with a specified mean and standard deviation.

role-model availability: Most simply defined by the number of eminent creators available during the developmental period of young talents growing up in the same domain of creativity; more sophisticated measures weight the count by eminence.

urbanization: The degree to which a given population becomes concentrated into cities and metropolitan areas.

Zeitgeist: From the German word for "spirit of the times," a general term for cultural, political, ideological, economic, and other environmental influences operating at the societal level.

REFERENCES

Albert, R. S. (1975). Toward a Behavioral Definition of Genius. *American Psychologist, 30*, 140–151.

Andersson, D. E., Andersson, Å. E., and Mellander, C. (Eds.). (2011). *Handbook of Creative Cities.* Cheltenham: Edward Elgar.

Borowiecki, K. J. (2014). Artistic Creativity and Extreme Events: The Heterogeneous Impact of War on Composers' Production. *Poetics, 47*, 83–105.

Candolle, A. de (1873). *Histoire des sciences et des savants depuis deux siècles.* Geneva: Georg.

Carneiro, R. L. (1970). Scale Analysis, Evolutionary Sequences, and the Rating of Cultures. In R. Naroll and R. Cohn (Eds.), *A Handbook of Method in Cultural Anthropology* (pp. 834–871). New York: Natural History Press.

Carson, S. H. (2014). Cognitive Disinhibition, Creativity, and Psychopathology. In D. K. Simonton (Ed.), *The Wiley Handbook of Genius* (pp. 198–221). Oxford: Wiley.

Cerulo, K. A. (1984). Social Disruption and Its Effects on Music: An Empirical Analysis. *Social Forces, 62*, 885–904.

Csikszentmihalyi, M. (2014). The Systems Model of Creativity and Its Applications. In D. K. Simonton (Ed.), *The Wiley Handbook of Genius* (pp. 533–545). Oxford: Wiley.

Damian, R. I., and Simonton, D. K. (2014). Diversifying Experiences in the Development of Genius and Their Impact on Creative Cognition. In D. K. Simonton (Ed.), *The Wiley Handbook of Genius* (pp. 375–393). Oxford: Wiley.

(2015). Psychopathology, Adversity, and Creativity: Diversifying Experiences in the Development of Eminent African Americans. *Journal of Personality and Social Psychology, 108*, 623–636.

Duckworth, A. (2016). *Grit: The Power of Passion and Perseverance.* New York: Scribner.

Feist, G. J. (1998). A Meta-Analysis of Personality in Scientific and Artistic Creativity. *Personality and Social Psychology Review, 2*, 290–309.

Galton, F. (1869). *Hereditary Genius: An Inquiry into Its Laws and Consequences.* London: Macmillan.

Ginsburgh, V., and Weyers, S. (2006). Persistence and Fashion in Art: Italian Renaissance from Vasari to Berenson and Beyond. *Poetics, 34*, 24–44.

Hellmanzik, C. (2014). Prominent Modern Artists: Determinants of Creativity. In D. K. Simonton (Ed.), *The Wiley Handbook of Genius* (pp. 564–585). Oxford: Wiley.

Jones, B. F., Reedy, E. J., and Weinberg, B. A. (2014). Age and Scientific Genius. In D. K. Simonton (Ed.), *The Wiley Handbook of Genius* (pp. 422–450). Oxford: Wiley.

Kozbelt, A. (2008). One-Hit Wonders in Classical Music: Evidence and (Partial) Explanations for an Early Career Peak. *Creativity Research Journal, 20,* 179–195.

 (2014). Musical Creativity over the Lifespan. In D. K. Simonton (Ed.), *The Wiley Handbook of Genius* (pp. 451–472). Oxford: Wiley.

Kroeber, A. L. (1917). The Superorganic. *American Anthropologist, 19,* 163–214.

 (1944). *Configurations of Culture Growth.* Berkeley: University of California Press.

Lamb, D., and Easton, S. M. (1984). *Multiple Discovery.* Avebury: Avebury.

Lehman, H. C. (1947). National Differences in Creativity. *American Journal of Sociology, 52,* 475–488.

Leung, A. K., Maddux, W. W., Galinsky, A. D., and Chiu, C. (2008). Multicultural Experience Enhances Creativity: The When and How. *American Psychologist, 63,* 169–181.

Martindale, C. (1976). Primitive Mentality and the Relationship between Art and Society. *Scientific Aesthetics, 1,* 5–18.

McCrae, R. R., and Greenberg, D. M. (2014). Openness to Experience. In D. K. Simonton (Ed.), *The Wiley Handbook of Genius* (pp. 222–243). Oxford: Wiley.

McKay, A. S., and Kaufman, J. C. (2014). Literary Geniuses: Their Life, Work, and Death. In D. K. Simonton (Ed.), *The Wiley Handbook of Genius* (pp. 473–487). Oxford: Wiley.

Merton, R. K. (1961). Singletons and Multiples in Scientific Discovery: A Chapter in the Sociology of Science. *Proceedings of the American Philosophical Society, 105,* 470–486.

Murray, C. (2003). *Human Accomplishment: The Pursuit of Excellence in the Arts and Sciences, 800 B.C. to 1950.* New York: HarperCollins.

Ogburn, W. K., and Thomas, D. (1922). Are Inventions Inevitable? A Note on Social Evolution. *Political Science Quarterly, 37,* 83–93.

Paulus, P. B., and Nijstad, B. A. (Eds.). (2019). *The Oxford Handbook of Group Creativity and Innovation* (pp. 271–284). New York: Oxford University Press.

Price, D. (1986). *Little Science, Big Science ... and Beyond.* New York: Columbia University Press.

Raskin, E. A. (1936). Comparison of Scientific and Literary Ability: A Biographical Study of Eminent Scientists and Men of Letters of the Nineteenth Century. *Journal of Abnormal and Social Psychology, 31,* 20–35.

Ritter, S. M., Damian, R. I., Simonton, D. K., van Baaren, R. B., Strick, M., Derks, J., and Dijksterhuis, A. (2012). Diversifying Experiences Enhance Cognitive Flexibility. *Journal of Experimental Social Psychology, 48,* 961–964.

Runco, M. A., Acar, S., and Cayirdag, N. (2017). Further Evidence That Creativity and Innovation Are Inhibited by Conservative Thinking: Analyses of the 2016 Presidential Election. *Creativity Research Journal, 29,* 331–336.

Saad, C. S., Damian, R. I., Benet-Martinez, V., Moons, W. G., and Robins, R. W. (2013). Multiculturalism and Creativity: Effects of Cultural Context, Bicultural Identity, and Cognitive Fluency. *Social Psychological and Personality Science, 4,* 36–374.

Simonton, D. K. (1975). Sociocultural Context of Individual Creativity: A Transhistorical Time-Series Analysis. *Journal of Personality and Social Psychology, 32,* 1119–1133.

 (1976). Philosophical Eminence, Beliefs, and Zeitgeist: An Individual-Generational Analysis. *Journal of Personality and Social Psychology, 34,* 630–640.

 (1977a). Creative Productivity, Age, and Stress: A Biographical Time-Series Analysis of 10 Classical Composers. *Journal of Personality and Social Psychology, 35,* 791–804.

 (1977b). Eminence, Creativity, and Geographic Marginality: A Recursive Structural Equation Model. *Journal of Personality and Social Psychology, 35,* 805–816.

(1979). Multiple Discovery and Invention: Zeitgeist, Genius, or Chance? *Journal of Personality and Social Psychology*, *37*, 1603–1616.

(1984a). Artistic Creativity and Interpersonal Relationships across and within Generations. *Journal of Personality and Social Psychology*, *46*, 1273–1286.

(1984b). Generational Time-Series Analysis: A Paradigm for Studying Sociocultural Influences. In K. Gergen and M. Gergen (Eds.), *Historical Social Psychology* (pp. 141–155). Hillsdale: Lawrence Erlbaum.

(1988). Galtonian Genius, Kroeberian Configurations, and Emulation: A Generational Time-Series Analysis of Chinese Civilization. *Journal of Personality and Social Psychology*, *55*, 230–238.

(1991a). Career Landmarks in Science: Individual Differences and Interdisciplinary Contrasts. *Developmental Psychology*, *27*, 119–130.

(1991b). Emergence and Realization of Genius: The Lives and Works of 120 Classical Composers. *Journal of Personality and Social Psychology*, *61*, 829–840.

(1992a). Gender and Genius in Japan: Feminine Eminence in Masculine Culture. *Sex Roles*, *27*, 101–119.

(1992b). The Social Context of Career Success and Course for 2,026 Scientists and Inventors. *Personality and Social Psychology Bulletin*, *18*, 452–463.

(1997a). Creative Productivity: A Predictive and Explanatory Model of Career Trajectories and Landmarks. *Psychological Review*, *104*, 66–89.

(1997b). Foreign Influence and National Achievement: The Impact of Open Milieus on Japanese Civilization. *Journal of Personality and Social Psychology*, *72*, 86–94.

(2000a). Creativity: Cognitive, Developmental, Personal, and Social Aspects. *American Psychologist*, *55*, 151–158.

(2000b). Methodological and Theoretical Orientation and the Long-Term Disciplinary Impact of 54 Eminent Psychologists. *Review of General Psychology*, *4*, 13–24.

(2008). Bilingualism and Creativity. In J. Altarriba and R. R. Heredia (Eds.), *An Introduction to Bilingualism: Principles and Processes* (pp. 147–166). Mahwah: Lawrence Erlbaum.

(2009). Varieties of (Scientific) Creativity: A Hierarchical Model of Disposition, Development, and Achievement. *Perspectives on Psychological Science*, *4*, 441–452.

(2010). Creativity As Blind-Variation and Selective-Retention: Combinatorial Models of Exceptional Creativity. *Physics of Life Reviews*, *7*, 156–179.

(2011). Big-C Creativity in the Big City: Definitions, Speculations, and Complications. In D. E. Andersson, Å. E. Andersson, and C. Mellander (Eds.), *Handbook of Creative Cities* (pp. 72–84). Cheltenham: Edward Elgar.

(2012a). Creative Productivity and Aging: An Age Decrement – or Not? In S. K. Whitbourne and M. Sliwinski (Eds.), *The Wiley-Blackwell Handbook of Adult Development and Aging* (pp. 477–496). New York: Wiley-Blackwell.

(2012b). Foresight, Insight, Oversight, and Hindsight in Scientific Discovery: How Sighted Were Galileo's Telescopic Sightings? *Psychology of Aesthetics, Creativity, and the Arts*, *6*, 243–254.

(2014). More Method in the Mad-Genius Controversy: A Historiometric Study of 204 Historic Creators. *Psychology of Aesthetics, Creativity, and the Arts*, *8*, 53–61.

(2018). Intellectual Genius in the Islamic Golden Age: Cross-Civilization Replications, Extensions, and Modifications. *Psychology of Aesthetics, Creativity, and the Arts*, *12*, 125–135.

(2019). Creativity in Sociocultural Systems: Cultures, Nations, and Civilizations. In P. B. Paulus and B. A. Nijstad (Eds.), *The Oxford Handbook of Group Creativity and Innovation* (pp. 271–284). New York: Oxford University Press.

Simonton, D. K., and Ting, S.-S. (2010). Creativity in Eastern and Western Civilizations: The Lessons of Historiometry. *Management and Organization Review*, *6*, 329–350.

Sorokin, P. A., and Merton, R. K. (1935). The Course of Arabian Intellectual Development, 700–1300 A.D. *Isis*, *22*, 516–524.

Spiller, G. (1929). The Dynamics of Greatness. *Sociological Review*, *21*, 218–232.

Sternberg, R. J., and Lubart, T. I. (1995). *Defying the Crowd: Cultivating Creativity in a Culture of Conformity*. New York: Free Press.

Szabo, A. T. (1985). Alphonse de Candolle's Early Scientometrics (1883, 1885) with References to Recent Trends in the Field (1978–1983). *Scientometrics*, *8*, 13–33.

Vohs, K., Redden, J., and Rahinel, R. (2013). Physical Order Produces Healthy Choices, Generosity, Conventionality, Whereas Disorder Produces Creativity. *Psychological Science*, *24*, 1860–1867.

Weiner, E. (2016). *The Geography of Genius*. New York: Simon & Schuster.

Yuasa, M. (1974). The Shifting Center of Scientific Activity in the West: From the Sixteenth to the Twentieth Century. In. N. Shigeru, D. L. Swain, and Y. Eri (Eds.), *Science and Society in Modern Japan* (pp. 81–103). Tokyo: University of Tokyo Press.

4 Assessment of Creativity

JONATHAN A. PLUCKER, MATTHEW C. MAKEL, AND MEIHUA QIAN

INTRODUCTION

Few topics within the study of creativity and innovation incite as much passion as **assessment** or measurement, the process of gathering data representing one's aptitudes, knowledge, attitudes, cognition, or potential. This appears to be especially true when the topic is discussed among non-academics who work in creative fields: A colleague once shared a story concerning his speaking about creativity with designers at a major entertainment company. He off-handedly mentioned measurement and . . . suffice it to say, he did not find the kingdom to be so magical from that point forward. The conventional wisdom is that creativity is too difficult to measure and many people are surprised to learn that creativity assessment has a long, rich history.

But why worry about creativity assessment at all? Why try to identify creative children or adults? Why not just let creativity exist unfettered, with no evaluation? These are reasonable (and common) questions, but they are based on the assumption that examining creativity inherently decreases or otherwise harms creativity, which further implies that nothing can be done to cultivate and grow creativity. Each of us makes judgments about creativity, either in examination of our own work or that of others. The purposes of creativity assessment vary widely, but they represent a range of important goals that are valuable for workforce development, education, and quality of life.

For example, standardized achievement test scores make up the vast majority of education data. Adding information on creativity could help promote a more well-rounded view of each student's development. In college admissions, inclusion of creativity measures could provide insight into applicants who would be most suitable for innovation-focused programs and eventually making creative contributions in their fields (Pretz and Kaufman, 2017; Sternberg, 2018a, 2018b). In the workplace, employers frequently list creativity and problem solving as important skills for their employees (e.g., National Association of Colleges and Employers, 2018). Creativity assessment could provide helpful information on which candidates to hire for new positions and how to create targeted professional development programs that improve employee creativity and innovation skills.

Attempts to measure creativity along what we would consider to be modern, scientific approaches date back over 100 years; some of our best researchers have done work on the topic, such as Guilford (1967) and Sternberg (2018a). Over the last 30 years, psychometric work has grown in interesting and promising ways. This expansion has been based largely on the work of Amabile (1983) and researchers and theorists who have promoted more-encompassing systems and sociocultural theories of creative development (e.g., Sternberg

Table 4.1 Framework for understanding approaches to creativity assessment

Category	Description	Typical approaches to assessment	Examples
Person	Creators' personality, motivation, and attitudes	Self-report scales Scales rated by others	Adjective check list (Domino, 1994; Gough, 1979) Creative personality scale (Kaufman and Baer, 2004)
Process	Cognitive dimensions of creativity	Cognitive tasks	SOI model (Guilford, 1967) TTCT (Torrance, 1974)
Product	The actual end result of creativity	Scales rated by others	Consensual Assessment Technique (CAT) (Amabile, 1983) Creative product semantic scale (Besemer and O'Quin, 1999)
Press/Place/ Environment	The context in which creativity is to occur	Rating scales	KEYS (Amabile et al., 1996)

and Lubart, 1995; Glăveanu, 2013). The argument can be made that the field of creativity assessment has never been as active and dynamic as it is today (Sternberg et al., 2012).

Traditional Areas of Psychometric Study

Psychometric methods in creativity research are typically grouped into four types of investigations: creative processes, personality and behavioral aspects of creativity, characteristics of **creative products**, and attributes of creativity-fostering environments. Unlike the more recent development of systems theories and multidisciplinary approaches, which consider varied perspectives, the psychometric approach has generally studied each of the four aspects in isolation. This section reviews seminal and recent work in each of these areas and concludes with a comparison among the specific areas of psychometric investigation.

Table 4.1 summarizes the roles of person, process, product, and environmental press in creativity.

Creative Processes

Researchers have used psychometric measures of **creative process** extensively for decades and they remain a popular measure of creative process and potential. However, these measures, used to quantify the creative process, are traditionally divergent thinking (DT) tasks and have been a lightning rod for criticism of the psychometric study of creativity.

These DT assessments ask participants to use "cognition that leads in various directions" (Runco, 1999, p. 577). In contrast to most standardized achievement or ability tests, DT tests require individuals to produce several responses to a specific prompt and not one correct answer.

The emphasis on quantity of responses is often referred to as **ideational fluency**, or simply ideation. The idea that "more is better" is a key component of ideation but is clearly not the sole component of the creative process. DT is often contrasted with **convergent thinking**, in which cognitive processes are used to produce one or very few possible solutions to a given problem (such as on most standardized tests).

Kaufman, Plucker, and Baer (2008) have noted that a great irony of the study of creativity is that so much time and energy have been devoted to the use of a single class of assessments. In fact, not only has the most energy been expended on DT tests; almost all of the earliest tests of **divergent thinking** remain in wide use in creativity research and education to this day. These include Guilford's (1967) structure of the intellect (SOI) divergent production tests, Torrance's (1974, 2008) Tests of Creative Thinking (TTCT), and Wallach and Kogan's (1965) and Getzels and Jackson's (1962) divergent thinking tasks. Even more recent DT measures, such as Hu and Adey's (2002) scientific creativity test, are clearly based on these earlier efforts.

Although the content and instructions of DT tests vary, how responses are categorized remains largely consistent. In general, DT tests ask for multiple responses to either figural or verbal prompts, and responses are scored for fluency, flexibility, originality, and elaboration of ideas. Fluency is operationally defined as the number of responses to a given stimulus. Originality is operationalized as the uniqueness of responses to stimuli. Flexibility is operationalized as the number and/or uniqueness of categories of responses to stimuli. Elaboration is operationalized as the extension of ideas within a specific category of responses to stimuli, "to fill [ideas] out with details" (Guilford, 1967, p. 138). For example, if a person was trying to decide what to buy as a birthday present for her brother, she could come up with as many ideas for presents as possible (fluency), presents that no one else would think of (originality), a list of different types of presents he may like (flexibility), or a list of the different basketball-related presents he might like (elaboration). However, in this example, as in life, choices have to be made eventually, and evaluative (convergent) thinking must be done to select the actual gift to be purchased.[1]

Major Approaches to DT Assessment

Guilford's (1967) SOI model proposed twenty-four distinct types of divergent thinking: one type for each combination of four kinds of content (Figural, Symbolic, Semantic, Behavioral) and six categories of product (Units, Classes, Relations, Systems, Transformations, Implications). For example, the SOI DT battery consists of several tests that ask participants

---

[1] See Acar and Runco (2015) for a promising, alternative approach.

to exhibit evidence of divergent production in several areas, including divergent production of semantic units (e.g., listing consequences of people no longer needing to sleep), of figural classes (finding as many classifications of sets of figures as possible), and of figural units (taking a simple shape and elaborating upon it as often as possible).

Tasks on the SOI are characterized by the need for trial-and-error strategies and flexible thinking. One well-known example of an SOI task is the Match Problem (divergent production of figural transformations). There are several versions of the Match Problem, but each is a variation on the basic theme of using seventeen matches to create a grid of two rows and three columns (i.e., six squares). Participants are asked to remove three matches so that the remaining matches form four complete squares. By asking participants to transform objects visually and spatially, Guilford was assessing flexibility. Other examples include the Sketches task (fluency with figural units), in which participants draw as many pictures as possible given a specific shape, such as a circle; the Alternate Letter Groups task (flexibility with figural classes), which requires participants to, given a set of letters, form subgroups of letters according to the figural aspects of the letters; and the Associations I task (originality with semantic transformations), in which a person, given two words, finds a third word that links the two (e.g., movie and fishing are linked by reel). Guilford's entire SOI divergent production battery consists of several dozen tests of the various divergent thinking components of the SOI model.

Guilford and his colleagues gathered enormous amounts of assessment data to validate the SOI model. Results are generally supportive of the SOI model (e.g., Chen and Michael, 1993). Although some researchers have suggested revisions to the model or concluded that the model has serious weaknesses (e.g., Sternberg and Grigorenko, 2000–2001), it inspired the development of more recent DT tests such as the **Torrance Tests of Creative Thinking** (TTCT).

The Torrance Tests of Creative Thinking are based upon many aspects of the SOI battery and today are by far the most commonly used DT assessments. Over the course of several decades, Torrance (1974) refined the administration and scoring of the TTCT, which may account for its enduring popularity. The battery includes Verbal and Figural tests that each include a Form A and Form B that can be used alternately. There are seven Verbal subtests consisting of: Asking, Guessing Causes, Guessing Consequences, Product Improvement, Unusual Uses,[2] Unusual Questions, and Just Suppose. The first three verbal subtests provide a picture to be used as a stimulus. For example, the image might be an elf gazing at the reflection in a pool of water with participants asked as many questions as they could about the image, guess causes for what made the image come to be, and guess the consequences that will result from the image.

The other four verbal subtests are independent and do not rely on an external stimulus. For Product Improvement, participants are given a toy and asked for different ways it could be improved. The Unusual Uses test requires participants to list different uses for an everyday object such as a cardboard box. A slight variation on this are the Unusual

---

[2] This subtest does not appear in later editions.

Questions tasks, which requests participants to ask as many questions as possible about an object. The final verbal subtest, Just Suppose, calls for participants to imagine what would happen if an improbable situation took place, such as if people no longer had to sleep.

There are three Figural subtests consisting of Picture Construction, Picture Completion, and Lines/Circles. Picture Construction requires participants to make a picture out of a basic shape, whereas the Picture Completion subtest provides a partially complete picture and asks participants to finish and name the drawing. The Lines/Circles subtest provides participants with either a set of lines or circles to modify and shape.

Administration, scoring, and score reporting of the TTCT are standardized with detailed norms. Although Torrance (1974) recommended that scorers be trained, he found that cursory levels of training (i.e., reading and understanding the scoring manual) allowed novice raters to produce scores associated with acceptable **reliability** estimates. His one caveat was that untrained raters tend to deviate from the scoring system when assessing originality, injecting their own personal judgments on the scoring of individual responses.

The original test produced scores in the traditional four DT areas of fluency, flexibility, originality, and elaboration. The streamlined scoring system introduced in the 1984 revision made significant changes, including the Figural tests being scored for resistance to premature closure and abstractness of titles in addition to the familiar scores of fluency, elaboration, and originality. Flexibility was removed because those scores tended to be largely undifferentiated from fluency scores (Hébert et al., 2002).

Psychometric Evidence

Evidence of reliability for DT assessments is substantial (e.g., Williams, 1980; Torrance, 1981; Acar and Runco, 2019), but the predictive and discriminant **validity** of divergent thinking tests has mixed support (cf. Thompson and Anderson, 1983; Bachelor, 1989; Zeng et al., 2011). Although the perceived lack of predictive validity (Baer, 1993; Weisberg, 1993) has led some researchers and educators to avoid the use of these tests, it is not universally accepted that psychometric measures of creative processes have poor predictive power. In fact, several studies provide at least limited evidence of discriminant and predictive validity for DT tests (Milgram and Hong, 1994; Yamada and Tam, 1996; Dumas and Runco, 2018). The evidence becomes more positive under certain sampling and assessment conditions recommended in the literature (e.g., samples of high IQ children or utilizing content-specific DT measures; see Clapham et al., 2005; Davidovitch and Milgram, 2006). Plucker (1999a), in a reanalysis of Torrance data using more sophisticated statistical techniques, found evidence that DT test scores were three times better than IQ test scores at predicting adult creative achievement.

A final concern with the psychometric measurement of creative processes involves how these batteries are scored. There is some evidence that alternatives to the traditional frequency tabulations of fluency, flexibility, originality, and elaboration should be considered, including the calculation of summative scores (i.e., totaling fluency, flexibility, and originality scores), uncommon scores (answers given by less than 5 percent of participants), weighted fluency scores, percentage scores, and scores based upon the entire body of each participant's answers as opposed to scoring individual responses in a list of ideas (e.g., Plucker et al., 2011, 2014; Silvia, 2011).

In summary, DT tests occupy much of the spotlight on research of the creative process. Although the ability to generate ideas is only one aspect of the creative process, its predominance implicitly devalues the role of creativity in the solving of problems. Although old habits die hard (and slowly), the field is starting to include both quantity and quality of outcome variables.

The Creative Person

A second major area of activity involves assessments of **creative personality**. Measures focusing on characteristics of the person typically focus on **self-report** or external ratings of past behavior or personality characteristics.

Personality Scales

Instruments intended to measure personality correlates of creative behavior are generally designed by studying individuals already deemed creative and then determining their common characteristics. These traits are then used as a reference for other children and adults under the assumption that individuals who compare favorably are predisposed to creative accomplishment. Such measures are quite common in creativity research and include the Self Report of Creative Traits (Runco, Acar, and Cayirdag, 2017), Big Five NEO-Five Factor Inventory (McCrae and Costa, 1997), work undertaken at the Institute of Personality Assessment and Research (MacKinnon, 1978), specific scoring dimensions of the Adjective Check List (Gough, 1979; Domino, 1994), and the Creative Personality Scale (Kaufman and Baer, 2004). After analyzing research that relied on these and related instruments, Davis (1992) concluded that personality characteristics of creative people include awareness of their creativity, originality, independence, risk taking, personal energy, curiosity, humor, attraction to complexity and novelty, artistic sense, open-mindedness, need for privacy, and heightened perception. Similarly, Feist (1998) found consistently that creative people tend to be "autonomous, introverted, open to new experiences, norm-doubting, self-confident, self-accepting, driven, ambitious, dominant, hostile, and impulsive" (p. 299) with openness, conscientiousness, self-acceptance, hostility, and impulsivity having the largest effect sizes (see also Batey and Furnham, 2006; Qian et al., 2010).

A meta-analysis has found that Big Five personality traits have stronger correlations to domain-general measures of creative self-beliefs than domain-specific traits (Karwowski and Lebuda, 2015). Of the Big Five personality traits, openness to experience was the most strongly related to creative self-beliefs; only neuroticism had a negative correlation (although this was weak, -.124). Additionally, openness to experience has been found to predict creative achievement, behaviors, and performance (Beaty et al., 2014; Kaufman, 2016).

Activity Checklists

In addition to personality traits, past behavior of creative individuals is also often examined to determine whether experience is associated with creative production. As a result, self-reports are relied upon for information about an individual's past behaviors and accomplishments that may reflect creative potential and achievement. Based on the assumption that "the best predictor of future creative behavior may be past creative behavior" (Colangelo et al., 1992, p. 158), several self-report biographical or activity inventories have been developed, such as the Creative Behavior Inventory (Hocevar, 1979). Hocevar and Bachelor (1989) and Plucker (1998, 1999b) believe self-reports of activities and attainments to be the preferable technique with which to measure creativity, and Silvia et al. (2012), after a comprehensive analysis, recommended self-reports as a promising creativity assessment technique.

Three examples of this type of instrument include the Creativity Achievement Questionnaire (CAQ; Carson et al., 2005), the Runco Ideational Behavior Scale (RIBS; Runco et al., 2000–2001), and the Kaufman Domains of Creativity Scale (K-DOCS; Kaufman, 2012). The CAQ assesses creativity with ninety-six items across ten domains that load onto an Arts (Drama, Writing, Humor, Music, Visual Arts, and Dance) and a Science (Invention, Science, and Culinary) factor. A respondent indicates the extent to which given items describe their creative achievements in each area. For example, within the Humor scale, items range from "I do not have recognized talent in this area" to "I have created jokes that are now repeated by others," "I have worked as a professional comedian," and "My humor has been recognized in a national publication." The CAQ is associated with high levels of evidence of reliability and with acceptable evidence of concurrent validity.

The RIBS was developed in response to a perceived need for a more appropriate criterion in studies of predictive validity for divergent thinking tests. Runco reasoned that a more appropriate criterion would be one that emphasizes ideation: the use of, appreciation of, and skill of generating ideas. Sample items include, "I think about ideas more often than most people" and "Sometimes I get so interested in a new idea that I forget about other things that I should be doing."

Runco et al. (2000–2001) examined the psychometric integrity of the RIBS, with results suggesting adequate evidence of reliability and construct validity. Plucker et al. (2006) subsequently used the RIBS as a criterion measure in a study of divergent thinking and time-on-task, with positive conclusions about the ability of DT assessments to predict ideational behavior; Runco et al. (2014) recently developed a brief version of the RIBS and gathered evidence of concurrent validity.

The K-DOCS (Kaufman, 2012) consists of fifty items measuring creativity in five broad domains: Self/Everyday, Scholarly, Performance (encompassing writing and music), Mechanical/ Scientific, and Artistic. Participants are asked to rate themselves on a Likert scale from 1 (much less creative) to 5 (much more creative) with regard to various creative behaviors such as "creating a tasty meal out of scattered leftovers" and "finding new ways to motivate myself to do something unpleasant." The K-DOCS is associated with acceptable internal consistency reliability and test-retest reliability (Kaufman, 2012; McKay et al., 2017). Sizable correlations between the five creativity domain scores and the Big Five personality traits, especially openness, also provided solid evidence of convergent validity (Kaufman, 2012).

One weakness of this approach is that administering self-report scales may not be logistically feasible with all groups, such as young children. In response to this need, several instruments have been developed to allow parents, teachers, other adults, and even peers to assess personality and past behavior correlates of creativity. Perhaps the most popular instrument within educational settings is the Scales for Rating the Behavioral Characteristics of Superior Students (SRBCSS; Renzulli et al., 2002). Teachers rate specific students on a six-point scale ranging from *never* to *occasionally* to *always*, with creativity scale items such as "The student demonstrates ... imaginative thinking ability," "... an adventurous spirit or a willingness to take risks," and "... the ability to adapt, improve, or modify objects or ideas."

Validity evidence of both self-reports and ratings by "familiar others" are inconclusive – with respect to creativity and to talent in general – with evidence supporting both validity (Plucker, 2004; McKay et al., 2017; Kaufman, 2019) and a lack thereof (Dollinger et al., 2007).

Attitudes

Theoretical and empirical support exists for a connection between **ideational attitudes** and ideational thinking (Acar and Runco, 2015). Although attempts to measure creative attitudes have not been widespread, considerable effort has been expended on the creation of attitude measures to evaluate attitudes toward interventions in business across cultures (Basadur et al., 2002) and identifying individuals who are predisposed to innovation or adaptation (Kirton, 2006).

For example, Basadur and colleagues have developed two scales that assess attitudes toward important aspects of divergent thinking, the six-item Preference for Active Divergence scale and the eight-item Preference for Premature Convergence (or premature closure) scale, with the former being indicative of positive DT attitudes and the latter being counterindicative (Basadur et al., 1999). Items on the Active Divergence scale include "One new idea is worth 10 old ones" and "I feel that all ideas should be given equal time and listened to with an open mind, regardless of how zany they seem to be." Items representing Premature Convergence include "Lots of time can be wasted on wild ideas" and "I wish people would think about whether or not an idea is practical before they open their mouths."

In the school setting, Runco et al. (2017) developed the Creative Attitudes and Values scale, a ten-item instrument to measure students' attitude toward divergent thinking. A sample item is: "Even if some method has worked well in the past, it is a good idea to question and perhaps change it on a regular basis." Every item has five response options: Never (0), Rarely (1), Sometimes (2), Mostly (3), and Always (4). In a related vein – but from a very different perspective – Hao et al. (2016) developed a measure of malevolent creativity providing scores on three scales: hurting people, lying, and playing tricks on people.

Tierney and Farmer (2011) and Schenkel et al. (2015), building on the work of Gist and Mitchell (1992), proposed the concept of creative self-efficacy as representing a person's beliefs about how creative they can be. Measures of creative self-efficacy are often brief; as an example, Beghetto (2006) used a three-item scale: "I am good at coming up with new ideas," "I have a lot of good ideas," and "I have a good imagination." In another study, Beghetto et al. (2011) used a five-item scale to measure students' creative efficacy in science: I am good at coming up with new ideas during science class, I have a good imagination during science class, I have a lot of good ideas during science class, I am good at coming up with my own science experiments, and I am good at coming up with new ways of finding solutions to science problems.

Karwowski (2014) also developed two measures, the ten-item Creative Mindsets Scale that assesses participant beliefs regarding the fixed vs. growth nature of creativity, and the eleven-item Short Scale of Creative Self that measures an individual's creative self-concept, including both creative self-efficacy (CSE) and creative personal identity (CPI). Sample items include "Some people are creative, others aren't – and no practice can change it" (Creative Mindsets), "I am good at proposing original solutions to problems" (CSE), and "I think I am a creative person" (CPI). All the items are answered using a five-point scale with 1 representing Definitely Not, and 5 being Definitely Yes.

All of these researchers have gathered evidence of reliability and validity, although the theoretical and psychometric distinctions between measures of creative self-efficacy and instruments such as the RIBS, which have similar items but are intended to measure different constructs, have yet to be clarified.

Creative Products

Assessment of creative products receives much less attention in the literature than assessment of personality, process, or even environmental variables, yet a case can be made that the ability to measure a product's creativity is among the most important aspects of creativity assessment in the real world. For example, if a company designs a new app or cell phone, being able to assess the degree of creativity in various designs may lead to substantial profit – and potential savings, as resources are not wasted on non-creative designs. In a different vein, the creativity of artistic products is often hotly debated; those debates are almost always subjective in nature and perhaps need not be.

From a psychological and educational perspective, Runco (1989) noted that analysis of creative products may address the measurement problems caused by the inconsistent psychometric quality of other forms of creativity measurement. More to the point, Baer and Kaufman (see Baer et al., 2004), among others, believe that product assessments are probably the most appropriate assessments of creativity. This logic is compelling: If one goal of creativity psychometrics is to predict who is most likely to produce creative works in the future, being able to create such products in the present is a key indicator.

Advanced techniques for the assessment of creative products clearly have a wide range of potential applications, and after some stagnation in the mid- to late-1990s, a number of potentially fruitful efforts have emerged in recent years. Although a number of high-quality product assessments have been developed, including the Creative Product Semantic Scale (Besemer and O'Quin, 1999) and the Student Product Assessment Form (Reis and Renzulli, 1991), the most active area is that of the Consensual Assessment Technique (CAT; see Amabile, 1983 for information on the early development of the methodology).

The CAT is an attempt to solve the "criterion problem" in creativity research: How do we know we are using the correct criteria of creativity when we design assessments? The criterion problem is a direct result of the field's difficulty defining its terms, which was discussed earlier in the chapter. Amabile (1982) hypothesized that "a product or response is creative to the extent that appropriate observers independently agree it is creative" (p. 1001). In other words, people know creativity when they see it, and the use of expert judges to evaluate a product's creativity should, theoretically, avoid criterion problems. Evidence of reliability has been found across a wide range of applications (Hennessey, 1994; Baer et al., 2004).

However, the use of expert judges is not without controversy. Early in the development of the CAT, evidence suggested that determining the necessary level of expertise for judges depends on a variety of factors, including the skill of the subjects, the target domain, and the purpose of the assessments (e.g., Runco et al., 1994; Amabile, 1996). Although Amabile (1996) recommends that experts have "at least some formal training and experience in the target domain" (p. 73), several researchers have examined the level of expertise that is necessary when using the CAT or similar assessment strategies. Indeed, researchers have learned a great deal about the use of expert judges to evaluate creative products. In general, expert and novice judges tend to produce quite different ratings of product creativity, although the domain in which the product is created impacts the degree to which the groups' ratings overlap. For example, Kaufman et al. (2008) found that expert and novice (e.g., college student) ratings of poetry barely correlated, yet Kaufman et al. (2009) found a higher correlation between the similar groups when evaluating the creativity of short stories. When using artistic products, Dollinger et al. (2004) found large correlations between artists and psychologists.

Recent research suggests that expertise, at least in this context, should be conceptualized as a continuum. When Kaufman et al. (2005) compared expert judges and quasi-experts (gifted high school writers), they found appreciably higher correlations between the two groups' ratings of creative writing products than previous research would have predicted. Similarly, Plucker et al. (2009) found that the movie ratings of professional movie critics (experts), film website users (novices), and college students (laypeople) fall on a continuum, with lowest ratings from critics and highest ratings from college students, with novices firmly in between the other two groups. Other researchers (Kaufman and Baer, 2012; Kaufman et al., 2013) further noted that the level of expertise required to evaluate creative work may differ across domains. These studies suggest both the level of expertise and nature of domains should be considered when selecting CAT raters and that novices do not appear to be the ideal CAT raters.

Two issues should be considered when evaluating the research on the CAT. First, the CAT, as it has been applied in various ways by researchers, is associated with convincing evidence of reliability. However, some researchers (e.g., Jeffries, 2017) have argued that the level of agreement among experts (i.e., inter-rater reliability) can be low, and the results are also heavily influenced by the instructions raters are provided with prior to their evaluation of the creative aspects of products. Moreover, evidence of validity is primarily found in the area of face validity, and several key aspects of validity such as generalizability and convergent and discriminant validity have not yet been examined.

This concern leads to the second issue, which involves questions about the appropriateness of using external judges to evaluate creativity. Runco and colleagues (Runco and Vega, 1990; Runco and Smith, 1992; Runco, McCarthy, and Svenson, 1994) have long questioned why "expert" opinion would be more valid or useful than self-ratings or the evaluations of peers, teachers, and other groups that are not necessarily experts. This is not a trivial concern: Given the expense and difficulty often encountered when planning and implementing studies involving expert raters, determining the appropriate level of expertise (if any) required for valid results when using CAT-like assessment strategies should continue to be a priority for researchers. At least, peer and teacher evaluations are based on long-term observations and should be considered along with "expert" ratings.

Consumer Product Design Models

As research on design has become more prevalent in the psychological and educational literature, the assessment of creative products from a design perspective has likewise become more common. As Christiaans (2002) has observed, "the result of a design activity is often expected to be original, adding value to the existing world of design. In the selection of designs for production in companies, for design awards, and in the field of design education, creativity assessment relies on human judgments" (p. 41). Although some researchers have used existing instruments and techniques (e.g., Christiaans used an approximation of the CAT and the Creative Product Semantic Scale), new models are also in development. A case in point is the research of Horn and Salvendy (2006), in which the researchers have questioned the applicability of existing product measures to the design context and propose an alternative model consisting of six components: Novelty (the newness of the product), Resolution (the ability of a product to resolve a problem), Emotion (the pleasure or arousal induced by the product), Centrality (ability to match consumer needs), Importance (importance to consumer needs), and Desire (how critical or desirable the product is). Then Horn and Salvendy (2009) reduced the six-dimensional model of product creativity to a more parsimonious three-dimensional model: Affect (emotional draw and feelings toward the product), Importance (importance or relevance to consumer needs), and Novelty (uniqueness and newness of a product). The increasing importance of design (see Worwood and Plucker, 2017) suggests this approach to creative product assessment will only increase in importance.

Creative Environments

Hunter et al. (2007), in their comprehensive review of research on situational influences on creativity, identified a number of environmental variables suspected to be related to creativity, including intra- and inter-group interactions, leadership, organizational structure, leadership, competition, and cohesion, among many others. A casual review of research literature in business and management shows many studies of how creativity and work environments are related (or not). Sternberg (2016) also discusses different kinds of environments and the extent to which they allow creativity.

Much of this research examines the correlation between successful work and situational variables and does not focus on assessments of **creative environments** per se. For example, Forbes and Domm (2004), in an approach influenced by the work of Amabile and her colleagues, developed an environment survey that required participants to rate the importance of items related to a recent, successful, creative project on which they worked. Six factors emerged from the data: mental involvement, intrinsic motivation, time and resource constraints, extrinsic motivation, external control, and team management.

One exception to this trend is the work of Amabile and her colleagues. Based on extensive research on organizational creativity, Amabile et al. (1996) developed the KEYS: Assessing the Climate for Creativity instrument to examine employees' perceptions of aspects of their work environment that may influence creative work – especially creative work by teams. They note that the self-report instrument is designed to assess "individuals' perceptions and the influence of those perceptions on the creativity of their work" (p. 1157). This instrument is associated with evidence of reliability and validity and is widely used by researchers.

Strengths and Weaknesses of Creativity Assessment

In reviewing the extensive literature, a number of clear strengths and weaknesses of creativity assessment become obvious. The sheer depth of psychometric work is impressive, with decades of studies and instrument development available. Indeed, a case can be made that many of the foundations of the field are based on this voluminous psychometric research; this work appears to be particularly influential outside of the United States.

Another strength is that, in certain contexts (e.g., samples of high IQ children, using content-specific DT measures), evidence of validity – including predictive validity – is rather convincing. A related weakness, of course, is that many popular instruments are not associated with convincing evidence or have been subjected to little psychometric evaluation.

Third, criticisms of creativity assessment aimed at divergent thinking are probably overblown. Although the field's reliance on divergent thinking is a weakness, those researchers interested in creativity should consider Guilford's (1968) observation that "most of our problem solving in everyday life involves divergent thinking. Yet in our educational practices, we tend to emphasize teaching students how to find conventional answers" (p. 8). This comment is as salient today as when Guilford first wrote it. For example, the past twenty years have seen an increasing emphasis on standardized tests in K–12 schools, yet employers continue to call for employees with creative skill sets. A better way forward involves strategies that move well beyond DT, such as multifaceted, multimodal assessment systems involving many of the other strong measures discussed in this chapter.

All of that said, many criticisms about creativity psychometrics are valid. Some should be relatively straightforward to address, others more difficult. First and foremost, for nearly half a century, scholars have been calling for more research on the criterion problem. This is the area that has received the most attention from researchers in recent years, although the needed psychometric work mentioned above is conspicuous in its absence.

The traditional criticisms about lack of predictive, discriminant, and construct validity evidence still hold true, although as noted above, there are many caveats and exceptions. But creativity assessment researchers still do not conduct evaluations of psychometric integrity very often, which adds to the problem both by failing to gather needed data and giving the impression that this type of work is unimportant. This research is needed for every type of assessment, from DT tests to the CAT. Other DT tasks not scored in this way (e.g., much of Guilford's work) are associated with more positive evaluations of construct validity than the TTCT. A potential solution is obvious: Score the TTCT without response set bias and examine the resulting construct validity evidence. Yet we have not been able to find any such studies in the more than thirty years since this hypothesis was discussed in the published literature. In a completely different area, CAT research is marked by a distinct lack of predictive validity studies, which is surprising given that many CAT advocates have stridently criticized DT assessments for their purported lack of evidence of this type. Addressing these criticisms should not be difficult, yet this research remains uncommon.

Another frequent criticism is that the field is living in the past, methodologically speaking: the almost exclusive reliance on classical test theory, the use of traditional assessment strategies, etc. These criticisms are not without warrant, and we would go further to call for explorations in the use of **biometric and neurocognitive methods**, those assessments that involve the direct measurement of biological characteristics and processes, which are gaining popularity in other fields but have generally not been applied in the assessment of creativity. Applying these methods will be expensive and time-consuming, but the potential benefits could be tremendous.

Such improvement in method, coupled with advancements in theory and reproducibility, will help lead creativity toward being more of a cumulative science (Makel and Plucker, 2014; Vartanian, 2014; Plucker, 2017). Despite all of the recent developments in creativity assessment, avenues for truly original approaches to creativity assessment remain. Psychometric limitations of creative assessment are likely what typically come to mind when considering limitations of assessment. But theoretical limitations are also important (Vartanian, 2014). Without developed theory, assessment is also stunted. Take, for example, the propulsion theory of creativity offered by Sternberg et al. (2001), in which eight qualitatively distinct kinds of creativity are posited. The idea of propulsion stems from the concept that creative ideas propel a field forward. The eight types are grouped into three categories: those that accept current paradigms (replication, redefinition, forward incrementation, advance forward incrementation), those that reject them (redirection, reconstruction/redirection, reinitiation), and those that synthesize them (integration). The distinctions are meant to differentiate type, not amount of creativity. Such a unique approach to creativity appears to be a promising foundation on which to build a new series of creative product assessments, yet no one beyond Sternberg and his colleagues appears to be willing to take the bait.

Finally, a major limitation on the usefulness of creativity assessments is the lack of instruments and strategies that can be scaled to use with large groups. For example, most DT assessments are easy to administer but extraordinarily time-intensive (and if we are being honest, dreary) to score. This makes them less than ideal for classroom use, let alone use in state-wide K–12 school accountability systems or college admissions (Plucker and Alanazi, 2019). Rapidly advancing technology has been suggested as a potential solution to this scaling problem. Regardless, the ability to "scale up" creativity assessments may very well determine whether these important measures become highly influential alternatives to achievement tests or remain useful, small-scale research tools with limited impact.

Our Research Contribution

Our team has conducted reviews of the creativity assessment research (Plucker and Alanazi, 2019; Plucker et al., 2019), developed creativity assessments and related strategies to fill needs in the field (Qian et al., 2010; Plucker et al., 2014; Qian et al., 2019), and used those and other instruments in our research (Plucker, 1999; Hartley and Plucker, 2014; Yi et al., 2015). We have also considered theoretical aspects of creativity, such as how creativity is and can be defined (Plucker et al., 2004) and the degree to which creativity is domain general or domain specific (Plucker, 2014; Worwood and Plucker, 2017; Qian and Plucker, 2018). Finally, we have explored the role of research within the field of creativity, with an emphasis on the use of open science strategies to promote high-quality, replicable research (Makel, 2014; Makel and Plucker, 2014; Plucker, 2017).

Critical/Creative Thinking Questions

1. What are ways you could use creativity assessment data in your field of interest?
2. What are two advantages and two disadvantages of classifying creativity assessments according to the categories of person, process, product, and press (environment)?
3. Some creativity assessments are associated with impressive reliability evidence but less convincing validity evidence. But is it possible to have an assessment with good evidence of validity but poor evidence of reliability?
4. How would a sociocultural scholar (e.g., Glăveanu) look at creativity assessment?

GLOSSARY

assessment: The process of gathering data representing one's aptitudes, knowledge, attitudes, cognition, or potential (often used interchangeably with the term, measurement).

biometric and neurocognitive methods: Assessments involving the direct measurement of biological characteristics and processes.

convergent thinking: Cognitive processes that produce one or very few possible solutions to a given problem.

creative environment: The social and physical context in which creativity occurs, also referred to as creative press.

creative person: Aspects of one's personality and motivation that are correlated with creativity.

creative process: Those aspects of creativity that focus on how an individual or group thinks about problem solving and ideation.

creative product: The tangible result of creativity and innovation, with "tangible" defined broadly.

divergent thinking tasks: Tests that require individuals to produce several responses to a specific prompt and not one correct answer. Often addressed in figural or verbal forms, and responses are generally scored for fluency, flexibility, originality, and elaboration.

ideational attitudes: An individual's feelings toward ideas and their ability to create them.

ideational fluency: The ability to create ideas, with high fluency representing a large number of ideas.

psychometric methods: Assessments that assess various aspects of the psychology of individuals.

reliability: The level at which the score on an assessment is consistent across multiple administrations of that assessment.

self-report assessments: Psychometric methods in which individuals rate themselves on specific characteristics, behaviors, and attitudes.

structure of the intellect: J. P. Guilford's model of human intelligence, which incorporates creativity into his conception of the intellect.

Torrance Tests of Creative Thinking: The most widely used assessment of divergent thinking.

validity: The degree to which a score on a specific assessment represents what it is intended to measure.

REFERENCES

Acar, S., and Runco, M. A. (2015). Thinking in Multiple Directions: Hyperspace Categories in Divergent Thinking. *Psychology of Aesthetics, Creativity, and the Arts*, 9, 41–53. doi.org/10.1037/a0038501.

(2019). Divergent Thinking: New Methods, Recent Research, and Extended Theory. *Psychology of Aesthetics, Creativity, and the Arts*, 13(2), 153–158. doi.org/10.1037/aca0000231.

Amabile, T. M. (1982). Social Psychology of Creativity: A Consensual Assessment Technique. *Journal of Personality and Social Psychology*, 43, 997–1013. doi.org/10.1037/0022-3514.43.5.997.

(1983). *The Social Psychology of Creativity*. New York: Springer-Verlag.

(1996). *Creativity in Context: Update to the Social Psychology of Creativity*. Nashville: Westview.

Amabile, T. M., Conti, R., Coon, H., Lazenby, J., and Herron, M. (1996). Assessing the Work Environment for Creativity. *Academy of Management Journal*, 39, 1154–1184. doi.org/10.2307/256995.

Bachelor, P. (1989). Maximum Likelihood Confirmatory Factor-Analytic Investigation of Factors within Guilford's Structure-of-Intellect Model. *Journal of Applied Psychology, 74,* 797–804. doi .org/10.1037/0021-9010.74.5.797.

Baer, J. (1993). *Creativity and Divergent Thinking: A Task-Specific Approach.* Mahwah: Lawrence Erlbaum Associates.

Baer, J., Kaufman, J. C., and Gentile, C. A. (2004). Extension of the Consensual Assessment Technique to Nonparallel Creative Products. *Creativity Research Journal, 16,* 113–117. doi.org/ 10.1207/s15326934crj1601_11.

Basadur, M., Pringle, P., and Kirkland, D. (2002). Crossing Cultures: Training Effects on the Divergent Thinking Attitudes of Spanish-Speaking South American Managers. *Creativity Research Journal, 14,* 395–408. doi.org/10.1017/CBO9780511763205.017.

Basadur, M., Taggar, S., and Pringle, P. (1999). Improving the Measurement of Divergent Thinking Attitudes in Organizations. *Journal of Creative Behavior, 33,* 75–111. doi.org/10.1002/j.2162-6057 .1999.tb01040.x.

Batey, M., and Furnham, A. (2006). Creativity, Intelligence, and Personality: A Critical Review of the Scattered Literature. *Genetic, Social, and General Psychology Monographs, 132,* 355–429. doi.org/ 10.3200/MONO.132.4.355-430.

Beaty, R. E., Nusbaum, E. C., and Silvia, P. J. (2014). Does Insight Problem Solving Predict Real-World Creativity? *Psychology of Aesthetics, Creativity, and the Arts, 8,* 287–292. doi.org/10.1037/ a0035727.

Beghetto, R. A. (2006). Creative Self-Efficacy: Correlates in Middle and Secondary Students. *Creativity Research Journal, 18,* 447–457. doi.org/10.1207/s15326934crj1804_4.

Beghetto, R. A., Kaufman, J. C., and Baxter, J. (2011). Answering the Unexpected Questions: Student Self-Beliefs and Teacher Ratings of Creativity in Elementary Math and Science. *Psychology of Aesthetics, Creativity, and the Arts, 5,* 342–349. doi.org/10.1037/a0022834.

Benedek, M., Mühlmann, C., Jauk, E., and Neubauer, A. C. (2013). Assessment of Divergent Thinking by Means of the Subjective Top-Scoring Method: Effects of the Number of Top-Ideas and Time-on-Task on Reliability and Validity. *Psychology of Aesthetics, Creativity, and the Arts, 7,* 341–349.

Besemer, S.P., and O'Quin, K. (1999). Confirming the Three-Factor Creative Product Analysis Matrix Model in an American Sample. *Creativity Research Journal, 12,* 287–296. doi.org/10.1207/ s15326934crj1204_6.

Carson, S. H., Peterson, J. B., and Higgins, D. M. (2005). Reliability, Validity, and Factor Structure of the Creative Achievement Questionnaire. *Creativity Research Journal, 17,* 37–50. doi.org/10.1207/ s15326934crj1701_4.

Chand, I., and Runco, M. A. (1992). Problem Finding Skills As Components in the Creative Process. *Personality and Individual Differences, 14,* 155–162. doi.org/10.1016/0191-8869(93)90185-6.

Chen S., A., and Michael, W. B. (1993). First-Order and Higher-Order Factors of Creative Social Intelligence within Guilford's Structure-of-Intellect Model: A Reanalysis of a Guilford Data Base. *Educational and Psychological Measurement, 53,* 619–641. doi.org/10 .1177/0013164493053003004.

Christiaans, H. H. C. M. (2002). Creativity As a Design Criterion. *Creativity Research Journal, 14,* 41–54. doi.org/10.1207/S15326934CRJ1401_4.

Clapham, M. M., Cowdery, E. M., King, K. E., and Montang, M. A. (2005). Predicting Work Activities with Divergent Thinking Tests: A Longitudinal Study. *Journal of Creative Behavior, 39,* 149–167. doi.org/10.1002/j.2162-6057.2005.tb01256.x.

Colangelo, N., Kerr, B., Hallowell, K., Huesman, R., and Gaeth, J. (1992). The Iowa Inventiveness Inventory: Toward a Measure of Mechanical Inventiveness. *Creativity Research Journal, 5,* 157–163. doi.org/10.1080/10400419209534429.

Davidovitch, N., and Milgram, R. M. (2006). Creative Thinking As a Predictor of Teacher Effectiveness in Higher Education. *Creativity Research Journal, 18,* 385–390. doi.org/10.1207/ s15326934crj1803_12.

Davis, G. A. (1992). *Creativity Is Forever,* 3rd ed. Dubuque: Kendall/Hunt.

Dollinger, S. J., Burke, P. A., and Gump, N. W. (2007). Creativity and Values. *Creativity Research Journal, 19,* 91–103. doi.org/10.1080/10400410701395028.

Dollinger, S. J., Urban, K. K., and James, T. A. (2004). Creativity and Openness: Further Validation of Two Creative Product Measures. *Creativity Research Journal, 16,* 35–47. doi.org/10.1207/ s15326934crj1601_4.

Domino, G. (1994). Assessment of Creativity with the ACL: An Empirical Comparison of Four Scales. *Creativity Research Journal, 7,* 21–33. doi.org/10.1080/10400419409534506.

Dumas, D., and Runco, M. (2018). Objectively Scoring Divergent Thinking Tests for Originality: A Re-Analysis and Extension. *Creativity Research Journal, 30*(4), 466–468.

Feist, G. J. (1998). A Meta-Analysis of Personality in Scientific and Artistic Creativity. *Personality and Social Psychology Review, 2*(4), 290–309. doi.org/10.1207/s15327957pspr0204_5.

Forbes, J. B., and Domm, D. R. (2004). Creativity and Productivity: Resolving the Conflict. *SAM Advanced Management Journal, 69*(2), 4–11.

Getzels, J. W., and Jackson, P. W. (1962). *Creativity and Intelligence: Explorations with Gifted Students.* San Francisco: Wiley.

Gist, M. E., and Mitchell, T. R. (1992). Self-Efficacy: A Theoretical Analysis of Its Determinants and Malleability. *Academy of Management Review, 17,* 183–211.

Glăveanu, V. P. (2013). Rewriting the Language of Creativity: The Five A's Framework. *Review of General Psychology, 17,* 69–81. doi:10.1037/a0029528.

Gough, H. G. (1979). A Creative Personality Scale for the Adjective Check List. *Journal of Personality and Social Psychology, 37,* 1398–1405. doi.org/10.1037/0022-3514.37.8.1398.

Guilford, J. P. (1967). *The Nature of Human Intelligence.* New York: McGraw-Hill.

  (1968). *Intelligence, Creativity and Their Educational Implications.* San Deigo: Robert R. Knapp.

Hartley, K. A., and Plucker, J. (2014). Teacher Use of Creativity-Enhancing Activities in Chinese and American Elementary Classrooms. *Creativity Research Journal, 26,* 389–399. doi:10.1080/ 10400419.2014.961771.

Hass, R. W. (2015). Feasibility of Online Divergent Thinking Assessment. *Computers in Human Behavior, 46,* 85–93. doi.org/10.1016/j.chb.2014.12.056.

Heausler, N. L., and Thompson, B. (1988). Structure of the Torrance Tests of Creative Thinking. *Educational and Psychological Measurement, 48,* 463–468. doi.org/10.1016/j.tsc.2017.11.005.

Hébert, T. P., Cramond, B., Spiers-Neumeister, K. L., Millar, G., and Silvian, A. F. (2002). *E. Paul Torrance: His Life, Accomplishments, and Legacy.* Storrs: The University of Connecticut, National Research Center on the Gifted and Talented.

Hennessey, B. A. (1994). The Consensual Assessment Technique: An Examination of the Relationship between Ratings of Product and Process Creativity. *Creativity Research Journal, 7,* 193–208. doi.org/10.1080/10400419409534524.

Hao, N., Tang, M., Yang, J., Wang, Q., and Runco, M. A. (2016). A New Tool to Measure Malevolent Creativity: The Malevolent Creativity Behavior Scale. *Frontiers in Psychology, 7,* Article 682. doi:10.3389/fpsyg.2016.00682.

Hocevar, D. (1979). "The Development of the Creative Behavior Inventory." Paper presented at the annual meeting of the Rocky Mountain Psychological Association. (ERIC Document Reproduction Service No. ED 170 350)

Hocevar, D., and Bachelor, P. (1989). A Taxonomy and Critique of Measurements Used in the Study of Creativity. In J. A. Glover, R. R. Ronning, and C. R. Reynolds (Eds.), *Handbook of Creativity* (pp. 53–75). New York: Plenum Press.

Horn, D., and Salvendy, G. (2006). Product Creativity: Conceptual Model, Measurement and Characteristics. *Theoretical Issues in Ergonomics Science, 7,* 395–412. doi.org/10.1080/14639220500078195.

(2009). Measuring Consumer Perception of Product Creativity: Impact on Satisfaction and Purchasability. *Human Factors and Ergonomics in Manufacturing, 19,* 223–240. doi:10.1002/hfm.20150.

Hu, W., and Adey, P. (2002). A Scientific Creativity Test for Secondary School Students. *International Journal of Science Education, 24,* 389–403. doi.org/10.1080/09500690110098912.

Hunter, S. T., Bedell, K. E., and Mumford, M. D. (2007). Climate for Creativity: A Quantitative Review. *Creativity Research Journal, 19,* 69–90. doi: 10.1080/10400410709336883.

Jeffries, K. K. (2017). A CAT with Caveats: Is the Consensual Assessment Technique a Reliable Measure of Graphic Design Creativity? *International Journal of Design Creativity and Innovation, 5,* 16–28. doi.org/10.1080/21650349.2015.1084893.

Karwowski, M. (2014). Creative Mindsets: Measurement, Correlates, Consequences. *Psychology of Aesthetics, Creativity, and the Arts, 8,* 62–70. doi:10.1037/a0034898.

Karwowski, M., and Lebuda, I. (2015). The Big Five, the Huge Two, and Creative Self-Beliefs: A Meta-Analysis. *Psychology of Aesthetics, Creativity, and the Arts, 10,* 214–232. doi.org/10.1037/aca0000035.

Kaufman, J. C. (2012). Counting the Muses: Development of the Kaufman-Domains of Creativity Scale (K-DOCS). *Psychology of Aesthetics, Creativity, and the Arts, 6,* 298–308. doi:10.1037/a0029751.

(2019). Self-Assessments of Creativity: Not Ideal, But Better Than You Think. *Psychology of Aesthetics, Creativity, and the Arts, 13,* 187–192. doi:10.1037/aca0000217.

Kaufman, J. C., and Baer, J. (2004). Sure, I'm creative – But Not in Mathematics!: Self-Reported Creativity in Diverse Domains. *Empirical Studies of the Arts, 22,* 143–155. doi:10.2190/26HQ-VHE8-GTLN-BJJM.

(2012). Beyond New and Appropriate: Who Decides What Is Creative? *Creativity Research Journal, 24,* 83–91. doi.org/10.1080/10400419.2012.649237.

Kaufman, J. C., Baer, J., and Cole, J. C. (2009). Expertise, Domains, and the Consensual Assessment Technique. *Journal of Creative Behavior, 43,* 223–233. doi.org/10.1002/j.2162-6057.2009.tb01316.x.

Kaufman, J. C., Baer, J., Cole, J. C., and Sexton, J. D. (2008). A Comparison of Expert and Nonexpert Raters Using the Consensual Assessment Technique. *Creativity Research Journal, 20,* 171–178. doi:10.1080/10400410802059929.

Kaufman, J. C., Baer, J., Cropley, D. H., Reiter-Palmon, R., and Sinnett, S. (2013). Furious Activity vs. Understanding: How Much Expertise Is Needed to Evaluate Creative Work? *Psychology of Aesthetics, Creativity, and the Arts, 7,* 332–340. doi.org/10.1037/a0034809.

Kaufman, J. C., Gentile, C. A., and Baer, J. (2005). Do Gifted Student Writers and Creative Writing Experts Rate Creativity the Same Way? *Gifted Child Quarterly, 49,* 260–265. doi.org/10.1177/001698620504900307.

Kaufman, J. C., Plucker, J. A., and Baer, J. (2008). *Essentials of Creativity Assessment*. San Francisco: Wiley.

Kaufman, S. B. (2016). Opening up Openness to Experience: A Four-Factor Model and Relations to Creative Achievement in the Arts and Sciences. *Journal of Creative Behaviors*, *47*, 233–255. doi.org/10.1002/jocb.33.

Kirton, M. J. (2006). *Adaptation-Innovation in the Context of Diversity and Change*. Abingdon: Routledge.

MacKinnon, D. W. (1978). *In Search of Human Effectiveness: Identifying and Developing Creativity*. Buffalo: The Creative Education Foundation.

Makel, M. C. (2014). The Empirical March: Making Science Better at Self-Correction. *Psychology of Aesthetics, Creativity, and the Arts*, *8*(1), 2–7. doi.org/10.1037/a0035803.

Makel, M. C., and Plucker, J. A. (2014). Creativity Is More Than Novelty: Reconsidering Replication As a Creativity Act. *Psychology of Aesthetics, Creativity, and the Arts*, *8*, 27–29.

McCrae, R. R., and Costa, P. T. (1997). Personality Trait Structure As a Human Universal. *American Psychologist*, *52*, 509–516.

McKay, A. S., Karwowski, M., and Kaufman, J. C. (2017). Measuring the Muses: Validating the Kaufman Domains of Creativity Scale (K-DOCS). *Psychology of Aesthetics, Creativity, and the Arts*, *11*, 216–230.

Milgram, R. M., and Hong, E. (1994). Creative Thinking and Creative Performance in Adolescents As Predictors of Creative Attainments in Adults: A Follow-up Study after 18 Years. In R. F. Subotnik and K. D. Arnold (Eds.), *Beyond Terman: Contemporary Longitudinal Studies of Giftedness and Talent* (pp. 212–228). New York: Ablex.

National Association of Colleges and Employers. (2018). Job Outlook 2018. www.naceweb.org/store/2017/job-outlook-2018/.

Plucker, J. A. (1998). Beware of Simple Conclusions: The Case for Content Generality of Creativity. *Creativity Research Journal*, *11*, 179–182.

1999a). Is the Proof in the Pudding? Reanalyses of Torrance's (1958 to Present) Longitudinal Study Data. *Creativity Research Journal*, *12*, 103–114.

(1999b). Reanalyses of Student Responses to Creativity Checklists: Evidence of Content Generality. *Journal of Creative Behavior*, *33*, 126–137.

(2004). Generalization of Creativity across Domains: Examination of the Method Effect Hypothesis. *Journal of Creative Behavior*, *38*, 1–12.

(2017). Toward a Science of Creativity: Considerable Progress But Much Work to Be Done. *Journal of Creative Behavior*, *51*, 301–304.

Plucker, J. A., and Alanazi, R. (2019). Is Creativity Compatible with Educational Accountability? Promise and Pitfalls of Using Assessment to Monitor and Enhance a Complex Construct. In I. Lebuda and V. P. Glăveanu (Eds.), *The Palgrave Handbook of Social Creativity Research* (pp. 501–514). New York: Palgrave Macmillan.

Plucker, J. A., Beghetto, R. A., and Dow, G. T. (2004). Why Isn't Creativity More Important to Educational Psychologists? Potentials, Pitfalls, and Future Directions in Creativity Research. *Educational Psychologist*, *39*(2), 83–96. doi.org/10.1207/s15326985ep3902_1

Plucker, J. A., Kaufman, J. C., Temple, J. S., and Qian, M. (2009). Do Experts and Novices Evaluate Movies the Same Way? *Psychology and Marketing*, *26*, 470–478.

Plucker, J. A., Qian, M., and Schmalensee, S. L. (2014). Is What You See What You Really Get? Comparison of Scoring Techniques in the Assessment of Real-World Divergent Thinking. *Creativity Research Journal*, *26* (2), 135–143.

Plucker, J. A., Qian, M., and Wang, S. (2011). Is Originality in the Eye of the Beholder? Comparison of Scoring Techniques in the Assessment of Divergent Thinking. *Journal of Creative Behavior*, *45*, 1–22.

Plucker, J. A., Runco, M. A., and Lim, W. (2006). Predicting Ideational Behavior from Divergent Thinking and Discretionary Time on Task. *Creativity Research Journal*, *18*, 55–63. doi:10.1207/s15326934crj1801_7.

Pretz, J. E., and Kaufman, J. C. (2017). Do Traditional Admissions Criteria Reflect Applicant Creativity? *The Journal of Creative Behavior*, *51*, 240–251. doi.org/10.1002/jocb.120.

Qian, M., and Plucker, J. A. (2018). Looking for Renaissance People: Examining Domain Specificity-Generality of Creativity Using Item Response Theory Models. *Creativity Research Journal*, *30*, 241–248. doi.org/10.1080/10400419.2018.1488348.

Qian, M., Plucker, J. A., and Shen, J. (2010). A Model of Chinese Adolescents' Creative Personality. *Creativity Research Journal*, *22*, 62–67. doi.org/10.1080/10400410903579585.

Qian, M., Plucker, J. A, and Yang, X. (2019). Evidence of the Psychometric Integrity of the Creative Personality Scale Using Item Response Theory Models. *Creativity Research Journal*, *31*, 349–355. doi.org/10.1080/10400419.2019.1647758.

Reis, S. M., and Renzulli, J. S. (1991). The Assessment of Creative Products in Programs for Gifted and Talented Students. *Gifted Child Quarterly*, *35*, 128–134.

Renzulli, J. S., Smith, L. H., White, A. J., Callahan, C. M., Hartman, R. K., and Westberg, K. L. (2002). *Scales for Rating the Behavioral Characteristics of Superior Students: Technical and Administration Manual*, rev. ed. Mansfield Center: Creative Learning Press.

Runco, M. A. (1989). The Creativity of Children's Art. *Child Study Journal*, *19*, 177–189.

(1999) Divergent Thinking. In M. A. Runco and S. Pritzker (Eds.), *Encyclopedia of Creativity*, vol. I (pp. 577–582). San Diego: Academic Press.

Runco, M. A., Acar, S., and Cayirdaga, N. (2017). A Closer Look at the Creativity Gap and Why Students Are Less Creative at School Than Outside of School. *Thinking Skills and Creativity*, *24*, 242–249.

Runco, M. A., McCarthy, K. A., and Svenson, E. (1994). Judgments of the Creativity of Artwork from Students and Professional Artists. *The Journal of Psychology*, *128*, 23–31.

Runco, M. A., Plucker, J. A., and Lim, W. (2000–2001). Development and Psychometric Integrity of a Measure of Ideational Behavior. *Creativity Research Journal*, *13*, 393–400.

Runco, M. A., and Smith, W. R. (1992). Interpersonal and Intrapersonal Evaluations of Creative Ideas. *Personality and Individual Differences*, *13*, 295–302.

Runco, M. A., and Vega, L. (1990). Evaluating the Creativity of Children's ideas. *Journal of Social Behavior and Personality*, *5*, 439–452.

Schenkel, M. T., Farmer, S. M., and Maslyn, J. M. (2015). From Harmonious Passion to Innovation: Examining the Roles of Creative Self-Efficacy and Leadership. *Academy of Management Proceedings*, *1*, 12909–12909.

Silvia, P. J. (2011). Subjective Scoring of Divergent Thinking: Examining the Reliability of Unusual Uses, Instances, and Consequences Tasks. *Thinking Skills and Creativity*, *6*, 24–30.

Silvia, P. J., Wigert, B., Reiter-Palmon, R., and Kaufman, J. C. (2012). Assessing Creativity with Self-Report Scales: A Review and Empirical Evaluation. *Psychology of Aesthetics, Creativity, and the Arts*, *6*, 19–34.

Sternberg, R. J. (2016). *What Universities Can Be: A New Model for Preparing Students for Active Concerned Citizenship and Ethical Leadership*. Ithaca: Cornell University Press.

(2018a). What's Wrong with Creativity Testing? *The Journal of Creative Behavior*. doi:10.1002/jocb.237.

(2018b). Yes, Creativity Can Predict Academic Success! Creativity. *Theories–Research-Applications*, *5*(2), 142–145. doi.org/10.1515/ctra-2018-0010.

Sternberg, R. J., Bonney, C. R., Gabora, L, and Merrifield, M. (2012). WICS: A Model for College and University Admissions. *Educational Psychologist*, *47*(1), 30–41.

Sternberg, R. J., and Grigorenko, E. L. (2000–2001). Guilford's Structure of Intellect Model and Model of Creativity: Contributions and Limitations. *Creativity Research Journal*, *13*, 309–316.

Sternberg, R. J., Kaufman, J. C., and Pretz, J. E. (2001). The Propulsion Model of Creative Contributions Applied to the Arts and Letters. *Journal of Creative Behavior*, *35*, 75–101.

Sternberg, R. J., and Lubart, T. I. (1995). *Defying the Crowd: Cultivating Creativity in a Culture of Conformity*. New York: Free Press.

Thompson, B., and Anderson, B. V. (1983). Construct Validity of the Divergent Production Subtests from the Structure-of-Intellect Learning Abilities Test. *Educational and Psychological Measurement*, *43*, 651–655.

Tierney, P., and Farmer, S. M. (2011). Creative Self-Efficacy Development and Creative Performance over Time. *Journal of Applied Psychology*, *96*, 277–293.

Torrance, E. P. (1974). *Torrance Tests of Creative Thinking: Norms-Technical Manual*. Scholastic Testing Service.

(1981). *Thinking Creatively in Action and Movement*. Bensonville: Scholastic Testing Service.

(2008). *Torrance Tests of Creative Thinking: Norms-Technical Manual, Verbal Forms A and B*. Scholastic Testing Service.

Vartanian, O. (2014). Toward a Cumulative Psychological Science of Aesthetics, Creativity, and the Arts. *Psychology of Aesthetics, Creativity, and the Arts*, *8*, 15–17.

Wallach, M. A., and Kogan, N. (1965). *Modes of Thinking in Young Children: A Study of the Creativity-Intelligence Distinction*. New York: Holt, Rinehart and Winston.

Weisberg, R. W. (1993). *Creativity: Beyond the Myth of Genius*. New York: W. H. Freeman and Company.

Williams, F. E. (1980). *Creativity Assessment Packet*. New York: DOK Publishers.

Worwood, M., and Plucker, J. A. (2017). Domain Generality and Specificity in Creative Design Thinking. In F. Darbellay, Z. Moody, and T. Lubart (Eds.), *Creativity, Design Thinking and Interdisciplinarity* (pp. 83–97). Singapore: Springer Nature Singapore.

Yamada, H., and Tam, A. Y.-W. (1996). Prediction Study of Adult Creative Achievement: Torrance's Longitudinal Study of Creativity Revisited. *Journal of Creative Behavior*, *30*, 144–149.

Yi, X., Plucker, J. A., and Guo, J. (2015). Modeling Influences on Divergent Thinking and Artistic Creativity. *Thinking Skills and Creativity*, *16*, 62–68.

Zeng, L., Proctor, R. W., and Salvendy, G. (2011). Can Traditional Divergent Thinking Tests Be Trusted in Measuring and Predicting Real-World Creativity? *Creativity Research Journal*, *23*, 24–37. doi:10.1080/10400419.2011.545713.

5 A Life-Span Developmental Approach to Creativity

ANNA N. N. HUI AND MAVIS W. J. HE

INTRODUCTION

There has been growing interest in understanding the life-span development of creativity (Hui, He, and Wong, 2019). Throughout the life course, creativity grows and declines and serves different purposes for different individuals, making creativity development a dynamic process. For example, a preschooler displays imagination by making up songs with interesting rhymes for self-expression. A school-age child develops a keen interest, out of curiosity, in digging deeper into topics such as planetology or paleontology. An adolescent experiments with new ideas in the pursuit of personal expression. A young adult shows independence in choosing his or her career to form a new identity. An established design engineer and his or her team create a new product to make a financial profit or to effect a social impact. An older adult engages in creative narrative expression to reinterpret the meaning of his or her life. Creativity is defined as novel and appropriate behaviors and within a continuum of impact in a field (Sternberg and Lubart, 1999; Piffer, 2012). Creativity engenders society's greatest achievements, business innovations, and personal **meaning-making**. This chapter takes the perspective of **life-span developmental psychology** to study the emergence of and changes in creative attitude, behaviors, and experiences in terms of nurturing potential and growth and of exploring the limits and decline of creativity through both the **person-centered approach** and the **function-centered approach**. The life-span developmental model of creativity postulates that the types of creativity expressed, how they are measured, and how they are valued vary in different life stages from childhood and adolescence to adulthood and late adulthood. Empirical evidence on the significant factors for the development of creativity across the life-span is also reviewed with reference to the critical issues in each life stage. The discussion also includes educational and practical implications as well as future research directions on creativity research.

Life-span developmental psychology studies the emergence of and change in attitude, behavior, and experience in terms of nurturing potential and growth and of exploring the limits and decline of psychological functions (Heckhausen, 2005). Life-span psychologists assume that development begins from conception and extends across the entire life cycle in nonlinear and dynamic ways, with goals of growth, maintenance, and regulation of loss

We would like to thank Prof. Wan-chi Wong from the Department of Educational Psychology, The Chinese University of Hong Kong for her contribution of ideas and academic mentoring to both authors in developing this student edition.

(Baltes, Staudinger, and Lindenberger, 1999). Life-span theory can be constructed in two ways: person-centered or function-centered (Baltes et al., 1999).

The person-centered approach to the development of creativity describes and connects states of development in order to generate a knowledge base about the overall pattern of creativity throughout the life course. An example is Tegano, Moran, and Sawyer's (1991) developmental criteria for creativity: Young children with creative potential display original and unusual ideas and achieve high ideational fluency, which refers to the generation of many different ideas. Schoolchildren with creative precursors propose high-quality and workable ideas in the process of discovering original solutions; and adults with creative behaviors contribute to society by translating their original ideas into tangible or intangible products with positive social impact. The complexity of creative products often increases when individuals acquire more domain-specific knowledge, master creative thinking skills more tactfully, and regulate higher task motivation successfully.

The function-centered approach to the development of creativity focuses on the mechanisms and processes of creativity and their functions for the individual and the society. For example, the "be creative" effect can be triggered by the processes of (1) explicitly instructing individuals to be inventive with various types of thinking styles (O'Hara and Sternberg, 2000–2001) and in various tasks (Nusbaum, Silvia, and Beaty, 2014); (2) training individuals to evaluate creative ideas and a solution's creativity (Storme et al., 2014); and (3) provoking one's intrinsic motivation to be creative (Moon, Hur, and Hyun, 2017). The functions of creativity may include self-expression, making an impact and effecting improvement in society (Moran, 2010), creating a "creator's identity" in eminent individuals or professionals, and construction of self in ordinary individuals (Hanson, 2012). These mechanisms and functions of creativity develop and change across the life-span, in which the corresponding research methods and measurements to creativity, as well as the critical conditions contributing to creativity also change accordingly (see Table 5.1).

The Development of Creativity in Childhood and Adolescence

Creativity can be developed at a young age, in which "**play**" has a significant role in the process. The development of creativity usually begins and develops through active engagement in different forms of play (Hoffmann and Russ, 2016). The desire or ability to play is a universal, natural, and lifelong social behavior that is essential to the learning process (Pramling and Carlsson, 2008), in which creativity manifests and proliferates as a result of new and personally meaningful interpretations of the process (Kaufman and Beghetto, 2009). Young children can engage in imaginative play as early as two years of age (Singer, 2009). Creativity is exhibited when a young child has the personal insight that a plastic toy banana can represent a cell phone or that a building block can be used as an imaginary cup (Beghetto et al., 2012). Play has positive effects on imagination, problem-solving, and the thinking skills associated with creativity (Hoffmann and Russ, 2016).

Table 5.1 Function, measurement, research approach, and critical factors of creativity development across the life-span

Life stage	Function of creativity	Measurements	Research approach	Critical factors
Early childhood	Self-expression	Personal interpretations of the play process	Cross-sectional; Experimental; Longitudinal	Positive effects of play on imagination; Creative personality traits; Divergent and possibility thinking; Task motivation; Childrearing practices; Positive teacher feedback based on the Goldilocks principle; Negative appraisals of school life as deterrent; Enrichment and stimulating activities
Childhood and adolescence	Self-expression; Identity formation	Standardized creativity tests, e.g., Torrance Tests of Creative Thinking; Test for Creative Thinking-Drawing Production; Consensual Assessment Techniques (CAT)		
Adulthood	Professional identity; Self enhancement; Society advancement	Creative personality scale; CAT; Standardized creativity tests; Self-reported, peer-reported; performance-based creativity, e.g., innovation or patents	Behavioral-genetic in twin studies; Cross-sectional; Longitudinal; Multitrait-multimethod analysis	**Creative personality traits;** Domain-specific expertise; Optimal-fit development; Confluence of intelligence, personality, expertise, cognitive style, motivation, and environment; Meaning-making in creative professional or leisure activities
Late adulthood	Self enhancement; Society betterment	CAT; Standardized creativity tests; Everyday problem-solving tests	Cross-sectional; Longitudinal; Case studies on eminent creative professionals	Continuous development of self-perceived creativity; Participation in creative training and activities, and collaborative problem-solving

The development of creativity in children and adolescents is not a continuous, smooth process; rather, there are sudden drops (slumps) at some times and increases at others (Alfonso-Benlliure and Santos, 2016). In a longitudinal study on a sample of over one hundred participants, Torrance (1963) found a first-grade slump in children's creative thinking when they entered formal schooling at approximately five years old. A few years later, Torrance (1968) reported another sudden drop among fourth graders, evidence for the so-called "fourth-grade slump," which occurs at the age of nine or ten (Runco, 2014). Following Torrance, many other researchers have further reported slumps in creativity development during childhood and adolescence (e.g., Krampen, 2012; He and Wong, 2015; Lin and Shih, 2016). These **creativity slumps** are usually associated with entry into formal schooling (i.e., age six or seven; Krampen, 2012), promotion to the fourth grade (age nine or ten; Lin and Shih, 2016), and the transition from primary to secondary school (i.e., age eleven or twelve; He and Wong, 2015). Furthermore, researchers have also observed individual differences in children's experiences of the slumps and in the development of their creativity, with some individuals more vulnerable to a slump than others (Barbot et al., 2016). Specifically, He and Wong (2015) adopted a sequential design to critically examine the longitudinal change in creativity for 514 students among three groups (i.e., transition group, primary non-transition group, and secondary non-transition group). They identified that individuals who had higher threat and overall perceived stressfulness and lower controllability showed negative self-appraisals about their school life and were more vulnerable to a creative slump during a school transition than others.

The important factors that are critical for facilitating or hindering the development of creativity in childhood and adolescence can be organized into two categories: individual (e.g., motivation, personality) and environmental (e.g., childrearing practices, teachers' feedback) factors (Beghetto and Kaufman, 2014). Key individual factors leading to the development of creativity include cognitive ability, such as divergent thinking (Kim, 2005); possibility thinking (Craft et al., 2013); task motivation (Hennessey and Amabile, 2010); and personality traits, such as openness to experience (Feist, 2010) and overexcitabilities (i.e., heightened sensitivity and intensity; He, Wong, and Chan, 2017). There are also empirical findings on the effective ways to foster a creativity-nurturing environment. For example, childrearing practices based on Carl Rogers's work (e.g., encouraging curiosity and exploration, letting children make decisions, and respecting children's opinions) lead to increased creative potential (Harrington, Block, and Block, 1987). Moreover, enrichment activities such as arts education are effective in fostering creativity development (Hui et al., 2015). Furthermore, stimulating activities that are effective for emotion regulation (e.g., pretend play; Hoffmann and Russ, 2016) or emotional arousal (e.g., listening to music; He, Wong, and Hui, 2017) also support the development of creativity.

In terms of fostering a creativity-nurturing environment, the role of teachers' positive feedback is especially highlighted in adolescence. Empirical findings showed that teachers' positive feedback (e.g., verbal encouragement on creative behaviors) was perceived by adolescent students to be the strongest predictor of their belief in the development of their own creativity (Beghetto, 2006). Effective feedback strategies also have been shown to play a positive role in enhancing adolescents' confidence in creative tasks (Visser, Chandler, and Grainger, 2017) as well as facilitating their creative performance (Deutsch, 2016). Beghetto and Kaufman (2007) believed that the **Goldilocks principle** (i.e., giving feedback with an optimal level of encouragement) can be applied to guiding the use of appropriate feedback with the aim of facilitating the development of creativity in children and adolescents and even in professionals and older adults. The Goldilocks principle proposes that effective feedback neither overencourages nor underencourages a student's creativity; rather, it should offer an optimal level of encouragement. Beghetto (2007) suggested that teachers should take time to hear students' ideas so that students feel comfortable to share their unique and personal meaningful ideas (i.e., mini-c creativity). They should also provide responses as follow-ups to challenge students to take intellectual risks and give them cues when their novel ideas may seem irrelevant. This cueing helps students further expand and polish their novel ideas to be original, meaningful, and appropriate to both others and themselves (i.e., little-c creativity). The optimal level will be effective and adequate enough to encourage students to be motivated to perform and enhance their creativity. Other researchers have also suggested that peer feedback should focus on the work (e.g., Kaufman, Gentile, and Baer, 2005), not the person (Dweck, 2002). Further research is needed to determine the "optimal level" of encouragement and identify further effective forms of feedback.

In summary, the development of creativity in childhood and adolescence emerges through play or schoolwork. It is also present during leisure time as personal creativity manifests in everyday creative efforts that transform experience and give it meaning and original interpretation (Runco 2014). Creativity serves as a means of self-expression of the individual's uniqueness (Paul and Kaufman, 2014) and gradually develops as a quality of character promoted in schools (Kieran, 2014). Measurements of creativity include standardized instruments, such as the Test for Creative Thinking-Drawing Production (TCT-DP; Urban and Jellen, 1995/2010), which is used in studies with young children (Hui et al., 2015), schoolchildren, and adolescents (He et al., 2017). There is also the **Consensual Assessment Technique** (CAT) developed by Amabile (1996) to have creative products such as collage, poetry, and artwork, judged by laypersons or professionals familiar with the involved domains. More assessment methods and instruments are reviewed by Baer and Kaufman (2019).

The Development of Creativity in Adulthood

Creativity continues to develop into adulthood. For example, in a forty-year longitudinal study that examined how creativity develops from adolescence to adulthood within individuals, the Torrance Tests for Creative Thinking (TTCT) done between 1958–1964 explained 23 percent of the variance in creative achievement that was reported by ninety-nine participants and rated by three expert judges in 1998. TTCT is the most widely used divergent thinking test to measure divergent thinking, which is the most significant type of thinking ability for creativity. This shows that the development of creative potential (as measured by the TTCT) for creative achievement seemed somewhat reliable across four decades (Cramond et al., 2005). There were also other correlates of creative achievement, for example, having living experience in foreign countries and having a mentor (Torrance, 2004). Similarly, creative engineering college students continued to engage in creative activities at work and were submitting more patent applications fifteen years later (Clapham et al., 2005). Another longitudinal study with a large sample of 307 British university students examined the relationship of creative thinking, personality traits, and academic performance over a period of four years (Chamorro-Premuzic, 2006). Creative thinking assessed using an alternate use test in the first year significantly predicted the originality of final-year projects, which could be regarded as creative outcomes. In addition, the creative-thinking scores correlated significantly with openness to experience in the academic performance of supervised dissertations rated by two independent raters.

Cross-sectional studies investigating age-related changes across young, middle, and late adulthood indicate peaks and slumps during the adult life stage (e.g., Palmiero, 2015). An integration of these cross-sectional studies illustrates a general developmental trend from a peak in young and middle adulthood to a decline in late adulthood (e.g., McCrae, Arenberg, and Costa, 1987; Palmiero, 2015). The longitudinal analysis of McCrae et al. (1987) revealed that the youngest age group (33–38 years) showed a significant improvement in total scores of fluency, including associational, expressional, ideational, and word fluency, while the oldest groups (69–74 years) exhibited a decline over a six-year interval. Interestingly, ideational fluency increased in all age groups, which may suggest that individuals of all ages possess the basic mechanisms for creative expression. Their creativity potentially could be further fostered through training. Environmental factors may account for the training effect on gains in creativity (Kientiz et al., 2014). Furthermore, Palmiero (2015) investigated age-related changes in creativity among 150 participants in 6 age groups (from 20 to 80 years with a 10-year interval) and discovered that the development of creativity reached a peak before 40 and remained relatively stable from 40 to 70, followed by a decline. Such findings appear to suggest that creativity can be maintained after middle age up to the age of 70; the argument regarding age-related decline in creativity may be questionable because evidence suggests no significant differences were found in creativity of middle-aged and older adults as measured by TTCT (Sharma and Babu, 2017), nor among young and older adults when using the consensual assessment techniques (Madore, Jing, and Schacter, 2016).

Twin studies based on a **behavioral-genetic design** have been shown to offer insight into the critical factors that may explain the development of creativity. A behavioral-genetic design examines both the influence of nature (genetics variance) and nurture (shared or non-shared environments) on creativity. Kandler et al. (2016) used a **multitrait-multimethod analysis** with two twin samples (monozygotic and dizygotic pairs) to examine the effects of genetic determinants (i.e., biological factors, personality traits, and intelligence) and environmental factors on individual differences in creativity. They adopted multiple methods to measure different types of creativity, including self-reported, peer-reported, and performance-based creativity (e.g., telling a joke, constructing a paper tower). The confirmatory factor analysis, a statistical technique to verify the two types of creativity proposed by the researchers, was performed to find how creativity as a psychological construct is organized in these observable variables of the creativity traits. Two distinct types of creativity were confirmed, namely: perceived (e.g., self-reported or peer/other-reported creativity) and assessed creativity (e.g., creativity assessed with standardized instruments). Whether one can identify creative individuals and predict their creative achievements by using creative assessment tests depends on individual differences in intelligence and personality traits that are highly correlated with creativity. In dizygotic twins, who have 50 percent similarity, and monozygotic twins, who share the same genetic makeup, are perceived to be creative differently; nonshared/individual-specific environmental factors, such as positive innovative climate, social support, autonomy of decision, could be used to explain genetic variance in perceived and measured creativity (Kandler et al., 2016).

Creativity in adulthood manifests in both professional careers and personal development. Professional creativity can be explained by expertise acquisition. Expertise is a unique variable related to the study of creative development and achievement in adults. Expertise is usually measured by accumulative products, deliberate practice, or cumulative experience (Simonton, 2000), extensive knowledge (Weisberg, 2015), or recognition as an expert in a specific field or domain (Baer, 2015). The amount and type of training to be acquired to attain expertise may be different from those required to achieve creativity. Taking music composition as an example: Continuous effort in composing a certain type of music genre may enhance mastery and expertise in the specific genre. If the creator keeps composing using the similar patterns without novel elements, the expertise cannot guarantee creative achievement. Simonton (2000) identified complex specialization ("overtraining") and versatility ("cross-training") as determinants of creative expertise. In his study of creative achievement among fifty-nine classical composers, Simonton (2000) found both inconsistency and consistency. More cumulative products in the same genre brought lower creativity, which might be caused by overtraining. However, cumulative generic production (i.e., composing pieces in different genres) exerted a stronger effect on creativity than genre-specific production, which might be explained by cross-training. The cross-over and mixing up different music genres and types shows novelty and vitality of the composer. The role of **domain-specific expertise** becomes increasingly salient in professional creativity as individuals engage in creative production (Baer, 2015; Weisberg, 2015). Reilly (2008) found that creative responses develop gradually, with enhanced expertise through professional training in group facilitation. Expertise in organizational leadership also had positive effects on both idea generation and idea implementation in a study with military experts conducted by Vincent et al. (2002).

Adult creativity requires other complex factors for continuous development, including intelligence, personality, expertise, cognitive style, motivation, and environment (Sternberg and Lubart, 1996). Barbot et al. (2016) used an **"optimal-fit" view** of creative development to explain individual difference in creativity. Optimal development is made possible under certain environmental factors and during the performance of specific tasks. An innovative personal style that is matched by an innovative work environment is also associated with novelty in creative products (Puccio, Talbot, and Joniak, 2000). Living abroad may be a contributory factor in some cases to adult creativity, as individuals who identified with both home and hosting cultures were more capable of integrating multiple perspectives when compared with those who identified with only a single culture (Tadmor, Galinsky, and Maddux, 2012).

Meaning-making plays an important role in influencing an adult's or a professional's engagement in a creative process or creative action (Chang, Wang, and Lee, 2016). Meaning-making can be defined as a cognitive framework that people can use to interpret their experiences and motivation (Park, 2010). Such a primary mechanism is mainly a sense-making and meaning-making process that affects one's willingness to engage in creative projects (Ford, 2000). According to Madjar, Greenberg, and Chen (2011), adults make sense and meaning by extracting cues from the environment and responding more positively to cues consistent with their personality. They found that individuals who are more willing to take risks tend to allocate more resources to creativity, present higher career commitment, and demonstrate more **radical creativity** (i.e., innovation), while the factors of organizational identification and creative coworkers are correlated with incremental creativity (i.e., adaptation). Radical creativity is defined as novel and useful ideas/procedures that bring innovative outcomes and substantial changes to existing procedures while incremental creativity offers only minor modifications to existing practice. As an individual grows older, the interpretation of contextual and personal factors influences intrinsic motivation and task commitment to professional creative tasks in young adults (Yeh and Lin, 2015), everyday creative behaviors in young adults (Silvia et al., 2014), and leisure-time creative tasks in older adults (Carlsen, 1995).

The Development of Creativity in Late Adulthood

Does creativity really show a decline in late adulthood? Some studies use a psychometric approach to creativity by administering standardized creativity tests to participants of various age groups, mostly divergent thinking tests such as the TTCT (e.g., Roskos-Ewoldsen, Black, and Mccown, 2008) and Wallach–Kogan Creativity Tests (WKCT; Kogan, 1973). These studies showed that older adults tend to score significantly lower in fluency, flexibility, and originality than young and middle-aged adults. However, mixed results were also observed, suggesting inconclusive findings. For example, Shimonaka and Nakazato (2007), after controlling for educational attainment, found no significant age difference among 412 adults aged 25–84 in fluency, flexibility, originality, or elaboration scores when using the S-A Creativity Test (devised by the Society for Creative Mind as originally formulated by Guilford, cited in Takeuchia et al., 2010).

The inconclusive findings lead to a prevalent criticism of the **peak and decline model** in creative abilities, pointing to its failure to control for certain confounding variables, such as cohort effects and education effects. For example, some researchers argued that the apparent decline of creativity in later adulthood may derive from scores on standardized creativity tests tending to favor children and adolescents, who are familiar with test-taking environments (Roskos-Ewoldsen et al., 2008). Older adults, who are no longer used to taking tests, often perform poorly on standardized tests (Lindauer, 2003). Similarly, other researchers have argued that the apparent decline in creativity as measured by general divergent-thinking tests could be seen not as a real decline but rather as a qualitative change toward engaging in specific domains in the creative process (Sasser-Coen, 1993). Indeed, studies examining the qualitative change in creativity among older artists and architects actually revealed a continuous development as the individuals aged (Dudek and Croteau, 1998; Lindauer, 2003). Binnewies, Ohly, and Niessen (2008) adopted the CAT to evaluate the quality of creative ideas generated at work by young and older nurses and found no significant relationship between creative ideas and age. Researchers suggest that expertise in pragmatics and domain-specific knowledge may compensate for the loss in fluency of divergent thinking as a mechanism of creativity. Older adults possess expertise in the pragmatics of life, such as life review and the everyday problems of life planning (Baltes, 1987). Adam-Price (1998) also pointed out that novelty and innovation may more often be associated with youthful creative thinking. Late-life creative thinking is characterized more by integrative or convergent ability, as is particularly evident in eminent creators (Gardner, 2011).

Older adults may even outperform young adults in **everyday creativity** when they must solve problems of daily life by adopting more problem-focused strategies to solve instrumental and interpersonal problems (Blanchard-Fields et al., 2007). Moreover, Artistico et al. (2003) observed that older adults actually scored higher than younger adults in perceived self-efficacy and performance in solving problems that were ecologically relevant specifically for older adults (e.g., wanting to be visited by relatives more often). They also found that self-efficacy perception varied as a function of the type of problem that the participants were dealing with. Moreover, in a recent life-span study on perceived creativity, Hui et al. (2014) also found that **self-perception of creative personality** was the highest in healthy older adults, when compared with mid-life, early, and emerging young adults.

Exploring the important factors that may account for the creativity reserve or even creativity gain in late adulthood is important. Meléndez et al. (2016) used education level, occupation, cognitive leisure activities, and vocabulary scores from a standardized intelligence test as observable variables and used them as the operational definition of cognitive resources. They found that significant predictors of creativity in older adults include the above cognitive resources and the personality trait of openness to new experiences. In another study with Chinese older adults, Zhang and Niu (2013) found two sets of positive factors favoring creativity development in late adulthood, including relatively stable factors, such as education and general health status, and relatively changeable factors, such as daily activities and a positive attitude toward aging. Other studies highlight the positive effects of other important variables, such as participation in creative and cultural activities (Hui, 2013), collaborative problem-solving programs (e.g., Stine-Morrow et al., 2008), and social and intellectual engagement (Parisi et al., 2007). In a randomized controlled trial study on the effects of participation in a creative arts program, Hui and Liang (2012) found significant gains in figural creativity and everyday problem-solving in the experimental group but not in the control group (whose members joined other recreational activities in an elderly community center, such as knitting and computer literacy). In a sample from Great Britain, Sweden,

Japan, and Brazil, Hannenmann (2006) found that participation in creative artistic activities could have a stimulating effect on creativity in patients with dementia.

Some eminent creative professionals are also known to continue producing legendary works and sometimes even their masterpieces into their old age. To name a few, Verdi composed "Ave Maria" at age eighty-five, Martha Graham performed until she was seventy-five and choreographed her 180th work at age ninety-five, Michelangelo worked on the Rondanini Pietà until shortly before his death at eighty-three, and Grandma Moses had her first art exhibition at age eighty (Hickson and Housley, 1997). The American architect Frank Lloyd Wright lived until the age of ninety-one and was creatively productive well into his eighties. The Guggenheim Museum in New York City, considered one of his masterpieces, was completed in the year of his death.

All in all, creativity in late adulthood continues to serve the function of self-expression in laypersons and of making contributions to society by eminent creative individuals. Creative participation and training may further strengthen personal creativity and enhance successful aging by providing new interpretations in life review.

Implications, Limitations, and Further Directions

Because of the uniqueness of each developmental period, creativity has diverse expressions in childhood, adolescence, adulthood, and late adulthood. The factors facilitating or hindering the development of creativity can also vary during different life stages. A life-span approach to understanding the development of creativity enables us to capture the patterns of possible growth and decline in human creativity through an interconnected time perspective. Such an approach also allows us to uncover the dynamics underlying the changes involved. The present chapter's review of the discourse and empirical evidence for the life-span approach to creativity reveals that such an approach can be enriching and thought-provoking, leading to a more thorough understanding of creativity development, on which basis a better cultivation of creative potential across the life-span is possible.

In its current form, the life-span approach to studying creativity has its limitations. The patterns or trends in the capacity for creativity, as identified by previous cross-sectional and longitudinal studies, are mainly based on psychometric tests that tend to be very limited and fail to capture the multidimensional nature of human creativity. In general, the evidence from research on measured creativity suggests a curvilinear relationship between age and creative performance, in which creativity increases from childhood to young adulthood and then begins to decline from middle age until late adulthood (see Kogan, 1973; Roskos-Ewoldsen et al., 2008). The latest research, however, has yielded insignificant differences when comparing creativity of younger and older adults (Madore, Jing, and Schacter, 2016; Sharma and Babu, 2017). It is worth noting the well-documented creativity slumps among children and adolescents indicated by empirical studies (Torrance, 1968; He and Wong, 2015; Alfonso-Benlliure and Santos, 2016), which demonstrate discontinuities alongside continuities in the development of creativity. Clearly, these kinds of knowledge concerning developmental trends are valuable. However, we also need to acknowledge the limitations of creativity tests for capturing the multifaceted, dynamic, and subtle aspects of creativity. Furthermore, the issues of individual difference are not sufficiently addressed in the literature on the growth or decline of creativity (Barbot et al., 2016). The question of whether individual differences may increase with age across the human life-span suggests interesting and important possibilities that have not yet been seriously investigated. Another limitation of the life-span approach to studying creativity lies in its lack of thorough deliberation on the nature of creativity, particularly regarding the psychological processes involved.

In spite of some limitations, the life-span approach can provide new insight into the meaning and process about the development of creativity, opening new avenues for cultivating the potential for creativity across the human life-span.

Our Research Contribution

We extended the research on a creativity slump in childhood to the critical period of school transitions in early adolescence. We continued the research on the effect of individual (e.g., overexcitability) and environmental factors (e.g., enrichment and stimulation) that facilitate creativity development in childhood and adolescence. We also provided new insights for creativity reserve and creativity gain in late adulthood in terms of self-perceived creativity and creative problem solving in daily life by studying how individuals of different age groups perceived creative personalities and how older adults suggested solutions to solve daily problems after taking part in a community art program. In our study on creative thinking in the transition from primary to secondary school (He and Wong, 2015), we extended the study of creative slump at the fourth grade to another significant school transition in early adolescence. By revealing that the major detrimental factors for hindering the development of creativity during school transition were negative stress appraisals of school life, we suggest that effective stress management is important for preventing creativity loss during school transition. Furthermore, we found empirical evidence that implies that educational resources on transitional support, social emotional learning on coping with heightened sensitivity and intensity in emotion (He, Wong, and Chan, 2017), and arts activities could be effective for emotional arousal and creativity enrichment as prevention or intervention strategies (Hui et al., 2015; He, Chan, and Wong, 2017; He, Wong, and Hui, 2017) for the development of creativity among adolescents and young adults. A recent life-span study found that older adults had higher self-perceived creative personality than adults in other age groups and that creativity can be sustained in late adulthood (Hui et al., 2014). Significant gains in figural creativity and everyday problem solving for older adults taking part in a community arts program (Hui and Liang, 2012) and participation in creative and cultural activities enhanced self-perceived creativity and quality of life (Hui, 2013).

Critical/Creative Thinking Questions

1. What is the relationship between age and creative performance?
2. What are the facilitators and inhibitors of creativity in different life stages?
3. Are there any general principles governing lifelong development in creativity?
4. What are the individual differences and similarities in the lifelong developmental process of creativity?
5. What are the degree and conditions of individual plasticity or modifiability regarding creative development?

GLOSSARY

behavioral-genetic design: A design that examines both the influence of nature (genetic variance) and nurture (shared or non-shared environments) on psychological constructs.

Consensual Assessment Technique: A group of experts or laypersons independently assess products with agreed criteria.

creative personality traits: Personality traits that are highly correlated with creativity.

creativity slump: A significant drop in creativity performance or expression.

domain-specific expertise: Expertise in a specific knowledge domain as measured by extensive knowledge, products, and practice.

everyday creativity: Novel and useful ideas that make small changes in daily life.

function-centered approach of life-span development: An approach that investigates the mechanisms and processes of a psychological construct and their functions for individuals and society.

Goldilocks principle of giving feedback: Effective feedback gives an optimal level of encouragement to increase a behavior – neither too much nor too little.

life-span developmental psychology: An approach that explores psychological changes from infancy to old age across different domains.

meaning-making: Individuals find meaning by seeing the worthiness of creativity and the purpose of their engagement in creative activities.

multitrait-multimethod analysis: An approach to examining construct validity by using more than one trait and more than one method.

"optimal-fit" view: The view that takes a developmental perspective that creative performance occurs in a given time when individual resources interact optimally with task characteristics given in specific domains.

peak and decline model: The model that assumes that adult creativity increases with age until a peak in mid-adulthood and then decreases with age from then.

person-centered approach of life-span development: An approach that examines how a psychological construct develops in an individual through the life course.

play: A range of activities understood as universal, innate, and lifelong, which are expressed in different forms including imaginative play and social play.

radical creativity: Novel and useful ideas/procedures that bring innovative outcomes and substantial changes to existing procedures.

self-perception of creative personality: Self-perception of creative personality is formed when one observes one's novel behaviors, forms a positive attitude toward creativity, and experiences positive affects in creative processes.

REFERENCES

Adam-Price, C. (Ed.). (1998). *Creativity and Successful Aging: Theoretical and Empirical Approaches.* New York: Springer-Verlag.

Alfonso-Benlliure, V., and Santos, M. R. (2016). Creativity Development Trajectories in Elementary Education: Differences in Divergent and Evaluative Skills. *Thinking Skills and Creativity*, *19*, 160–174.

Amabile, T. M. (1996). *Creativity in Context: Update to the Social Psychology of Creativity.* Boulder: Westview.

Artistico, D., Cervone, D., and Pezzuti, L. (2003). Perceived Self-Efficacy and Everyday Problem Solving among Young and Older Adults. *Psychology and Aging*, *18*, 68–79.

Baer, J. (2015). The Importance of Domain-Specific Expertise in Creativity. *Roeper Review: A Journal on Gifted Education*, *37*, 165–178.

Baer, J., and Kaufman, J. C. (2019). Assessing Creativity with the Consensual Assessment Technique. In I. Lebuda and V. P. Glăveanu (Eds.), *The Palgrave Handbook of Social Creativity Research* (pp. 27–37). Basingstoke: Palgrave Macmillan.

Baltes, P. B. (1987). Theoretical Propositions of Life-Span Developmental Psychology: On the Dynamics between Growth and Decline. *Developmental Psychology*, *23*, 611–626.

Baltes, P. B., Staudinger, U. M., and Lindenberger, U. (1999). Lifespan Psychology: Theory and Application to Intellectual Functioning. *Annual Review of Psychology*, *50*, 471–507.

Barbot, B., Lubart, T. I., and Besançon, M. (2016). "Peaks, Slumps, and Bumps": Individual Differences in the Development of Creativity in Children and Adolescents. *New Directions for Child and Adolescent Development*, *151*, 33–45.

Beghetto, R. A. (2006). Creative Self-Efficacy: Correlates in Middle and Secondary Students. *Creativity Research Journal*, *18*, 447–457.

  (2007). Ideational Code-Switching: Walking the Talk about Supporting Student Creativity in the Classroom. *Roeper Review*, *29*(4), 265–270.

Beghetto, R. A., and Kaufman, J. C. (2007). Toward a Broader Conception of Creativity: A Case for "mini-c" Creativity. *Psychology of Aesthetics, Creativity, and the Arts*, *1*, 73–79.

Beghetto, R. A., Kaufman, J. C., Hegarty, B., Hammond, H., and Wilcox-Herzog, A. (2012). Cultivating Creativity, Play and Leisure in Early Childhood Education: A 4 C Perspective. In O. N. Saracho and B. Spodek (Eds.), *Contemporary Perspectives on Creativity in Early Childhood Education*. Information Age Publishing.

Binnewies, C., Ohly, S., and Niessen, C. (2008). Age and Creativity at Work: The Interplay between Job Resources, Age and Idea Creativity. *Journal of Managerial Psychology*, *23*, 438–457.

Blanchard-Fields, F., Mienaltowski, A., and Seay, R. B. (2007). Age Differences in Everyday Problem-Solving Effectiveness: Older Adults Select More Effective Strategies for Interpersonal Problems. *Journal of Gerontology: Series B: Psychological Sciences and Social Sciences*, *62*, 61–64.

Carlsen, M. B. (1995). Meaning-Making and Creative Aging. In R. A. Neimeyer and M. J. Mahoney (Eds.), *Constructivism in psychotherapy* (pp. 127–153). Washington, DC: American Psychological Association.

Chamorro-Premuzic, T. (2006). Creativity versus Conscientiousness: Which Is a Better Predictor of Student Performance? *Applied Cognitive Psychology*, *20*, 521–531.

Chang, S.-H., Wang, C.-L., and Lee, J.-C. (2016). Do Award-Winning Experiences Benefit Students' Creative Self-Efficacy and Creativity? The Moderated Mediation Effects of Perceived School Support for Creativity. *Learning and Individual Differences*, *51*, 291–298.

Clapham, M. M., Cowdery, E. M., King, K. E., and Montang, M. A. (2005). Predicting Work Activities with Divergent Thinking Tests: A Longitudinal Study. *Journal of Creative Behavior*, *39*, 149–167.

Craft, A., Cremin, T., Burnard, P., Dragovic, T., and Chappell, K. (2013). Possibility Thinking: Culminative Studies of an Evidence-Based Concept Driving Creativity? *Education 3–13*, *41*, 538–556.

Cramond, B., Matthews-Morgan, J., Bandalos, D., and Zuo, L. (2005). A Report on the 40-Year Follow-up of the Torrance Tests of Creative Thinking: Alive and Well in the New Millennium. *Gifted Child Quarterly*, *49*, 283–291.

Deutsch, D. (2016). Authentic Assessment in Music Composition: Feedback That Facilitates Creativity. *Music Educators Journal*, *102*, 53–59.

Dudek, S., and Croteau, H. (1998). Aging and Creativity in Eminent Architects. In C. Adams-Price (Ed.), *Creativity and Successful Aging: Theoretical and Empirical Approaches* (pp. 117–152). New York: Springer.

Dweck, C. (2002). Beliefs That Make Smart People Dumb. In R. J. Sternberg (Ed.), *Why Smart People Can Be So Stupid* (pp. 24–41). New Haven: Yale University Press.

Feist, G. J. (2010). The Function of Personality in Creativity: The Nature and Nurture of the Creative Personality. In J. C. Kaufman and R. J. Sternberg (Eds.), *The Cambridge Handbook of Creativity* (pp. 113–130). New York: Cambridge University Press.

Ford, C. M. (2000). Dialogue: Creative Developments in Creative Theory. *Academy of Management Review*, *25*, 284–287.

Gardner, H. (2011). *Creating Minds: An Anatomy of Creativity Seen through the Lives of Freud, Einstein, Picasso, Stravinsky, Eliot, Graham, and Gandhi*. New York: Basic Books.

Hannenmann, B. T. (2006). Creativity with Dementia Patients: Can Creativity and Art Stimulate Dementia Patients Positively? *Gerontology*, *52*, 59–65.

Hanson, M. H. (2012). Author, Self, Monster: Using Foucault to Examine Functions of Creativity. *Journal of Theoretical and Philosophical Psychology*, *33*, 18–31.

Harrington, D. M., Block, J. W., and Block, J. (1987). Testing Aspects of Carl Rogers' Theory of Creative Environments: Childrearing Antecedents of Creative Environments in Young Adolescents. *Journal of Personality and Social Psychology*, *52*, 851–856.

He, W. J., and Wong, W. C. (2015). Creativity Slump and School Transition Stress: A Sequential Study from the Perspective of the Cognitive-Relational Theory of Stress. *Learning and Individual Differences*, *43*, 185–190.

He, W. J., Wong, W. C., and Chan M. K (2017). Overexcitabilities As Important Psychological Attributes of Creativity: A Dabrowskian Perspective. *Thinking Skills and Creativity*, *25*, 27–35.

He, W. J., Wong, W. C., and Hui, A. N. N. (2017). Emotional Reactions Mediate the Effect of Music Listening on Creative Thinking: Perspective of the Arousal-and-Mood Hypothesis. *Frontiers in Psychology*. doi.org/10.3389/fpsyg.2017.01680.

Heckhausen, J. (2005). Psychological Approaches to Human Development. In M. L. Johnson (Ed.), *The Cambridge Handbook of Age and Ageing* (pp. 180–272). Cambridge: Cambridge University Press.

Hennessey, B. A., and Amabile, T. M. (2010). Creativity. *Annual Review of Psychology*, *61*, 569–598.

Hickson, J., and Housley, W. (1997). Creativity in Later Life. *Educational Gerontology*, *23*, 539–547.

Hoffmann, J., and Russ, S. (2016). Fostering Pretend Play Skills and Creativity in Elementary School Girls: A Group Play Intervention. *Psychology of Aesthetics, Creativity, and the Arts*, *10*, 114–125.

Hui, A. N. N. (2013). Creativity and Leisure: An Activity and Engagement Perspective. *Journal of Nutrition, Health and Aging*, *17*(Suppl. 1), S125.

Hui, A. N. N., He, M. W. J., and Wong, W. C. (2019). Understanding the Development of Creativity across the Lifespan. In J. C. Kaufman and R. J. Sternberg (Eds.). *The Cambridge Handbook of Creativity*. New York: Cambridge University Press.

Hui, A. N. N., He, M. W. J, and Ye, S. S. (2015). Arts Education and Creativity Enhancement in Young Children in Hong Kong. *Educational Psychology*, *35*, 315–327.

Hui, A. N. N., and Liang, E. (2012). "Creativity As a Reserve Capacity in Older Adults and a Virtue in Positive Psychology." Symposium presentation, Second China International Conference on Positive Psychology, Beijing, China.

Hui, A. N. N., Yeung, D. Y., Sue-Chan, C., Chan, K., Hui, D., and Cheng, S. T. (2014). Gains and Losses in Creative Personality As Perceived by Adults across the Life Span. *Developmental Psychology*, *50*, 709–713.

Jaquish, G. A., and Ripple, R. E. (1981). Cognitive Creative Abilities and Self-Esteem across the Adult Life-Span. *Human Development*, *24*, 110–119.

Kandler, C., Riemann, R., Angleitner, A., Spinath, F. M., Borkenau, P., and Penke, L. (2016). The Nature of Creativity: The Roles of Genetic Factors, Personality Traits, Cognitive Abilities, and Environmental Sources. *Journal of Personality and Social Psychology*, *111*, 230–249.

Kaufman, J. C., and Beghetto, R. A. (2009). Beyond Big and Little: The Four C Model of Creativity. *Review of General Psychology*, *13*, 1–12.

Kaufman, J. C., Plucker, J. A., and Baer, J. (2008). *Essentials of Creativity Assessment*. Hoboken: John Wiley & Sons.

Kientiz, E., Quintin, E.-M., Saggar, M., Bott, N. T., Royalty, A. et al. (2014). Targeted Intervention to Increase Creative Capacity and Performance: A Randomized Controlled Pilot Study. *Thinking Skills and Creativity*, *13*, 57–66.

Kieran, M. (2014). Creativity As a Virtue of Character. In E. S. Paul and S. B. Kaufman (Eds.), *The Philosophy of Creativity: New Essays* (pp. 125–144). New York: Oxford University Press.

Kim, K. H. (2005). Can Only Intelligent People Be Creative? *Journal of Secondary Gifted Education*, *16*, 57–66.

Kogan, N. (1973). Creativity and Cognitive Style: A Life-Span Perspective. In P. B. Baltes and K. W. Schaie (Eds.), *Life-Span Developmental Psychology: Personality and Socialization* (pp. 145–178). New York: Academic Press.

Krampen, G. (2012). Cross-Sequential Results on Creativity Development in Childhood within Two Different School Systems: Divergent Performances in Luxembourg versus German Kindergarten and Elementary School Students. *European Journal of Psychology*, *8*, 423–448.

Lin, W. L., and Shih, Y. L. (2016). The Developmental Trends of Different Creative Potentials in Relation to Children's Reasoning Abilities: From a Cognitive Theoretical Perspective. *Think Skills and Creativity*, *22*, 36–47.

Lindauer, M. S. (2003). *Aging, Creativity, and Art: A Positive Perspective on Late-Life Development*. New York: Kluwer Academic and Plenum Publishers.

Madjar, N., Greenberg, E., and Chen, Z. (2011). Factors for Radical Creativity, Incremental Creativity, and Routine, Noncreative Performance. *Journal of Applied Psychology*, *96*, 730–743.

Madore, K. P., Jing, H. G., and Schacter, D. L. (2016). Divergent Creative Thinking in Young and Older Adults: Extending the Effects of an Episodic Specificity Induction. *Memory and Cognition, 44*(6), 974–988. doi:10.3758/s13421-016-0605-z.

McCrae, R. R., Arenberg, D., and Costa, P. T. Jr. (1987). Declines in Divergent Thinking with Age: Cross-Sectional, Longitudinal, and Cross-Sequential Analyses. *Psychology and Aging, 2*, 130–137.

Meléndez, J. C., Alfonso-Benlliure, V., Mayordomo, T., and Sales, A. (2016). Is Age Just a Number? Cognitive Reserve As a Predictor of Divergent Thinking in Late Adulthood. *Creativity Research Journal, 28*, 435–441.

Moon, T. W., Hur, W. M., and Hyun, S. H. S. (2017). How Service Employees' Work Motivations Lead to Job Performance: The Role of Service Employees' Job Creativity and Customer Orientation. *Current Psychology*. doi.org/10.1007/s12144–017-9630-8.

Moran, S. (2010). The Roles of Creativity in Society. In J. C. Kaufman and R. J. Sternberg (Eds.), *The Cambridge Handbook of Creativity* (pp. 74–90). Cambridge: Cambridge University Press.

Nusbaum, E. C., Silvia, P. J., and Beaty, R. E. (2014). Ready, Set, Create: What Instructing People to "Be Creative" Reveals about the Meaning and Mechanisms of Divergent Thinking. *Psychology of Aesthetics, Creativity, and the Arts, 8*, 423–432.

O'Hara, L. A., and Sternberg, R. J. (2000–2001). It Doesn't Hurt to Ask: Effects of Instructions to Be Creative, Practical, or Analytical on Essay–Writing Performance and Their Interaction with Students' Thinking Styles. *Creativity Research Journal, 13*(2), 197–210.

Palmiero, M. (2015). The Effects of Age on Divergent Thinking and Creative Objects Production: A Cross-Sectional Study. *High Ability Studies, 26*, 93–104.

Parisi, J. M., Greene, J. C., Morrow, D. G., and Stine-Morrow, E. A. L. (2007). The Senior Odyssey: Participant Experiences of a Program of Social and Intellectual Engagement. *Activities, Adaptation and Aging, 31*, 31–49.

Park, C. L. (2010). Making Sense of the Meaning Literature: An Integrative Review of Meaning Making and Its Effect on Adjustment to Stressful Events. *Psychological Bulletin, 136*(2), 257–301.

Paul, E. S., and Kaufman, S. B. (Eds.). (2014). *The Philosophy of Creativity: New Essays*. New York: Oxford University Press.

Piffer, D. (2012). Can Creativity Be Measured? An Attempt to Clarify the Notion of Creativity and General Directions for Future Research. *Thinking Skills and Creativity, 7*, 258–264.

Pramling, S. I., and Carlsson, A. M. (2008). The Playing Learning Child: Towards a Pedagogy of Early Childhood. *Scandinavian Journal of Educational Research, 52*, 623–641.

Puccio, G. J., Talbot, R. J., and Joniak, A. J. (2000). Examining Creative Performance in the Workplace through a Person–Environment Fit Model. *Journal of Creative Behavior, 34*, 227–247.

Ramos, S. J., and Puccio, G. J. (2014). Cross-Cultural Studies of Implicit Theories of Creativity: A Comparative Analysis between the United States and the Main Ethnic Groups in Singapore. *Creativity Research Journal, 26*, 223–228.

Reilly, R. C. (2008). Is Expertise a Necessary Precondition for Creativity? A Case of Four Novice Learning Group Facilitators. *Thinking Skills and Creativity, 3*, 59–76.

Roskos-Ewoldsen, B., Black, S. R., and Mccown, S. M. (2008). Age-Related Changes in Creative Thinking. *Journal of Creative Behavior, 42*, 33–59.

Runco, M. A. (2014). *Creativity. Theories and Themes: Research, Development, and Practice*. Burlington: Elsevier Academic Press.

Sasser-Coen, J. R. (1993). Qualitative Changes in Creativity in the Second Half of Life: A Life-Span Developmental Perspective. *Journal of Creative Behavior, 27*, 18–27.

Sharma, S., and Babu, N. (2017). Interplay between Creativity, Executive Function and Working Memory in Middle-Aged and Older Adults. *Creativity Research Journal, 29*(1), 71–77.

Shimonaka, Y., and Nakazato, K. (2007). Creativity and Factors Affecting Creative Ability in Adulthood and Old Age. *Japanese Journal of Educational Psychology*, *55*, 231–243.

Silvia, P. J., Beaty, R. J., Nusbaum, E. C., Eddington, K. M., Levin-Aspenson, H., and Kwapil, T. R. (2014). Everyday Creativity in Daily Life: An Experience-Sampling Study of "little c" Creativity. *Psychology of Aesthetics, Creativity, and the Arts*, *8*, 183–188.

Simonton, D. K. (2000). Creative Development As Acquired Expertise: Theoretical Issues and an Empirical Test. *Developmental Review*, *20*, 283–318.

Singer, J. L. (2009). Researching Imaginative Play and Adult Consciousness: Implications for Daily and Literary Creativity. *Psychology of Aesthetics, Creativity, and the Arts*, *3*, 190–199.

Sternberg, R. J., and Lubart, T. I. (1996). Investing in Creativity. *American Psychologist*, *51*, 677–688.

  (1999). The Concept of Creativity: Prospects and Paradigms. In R. J. Sternberg (Ed.), *Handbook of Creativity* (pp. 3–15). Cambridge: Cambridge University Press.

Stine-Morrow, E. A. L., Parisi, J. M., Morrow, D. G., and Park, D. C. (2008). The Effects of an Engaged Lifestyle on Cognitive Vitality: A Field Experiment. *Psychology and Aging*, *23*, 778–786.

Storme, M., Myszkowski, N., Çelik, P., and Lubart, T. (2014). Learning to Judge Creativity: The Underlying Mechanisms in Creativity Training for Non-Expert Judges. *Learning and Individual Differences*, *32*, 19–25.

Tadmor, C. T., Galinsky, A. D., and Maddux, W. W. (2012). Getting the Most out of Living Abroad: Biculturalism and Integrative Complexity as Key Drivers of Creative and Professional Success. *Journal of Personality and Social Psychology*, *103*, 520–542.

Takeuchi, H., Taki, Y., Sassa, Y., Hashizume, H., Sekiguchi, A., Fukushima, A., and Kawashima, R. (2010). White Matter Structures Associated with Creativity from Diffusion Tensor Imaging. *Neuroimage*, *51*, 11–18.

Tegano, D. W., Moran, J. D., and Sawyers, J. K. (1991). *Creativity in Early Childhood Classrooms*. Washington, DC: NEA Professional Library, National Education Association.

Torrance, E. P. (1963). *Education and the Creative Potential*. Minneapolis: University of Minnesota Press.

  (1968). A Longitudinal Examination of the Fourth Grade Slump in Creativity. *Gifted Child Quarterly*, *12*, 195–199.

  (2004). Predicting the Creativity of Elementary School Children (1958–80) – and the Teacher Who "Made a Difference". In D. J. Treffinger (Ed.), *Creativity and Giftedness* (pp. 35–49). Thousand Oaks: Corwin Press.

Urban, K. K., and Jellen, H. G. (1995/2010). *Test for Creative Thinking – Drawing Production (TCT–DP). Manual*. Frankfurt am Main: Pearson Assessment and Information GmbH.

Vincent, A. S., Decker, B. P., and Mumford, M. D. (2002). Divergent Thinking, Intelligence, and Expertise: A Test of Alternative Models. *Creativity Research Journal*, *14*, 163–178.

Visser, I., Chandler, L., and Grainger, P. (2017). Engaging Creativity: Employing Assessment Feedback Strategies to Support Confidence and Creativity in Graphic Design Practice. *Art, Design and Communication in Higher Education*, *16*, 53–67.

Weisberg, R. W. (2015). Expertise, Nonobvious Creativity, and Ordinary Thinking in Edison and Others: Integrating Blindness and Sightedness. *Psychology of Aesthetics, Creativity, and the Arts*, *9*, 15–19.

Yeh, Y., and Lin, C. F. (2015). Aptitude-Treatment Interactions during Creativity Training in E-Learning: How Meaning-Making, Self-Regulation, and Knowledge Management Influence Creativity. *Educational Technology and Society*, *18*, 119–131.

Zhang, W., and Niu, W. H. (2013). Creativity in the Later Life: Factors Associated with the Creativity of the Chinese Elderly. *Journal of Creative Behavior*, *47*, 60–76.

6 Neuroscience of Creativity

OSHIN VARTANIAN

INTRODUCTION

There has been long-standing interest in the biological bases of creativity and genius throughout history. Much of the earlier work in this area involved efforts to understand the genetic bases of creativity. More recently, however, and due in major part to technological advances in modern neuroimaging and theoretical advances in psychology, the focus has shifted to studying the relationship between creativity and brain structure and function – represented by a burgeoning discipline referred to as the **neuroscience of creativity**. Because it is always important to understand the historical roots of ideas, I will review some important early ideas introduced by Sir Francis Galton that were meant to measure the heritability of genius. I will argue that creativity is most likely an emergenic trait, meaning that it is expressed in a number of independent subtraits or abilities that are simultaneously present in a person. This idea holds also for the neurological bases of creativity, because at the level of the brain, it has also been shown that creativity emerges not as a function of a single brain region, process, or mechanism but rather as an emergent property of the dynamic interplay between spontaneous and controlled processes. In this sense, the neural bases of creativity also appear to be componential. In this chapter, I will conduct a selective review of some of the key empirical work from neuroimaging to highlight the contributions of this research to our understanding of creativity. Toward that end, I will review findings from early brain-mapping approaches and will end with presenting contemporary models based on network dynamics (i.e., interactions among networks).

Have you ever thought about what makes a person creative? Answering this question lies at the heart of what creativity researchers are interested in studying. Not surprisingly, this question can be approached from various perspectives, many of which are covered in the present book. For example, we can consider specific personality characteristics that can contribute to a person being more or less creative. Indeed, we know that people who score higher on the factor *openness to experience* exhibit greater levels of creativity regardless of whether the focus is on creative self-beliefs, creative performance (e.g., divergent thinking), or creative achievement (Silvia et al., 2009; Karwowski and Lebuda, 2016). This suggests that something about one's personality can have an impact on whether one thinks or behaves creatively. Similarly, we can consider whether certain mental capacities can help a person exhibit creativity. For example, studies have shown that there is a positive correlation between creativity and *working memory capacity* – defined as the ability to maintain and manipulate information in the focus of attention (De Dreu et al., 2012). This is perhaps not surprising, given that greater working memory capacity can enable a person to maintain task focus for longer periods of time, thereby increasing the likelihood that a creative solution can be found. The focus of this chapter, however, is on yet another perspective that has interested creativity researchers for a long time; namely, whether there is something in our biology that distinguishes more from less creative people. In other words, can we examine a person biologically – either in terms of their present state or their history – in order to glean insights about their creativity? My aim in this chapter will be to trace the history of this interesting question in psychology and to provide you with a contemporary picture of what we know about the relationship between creativity and brain function. I hope that you will come away with a greater appreciation of the role that your brain plays in how creative you are.

Creativity: Nature or Nurture?

Before we enter into a discussion of the biological bases of creativity, it is important to clear up a few misconceptions first. Perhaps the most common misconception is that a focus on the biological bases of higher-order cognitive constructs (e.g., creativity, intelligence, etc.) is an inherently reductionistic exercise – meaning that it attempts to reduce knowledge about higher-order constructs in a particular domain (i.e., psychology) to seemingly more fundamental levels of knowledge represented by another domain (e.g., biology) (see Brigandt and Love, 2017). According to **biological reductionism**, everything about the psychology of creativity can be understood and explained if one were to understand its biological bases – from the molecular level all the way to brain structure and function. Although biological reductionism has had its advocates in the past, it does not play a role in contemporary conceptions of the **neuroscience of creativity** – the discipline concerned with understanding the neurological bases of creativity in terms of both brain structure and function (see Vartanian, Bristol, and Kaufman, 2013; Abraham, 2018; Jung and Vartanian, 2018). Rather, there is general consensus among researchers in the field that to gain a complete explanation of creativity, it is necessary to understand its various causes along different levels of analysis, from the biological all the way to the cultural levels.

Second, a historically old and related argument has revolved around whether creativity and genius are influenced by nature or nurture (see Vartanian, 2011) – where "nature" is commonly understood to mean determined by genes, whereas nurture is commonly understood to mean determined by the environment. Scientific interest in this question must be traced back to Sir Francis Galton's seminal book *Hereditary Genius*, published in 1869. Galton believed that genius was a biologically transmitted trait and that it would run in families. Galton's own lineage may have prompted him to ponder this hypothesis, given that his blood relations included his grandfather Erasmus Darwin, his cousin Charles Darwin, Charles's scientifically eminent sons Francis the botanist, Leonard the eugenicist, Sir George the physicist, as well as the latter's son Sir Charles Galton Darwin the physicist. However, Galton was in need of a mechanism to explain how genius would be passed on from one generation to the next. He used **Lamarckianism** as his explanatory mechanism for evolutionary change, according to which organs that assist an organism are strengthened and passed on to their offspring, or else they atrophy through disuse. Galton's own research in support of his hypothesis was plagued by shortcomings. For starters, he defined genius in terms of achieved distinction or reputation, specifically "the opinion of contemporaries, revised by posterity ... the reputation of a leader of opinion, of an originator, of a man to whom the world deliberately acknowledges itself largely indebted." Not surprisingly, the characterization of some people as born geniuses based on this ambiguous definition is questionable. Furthermore, there were questions about the actual relatedness of some individuals. This meant that on the whole, the evidence was not very convincing.

Sir Francis Galton is also considered to have conducted the first investigation to attempt to study highly creative individuals *directly* to figure out the causes of their creativity (Simonton, 2001). In a monograph published in 1874 entitled *English Men of Science: Their Nature and Nurture*, Galton reported the results of a study in which he surveyed elected Fellows of the Royal Society using a questionnaire he had devised himself. The aim of the questionnaire was to measure the relative contributions of nature and nurture to eminence in science, and it addressed a wide host of developmental issues including the distribution of ability in the family, birth order, and educational experience, among others. This work represents an early intellectual contribution to resolving the extent to which individual differences in creativity (as well as other traits and abilities) are a function of genetic endowment or environmental influences in eminent people.

We now know that creativity and genius do not run in families, and this is because creativity is most likely an emergenic trait (Waller et al., 1993; Martindale, 1999). **Emergenesis** refers to a process whereby a trait is expressed if and only if a number of independent subtraits or abilities are simultaneously present (Lykken et al., 1992). Because the relationship among the subtraits is not additive but multiplicative in nature, the absence of any one component is sufficient to block the occurrence of the emergenic trait altogether. Thus, even though many of the subtraits may themselves be normally distributed throughout the population, the emergenic trait itself shows a **log-normal distribution** (skewed distributions that arise as the multiplicative product of many independent random variables).

Emergenesis makes it extremely uncommon for any individual to possess simultaneously all the necessary subtraits for the expression of an emergenic trait such as high-level creativity or genius. In fact, emergenesis explains why, contrary to Galton's assertion, creative achievement does not run in families: Even though 30–60 percent of the variance in most personality traits and cognitive abilities can be accounted for genetically (Plomin, Owen, and McGuffin, 1994), and members of a given family possess genetic similarities, it is unlikely that they will possess *all* the necessary characteristics for the expression of creative behavior (Vartanian, 2011). As I will attempt to demonstrate later in the chapter, the view that not one trait but a combination of traits and abilities (and their genetics bases) interacts to support creativity is also the picture that has emerged from the neuroscience of creativity. Specifically, there is strong evidence to suggest that creativity does not depend on any single brain structure but rather emerges as a function of the dynamic interplay among a number of structures in the brain. This interactive, componential view will be the key takeaway message from this chapter regarding the neural bases of creativity.

What Are the Big Aims of the Neuroscience of Creativity?

At the outset, it is important to take a moment to reflect on what the big aims of the neuroscience of creativity are. I believe that three aims have motivated much of the work in this area over the last two decades. The first aim has to do with understanding what *causes* creativity. According to the classic Aristotelian model (see Killeen, 2001), a complete explanation of a phenomenon requires an understanding of four different types of causes that lead to its instantiation: (a) *efficient causes* represent the triggers that are sufficient to generate or prevent an effect against its causal background; (b) *final causes* are the functional explanations that address purposive questions (e.g., "What is it supposed to do?"); (c) *formal causes* are models that specify the transition from efficient causes to final causes; and (d) *material causes* are explanations of the substrates that comprise a phenomenon or give rise to it, an exclusive focus on which is known as *reductionism*. In this sense, it can be argued that by elucidating the material causes of creativity in terms of its brain correlates, research in the neuroscience of creativity can contribute to a more complete explanation of the phenomenon of creativity by revealing its material bases.

Of course, in isolation, neuroimaging data are correlational in nature and unable to reveal the causes of the behaviors under consideration. However, in combination with complementary approaches that can be used to test causal hypotheses (e.g., patient studies involving loss of function due to focal brain damage), neuroimaging data can reveal structures that are both necessary and sufficient for the realization of specific cognitive functions. In addition, novel analytic approaches that can be applied to brain imaging data such as Dynamic Causal Modeling can be used to test causal hypotheses regarding brain function – where, in accordance with control theory, a cause is understood to mean activity in one brain region controlling activity in another brain region. This method has already been used to test specific hypotheses about causal pathways in the brain during divergent thinking (Vartanian et al., 2018).

The second aim that has motivated the search for the neural correlates of creativity revolves around the extent to which brain data can be used to falsify central ideas and theories in the psychology of creativity. For example, brain data can be used to determine whether neural structures that are involved in creativity exhibit **domain generality versus domain specificity** – meaning whether "creativity is a general, domain-transcending set of skills, aptitudes, traits, propensities, and motivations that can be productively deployed in any domain – or, conversely, whether the skills, aptitudes, traits, propensities, and motivations that lead to creative performance vary from domain to domain" (Baer, 2010, p. 321). This potential application is important because it can shed light on this central and historically important question in the psychology of creativity in new ways (Kaufman and Baer, 2005; Baer, 2015). Simply put, if it were the case that at the level of the brain two variants of creativity exhibit domain specificity (i.e., creativity in domains A and B do not exhibit structural and functional overlap), then this would represent inconsistent evidence with the idea that the psychological processes that underlie those two types of creativity exhibit domain generality. As such, alongside behavioral data, brain data offer an additional type of data that can be used for the falsification of ideas and theories – a critical process for improving the quality of the science of creativity.

Third, an overarching theme of research in the cognitive neuroscience of creativity is to offer better mechanistic explanations of some of the core constructs that drive research in the psychology of creativity. Simonton (2018) has identified two major candidates for this endeavor, including (a) what is a creative idea, and (b) what are the processes that lead to the emergence of a creative idea. In terms of the latter, as we shall see, there is growing evidence to suggest that creative ideas emerge from the interaction of multiple large-scale brain networks. Perhaps even more remarkably, the same large-scale networks appear to be at play across a wide range of tasks, ranging from divergent thinking to musical improvisation and creative drawing. In contrast, we have made relatively less progress in gaining a better understanding of the neural representation of creative ideas (i.e., what are the functional and structural correlates of a creative idea in the brain). Part of this shortcoming might be related to the limitations of the types of tasks and samples that have been studied in neuroimaging studies of creativity. Specifically, truly creative ideas and the people who exhibit them might be too singular for the types of designs and analytic approaches that typify neuroimaging studies. As noted by Simonton (2018, p. 15), "those measures that emphasize personal creativity will come closest to the creative process going on in a creator's head, whereas those that emphasize consensual creativity are contaminated with sundry social, cultural, economic, political, and historical factors that may have nothing to do with either psychology or neuroscience [see also Simonton, 2010]." Nevertheless, at least, in principle, there is no reason to assume that methodological approaches cannot be developed that can identify the neural representation of creative ideas emerging in truly creative people in different contexts, and this remains one of the long-term goals of this research program. Indeed, at least one recent study has already examined the neural correlates of divergent and convergent thinking in a sample of high-level creative achievers who included internationally acclaimed persons in multiple disciplines spanning the visual arts (e.g., painting, drawing, sculpture, photography, graphic design and animation) and the sciences (e.g., biology, neuroscience, chemistry and mathematics) (Japardi et al., 2018). The results of that study have shown that there is remarkable overlap in the neural systems that support creativity in average and above-average individuals.

Neuroscience of Creativity: From Brain Mapping to Network Dynamics

As a discipline, the neuroscience of creativity is relatively new. Indeed, as recently as 1999, when Colin Martindale reviewed the empirical evidence in support of the biological bases of creativity for the *Handbook of Creativity* (Sternberg, 1999), not a single brain-scanning study involving a modern neuroimaging approach had been published that focused on creativity (Martindale, 1999). Nevertheless, despite its youth, the discipline appears to have undergone two stages of progressive maturation.

The first stage was primarily characterized by brain mapping approaches. Motivated by new brain imaging technologies at their disposal, researchers conducted numerous studies to isolate regions of the brain that were involved in creative idea generation. The majority of the studies relied on functional magnetic resonance imaging (fMRI), a method that measures brain activation *indirectly*. Specifically, when neurons in a particular region of the brain need to work harder to satisfy task demands, their metabolic demands are greater. In order to satisfy those greater metabolic demands, more blood is supplied to those regions to deliver the necessary oxygen for cellular function. In turn, the uptake of oxygen from the blood by the cells causes a change in the proportion of oxygenated versus deoxygenated hemoglobin levels in the blood, and the magnetic signature of that change is detected by the scanner. In other words, with fMRI we infer brain activation rather than measure it directly. The advantage of this method is that it is noninvasive and offers very high spatial resolution (i.e., information about where the activation is occurring).

Not surprisingly, those early studies used a plethora of tasks to measure the neural correlates of creative idea generation, including divergent thinking, drawing, finding pragmatic links between incoherent sentences, and solving anagrams and insight tasks, among others. Aside from fMRI, the neuroimaging methods also included positron emission tomography (PET), electroencephalography (EEG), event-related potentials (ERP), near infrared spectroscopy (NIRS), diffusion tensor imaging (DTI), and single-photon emission computed tomography (SPECT). PET is a functional imaging technique that uses radioactive tracers to detect metabolic changes in the brain. EEG represents recordings of the electrical activity measured along the scalp (produced by the synchronous firing of groups of neurons within the brain), whereas ERPs are calculated based on EEG and represent changes in electrical activity in relation to specific stimuli. NIRS computes ratios of oxygenated and deoxygenated hemoglobin at the scalp and thereby provides a measure of brain activity based on its hemodynamics (i.e., dynamics of blood flow). Like PET, SPECT also uses a radioactive tracer but is used to show how blood flows through arteries and veins. Finally, DTI is an MRI-based imaging method that enables one to study brain network connectivity by mapping white matter tracts. Needless to say, all of these methods have intricate analytic workflows, variable signal-to-noise ratios, and exhibit vast differences in temporal and spatial resolution. As such, the early results were characterized by large amounts of variability and inconsistency (for descriptive reviews, see Arden et al., 2010; Dietrich and Kanso 2011).

Fortunately, we have at our disposal very handy tools for the **meta-analysis** of neuroimaging data. In the behavioral sciences, what a meta-analysis allows one to do is to derive an average effect size for a particular phenomenon across many studies. This way researchers can tell whether, despite variations in methodology across studies, a particular phenomenon is reliable or not. The focus in meta-analysis of neuroimaging data is somewhat different, which is to isolate, across studies, regions of the brain that are reliably activated in relation to a manipulation of interest. Four such large-scale quantitative meta-analyses of the neuroimaging literature were conducted early on that were immensely helpful in isolating the neural correlates of creativity based on early brain mapping studies. First, Gonen-Yaacovi et al. (2013) conducted a meta-analysis of thirty-four neuroimaging studies that had focused on creativity. Across all studies, creativity was shown to engage the entire brain. However, when the researchers compared different types of creativity to each other, they found reliable differences in their neural correlates. For example, tasks that required verbal processing activated a dissociable set of regions than tasks that activated nonverbal (e.g., visuospatial) processing. Similarly, tasks that required the generation of responses (e.g., divergent thinking) activated a dissociable set of regions than tasks that required the combination of remote semantic associations. An example of the latter task is the Remote Associates Task, in which the participants are presented with three stimulus words on each trial (e.g., cottage, Swiss, cake) and asked to generate a response that is associated with all three stimuli (i.e., cheese) (Mednick, Mednick, and Mednick, 1964). The likely explanation for these dissociations is that the neural correlates of verbal vs. nonverbal and generation vs. combination tasks vary because the cognitive processes that underlie them are different. For example, whereas creativity in the verbal domain likely requires the involvement of linguistic regions in the frontal and temporal lobes, nonverbal tasks likely require the involvement of superior parietal regions that support visuospatial processing.

Interestingly, largely similar results were reported by three other meta-analyses. First, Boccia et al. (2015) focused on forty-five neuroimaging studies of creativity. Unlike Gonen-Yaacovi et al. (2013), they opted to carve the studies into three bins and found dissociable patterns of brain activation for creativity in the musical, verbal, and visuospatial domains. This prompted the authors to conclude that "this evidence suggests that creativity relies on multi-componential neural networks and that different creativity domains depend on different brain regions" (p. 1). These inferences are consistent with a componential view of creativity specifically (Amabile, 2013) and of problem-solving ability more generally (Sternberg, 1980). In other words, given that, as a higher-order cognitive ability, creativity is likely decomposable into specific sub-processes (e.g., semantic memory, attention, etc.), regions of the brain that exhibit a degree of functional specificity in relation to those sub-processes appear to contribute to the types of creativity that draw on those functions. This conclusion was also supported by another meta-analysis that focused specifically on divergent thinking studies (Wu et al., 2015). They found that divergent thinking was associated with engagement of the lateral prefrontal cortex, posterior parietal cortex, anterior cingulate cortex, several regions in the temporal cortex, and left fusiform gyrus – regions that have been implicated in several sub-processes that support divergent thinking including memory, attention, and executive functions.

The final meta-analysis, conducted by Vartanian (2012), addressed the same issue but focused more narrowly on fMRI studies of analogy and metaphor. Analogy and metaphor have been linked historically, theoretically, and empirically with creativity (Dunbar, 1977; Gentner et al., 2001; Green et al., 2012). The link between analogy and creativity becomes obvious when we consider its definition: Analogical reasoning occurs whenever we aim to understand novel situations by drawing parallels to earlier situations (Sternberg, 1977). This type of reasoning has played an important role in creative scientific discovery; perhaps the most important example was Bohr's conceptualization of the motion of the electron around the nucleus of the hydrogen atom (target domain) by drawing a parallel with the motion of planets around the sun in the solar system (source domain). Although several different models of analogical reasoning exist (e.g., Gentner, 1998), there is broad agreement that two of its necessary cognitive subcomponents include (a) retrieval of relevant content from long-term memory based on current content in working memory, and (b) mapping (i.e., aligning) the representational content of cases in working memory and projecting inferences from one case to another. There is now substantial evidence to suggest that the core maintenance and manipulation functions of working memory are represented within the fronto-parietal system in the brain (Baddeley, 2003). In addition, converging neuropsychological (Waltz et al., 1999), neuroimaging (Christoff et al., 2001), and developmental (Crone et al., 2009) evidence has pointed to the role of the rostrolateral prefrontal cortex (RLPFC) in structural alignment across relations – termed *relational integration* (Bunge, Helskog, and Wendelken, 2009). As such, Vartanian (2012) predicted that across analogy studies, one would expect to observe activations in regions within the fronto-parietal working memory system and the RLPFC.

How about metaphor? Because metaphors can serve as vehicles for contemplating concepts at higher levels of abstraction, they make category membership more flexible, which in turn can contribute to a defining feature of creative cognition that involves the flexible manipulation of concepts (Vartanian and Goel, 2005; Vartanian, 2009). For example, how does one understand an utterance such as "lawyers are sharks"? According to classic standard pragmatic models of metaphor comprehension, people extract metaphoric meaning only after failure to extract a literal meaning (Grice, 1975). Given that the literal meaning (i.e., lawyers are marine creatures) is nonsensical, the metaphoric meaning (i.e., lawyers are predatory animals) follows. According to this account, one should expect to observe greater demands on working memory and text comprehension resources for metaphorical than for literal meaning. More contemporary models have deemphasized processing differences between literal and metaphoric meaning while maintaining the existence of qualitative differences involving categorization and abstraction between the two types of processes (Glucksberg, 2003). Nevertheless, one would predict the engagement of the fronto-parietal working memory and temporal lobe structures involved in linguistic comprehension in relation to processing of metaphor (see Mashal et al., 2007).

Vartanian (2012) predicted that one should expect to observe (a) a consistent and theoretically derived set of brain activations *within* each task (because of similar cognitive components) (Hypothesis 1), but (b) dissociable sets of brain activations *between* tasks (because they rely on different cognitive sub-processes) (Hypothesis 2). His meta-analysis of the analogy and metaphor literatures – based on ten fMRI studies within each category – supported both hypotheses. Specifically, as predicted, analogy was associated with reliable activation in left RLPFC and dorsolateral PFC across studies. In contrast, metaphor was associated with reliable activation in left dorsolateral PFC and temporal pole – a well-established hub for text comprehension (Ferstl et al., 2008). In addition, and contrary to expectation, activation was also observed in the cingulate gyrus for metaphor. This structure is known to be an important part of the brain's frontal attentional control system (Carter et al., 1997), and its activation is consistent with the idea that metaphor requires more attention than the corresponding control conditions across studies. Overall, the results of Vartanian (2012) demonstrated that when the cognitive task and imaging modality are kept consistent, reliable patterns of neural activation emerge across studies of processes related to creativity.

The major takeaway points from the early brain mapping approaches were that there is no single region that underlies creativity in the brain and that the neural correlates of creativity are process-specific. The second and current stage of the discipline is characterized by a move away from focusing on isolated regions to a greater appreciation of the interaction of large-scale brain networks that support creativity – a development that was greatly facilitated by our understanding of brain function at rest. Specifically, **resting-state connectivity** is a technique using which one can identify brain regions that exhibit similar patterns of fMRI activity fluctuations and can therefore be grouped into large-scale brain systems called "networks." One of the major technological advances in neuroimaging research has involved the use of this technique to study the interactions (i.e., dynamics) of these large-scale brain networks in the service of various types of thinking, including creative cognition (Zabelina and Andrews-Hanna, 2016).

Two such networks that appear to play a particularly important role in creative cognition involve the default-mode network (DN) and the executive control network (ECN) (Beaty et al., 2016). Activity in the DN is associated with spontaneous and self-generated thought. In contrast, activity in the ECN is associated with tasks that necessitate externally directed attention (i.e., cognitive control) (see Chrysikou, 2018). Beaty et al. (2015) used whole-brain functional connectivity analysis to highlight a network of brain regions associated with divergent thinking, which included several regions within the DN and ECN, as well as structures within the salience network such as the insula, shown to be involved in high-level cognitive control and attentional processes (Menon and Uddin, 2010). The brain's salience network has an important role to play in many types of higher-order cognition because it is involved in the detection and allocation of neural resources to behaviorally relevant stimuli (Bressler and Menon, 2010; Uddin, 2015). As such, it can trigger the engagement of other networks based on the relevance (i.e., salience) of the task at hand.

Beaty et al.'s analyses revealed direct functional connections between these three networks in the service of divergent thinking. Specifically, posterior cingulate cortex (PCC) – a region that lies within the DN – exhibited increased functional coupling with regions of the ECN including the dorsolateral prefrontal cortex, as well as regions within the salience network such as the bilateral insula. Finally, using dynamic functional connectivity analysis conducted in the course of engagement in a divergent thinking task (i.e., Alternate Uses Task),

Beaty et al. were able to show that the time course of the coupling between the PCC and regions within the salience and ECN varies as a function of the phase of the task. Specifically, the PCC showed early coupling with the insula and later coupling with the right dorsolateral PFC among other regions. There is evidence to show that one of the roles of the salience network is to facilitate switches between DN and ECN (Cocchi et al., 2013). As such, its early involvement in the Alternate Uses Task could be to facilitate later coupling between DN and ECN.

Data from several recent fMRI studies on musical improvisation (Pinho et al., 2016) and poetry composition (Liu et al., 2015) have shown that engagement across numerous creativity tasks is associated with dynamic coupling between the DN and ECN (reviewed in Beaty et al., 2016). In this context, DN activity is perceived to reflect the spontaneous generation of ideas or information derived from long-term memory, whereas activity in the ECN is understood to reflect evaluative processes that constrain thinking to meet specific task goals. Not only does this dynamic interplay between generative and evaluative processes have a long history in creativity research (Campbell, 1960; Martindale, 2007; Simonton, 2010), but numerous classical models of cognition emphasized the ability of creative people to navigate back and forth in the service of novel idea generation (see Kris, 1952). In this sense, the interplay between the DN and ECN can be perceived as the interplay between controlled and spontaneous thought processes in the service of novel and useful idea generation.

The dynamic interplay between DN and ECN is also apparent when one focuses on resting-state rather than task-related data. For example, Beaty et al. (2014) reported that, compared with less creative people, more creative people exhibit increased coupling of DN regions with the left inferior frontal gyrus – a region within ECN whose involvement in divergent thinking tasks is frequently attributed to its role in cognitive control. The close coupling of these two networks at rest suggests that there might be stable functional differences involving the coupling of the DN and ECN that distinguish more from less creative people.

Whereas the studies discussed thus far have demonstrated that the DN and ECN interact in the course of creative cognition, the precise nature of this interaction has not been made clear. At least a couple of possibilities exist in terms of how these two networks might exert control over each other in the service of creativity. According to one model, kernel ideas emerge in nodes within the posterior brain regions including the temporal and parietal lobes, whereas nodes within the frontal lobes exert control over those regions to ensure that the originated ideas meet the relevant tasks demands. Thus, according to this *unidirectional* model, the frontal lobes exert control over the temporal and parietal lobes during creative cognition. According to another model, however, it could be that the posterior and frontal lobes exert control over each other in the form of feedback loops in the course of creative cognition. According to this *bidirectional* model, the temporal and parietal lobes also exert control over brain activity in the frontal lobes in successive generation-evaluation cycles. Vartanian et al. (2018) used Dynamic Causal Modeling to test these two possibilities head-to-head using fMRI data collected in the course of the Alternate Uses Task. Dynamic Causal Modeling is an analytic tool that enables one to test whether certain regions in the brain exert control over the activity of other region(s) in the brain during engagement in any task. The results from the study offered stronger support for the unidirectional than the bidirectional model by demonstrating that the inferior frontal gyrus exerts control over the middle temporal gyrus and the inferior parietal lobule. As such, we have a better mechanistic understanding of the specific nature of the interaction between frontal and posterior lobes during creative cognition. However, it must be emphasized that if the nature of the task were to change, the observed pattern might have differed as a result. Specifically, if instead of the Alternate Uses Task the researchers had relied on a task that requires greater back-and-forth between idea generation and refinement cycles (e.g., creative story generation), a bidirectional pattern of influence between the DN and ECN might have emerged.

Recently, Beaty, Seli, and Schacter (2019) have offered an up-to-date account of the network dynamics account of creative cognition in the brain. Specifically, having reviewed the experimental studies examining cognitive mechanisms of network interactions and correlational studies assessing network dynamics associated with individual creative abilities, their review identified three classes of cognitive processes that contribute to network interactions during creative performance: (1) goal-directed memory retrieval, (2) prepotent-response inhibition, and (3) internally focused attention. Regarding goal-directed memory retrieval, there is increasing evidence to suggest that people who have been primed to draw on their episodic memory generate more novel and useful responses during divergent thinking tasks and that there was stronger functional connectivity between the DN and ECN following such episodic memory induction (Madore, Addis, and Schacter, 2015; Schacter and Madore, 2016; Madore et al., 2019). This suggests that in the context of divergent thinking the "DN-ECN coupling appears to reflect goal-directed retrieval processes recruited to strategically search, select, and combine elements of past experience during divergent thinking" (Beaty et al., 2019, p. 23).

Regarding prepotent-response inhibition, there is emerging evidence to suggest that people who perform well on divergent thinking tasks are better able to suppress interference from dominant or salient response tendencies (e.g., obvious concepts or ideas) (Benedek et al., 2014). In turn, this makes it more likely that they report original and novel ideas. Furthermore, functional connectivity analyses have revealed that the strength of the DN-ECN coupling reveals the extent to which prepotent-responses are inhibited, suggesting that the DN is where automatic responses arise, which are in turn inhibited by the ECN (Beaty et al., 2017; Vatansever, Menon, and Stamatakis, 2017).

Finally, as has been suggested above, at least to a certain extent creative cognition involves attending to internally generated thoughts (for review, see Benedek, 2018). In addition, divergent thinking requiring internal attention has been associated with greater activation in the right anterior inferior parietal lobule (IPL), which represents a part of the ECN, as well as a stronger functional coupling between the right anterior IPL and the visual cortex in the internal condition (Benedek et al., 2016). This suggest that the ECN may play a role in the regulation of the focus of attention during divergent thinking by attenuating sensory input (from the visual cortex) and directing attention to internally generated thought processes. The continued development of a network dynamics model of creative cognition suggests that aside from the well-established DN-ECN coupling, it is also important to consider the extent to which the ECN exerts top-down control over the sensory cortices (e.g., visual cortex) to reduce the impact of external input and to keep attention focused on internally generated thought processes.

CONCLUSION

The present review of the neuroscience of creativity has been necessarily selective. For example, it was not possible to review the important work conducted on brain *structure* that is an important complement to research on functional neuroimaging (see Jung et al., 2013), nor was there room to discuss the ways in which patient data in neuropsychology have enriched our understanding of the role of the brain in creativity (e.g., Miller et al., 1998). Nevertheless, the available data from functional neuroimaging strongly suggest that creativity is a product of the interaction of large-scale systems in the brain that support spontaneous and controlled processes, in accordance with componential models of creativity. It is hoped that future research in this area will contribute to a more comprehensive causal understanding of the neurological processes that drive creativity.

My Research Contribution

Our thinking is usually constrained by various explicit or implicit factors. For example, some tasks impose explicit and specific requirements for allowable solutions – requirements that are meant to guide our search for solutions. In other cases, as is oftentimes the case with problems that require insight for solution, the representation of the problem itself imposes implicit constraints on thinking, leading the problem solver astray. I am interested in understanding how thinkers break free from such constraints in order to think more creatively and flexibly and in the neural systems that support such transitions. Specifically, for almost two decades, I have presented people in the fMRI scanner with problems that either do or do not require that constraints be broken for successful solution. Further, I have examined the neural systems that come online when those constraints are overcome. My main research contribution has been to show that the right inferior frontal gyrus plays a key role in modulating the constraints placed on the problem space. This is an interesting finding because this region plays a key role in inhibition in the cognitive, affective, and behavioral domains: When people have a lesion in this region, they cannot suppress inappropriate actions; in turn, when neurologically heathy people

(cont.)

inhibit or disinhibit their behavior appropriately, this region exhibits greater activation. In summary, it appears that a region that regulates suppression of behavior also plays a part in reducing the constraints that are placed on thinking during creative cognition.

Critical/Creative Thinking Questions

1. Does the neural machinery that supports creativity in truly eminent people work differently than the neural machinery that supports creativity in regular people? Another way to think about this question is to ask whether you expect the building blocks of creativity (e.g., memory, attention, etc.) to be the same or different in the two groups.
2. Are creative artists and creative scientists similar or different in the way they solve problems in their respective domains? In other words, is creativity a domain-general or domain-specific ability, and are its neural correlates the same or different as a result?
3. What can we learn about the psychology and neuroscience of creativity by studying other higher-order cognitive processes such as reasoning, planning, and judgment and decision-making? From an evolutionary perspective, would you expect those abilities to be built on largely similar or different components? Why is that important?
4. Is it necessary to understand the workings of the brain in order to understand the psychology of creativity? What are some of the insights that we might miss if our models of creativity did not involve any knowledge about the brain?
5. Creativity appears to be an emergent property of the dynamic interplay between spontaneous and controlled processes in the brain. However, how is the switching between spontaneous and controlled processes regulated? Is it determined deliberately by the thinker or intuitively by features of the problem space?

GLOSSARY

biological reductionism: Reducing knowledge about a higher-order construct in a domain (i.e., psychology) to seemingly more fundamental levels of knowledge represented by another domain (e.g., biology).

domain generality versus domain specificity: The question about whether creativity is a general, domain-transcending set of skills, aptitudes, traits, propensities, and motivations, or whether the skills, aptitudes, traits, propensities, and motivations that lead to creativity vary from domain (e.g., arts) to domain (e.g., sciences).

emergenesis: A process whereby novel or emergent properties arise from the interaction of more elementary (and partly genetic) properties.

Lamarckianism: Lamarckianism is an explanatory mechanism for evolutionary change, according to which organs that assist an organism are strengthened and passed on to their offspring, or else they atrophy through disuse. Such acquired characteristics are inherited.

log-normal distribution: A skewed distribution that arises as the multiplicative product of many independent random variables. Log-normal distributions are skewed to the right, although the logarithm of the random variable is normally distributed.

meta-analysis: The meta-analysis of functional neuroimaging data involves the identification of brain regions that exhibit reliable activation across multiple studies that manipulated a variable of interest (e.g., creativity).

neuroscience of creativity: The discipline concerned with understanding the neurological bases of creativity in terms of both brain structure and function.

resting-state connectivity: Resting-state connectivity is a technique using which one can identify brain regions that exhibit similar patterns of fMRI activity fluctuations and can therefore be grouped into large-scale brain systems called "networks."

REFERENCES

Abraham, A. (2018). *The Neuroscience of Creativity*. New York: Cambridge University Press.

Amabile, T. M. (2013). Componential Theory of Creativity. In E. H. Kessler (Ed.), *Encyclopedia of Management Theory* (pp. 134–139) Los Angeles: Sage.

Arden, R., Chavez, R. S., Grazioplene, R., and Jung, R. E. (2010). Neuroimaging Creativity: A Psychometric View. *Behavioural Brain Research*, *214*, 143–156.

Baddeley, A. (2003). Working Memory: Looking Back and Looking Forward. *Nature Reviews Neuroscience*, *4*, 829–839.

Baer, J. (2010). Is Creativity Domain Specific? In J. C. Kaufman and R. J. Sternberg (Eds.), *The Cambridge Handbook of Creativity* (pp. 321–342). New York: Cambridge University Press.
  (2015). *Domain Specificity of Creativity*. San Diego: Academic Press.

Beaty, R. E., Benedek, M., Kaufman, S. B., and Silvia, P. J. (2015). Default and Executive Network Coupling Supports Creative Idea Production. *Scientific Reports*, *5*, Article 10964.

Beaty, R. E., Benedek, M., Silvia, P. J., and Schacter, D. L. (2016). Creative Cognition and Brain Network Dynamics. *Trends in Cognitive Sciences*, *20*, 87–95.

Beaty, R. E., Benedek, M., Wilkins, R. W., Jauk, E., Fink, A., Silvia, P. J., Hodges, D. A., Koschutnig, K., and Neubauer, A. C. (2014). Creativity and the Default Network: A Functional Connectivity Analysis of the Creative Brain at Rest. *Neuropsychologia*, *64*, 92–98.

Beaty, R. E., Christensen, A. P., Benedek, M., Silvia, P. J., and Schacter, D. L. (2017). Creative Constraints: Brain Activity and Network Dynamics Underlying Semantic Interference during Idea Production. *NeuroImage*, *148*, 189–196.

Beaty, R. E., Seli, P., and Schacter, D. L. (2019). Network Neuroscience of Creative Cognition: Mapping Cognitive Mechanisms and Individual Differences in the Creative Brain. *Current Opinion in Behavioral Sciences*, *27*, 22–30.

Benedek, M. (2018). Internally Directed Attention in Creative Cognition. In R. E. Jung and O. Vartanian (Eds.), *The Cambridge Handbook of the Neuroscience of Creativity* (pp. 180–194). New York: Cambridge University Press.

Benedek, M., Jauk, E., Beaty, R. E., Fink, A., Koschutnig, K., and Neubauer, A. C. (2016). Brain Mechanisms Associated with Internally Directed Attention and Self-Generated Thought. *Scientific Reports*, *6*, 22959.

Benedek, M., Jauk, E., Sommer, M., Arendasy, M., and Neubauer, A. C. (2014). Intelligence, Creativity, and Cognitive Control: The Common and Differential Involvement of Executive Functions in Intelligence and Creativity. *Intelligence*, *46*, 73–83.

Boccia, M., Piccardi, L., Palermo, L., Nori, R., and Palmiero, M. (2015). Where Do Bright Ideas occur in Our Brain? Meta-Analytic Evidence from Neuroimaging Studies of Domain-Specific Creativity. *Frontiers in Psychology*, *6*, Article 1195.

Bressler, S., and Menon, V. (2010). Large-Scale Brain Networks in Cognition: Emerging Methods and Principles. *Trends in Cognitive Sciences*, *14*, 277–290.

Brigandt, I., and Love, A. (2017). Reductionism in Biology. In E. N. Zalta (Ed.), *The Stanford Encyclopedia of Philosophy* (Spring 2017 Edition). https://plato.stanford.edu/archives/spr2017/entries/reduction-biology/.

Bunge, S. A., Helskog, E. H., and Wendelken, C. (2009). Left, But Not Right, Rostrolateral Prefrontal Cortex Meets a Stringent Test of the Relational Integration Hypothesis. *NeuroImage*, *46*, 338–342.

Campbell, D. T. (1960). Blind Variation and Selective Retention in Creative Thought As in Other Knowledge Processes. *Psychological Review*, 67, 380–400.

Carter, C. S., Mintun, M., Nichols, T., and Cohen, J. D. (1997). Anterior Cingulate Gyrus Dysfunction and Selective Attention Deficits in Schizophrenia: [15O]H2O PET Study during Single-Trial Stroop Task Performance. *American Journal of Psychiatry*, *154*, 1670–1675.

Christoff, K., Prabhakaran, V., Dorfman, J., Zhao, Z., Kroger, J. K., Holyoak, K. J., and Gabrieli, J. D. E. (2001) Rostrolateral Prefrontal Cortex Involvement in Relational Integration during Reasoning. *NeuroImage*, *14*, 1136–1149.

Chrysikou, E. G. (2018). The Costs and Benefits of Cognitive Control for Creativity. In R. E. Jung and O. Vartanian (Eds.), *The Cambridge Handbook of the Neuroscience of Creativity* (pp. 299–317). New York: Cambridge University Press.

Cocchi, L., Zalesky, A., Fornito, A., and Mattingley, J. B. (2013) Dynamic Cooperation and Competition between Brain Systems during Cognitive Control. *Trends in Cognitive Sciences*, *17*, 494–501.

Crone, E. A., Wendelken, C., van Leijenhorst, L., Honomichl, R. D., Christoff, K., and Bunge, S. A. (2009). Neurocognitive Development of Relational Reasoning. *Developmental Science*, *12*, 55–66.

De Dreu, C. K. W., Nijstad, B. A., Baas, M., Wosink, I., and Roskes, M. (2012). Working Memory Benefits Creative Insight, Musical Improvisation, and Original Ideation through Maintained Task-Focused Attention. *Personality and Social Psychology Bulletin*, 38, 656–669.

Dietrich, A., and Kanso, R. (2010). A Review of EEG, ERP, and Neuroimaging Studies of Creativity and Insight. *Psychological Bulletin*, *136*, 822–848.

Dunbar, K. (1997). How Scientists Think: Online Creativity and Conceptual Change in Science. In T. B. Ward, S. M. Smith, and S. Vaid (Eds.), *Conceptual Structures and Processes: Emergence, Discovery and Change* (pp. 461–493). Washington, DC: APA Press.

Ferstl, E. C., Neumann, J., Bogler, C., and von Cramon, D. Y. (2008). The Extended Language Network: A Meta-Analysis of Neuroimaging Studies on Text Comprehension. *Human Brain Mapping*, *29*, 581–593.

Galton, F. (1869). *Hereditary Genius*. New York: Friedmann.
  (1874). *English Men of Science: Their Nature and Nurture*. London: Macmillan & Co.

Gentner, D. (1998). Analogy. In W. Bechtel and G. Graham (Eds.), *A Companion to Cognitive Science* (pp. 107–113). Oxford: Blackwell.

Gentner, D., Bowdle, B., Wolff, P., and Boronat, C. (2001). Metaphor Is Like Analogy. In D. Gentner, K. J. Holyoak, and B. Kokinov (Eds.), *The Analogical Mind: Perspectives from Cognitive Science* (pp. 199–253). Cambridge, MA: MIT Press.

Glucksberg, S. (2003). The Psycholinguistics of Metaphor. *Trends in Cognitive Sciences*, 7, 92–97.

Gonen-Yaacovi, G., de Souza, L. C., Levy, R., Urbanski, M., Josse, G., and Volle, E. (2013). Rostral and Caudal Prefrontal Contribution to Creativity: A Meta-Analysis of Functional Imaging Data. *Frontiers in Human Neuroscience*, 7, Article 465.

Green, A. E., Kraemer, D. J., Fugelsang, J. A., Gray, J. R., and Dunbar, K. N. (2012). Neural Correlates of Creativity in Analogical Reasoning. *Journal of Experimental Psychology: Learning, Memory, and Cognition*, 38, 264–272.

Grice, H. P. (1975). Logic and Conversation. In P. Cole and J. Morgan (Eds.), *Syntax and Semantics: Speech Acts*, vol. 3 (pp. 41–58). New York: Academic Press.

Japardi, K., Bookheimer, S., Knudsen, K., Ghahremani, D. G., and Bilder, R. M. (2018). Functional Magnetic Resonance Imaging of Divergent and Convergent Thinking in Big-C Creativity. *Neuropsychologia*, 118, 59–67.

Jung, R. E., Mead, B. S., Carrasco, J., and Flores, R. A. (2013). The Structure of Creative Cognition in the Human Brain. *Frontiers in Human Neurosciences*, 7, Article 330.

Jung, R. E., and Vartanian, O. (Eds.). (2018). *The Cambridge Handbook of the Neuroscience of Creativity*. New York: Cambridge University Press.

Karwowski, M., and Lebuda, I. (2016). The Big Five, the Huge Two, and Creative Self-Beliefs: A Meta-Analysis. *Psychology of Aesthetics, Creativity, and the Arts*, 10, 214–232.

Kaufman, J. C., and Baer, J. (Eds.). (2005). *Creativity across Domains: Faces of the Muse*. Mahwah: Lawrence Erlbaum.

Killeen, P. R. (2001). The Four Causes of Behavior. *Current Directions in Psychological Science*, 10, 136–140.

Kris, E. (1952). *Psychoanalytic Explorations in Art*. New York: International Universities Press.

Liu, S., Erkkinen, M. G., Healey, M. L., Xu, Y., Swett, K. E., Chow, H. M., and Braun, A. R. (2015). Brain Activity and Connectivity during Poetry Composition: toward a Multidimensional Model of the Creative Process. *Human Brain Mapping*, 36, 3351–3372.

Lykken, D. T., McGue, M., Tellegen, A., and Bouchard, T. J. Jr. (1992). Emergenesis: Genetic Traits That May Not Run in Families. *American Psychologist*, 47, 1565–1577.

Madore, K. P., Addis, D. R., and Schacter, D. L. (2015). Creativity and Memory: Effects of an Episodic Specificity Induction on Divergent Thinking. *Psychological Science*, 26, 1461–1468.

Madore, K. P., Thakral, P. P., Beaty, R. E., Addis, D. R., and Schacter, D. L. (2019). Neural Mechanisms of Episodic Retrieval Support Divergent Creative Thinking. *Cerebral Cortex*, 29, 150–166.

Martindale, C. (1999). Biological Bases of Creativity. In R. J. Sternberg (Ed.), *Handbook of Creativity* (pp. 137–152). New York: Cambridge University Press.

  (2007). Creativity, Primordial Cognition, and Personality. *Personality and Individual Differences*, 43, 1777–1785.

Mashal, N., Faust, M., Hendler, T., and Jung-Beeman, M. (2007). An fMRI Investigation of the Neural Correlates Underlying the Processing of Novel Metaphorical Expressions. *Brain and Language*, 100, 115–126.

Mednick, M. T., Mednick, S. A., and Mednick, E. V. (1964). Incubation of Creative Performance and Specific Associative Priming. *The Journal of Abnormal and Social Psychology*, 69, 84–88.

Menon, V., and Uddin, L. Q. (2010). Saliency, Switching, Attention and Control: A Network Model of Insula Function. *Brain Structure and Function*, 214, 655–667.

Miller, B. L., Cummings, J., Mishkin, F., Boone, K., Prince, F., Ponton, M., and Cotman, D. (1998). Emergence of Artistic Talent in Frontotemporal Dementia. *Neurology, 51*, 978–982.

Pinho, A. L., Ullén, F., Castelo-Branco, M., Fransson, P., and de Manzano, Ö. (2016). Addressing a Paradox: Dual Strategies for Creative Performance in Introspective and Extrospective Networks. *Cerebral Cortex, 26*, 3052–3063.

Plomin, R., Owen, M. J., and McGuffin, P. (1994). The Genetic Basis of Complex Human Behaviors. *Science, 264*, 1733–1739.

Schacter, D. L., and Madore, K. P. (2016). Remembering the Past and Imagining the Future: Identifying and Enhancing the Contribution of Episodic Memory. *Memory Studies, 9*, 245–255.

Silvia, P. J., Nusbaum, E. C., Berg, C., Martin, C., and O'connor, A. (2009). Openness to Experience, Plasticity, and Creativity: Exploring Lower-Order, Higher-Order, and Interactive Effects. *Journal of Research in Personality, 43*, 1087–1090.

Simonton, D. K. (2001). "The Psychology of Creativity: A Historical Perspective." Presentation given at the Green College Lecture Series on the Nature of Creativity: History, Biology, and Socio-Cultural Dimensions, University of British Columbia, Vancouver, BC.

(2010). Creative Thought As Blind-Variation and Selective-Retention: Combinatorial Models of Exceptional Creativity. *Physics of Life Reviews, 7*, 156–179.

(2018). Creative Ideas and the Creative Process: Good News and Bad News for the Neuroscience of Creativity. In R. E. Jung, and O. Vartanian (Eds.), *The Cambridge Handbook of the Neuroscience of Creativity* (pp. 9–18). New York: Cambridge University Press.

Sternberg, R. J. (1977). Component Processes in Analogical Reasoning. *Psychological Review, 84*, 353–378.

(1980). Sketch of a Componential Subtheory of Human Intelligence. *Behavioral and Brain Sciences, 3*, 573–584.

(Ed.). (1999). *Handbook of Creativity*. New York: Cambridge University Press.

Uddin, L. Q. (2015). Salience Processing and Insular Cortical Function and Dysfunction. *Nature Reviews Neuroscience, 16*, 55–61.

Vartanian, O. (2009). Variable Attention Facilitates Creative Problem Solving. *Psychology of Aesthetics, Creativity, and the Arts, 3*, 57–59.

(2011). Nature and Nurture. In M. Runco and S. Pritzker (Eds.), *Encyclopedia of Creativity*, 2nd ed. (pp. 175–178). San Diego: Academic Press.

(2012). Dissociable Neural Systems for Analogy and Metaphor: Implications for the Neuroscience of Creativity. *British Journal of Psychology, 103*, 302–316.

Vartanian, O., Beatty, E. L., Smith, I., Blackler, K., Lam, Q., and Forbes, S. (2018a). One-Way Traffic: The Inferior Frontal Gyrus Controls Brain Activation in the Middle Temporal Gyrus and Inferior Parietal Lobule during Divergent Thinking. *Neuropsychologia, 118*, 68–78.

Vartanian, O., Bristol, A. S., and Kaufman, J. C. (Eds.). (2013). *Neuroscience of Creativity*. Cambridge, MA: The MIT Press.

Vartanian, O., and Goel, V. (2005). Task Constraints Modulate Activation in Right Ventral Lateral Prefrontal Cortex. *Neuroimage, 27*, 927–933.

Vatansever, D., Menon, D. K., and Stamatakis, E. A. (2017). Default Mode Contributions to Automated Information Processing. *Proceedings of the National Academy of Sciences USA, 114*, 12821–12826.

Waller, N. G., Bouchard, T. J. Jr., Lykken, D. T., Tellegen, A., and Blacker, D. M. (1993). Creativity, Heritability, Familiality: Which Word Does Not Belong? *Psychological Inquiry, 4*, 235–237.

Waltz, J. A., Knowlton, B. J., Holyoak, K. J., Boone, K. B., Mishkin, F. S., de Menenzes Santos, M., Thomas, C. R., and Miller, B. L. (1999). A System for Relational Reasoning in Human Prefrontal Cortex. *Psychological Science*, *10*, 119–125.

Wu, X., Yang, W., Tong, D., Sun, J., Chen, Q., Wei, D., Zhang, Q., Zhang, M., and Qiu, J. (2015). A Meta-Analysis of Neuroimaging Studies on Divergent Thinking Using Activation Likelihood Estimation. *Human Brain Mapping*, *36*, 2703–2718.

Zabelina, D. L., and Andrews-Hanna, J. (2016). Dynamic Network Interactions Supporting Internally-Oriented Cognition. *Current Opinion in Neurobiology*, *40*, 86–93.

7 Creativity and Cognition, Divergent Thinking, and Intelligence

ANNE M. ROBERTS, ROBERT J. STERNBERG, MARK A. RUNCO, SELCUK ACAR, THOMAS B. WARD, YULIYA KOLOMYTS, AND JAMES C. KAUFMAN

INTRODUCTION

Creativity appears to be an important part of cognitive capacities and problem solving. **Creativity** is one's ability to generate ideas that are novel, surprising, and compelling (Kaufman and Sternberg, 2010). This chapter will focus on the **creative-cognitive approach**, which seeks to further understand how human minds produce creative ideas.

Other species exhibit innovative behaviors that fit the definition of creativity presented above (see, e.g., contributions to Kaufman and Kaufman, 2015), but the cumulative production of ever more complex concepts and artifacts is unique to humans. For example, many species use and modify found objects as tools to accomplish particular goals, but only humans have extensively refined those types of initial innovations, developed new ones, systematically changed the materials from which such tools are made, and so on (Kaufman, 2016).

This chapter will explore in depth the relationship between cognition and creativity. First, we will explore the relationship between creativity and intelligence. **Intelligence** is one's ability to learn, think, and adapt to the environment (Sternberg and Kaufman, 2011; Sternberg, 2021). Next, we will discuss cognitive theories and studies of the creative process. Finally, we will highlight **divergent thinking (DT)**, or the ability to think of as many different possible solutions as possible to an open question or problem. As part of creativity research, divergent thinking has been studied for its relationship to intelligence.

Creativity and Intelligence

How do we distinguish between what it means to be creative, intelligent, and wise? Sternberg (1985b) performed a series of studies to investigate the relationships among intelligence, creativity, and wisdom. **Wisdom** is one's ability to seek a common good, to understand multiple points of view, and to balance one's own interests with those of others and of larger entities (Sternberg and Jordan, 2005). He first asked laypeople to list behaviors that ideally characterized an intelligent, creative, or wise person. These lists were used to examine underlying dimensions of each construct. For creativity, people used the following descriptors:

- **non-entrenchment:** someone who thinks in a nonconformist, unorthodox way, and who takes chances and is not afraid to defy conventional ways of thinking;
- **integration and intellectuality:** someone who makes connections, as well as distinctions, between ideas and things, who can synthesize information in a new way, and who can grasp abstract ideas;
- **aesthetic taste and imagination:** someone who has good taste and aesthetic imagination, who has good taste, and an appreciation of art, music, and related forms of expression; and
- **decisional skill and flexibility:** someone who weighs the pros and cons of a decision but then follows his or her gut feelings and has the ability to change direction in his or her thinking – who does not get stuck in seeing things in specific ways.

These dimensions were somewhat different from those for either intelligence or wisdom. For intelligence, the dimensions were practical problem-solving ability, verbal ability, intellectual balance and integration, goal orientation and attainment, contextual intelligence, and fluid thought. The need for integration was common to both creativity and intelligence, and fluid thought is important to both as well. For wisdom, the dimensions were reasoning ability, sagacity, learning from ideas and environment, judgment, efficient use of information, and perspicacity (shrewdness). Creativity came out in the dimensions as less similar to wisdom than to intelligence. Certainly, reasoning and learning from ideas and environment would be relevant to creativity but, in terms of the dimensions, there was not much overlap.

Explicit Theories of Intelligence That Include Creativity and Wisdom

Although there are many theories of intelligence, we have selected four that we believe offer different perspectives on how creativity is related to intelligence: the structure of intellect model (SOI; Guilford, 1967), the Cattell–Horn–Carroll theory (Horn and Cattell, 1966; McGrew, 2009), the multiple intelligences (MI; Gardner, 2011) model, and the wisdom-intelligence-creativity synthesized (WICS; Sternberg, 2003) model.

Structure of Intellect (SOI): Guilford's Pioneering Model. Guilford's structure of intellect model was perhaps the first that explicitly showed the relationship between intelligence and creativity; however, it did not attempt to account for wisdom.

J. P. Guilford (1967) proposed a model with 120 distinct abilities (he would later expand the model to include 180; Guilford, 1988). The basic theory aligns abilities along three dimensions: operations, products, and contents. In the best-known version of the model, there are five operations, six products, and four contents. The five operations are cognition, memory, divergent production, convergent production, and evaluation. The six products include units, classes, relations, systems, transformations, and implications. The four contents are figural, symbolic, semantic, and behavioral. Since these dimensions are completely crossed with each other, they yield a total of $5 \times 6 \times 4$, or a total of 120 different abilities. For example, inferring a relation in a verbal analogy (such as the relation between BLACK and WHITE in BLACK: WHITE: HIGH: LOW) would involve cognition of semantic relations.

In Guilford's model, creativity is especially related to divergent production. It could involve divergent production of semantic content (e.g., word fluency in writing), of symbolic content (e.g., in generating a new mathematical proof), of figural content (e.g., painting pictures), or of behavioral content (e.g., an unexpected gesture toward another person). Guilford's tests of creativity (see also Chapter 4) were generally divergent thinking tests; for example, thinking of unusual uses of a paperclip. According to Guilford, therefore, creativity can largely be understood as part of the general structure of intellect.

Guilford (1967) gave the field a huge push forward with his ideas about creativity as a natural resource and for his contribution in distinguishing between divergent thinking (of as many different ideas as possible) and convergent thinking (arriving at a single, hopefully correct answer to a problem). **Convergent thinking (CT)** can be defined as choosing which idea or answer is most worth pursuing. What really caught on was the definition of divergent thinking (DT), or what Guilford called "divergent production." This was an enormously attractive idea because it clarified what was (or could be) unique about creative cognition.

Cattell–Horn–Carroll Theory: Origins in *g*, Development, and Use. Much of the early work on intelligence assumed the existence of a **general intelligence factor (g)**, which considers intelligence as one interrelated broad construct or the capacity to learn from experiences and being able to adapt to the contextual environment (Spearman, 1904; Sternberg, 2018). Although many current researchers still rely largely or exclusively on *g* (e.g., Gottfredson, 2016), most have moved to more nuanced approaches. Much of the research on the relationship between intelligence and creativity is based on studies that use a *g*-based approach.

For example, most studies and some meta-analysis studies that use the *g* factor to measure the relationship between intelligence and creativity have found a mild positive correlation, or association (Wallach and Kogan, 1965; Barron and Harrington, 1981; Kim, 2005). The threshold theory, at one point the predominant view, posited that there was a positive relationship between creativity and intelligence up to a person's IQ of about 120 (Getzels and Jackson, 1962). Kim's (2005) meta-analysis (a statistical procedure that looks at a great deal of data across multiple empirical studies) found that the (small) correlation between creativity and intelligence did not change, regardless of whether a person's IQ was low or high. Again, however, her meta-analysis was largely based on studies using a *g* measure.

Slowly, creativity research has been moving beyond *g*. A theory used in many studies of creativity is the Cattell–Horn–Carroll (CHC) theory (McGrew, 2009; Schneider and McGrew, 2012). This theory grew out of the Cattell–Horn theory of fluid (*Gf*) and crystallized (*Gc*) intelligences (Horn and Cattell, 1966), and Carroll's (1993) three-stratum theory, which proposed a hierarchy of intellectual abilities. Both theories had their roots in *g*.

The Cattell-Horn theory started with Raymond B. Cattell and his student, John L. Horn, drawing on the general ability factor (*g*), and expanding it to **fluid intelligence (Gf)**, and **crystallized intelligence (Gc)**. According to their theory, fluid intelligence is solving problems with new stimuli. Fluid intelligence can help a person in solving novel problems. Crystallized intelligence, on the other hand, encompasses acquired knowledge and learning, such as retaining material taught in school (Willis et al., 2011). The expanded CHC theory includes other abilities beyond *Gf* and *Gc*. These include, for example, short-term memory (*Gsm*), long-term storage and retrieval (*Glr*), processing speed (*Gs*), and visual processing (*Gv*) (van Aken et al., 2017).

The CHC model offers a more comprehensive approach to intelligence. As we will discuss, creativity's exact place in the model is problematic. However, we believe the more nuanced approach offered by the CHC model is nonetheless an improvement over *g* approaches. Batey and Furnham (2006) suggested that *Gf* and *Gc* in creative domains may vary according to the age of a creative person. They theorized that *Gf* might be more important earlier in life, whereas *Gc* would be more valuable later on in life. This pattern might reflect someone becoming more experienced in a creative domain (Kaufman and Beghetto, 2009). Many studies that aim to move beyond *g* stick to *Gf* and *Gc*. Some find that creativity is more related to *Gf* than *Gc* (e.g., Batey et al., 2009), whereas others find *Gc* is more related to *Gf* (e.g., Cho et al., 2010).

Curiously and counterintuitively, the new CHC model places creativity within the *Glr* ability (Kaufman, 2015). *Glr* comprises two components: learning efficiency and fluency. The underlying logic is that being creative entails encoding and remembering a wide variety of information and then being able to remember relevant information that may solve a problem at hand (Kaufman et al., 2011). Someone with a wide range of knowledge to draw from and the ability to connect disparate concepts could be more creative. There have been studies linking *Glr* to rated creative performance (Avitia and Kaufman, 2014) and divergent thinking (Benedek et al., 2012). In recent years, *Glr* has been split into *Gl* (learning efficiency) and *Gr* (retrieval fluency), with creativity, particularly divergent thinking, being associated with *Gr* (Kaufman et al., 2019).

Although *Glr*/*Gr* is clearly related to creativity in some way (particularly given the small, but notable, empirical support), it seems simplistic to take such a limited view of the construct. In addition to the research on *Gc* and *Gf*, there have also been studies that connect *Gs* to creativity (e.g., Vartanian et al., 2007). Yet our concern is not alleviated by creativity's various relationships to three additional abilities. All these connections conceptually are focused on small aspects of creativity (working with something new, using acquired knowledge, being able to retrieve the right information at the right time). Until the CHC theory is expanded further, creativity is poorly represented.

Multiple Intelligences Theory (MI – Gardner). MI theory (Gardner, 2011) holds that intelligence is not a single thing but rather that there are eight domains related to intelligence. Some of these eight are measured by conventional IQ tests; others are not. Gardner (2011) suggests portfolios, or other supplemental materials, could be used for this purpose.

- **linguistic intelligence:** This involves the use of words and language in general. Linguistic intelligence allows us to listen, read, speak, and write effectively. Most IQ tests measure linguistic intelligence, as do many achievement-oriented tests, such as the SAT and the ACT. School achievement tests often draw heavily on linguistic intelligence.
- **logical-mathematical intelligence:** This type of intelligence is used to solve logic and mathematical problems. It is heavily involved in school subjects, such as arithmetic at the lower grade levels, and later in algebra, geometry, calculus, and trigonometry. Logical-mathematical intelligence is measured by many intelligence tests, as well as by achievement-oriented tests, such as the SAT and ACT.
- **visual-spatial intelligence:** Visual-spatial intelligence involves mentally rotating objects in one's head – for example, imagining how to fit suitcases into the trunk of a car or imagining what a building project will look like when it is done. It is quite comparable to CHC's ability of *Gv*.
- **bodily-kinesthetic intelligence:** This kind of intelligence involves the control and management of one's bodily movements and the positioning of them in space. It is used in sports, such as dance, basketball, soccer, swimming, and tennis. Unlike the three intelligences discussed above, bodily-kinesthetic intelligence is not measured by conventional tests of intelligence.
- **interpersonal intelligence**: This intelligence is used to relate to other people. It involves recognizing other people's emotions, moods, and motives and then responding appropriately. It overlaps with the construct of emotional intelligence.
- **intrapersonal intelligence:** Understanding oneself is central to this type of intelligence. People who are high in intrapersonal intelligence are self-reflective and understand their strengths, as well as their weaknesses.
- **musical intelligence:** This intelligence type involves the understanding and production of music. It is used in singing, playing musical instruments, reading music, and appreciating music.
- **naturalist intelligence:** This final type of intelligence is used to recognize patterns in nature. Examples would include recognizing kinds of rocks, classifying plants, or differentiating among the leaves of different kinds of trees.

Gardner (2011) has used MI theory as a basis for understanding creativity. Specifically, he has illustrated how each of the seven great creators used one of the intelligences to pursue an extraordinarily creative career. For example, Gardner has suggested that Stravinsky was extremely high in musical intelligence, Martha Graham in bodily-kinesthetic intelligence, Einstein in logical-mathematical intelligence, and so forth.

The empirical evidence for the central claim that the intelligences are independent from one another appears to be weak. Visser, Ashton, and Vernon (2006) conducted an investigation of the theory and failed to find evidence for the independence of the intelligences. Psychometric evidence comparing different abilities overwhelmingly suggests that – under most circumstances – most mental abilities are at least moderately correlated with each other (although, it should be noted, Gardner would not consider these types of tests as being the best way to answer this question). Moreover, current neuropsychological evidence (Haier, 2016) is less consistent with Gardner's theory. It suggests that various abilities are widely distributed across the brain – that rather than there being distinct areas of the brain responsible for particular skills, many different parts of the brain contribute to each of the variety of the skills we obtain.

Wisdom-Intelligence-Creativity Synthesized (WICS – Sternberg). Sternberg (2003, 2005, 2007, 2009) has proposed a model called WICS, or Wisdom, Intelligence, Creativity Synthesized. Of existing models, it is perhaps the one that most directly addresses the relationship between creativity and intelligence, on the one hand, and creativity and wisdom, on the other (see also Niu and Sternberg, 2003).

The theory proposes that there is a set of information-processing components that underlie all higher cognitive processes, including those of **metacomponents** (executive processes), **performance components** (which execute the instructions of the metacomponents), and **knowledge-acquisition components** (which learn how to solve the relevant problem in the first place) (Sternberg, 1984, 1985c, 1986). The metacomponents include (1) recognizing the existence of a problem, (2) defining or redefining the problem, (3) mentally representing the problem, (4) formulating a strategy for solving the problem, (5) monitoring problem solving while it is ongoing, and (6) evaluating the problem solving after it is done.

In the original version of the theory (Sternberg, 1984), these components are used for creative, analytical, and practical thinking. They are used creatively for relatively novel tasks and situations. They are used analytically for somewhat familiar but abstract problems. They are used practically to adapt to, shape, and select real-world environments (Sternberg, 1985a, 1985c, 1997; Sternberg and Smith, 1985). In the augmented version of the theory (Sternberg, 2003, 2020), the metacomponents are used for wise thinking as well. In other words, people are creative when they generate new, surprising, and compelling ideas; analytical when they evaluate whether their ideas are good ones; practical (showing common sense) when they implement their ideas or persuade others of the value of the ideas; and wise when they apply the ideas for a common good. This involves balancing their own interests with others and higher-order interests, over the long-term, as well as the short-term period, through the infusion of positive ethical values.

Sternberg (2010; Sternberg and the Rainbow Project Collaborators, 2006) implemented the original theory by administering tests of creative, as well as analytical and practical skills, to high school seniors and college freshmen from across the United States. The students varied widely in geographic area, socioeconomic status, and ethnicity. The creative tests loaded on a factor separate from that of analytical tests. However, the only creative tests that were successful were the performance-based ones. Multiple-choice creative tests proved to load onto the general factor as much as the analytical tests. The creative tests roughly doubled prediction of freshman-year GPA. Moreover, including tests of creative and practical thinking reduced ethnic-group differences, although they did not eliminate these differences completely. A later version of the work, the Kaleidoscope Project at Tufts University, added assessment of wisdom to the mix (Sternberg, 2010).

Therefore, in the revised WICS theory, creative and wise thinking are included in the augmented theory of successful intelligence. However, this theory does not give a full picture of the nature of creative or wise thought, leaving us with the question: Why?

According to **Sternberg's balance theory of wisdom** (Sternberg, 1998, 2001a, 2001b, 2019), a part of WICS, the application of intelligence, creativity, and knowledge is mediated (an underlying process that influenced the previously stated variables) by positive ethical values toward the achievement of a common good through a balance among the following: (1) intrapersonal, (2) interpersonal, and (3) extra-personal interests, over the (1) short- and (2) long-term periods.

Wisdom is not only about maximizing one's own or someone else's self-interest but also about balancing various self-interests (intrapersonal) with the interests of others (interpersonal) and of other aspects of the context in which one lives (extra-personal), such as one's city or country or environment or even religious beliefs, including God. Wise people, such as Nelson Mandela, Eleanor Roosevelt, Martin Luther King, or Greta Thunberg, see far beyond their own personal interests to the interests of others and of society as well.

Although Sternberg has amassed a large body of evidence to support his theory, the theory is not without its critics. For example, Gottfredson (2003) has argued that the evidence for a separate construct, or category, of practical intelligence is not sufficiently compelling. These are legitimate arguments over questions regarding data. However, one simply might ask oneself whether the academics one knows with very high IQs are equally impressive, on average, in their practical intelligence – in their relations with others or perhaps their self-understanding. How many of the most successful academics, for example, would be equally successful CEOs, or even vice presidents for public relations? There is still much to debate in this area.

Cognitive Approaches to Creativity

The **creative cognition approach** is concerned primarily with understanding how human minds produce creative ideas (Finke et al., 1992). It examines how basic mental processes are applied to existing knowledge to generate ideas that have some degree of novelty and worth (Finke et al., 1992). In that sense, it represents what Sternberg and Lubart (1996) referred to as a unidisciplinary approach. It is intended to complement other unidisciplinary approaches, such as personality (Feist, 1998), social (Amabile, 1983), and cultural (Lubart, 2010) approaches, as well as to provide details about how individuals use knowledge, which may be relevant to aspects of some confluence models (e.g., Lubart and Sternberg, 1995; Amabile and Pratt, 2016).

The creative cognition approach is consonant with the broadly agreed upon notion that existing knowledge plays a role in creativity (Feldhusen, 1995; Sternberg and Lubart, 1995; Sternberg, 2018). It examines how that knowledge may be either helpful or harmful to creative functioning.

Distinctions among levels of creativity raise an important question about the creative cognition approach, namely, whether or not the types of processes that can be examined readily in laboratory studies are the same as those that operate to produce other levels of creative accomplishment (see, e.g., Simonton, 1997; Ward, 2018). As a means of answering that question, creative cognition researchers have used a convergence strategy, considering the extent to which patterns observed in the laboratory are consistent with observations from other modes of inquiry, such as anecdotal and historical accounts of real-world creativity (e.g., Ward et al., 1995; Weisberg, 2006).

Additional approaches include testing Pro-c participants (e.g., design engineers, elite actors) using surveys or controlled experimental situations (e.g., Jansson and Smith, 1991; Purcell and Gero, 1996; Goodman and Kaufman, 2014), documenting Pro-c activities in-vivo as people perform real-world creative tasks (e.g., Christensen and Schunn, 2005) and performing content analyses on large-scale collections of real-world creative products (e.g., Sawyer, 2012; Chan and Schunn, 2015).

A topic of particular interest in creative cognition has been the role of existing conceptual structures in guiding and constraining creative activities. A wealth of research in mainstream cognitive psychology has identified key organizing attributes of such knowledge structures.

Laboratory Studies

In an early study on the role of conceptual structure in imagination, Ward (1994) had students in psychology classes imagine life on other planets different from Earth. They were instructed to draw and describe a member of one species of animals that might live on the planet and then to draw and describe both another member of the same species and a member of a different species. The vast majority of students developed creatures that had eyes and legs and that were bilaterally symmetric. The ubiquitous presence of eyes and legs is readily predictable based on the properties people list as being characteristic of animals (Ashcraft, 1978).

The tendency of newly generated ideas to closely mirror the properties of the domains from which they are generated has been called **structured imagination** (Ward, 1994). It is a robust tendency, occurring even when instructions encourage participants to deviate from existing ideas (Ward and Sifonis, 1997). It also occurs across multiple conceptual domains (Rubin and Kontis, 1983; Ward et al., 2002; Ward, 2008), different cultures (Yi et al., 2013), and different age and ability groups (Ward et al., 1999). It is also observed in virtual environments where real-world constraints need not apply (Ward, 2015) and with other modes of production, such as having participants perform the creature generation task using Spore, a video game that allows players to develop novel species for later interaction with other species (Cockbain et al., 2014).

The Ward (1994) findings and the results of subsequent studies led to the development of the **path of least resistance model** (Ward, 1994; Ward et al., 2002). The model states that when people develop new ideas for a particular domain, the predominant tendency is to access fairly specific, basic-level exemplars from that domain as starting points and to project many of the stored properties of those exemplars onto the novel ideas being developed. For example, in imagining new types of animals, the predominant tendency would be for people to retrieve particular, basic-level animals, such as dogs and elephants, and to pattern their novel creatures after those instances. Category instances that come to mind most readily should be the ones most often used as starting points in creative tasks.

The most direct test of the predictions of the path of least resistance model is the set of studies by Ward et al. (2002). For each of the three distinct conceptual domains of animals, fruit, and tools, they had separate groups of college students perform a noncreative task of listing as many examples of the domain as they could and a creative task of imagining novel examples of those categories that might exist on another planet. Data from the listing task were used to derive a measure of representativeness, namely, Output Dominance (the number of participants who listed any given exemplar). Exemplars listed by more people can reasonably be interpreted as more accessible and be taken as more representative of the domain. In the creative imagination task, after producing their novel products, participants described the kinds of things they used as the basis for their ideas.

Consistent with the predictions of the path of least resistance model, Ward et al. (2002) found that approximately two-thirds of the participants reported relying on basic level instances in generating their own ideas, and Output Dominance and Imagination Frequency were positively correlated. In other words, most people relied on specific known instances and those instances were the ones that were most accessible within the categories.

Evidence from Pro-c (Professional) Instances

One concern about the research findings discussed in the previous section is that the participants were college students, not selected for special skills, high levels of creativity, or motivation to achieve in the domains under investigation (e.g., imagining life forms on other planets). They also had limited time, typically developing ideas in single sessions lasting less than an hour. In contrast, higher-level real-world creativity can involve more complex problems, with an extended period of effort performed by professionals with a high level of motivation to succeed in their domains, operating at what Kaufman and Beghetto (2009) describe as the Pro-c level of creativity.

With those types of concerns in mind, Ward (1994) examined creatures envisioned by professional science-fiction writers for the same types of properties as those included by college students in laboratory studies. Specifically, he examined paintings shown in the book *Barlowe's Guide to Extraterrestrials* (Barlowe and Summers, 1979). Barlowe, a painter, had chosen to depict creatures from the science-fiction literature that "challenged the imagination" (p. 9). Coding revealed that roughly three-fourths of them possessed the eyes, legs, and symmetry that so dominated the college students' creatures. Thus, structured imagination is not limited to college students performing contrived tasks within limited amounts of time.

In addition, there are interesting anecdotal/historical accounts that reveal negative influences from reliance on specific known instances. For example, in the 1830s, when passenger rail travel was just getting started in the United States, designers seem to have patterned the first railway passenger cars directly on horse-drawn stagecoaches of the day, including the fact that conductors had to sit on the outside of the car (White, 1978). This approach was efficient in the sense that railway passenger cars became available quickly, but because the conductors were seated on the outside, several of them fell off and were killed.

In the railway passenger car case, accessing and relying on a specific exemplar of earlier knowledge got in the way of innovation. However, history is replete with examples of major advances occurring through a slow incremental process of patterning new ideas after very specific earlier ones (see, e.g., Ward et al., 1995; Weisberg, 2006). As shown in laboratory studies (e.g., Ward, 2008), the approach of relying heavily on specific existing products in developing new ones may favor practicality over extreme, but potentially impractical, originality.

Importantly, the historical case described in this section highlights a distinction between cognitive processes of introducing incremental advances on specific previous ideas and the potential far-reaching, Big-C impacts (when someone's creative contributions continue to be remembered and influential for generations after the creator's death) of those modifications. As eloquently stated by Weisberg (2006), "one must keep separate the importance of a product, which may be extraordinary, and thought processes that brought it about, which may be very ordinary" (p. 31).

To summarize, research using the creative cognition convergence approach does reveal commonalties between the findings from laboratory studies employing convenience samples in artificial tasks and those from content analyses and anecdotal accounts of higher-level creativity. There is a general tendency among people approaching creative tasks to rely on specific domain instances in developing new products, and that tendency is typically associated with less originality but greater utility of the resulting products.

Conformity Effects

A related line of research has also examined how knowledge can be made more accessible by exposure to examples. As a starting point, Smith, Ward, and Schumacher (1993) had undergraduate students from psychology classes develop ideas for alien life-forms and novel toys. Prior to performing the task, participants in the experimental condition were shown three examples each of novel aliens and toys, whereas those in a control condition were not shown examples. Across three experiments, participants who saw examples were significantly more likely to include properties of the examples in their own designs, even when asked to develop ideas as different as possible from the examples. The **conformity effect** is the tendency to copy the properties of the examples, and it has been replicated across multiple studies that include different knowledge domains, task instructions, and task variations (Marsh et al., 1999; Landau and Lehr, 2004; Chrysikou and Weisberg, 2005).

Several recent studies also have shown that examples that violate constraints or are otherwise creative can increase the unusualness or creativity of participants' creations. Yi, Plucker, and Guo (2015), for instance, had participants develop alien creatures and collages either with or without exposure to examples, but, in contrast to previous studies, the examples chosen had previously been rated as highly creative. The results showed that those viewing these examples generated products that were rated more creative.

Design Fixation in Pro-c Individuals

Research on the conformity effect has relied on non-specialist samples of undergraduate students, typically recruited from psychology classes. However, a parallel line of research has examined similar phenomena in individuals with advanced training or work experience in engineering domains, who can be regarded as operating at the Pro-c level. In a seminal study, Jansson and Smith (1991) had practicing mechanical engineers and advanced mechanical engineering students perform a variety of creative generation tasks, such as developing ideas for novel car-mounted bicycle racks, spill-proof coffee cups, and devices to assist blind individuals in measuring quantities for cooking. Prior to completing their own designs, some of the participants were shown examples of previous attempted designs.

A crucial aspect of the examples is that they had design flaws built into them. For instance, the spill-proof coffee cup had a straw that would leak if the cup were tipped over and would make the coffee too hot to drink by not allowing the passage of air across the liquid. Although the participants were alerted to the flaws and were instructed not to copy them, many of them nevertheless incorporated the flaws into their own designs. In addition, those shown the examples generated a narrower range of designs than participants who were not shown examples, tending instead to generate ideas of the same basic type as the examples.

Jansson and Smith referred to copying the examples' properties as design fixation, and the work sparked efforts to replicate the findings and identify the factors underlying such effects. As a case in point, Purcell and Gero (1996) noted that, in contrast to Jansson and Smith's robust findings with mechanical engineers, fixation effects for students in architecture and industrial design are slight and limited to designs with which they are already most familiar. Mechanical engineering students, in contrast, show fixation for examples with which they are unfamiliar, as long as the designs use typical mechanical engineering design principles.

Taken together, the findings suggest that the examples activate existing knowledge, which then is incorporated into the participants' designs. Without the domain-specific mechanical engineering knowledge about the principles operating in the examples, industrial design students are influenced by general, surface-level knowledge about objects they have encountered before, whereas the mechanical engineers are influenced by the domain-specific principles of their discipline embodied in those objects. In either case, the effect of the examples is due to knowledge activation.

Overcoming Fixation via Incubation

The fact that people can be fixated on chronically accessible ideas or on ideas made more accessible by way of examples raises the question of how such fixation might be overcome to yield better creative performance. One possibility is **idea incubation**, a temporary withdrawal from ordinary attempts at solving a problem, initially suggested by Wallas (1926) nearly a century ago. An oft-cited anecdotal account (possibly apocryphal) of incubation is Archimedes' "Eureka" realization while bathing that the principle of displacement could be used to measure the volume of Hiero's crown, which could be combined with its weight to determine if it was pure gold.

One prominent view of incubation effects is **Smith's forgetting fixation theory**, which states that activities that temporarily distract a problem solver can lead to forgetting of interfering information, which then leads to a greater likelihood of retrieving new, relevant information (Smith and Blankenship, 1991; Smith, 1995). In a more recent test of this view, Kohn and Smith (2009) had participants attempt to solve Remote Associates Test (RAT) problems in which they had to determine one word that would form a compound word or a two-word phrase with each of three presented words (e.g., walk for the triad cat, board, and sleep, forming catwalk, boardwalk, and sleepwalk). Participants showed a significantly higher resolution rate in the incubation condition than the no-incubation condition only when fixation was induced by the related version of the prior two-word phrase generation task. The results imply that incubation effects are largely due to people forgetting interfering information and are less likely to occur when people are not initially fixated.

Another process that has been of considerable interest in explicating creativity is **conceptual combination**, whereby previously separate ideas, concepts, or other forms are mentally merged. The elements to be combined can be words, concepts, visual forms, and other simple elements or, at a more abstract level, they can be hypothetical scientific constructs, musical styles, artistic genres, and so on. Whether in science, technology, art, music, literature, or other creative realms, combinations are seen as stimulants to creativity and have been mentioned frequently in historical accounts of creative accomplishments (e.g., Rothenberg, 1979; Sternberg and Davidson, 1982; Thagard, 1984; Ward et al., 1995).

Rothenberg, in particular, has argued that simultaneously entertaining or integrating two opposing ideas, a process termed Janusian thinking, underlies creative acts as diverse as the paintings of da Vinci, the symphonies of Mozart, and the scientific reasoning of Einstein. In addition, combining concepts is a crucial component in several process models of creative functioning (e.g., Sternberg, 1988).

Conceptual combination is directly relevant as a process underlying creativity because combinations are not mere summations of the elements being merged. Instead, they can yield emergent features. That is, combinations can produce or highlight properties that are either absent from or very low in salience for the representations of either of their component elements. Even a simple combination such as "pet bird" might include an emergent property, namely, "talks," which would not typically be thought of as an attribute of "pets" or "birds" in general.

Another generative process with a special link to creativity that has undergone careful experimental examination is **analogical reasoning**, the application of structured knowledge from a familiar domain, called the source domain, to a novel or less familiar one, called the target domain (see, e.g., Gentner et al., 2001). The emphasis on structured knowledge is important because it allows a formal description of the domains and the processes involved in connecting them. Consider, for example, Robbins, Laurents, Bernstein, and Sondheim's adaptation of Shakespeare's *Romeo and Juliet* to the context of a 1950s New York City gang conflict in *West Side Story*. The analogy can be described in terms of aligning the two domains to find corresponding objects (e.g., Romeo and Tony, Juliet and Maria), relations (e.g., Romeo loves Juliet and Tony loves Maria), and higher-order relation (e.g., a clash between love for each other and hate between the groups they are affiliated with).

Commonly cited real-world examples of analogy in creative endeavors abound, such as Rutherford's use of a solar system as a model for how the hydrogen atom was structured, Kepler's reasoning about planetary motion (Gentner et al., 1997), and the Wright brothers' efforts to craft a workable flying machine (Crouch, 1992). Not surprisingly, then, analogy has been a key ingredient in proposals for enhancing creativity (e.g., Gordon, 1961) and has been listed as a component process in cognitive process models of creativity (e.g., Finke et al., 1992).

A host of other processes that have been investigated by cognitive psychologists also have the potential to serve creative purposes. These include problem-finding (see e.g., Sternberg, 1988; Runco and Chand, 1994), the reorganization of existing category knowledge to form ad hoc or goal-derived categories to meet a particular need (Smith et al., 2017), metaphoric interpretation, which can yield emergent properties (e.g., Tourangeau and Rips, 1991), and unexpected observation reasoning (Dunbar, 1997).

Despite the progress made in understanding these processes and the ones considered in more detail in this chapter, much remains to be done to understand the cognition of creativity. Applying a convergence approach and bringing together the ecological validity of real-world examples with the experimental rigor of behavioral cognitive science research and detailed observations of corresponding brain activity can provide the path to continued progress on this important goal.

Divergent Thinking

Neuroscientific investigations also offer insights into how **divergent thinking (DT)**, or the ability to think of as many different possible solutions as possible to an open question or problem, works. The neuroscientific research on creativity is progressing as fast as any other area of research in the field of creativity and great strides are being made – but there are serious concerns. One concern is that many neuroscientific studies of DT focus on one type of DT test (e.g., Uses or Titles) and many only examine one measured index (e.g., fluency). This seriously limits generalizations; findings will not apply accurately to other tests or to creativity in the natural environment (Runco et al., 2016).

In addition, DT is easily inhibited by wrong directions, by test-like testing conditions, and by evaluations and judgments. It is a sensitive process and the experimental conditions used for neuroscientific research are often rigid (e.g., timed tests). This may very well preclude results with external validity (real-world application). Again, what we discover about DT when the individual is in the lab may not tell us much about what the same person can do when he or she is in a relaxed or even playful setting. Neuroscientific research on DT is exciting but it is in its early stages and needs to be better integrated with the other research on DT. Research has underlined the involvement of multiple and simultaneous activity across different regions of the human brain – specifically the coupling of default and executive networks (Beaty et al., 2015). The default network is engaged in spontaneous thought (e.g., mind-wandering, daydreaming) whereas the executive network is activated during external task cognitive demands are in place. DT performance benefits from the synchronization of these two networks.

Divergent Thinking, Personality, Attitudes, and Cognitive Style

Research on DT reflects personality, attitudinal, and thinking style correlates, or associations. These attributes are best viewed as correlates because it is not perfectly clear if there is a causal relationship and if personality and the other factors actually influence DT. If they are necessary, they would be involved all the time and, when they were not present, there would be no creativity.

There are two personality traits, and an associated attitude trait, for which enough evidence exists to infer that they are causally and functionally tied to DT and creativity and not just mere correlates. These are openness to experience and cognitive flexibility. We will put them into a broad context because the empirical work on personality and DT is extensive.

The Big Five Personality Approach is one of the oldest approaches used in studies of creativity (Feist, 1998; Karwowski and Lebuda, 2016). The Big Five Personality Approach, which includes openness to experience, conscientiousness, extraversion, agreeableness, and neuroticism, is described in detail in Hoffmann, Ivcevic, and Feist (see Chapter 9). Walker and Jackson (2014) investigated correlations between DT (i.e., fluency and originality) and the Big Five traits. Only openness to experience was significantly related to DT (both fluency and originality). Batey, Chamorro-Premuzic, and Furnham (2009), on the other hand, found a significant relationship between extraversion – but not openness to experience – and fluency at least when they used the Uses task for DT. This reminds us of the important point that there are differences between various DT tasks.

Runco et al. (2015) found that Uses is not the most reliable measure of DT, even though it may be the most commonly used. Differences among DT tests are very frequently found (Wallach and Kogan, 1965; Runco and Albert, 1985). These differences have even been used to question the construct validity (the degree to which the test measures what it claims to measure) of DT (Cronbach, 1970). Some variation among DT tests is to be expected, given theories of DT, but it is clear that findings from research relying on any one DT test may very well not generalize to findings from a different DT test. This is particularly true when one test is verbal and one is figural (Runco and Albert, 1985). The neuroscience research revealed that verbal and figural stimuli trigger different kinds of activation in the brain (see Dietrich and Kanso, 2010; Gonen-Yaacovi et al., 2013) and may explain why there are different outcomes between the two.

Acar and Runco (2015) recently investigated DT and personality using a new approach, based directly on personality theories of creativity. Instead of using the traditional four indices (i.e., fluency, flexibility, originality, elaboration) for DT, they focused on the literal definition of the term "divergent thinking," and cited earlier research, which denotes thinking in different directions. That sounds like an obvious point, but Acar and Runco cited earlier research that defined original ideation not in terms of divergence but just in terms of statistical infrequency.

Indeed, one of the theories used to support DT early on was that of Mednick (1962) and this is exactly what he proposed – that thinking is a matter of chaining ideas together, one after another, and original ideas are remote and found only after obvious ideas. Original ideas are far removed from the starting point – that is, remote. This idea of remote associates has been supported many times over (Mednick, 1962; Milgram and Rabkin, 1980; Runco, 1986) and the recent work used semantic distance (i.e., remotely related ideas generated for any given stimuli) as a novel way of measuring original thinking (Acar and Runco, 2014; Dumas and Dunbar, 2014; Beketayev and Runco, 2016; Hass, 2017).

Computer Assessments of Divergent Thinking

Technological advances have contributed both to refined scoring methods for DT and to the testing of predictions found in DT theory. Acar and Runco (2014), for example, utilized the sizable lexical and associative networks that are now available online (e.g., WordNet, Idea Fisher, Word Association Network) to examine the associative processes underlying DT. The associative basis of DT has been recognized since the early days of DT testing (Mednick, 1962; Milgram and Rabkin, 1980; Runco, 1986), and the newer results are quite consistent with what was predicted early on. In particular, distant associations and ideas found only after some time has passed tend to be, on average, the most original.

Acar and Runco (2017) used think-aloud in their work on flexibility. They tested the idea that the time elapsing between the ideas, or latency, represented useful information about creative cognition. Acar and Runco also explored the possibility that latency would vary between verbal and figural tasks of DT. They found that latency was associated with ideational, semantic shifts. This finding supports the claim that verbal and figural DT tasks trigger somewhat different cognitive processes (Runco and Albert, 1985; Richardson, 1986). This work on DT presents a scoring method that can be automatized. It replicated earlier findings and offered some new information (e.g., lagged time between ideas) about the processes underlying DT. Acar and Runco (2017) argued that longer time elapsing between any adjacent two ideas given for DT implies longer mental leap in the semantic space resulting in change from one conceptual category to another. This is consistent with the existing theories on the role of executive functions in DT because spending longer time for a new idea may indicate a higher level of cognitive effort and the engagement of controlled cognitive processes.

Enhancing Divergent Thinking

Divergent thinking is indicative of the potential for creative thinking and can be assessed in an objective and reliable fashion. It will come as no surprise, then, that quite a bit of research has focused on the enhancement of DT as a step toward enhancing creativity. Even the research on explicit instructions (e.g., Harrington, 1975; Runco, 1986) was often justified as helping to answer questions about the best enhancement techniques. The most typical way to support DT is through training that emphasizes tactics that allow the individual to generate numerous potential solutions, embrace wild ideas, and seek novelty. Meta-analyses (or statistical methods to combine the results from multiple studies) determined that such training is effective (Scott, Leritz, and Mumford, 2004a, 2004b). On the other hand, the practice and training of ideation per se (Runco et al., 2005) also leads to improvements in DT.

Computers have been used in some of the more recent attempts to enhance DT. Viriyayudhakorn, Kunifuji, and Ogawa (2011) tested the usefulness of four Wikipedia-based DT support engines to facilitate making connections on some DT tasks. They found that the related keywords helped in making more original associations. Using a similar method called Extenics, or the science of studying the possibility of extending rules and methods of developing innovation with patterns (Yang and Li, 2012), Niu et al. (2014) improved DT outcomes in a way that responses were extended beyond participants' personal experiences. This is important because DT benefits from experience (Runco and Acar, 2010).

If experience plays a role in DT, perhaps an intervention facilitating better use of memory would support DT performance. Ritter et al. (2012) described how active involvement in diverse and unusual experiences improves cognitive flexibility. Damian and Simonton (2014) described much of the same but added that diversifying experiences are beneficial for creativity in part because they challenge conventional and routine forms of thinking. Trauma, psychopathology, minority status, **cognitive disinhibition**, bilingualism, and multiculturalism represent some forms of diversification (see Runco, 1994).

The nature of the idea incubation is sometimes manipulated in investigations of enhancement. Hao et al. (2015), for example, compared individuals who worked on DT tasks without interruption with those who were in one of three incubation conditions, including positive, negative, and neutral emotional states. They found that originality was indeed higher after incubation and highest in the positive emotion condition. Fluency was unrelated to incubation.

Gilhooly et al. (2012) also examined incubation of ideas and DT and reported that the effects are larger when incubation is experienced immediately rather than delayed. Meditation is relevant, in part, because it can provide an opportunity for idea incubation.

Judgments, Selection, and Evaluation of Ideas

The role of judgment in the creative process requires that evaluations of ideas are postponed. There are concerns, however, due to judgments that are very difficult to postpone or control in any way. Humans are social animals and often use very subtle nonverbal cues, so even if team members in a brainstorming group do not say something judgmental about an idea, group members are likely to pick up on subtle cues and infer if there is any criticism, even if it goes unstated.

The realistic view is that some judgment is involved in all creative problem-solving. It is good to have original ideas, but it is also vital to know which ideas are the most original (and useful). For this reason, the more realistic and comprehensive theories of the creative process include idea evaluation as a stage or component (Runco and Chand, 1994), to go along with idea generation. This is not a new idea, either; Wallas (1926) had a verification stage in his model of the creative process. It followed preparation, incubation, and illumination stages.

Several investigations have examined ideation judgment as part of DT and creativity. One series of studies started in 1990 and used the results from DT tests as targets for judgments and evaluations. Runco and Vega (1990) were concerned about the fourth-grade slump in creativity (Torrance, 1968) and postulated that, when it does indeed occur, one influence may be that children become more conventional in their thinking, in response to parents' and teachers' expectations, which could make them more selective and judgmental. Runco and Vega found that their method for assessing judgments of ideas was reliable, as the assessment tool produced stable and consistent results.

DT is meaningful to, but not involved in, all creative behavior. In short, DT is not synonymous with creativity. Rather, empirical work showed only limited relationships between DT and various indicators of creativity. The synthesis holds that DT is involved in many creative efforts, but it really is just an estimate of the potential for creative problem-finding and problem-solving. It is best viewed as an estimate because, like all tests, DT tests sample behavior. They are not comprehensive and are given under artificial conditions – namely, the testing environment. All test settings differ from the natural environment and, as such, generalization is a concern with all tests. There are ways to ensure generalization from test scores, but we saw that the only reasonable view of DT is that it is sometimes involved in actual creative performances, but not always. In other words, some kinds of creativity rely, in part, on DT.

CONCLUSION

Creativity is closely related, but far from redundant, to intelligence and wisdom. This chapter reflected on the creative cognition approach and how research studies have shown that basic mental processes are applied to existing knowledge to create new and task-appropriate ideas. These ideas can be facilitated using constraints, which might or might not be conducive to practical and appropriate uses of these newly designed ideas. Judgments of these developed ideas require that evaluations of these ideas are postponed (explicitly and implicitly). In addition, studies have shown that there is a tendency for newly generated ideas to closely reflect the domain properties from which they are generated, also known as structured imagination. The creativity models written about also discuss the relationship of how we view intelligence, wisdom, and the creative process, and what assessment tools we decide to use to measure divergent thinking skills in the context of this creative process.

Our Research Contribution

As we have discussed, DT contributes to some expressions of creativity but is far from synonymous with creativity. Even creative thinking requires motivation, attitudes, judgments, and so on. One of Acar and Runco's foci is on how DT can be enhanced, and DT tests can now be administered and scored by computer. They suggest it is best to consider the various dimensions of DT rather than focus on fluency alone. This is especially clear because originality is a bigger part of definitions of creativity than is fluency and the two are far from redundant. Care must be taken when assessing DT because there are differences among DT tests. Some rely on experience more than others, for example.

There are many different kinds of DT tasks and ways to administer them, such as the different amount of time allowed for tasks and various instructions provided. Recently, Acar, Runco, and Park (2020) conducted a meta-analysis on the impact of different explicit instructions on DT outcomes. They found that creative instructions, as well as those emphasizing quality, tend to increase the DT outcomes when they are presented along with quantity instructions, whereas instructions that were original tended to diminish them. Interestingly, although originality is the backbone of creativity, asking for it explicitly may not be the best way to get at it. In fact, Acar, Burnett, and Cabra (2017) found that average ratings of the exact same products or ideas tend to be consistently lower for originality than creativity.

Critical/Creative Thinking Questions

1. Explain how intelligence, creativity, and cognition are related based on evidence from the chapter. How would you describe these similarities and differences to people with no background knowledge on creativity research?
2. The Cattell–Horn–Carroll (CHC) theory places creativity within the *Glr* ability (learning efficiency and fluency of remembering relevant information). How would researchers who use the CHC theory view someone's creative ability in problem solving that is not in their area of expertise (or where they do not have a lot of background knowledge)?
3. For the structure of intellect (SOI) model, Guilford included convergent thinking as part of his model in addition to divergent thinking. Convergent thinking, or choosing the best alternative out of many possible ideas, is often overlooked in creativity research. What possible situations would require convergent thinking skills and how would creatively choosing the best idea be beneficial in that situation?
4. The path of least resistance model focuses on the pattern of when people create new ideas for a specific domain; they tend to access specific, basic-level examples from that domain as the starting point. Then, soon after, many of the properties of these examples are added onto the new ideas being developed. Adding constraints can increase originality but decrease practical, or appropriate, solutions. Which method (constraints or no constraints) would you choose for creating new ideas and why?
5. Which divergent thinking (DT) skills assessment from this chapter would you choose to measure your peers' DT skills in one of your college classes? Is the DT skills assessment computerized or on paper? Why would you choose this measure and what specifically would you hope to measure using this assessment?

GLOSSARY

analogical reasoning: The application of structured knowledge from a familiar domain, called the source domain, to a novel or less familiar one, called the target domain.

Cattell–Horn–Carroll (CHC) theory: This theory emerged from the Cattell–Horn theory of fluid (*Gf*) and crystallized (*Gc*) intelligences and Carroll's three-stratum theory; it expanded the original models to incorporate sixteen broad and narrow abilities.

conceptual combination: Previously separate ideas, concepts, or other forms are mentally merged.

conformity effect: The tendency to copy the properties of the examples provided.

convergent thinking (CT): Choosing which idea or answer is most worth pursuing.

creative-cognition approach: Seeks to further understand how human minds produce creative ideas.

creativity: One's ability to generate ideas that are novel, surprising, and compelling.

crystallized intelligence (Gc): Includes the process of knowledge acquisition and learning new skills.

divergent thinking (DT): The ability to think of as many different possible solutions as possible to an open question or problem.

fluid intelligence (Gf): Involves inductive, deductive, and quantitative reasoning with new content and systems to be learned. Fluid intelligence can help a person in solving novel problems, as well as encoding their short-term memories.

general intelligence factor (*g*): One's general mental capacity that influences cognition.

idea incubation: A temporary withdrawal from ordinary attempts at solving a problem.

intelligence: One's ability to learn, think, and adapt to the environment.

metacomponents (executive processes), **performance components** (execute the instructions of the meta-components), and **knowledge-acquisition components** learn how to solve the relevant problem).

multiple intelligences theory (MI): Gardner created this theory that involves eight distinct types of intelligences, including linguistic, logical-mathematical, visual-spatial, bodily-kinesthetic, interpersonal, intrapersonal, musical, and naturalist intelligence.

path of least resistance model: Created by Ward, this model states that when people develop new ideas for a particular domain, the predominant tendency is to access fairly specific, basic-level exemplars from that domain as starting points and to project many of the stored properties of those exemplars onto the novel ideas being developed.

Smith's forgetting fixation theory: States that activities that temporarily distract a problem solver can lead to forgetting of interfering information, which then leads to a greater likelihood of retrieving new, relevant information.

Sternberg's balance theory of wisdom: Part of WICS, this theory involves the application of intelligence, creativity, and knowledge, as mediated (an underlying process that influenced the previously stated variables) by positive ethical values toward the achievement of a common good through a balance among the following: (1) intrapersonal, (2) interpersonal, and (3) extra-personal interests, over (1) short- and (2) long-term periods.

structured imagination: The tendency of newly generated ideas to closely mirror the properties of the domains from which they are generated.

structure of intellect (SOI) model: This model explicitly shows the relationship between intelligence and creativity.

wisdom: One's ability to seek a common good, to understand multiple points of view, and to balance one's own interests with those of others and of larger entities.

wisdom-intelligence-creativity synthesized (WICS) model: Sternberg devised this model that proposes that there is a set of information-processing components that underlie all higher cognitive processes, including metacomponents, performance components, and knowledge-acquisition components.

REFERENCES

Acar, S., Burnett, C., and Cabra, J. F. (2017). Ingredients of Creativity: Originality and More. *Creativity Research Journal, 29*(2), 133–144.

Acar, S., and Runco, M. A. (2014). Assessing Associative Distance among Ideas Elicited by Tests of Divergent Thinking. *Creativity Research Journal, 26*, 229–238.

(2015). Thinking in Multiple Directions: Hyperspace Categories in Divergent Thinking. *Psychology of Aesthetics, Creativity, and the Arts, 9*, 41–53.

(2017). Latency Predicts Category Switch in Divergent Thinking. *Psychology of Aesthetics, Creativity, and the Arts, 11*, 43–51.

Acar, S., Runco, M. A., and Park, H. (2020). What Should People Be Told When They Take a Divergent Thinking Test? A Meta-Analytic Review of Explicit Instructions for Divergent

Thinking. *Psychology of Aesthetics, Creativity, and the Arts*, *14*(1), 39–49. doi.org/10.1037/aca0000256.

Amabile, T. M. (1983). Social Psychology of Creativity: A Componential Conceptualization. *Journal of Personality and Social Psychology*, 45, 357–377.

    (1996). *Creativity in Context: Update to "The Social Psychology of Creativity"*. Boulder: Westview Press.

Amabile, T. M., and Pratt, M. G. (2016). The Dynamic Componential Model of Creativity and Innovation in Organizations: Making Progress, Making Meaning. *Research in Organizational Behavior, 36*, 157–183.

Ashcraft, M. H. (1978). Property Norms for Typical and Atypical Items from 17 Categories: A Description and Discussion. *Memory and Cognition, 6*(3), 227–232. doi.org/10.3758/BF03197450.

Avitia, M. J., and Kaufman, J. C. (2014). Beyond *g* and *c*: The Relationship of Rated Creativity to Long-Term Storage and Retrieval (*Glr*). *Psychology of Aesthetics, Creativity, and the Arts, 8*(3), 293.

Barlowe, W. D., and Summers, I. (1979). *Barlowe's Guide to Extraterrestrials*. New York: Workman Publishing.

Barron, F., and Harrington, D. M. (1981). Creativity, Intelligence, and Personality. *Annual Review of Psychology, 32*, 439–476. dx.doi.org/10.1146/annurev.ps.32.020181.002255.

Batey, M., and Furnham, A. (2006). Creativity, Intelligence and Personality: A Critical Review of the Scattered Literature. *Genetic, Social, and General Psychology Monographs, 132*, 355–429.

Batey, M., Chamorro-Premuzic, T., and Furnham, A. (2009). Intelligence and Personality As Predictors of Divergent Thinking: The Role of General, Fluid and Crystallised Intelligence. *Thinking Skills and Creativity, 4*, 60–69.

Beaty, R. E., Benedek, M., Kaufman, S. B., and Silvia, P. J. (2015). Default and Executive Network Coupling Supports Creative Idea Production. *Scientific Reports, 5*, 10964.

Beketayev, K., and Runco, M. A. (2016). Scoring Divergent Thinking Tests by Computer with a Semantics-Based Algorithm. *Europe's Journal of Psychology, 12*(2), 210.

Benedek, M., Könen, T., and Neubauer, A. C. (2012). Associative Abilities Underlying Creativity. *Psychology of Aesthetics, Creativity, and the Arts, 6*, 273–281.

Carroll, J. B. (1993). *Human Cognitive Abilities: A Survey of Factor-Analytic Studies*. Cambridge: Cambridge University Press.

Chan, J., and Schunn, C. (2015). The Importance of Iteration in Creative Conceptual Combination. *Cognition, 145*,104–115. doi.org/10.1016/j.cognition.2015.08.008.

Cho, S. H., Nijenhuis, J. T., van Vianen, A. E., Kim, H. B., and Lee, K. H. (2010). The Relationship between Diverse Components of Intelligence and Creativity. *The Journal of Creative Behavior, 44* (2), 125–137.

Christensen, B. T., and Schunn, C. D. (2005). Spontaneous Access and Analogical Incubation Effects. *Creativity Research Journal, 17*, 207–220.

Chrysikou, E. G., and Weisberg, R. W. (2005). Following the Wrong Footsteps: Fixation Effects of Pictorial Examples in a Design Problem-Solving Task. *Journal of Experimental Psychology: Learning, Memory, and Cognition, 31*(5), 1134–1148.

Cockbain, J., Vertolli, M. O., and Davies, J. (2014). Creative Imagination Is Stable across Technological Media: The Spore Creature Creator versus Pencil and Paper. *The Journal of Creative Behavior, 48*(1), 13–24. doi.org/10.1002/jocb.38.

Cronbach L. J. (1970). *Essentials of Psychological Testing*. Harper & Row.

Crouch, T. D. (1992). Why Wilbur and Orville? Some Thoughts on the Wright Brothers and the Process of Invention. In R. J. Weber and D. N. Perkins (Eds.), *Inventive Minds* (pp. 80–92). Oxford: Oxford University Press.

Damian, R. I., and Simonton, D. K. (2014). Diversifying Experiences in the Development of Genius and Their Impact on Creative Cognition. In D. K. Simonton (Ed.), *The Wiley Handbook of Genius* (pp. 375–394). New York: Wiley-Blackwell.

Dietrich, A., and Kanso, R. (2010). A Review of EEG, ERP, and Neuroimaging Studies of Creativity and Insight. *Psychological bulletin*, *136*(5), 822.

Dumas, D., and Dunbar, K. N. (2014). Understanding Fluency and Originality: A Latent Variable Perspective. *Thinking Skills and Creativity*, *14*, 56–67.

Dunbar, K. (1997). How Scientists Think: On-line Creativity and Conceptual Change in Science. In T. B. Ward, S. M. Smith, and J. Vaid (Eds.), *Creative Thought: An Investigation of Conceptual Structures and Processes* (pp. 461–494). Washington, DC: American Psychological Association.

Feist, G. J. (1998). A Meta-Analysis of Personality in Scientific and Artistic Creativity. *Personality and Social Psychology Review*, *2*(4), 290–309.

Feldhusen, J. F. (1995). Creativity: A Knowledge Base, Metacognitive Skills, and Personality Factors. *Journal of Creative Behavior*, *29*(4), 255–268.

(2002). Creativity: The Knowledge Base and Children. *High Ability Studies*, *13*(2), 179–183.

Finke, R. A., Ward, T. B., and Smith, S. M. (1992). *Creative Cognition: Theory, Research, and Applications*. Cambridge, MA: MIT Press.

Gardner, H. (2011). *Frames of Mind: The Theory of Multiple Intelligences*, rev. ed. New York: Basic.

Gentner, D., Holyoak, K., and Kokinov, B. (2001). *The Analogical Mind: Perspectives from Cognitive Science*. Cambridge, MA: MIT Press.

Getzels, J. W., and Jackson, P. W. (1962). *Creativity and Intelligence: Explorations with Gifted Students*. New York: Wiley.

Gilhooly, K. J., Georgiou, G. J., Garrison, J., Reston, J. D., and Sirota, M. (2012). Don't Wait to incubate: Immediate versus Delayed Incubation in Divergent Thinking. *Memory and Cognition*, *40*, 966–975.

Gonen-Yaacovi, G., De Souza, L. C., Levy, R., Urbanski, M., Josse, G., and Volle, E. (2013). Rostral and Caudal Prefrontal Contribution to Creativity: A Meta-Analysis of Functional Imaging Data. *Frontiers in Human Neuroscience*, *7*, 465.

Goodman, G., and Kaufman, J. C. (2014). Gremlins in My Head: Predicting Stage Fright in Elite Actors. *Empirical Studies of the Arts*, *32*, 133–148.

Gordon, W. (1961). *Synectics: The Development of Creative Capacity*. New York: Harper & Row.

Gottfredson, L. S. (2003). Dissecting Practical Intelligence Theory: Its Claims and Evidence. *Intelligence*, *31*, 347–397.

(2016). A *g* Theorist on Why Kovac's and Conway's Process Overlap Theory Amplifies, Not Opposes, *g* Theory. *Psychological Inquiry*, *27*, 210–217.

Guilford, J. P. (1967). *The Nature of Human Intelligence*. New York: McGraw-Hill.

(1988). Some Changes in the Structure-of-Intellect Model. *Educational and Psychological Measurement*, *48*, 1–4.

Haier, R. J. (2016). *The Neuroscience of Intelligence*. Cambridge: Cambridge University Press.

Hao, N., Liu, M., Ku, Y., Hu, Y., and Runco, M. A. (2015). Verbal Divergent Thinking Facilitated by a Pleasurable Incubation Interval. *Psychology of Aesthetics, Creativity, and the Arts*, *9*, 286–295.

Harrington, D. M. (1975). Effects of Explicit Instructions to "Be Creative" on the Psychological Meaning of Divergent Thinking Test Scores. *Journal of Personality*, *43*, 434–454.

Hass, R. W. (2017). Tracking the Dynamics of Divergent Thinking via Semantic Distance: Analytic Methods and Theoretical Implications. *Memory and Cognition*, *45*(2), 233–244.

Horn, J. L., and Cattell, R. B. (1966). Refinement and Test of the Theory of Fluid and Crystallized Intelligence. *Journal of Educational Psychology*, *57*, 253–270.

Jansson, D. G., and Smith, S. M. (1991). Design Fixation. *Design Studies*, *12*, 3–11.

Karwowski, M., and Lebuda, I. (2016). The Big Five, the Huge Two, and Creative Self-Beliefs: A Meta-Analysis. *Psychology of Aesthetics, Creativity, and the Arts*, *10*(2), 214–232. doi.org/10.1037/aca0000035.

Kaufman, J. C. (2016). *Creativity 101*. New York: Springer Publishing Company.

Kaufman, A. B., and Kaufman, J. C. (2015). *Animal Creativity and Innovation*. Academic Press.

Kaufman, A. S., Schneider, W. J., and Kaufman, J. C. (2019). Psychometric Approaches to Intelligence. In R. J. Sternberg (Ed.), *Human Intelligence* (pp. 67–103). Cambridge: Cambridge University Press.

Kaufman, J. C., and Beghetto, R. A. (2009). Beyond Big and Little: The Four C Model of Creativity. *Review of General Psychology*, *13*, 1–12.

(2013). In Praise of Clark Kent: Creative Metacognition and the Importance of Teaching Kids When (Not) to Be Creative. *Roeper Review*, *35*(3), 155–165.

Kaufman, J. C., Kaufman, S. B., and Lichtenberger, E. O. (2011). Finding Creativity on Intelligence Tests via Divergent Production. *Canadian Journal of School Psychology*, *26*, 83–106.

Kaufman, J. C., and Sternberg, R. J. (Eds.) (2010). *The Cambridge Handbook of Creativity*. Cambridge: Cambridge University Press.

Kim, K. H. (2005). Can Only Intelligent People Be Creative? A Meta-Analysis. *Journal of Secondary Gifted Education*, *16*, 57–66.

Kohn, N. W., and Smith, S. M. (2009). Partly versus Completely out of Your Mind: Effects of Incubation and Distraction on Resolving Fixation. *Journal of Creative Behavior*, *43*, 102–118. doi.org/10.1002/j.2162-6057.2009.tb01309.x.

Landau, J. D., and Lehr, D. P. (2004). Conformity to Experimenter-Provided Examples: Will People Use an Unusual Feature? *Journal of Creative Behavior*, *38*, 180–191.

Lee, S. A., and Dow, G. T. (2011). Malevolent Creativity: Does Personality Influence Malicious Divergent Thinking? *Creativity Research Journal*, *23*, 73–82.

Lubart, T. (2010). Cross-Cultural Perspectives on Creativity. In J. C. Kaufman and R. J. Sternberg (Eds.), *The Cambridge Handbook of Creativity* (pp. 265–278). Cambridge: Cambridge University Press.

Lubart, T. I., and Sternberg, R. J. (1995). An Investment Approach to Creativity. In S. M. Smith, T. B., Ward, and R. A. Finke (Eds.), *The Creative Cognition Approach* (pp. 269–302). Cambridge, MA: MIT Press.

Marsh, R. L., Ward, T. B., and Landau, J. D. (1999). The Inadvertent Use of Prior Knowledge in a Generative Cognitive Task. *Memory and Cognition*, *27*, 94–105.

McGrew, K. S. (2009). CHC Theory and the Human Cognitive Abilities Project: Standing on the Shoulders of the Giants of Psychometric Intelligence Research. *Intelligence*, *37*, 1–10.

Mednick, S. (1962). The Associative Basis of the Creative Process. *Psychological Review*, *69*, 220–232.

Milgram, R. M., and Rabkin, L. (1980). Developmental Test of Mednick's Associative Hierarchies of Original Thinking. *Developmental Psychology*, *16*, 157–158.

Niu, W., and Sternberg, R. J. (2003). Societal and School Influences on Student Creativity: The Case of China. *Psychology in the Schools*, *40*(1), 103–114.

Purcell, A. T., and Gero, J. S. (1996). Design and Other Types of Fixation. *Design Studies*, *17*, 363–383.

Rhodes, M. (1961). An Analysis of Creativity. *Phi Delta Kappan, 42*, 305–310.

Richardson, A. G. (1986). Two Factors of Creativity. *Perceptual and Motor Skills, 63*, 379–384.

Ritter, S. M., Damian, R. I., Simonton, D. K., van Baaren, R. B., Strick, M., Derks, J., and Dijksterhuis, A. (2012). Diversifying Experiences Enhance Cognitive Flexibility. *Journal of Experimental Social Psychology, 48*, 961–964.

Rothenberg, A. (1979). *The Emerging Goddess*. Chicago: University of Chicago Press.

Rubin, D. C., and Kontis, T. C. (1983). A Schema for Common Cents. *Memory and Cognition, 11*, 335–341.

Runco, M. A. (1986). Flexibility and Originality in Children's Divergent Thinking. *Journal of Psychology, 120*, 345–352.

(1994). *Problem Finding, Problem Solving, and Creativity*. Westport: Ablex.

(2007). A Hierarchical Framework for the Study of Creativity. *New Horizons in Education, 55*, 1–9.

Runco, M. A., and Acar, S. (2010). Do Tests of Divergent Thinking Have an Experiential Bias? *Psychology of Art, Creativity, and Aesthetics, 4*, 144–148. dx.doi.org/10.1037/a0018969.

Runco, M. A., and Albert, R. S. (1985). The Reliability and Validity of Ideational Originality in the Divergent Thinking of Academically Gifted and Nongifted Children. *Educational and Psychological Measurement, 45*, 483–501.

Runco, M. A., and Chand, I. (1994). Conclusions concerning Problem Finding, Problem Solving, and Creativity. In M. A. Runco (Ed.), *Problem Finding, Problem Solving, and Creativity* (pp. 217–290). Westport: Ablex.

Runco, M. A., and Vega, L. (1990). Evaluating the Creativity of Children's Ideas. *Journal of Social Behavior and Personality, 5*, 439–452.

Sawyer, R. K. (2012). *Explaining Creativity: The Science of Human Innovation*, 2nd ed. Oxford: Oxford University Press.

Schneider, W. J., and McGrew, K. S. (2012). The Cattell-Horn-Carroll Model of Intelligence. In D. P. Flanagan and P. L. Harrison (Eds.), *Contemporary Intellectual Assessment: Theories, Tests, and Issues* (pp. 99–144). New York: Guilford Press.

Scott, G., Leritz, L. E., and Mumford, M. D. (2004a). The Effectiveness of Creativity Training: A Quantitative Review. *Creativity Research Journal, 16*, 361–388.

(2004b). Types of Creativity Training: Approaches and Their Effectiveness. *Journal of Creative Behavior, 38*, 149–179.

Simonton, D. K. (1997). Creativity in Personality, Developmental, and Social Psychology: Any Links with Cognitive Psychology. In T. B. Ward, S. M. Smith, and J. Vaid (Eds.), *Creative Thought: An Investigation of Conceptual Structures and Processes* (pp. 309–324). Washington, DC: American Psychological Association.

Smith, S. M. (1995). Fixation, Incubation, and Insight in Memory and Creative Thinking. In S. M. Smith, T. B. Ward, and R. A. Finke (Eds.), *The Creative Cognition Approach* (pp. 135–156). Cambridge, MA: MIT Press.

Smith, S. M., and Blankenship, S. E. (1991). Incubation and the Persistence of Fixation in Problem Solving. *American Journal of Psychology, 104*, 61–87.

Smith, S. M., Ward, T. B., and Schumacher, J. S. (1993). Constraining Effects of Examples in a Creative Generation Task. *Memory and Cognition, 21*, 837–845.

Spearman, C. (1904). "General Intelligence," Objectively Determined and Measured. *The American Journal of Psychology, 15*, 201–292.

Sternberg, R. J. (1984). Toward a Triarchic Theory of Human Intelligence. *Behavioral and Brain Sciences, 7*, 269–287.

(1985a). Human Intelligence: The Model Is the Message. *Science, 230*, 1111–1118.

(1985b). Implicit Theories of Intelligence, Creativity, and Wisdom. *Journal of Personality and Social Psychology*, *49*(3), 607–627.

(1985c). Teaching Critical Thinking, Part 1: Are We Making Critical Mistakes? *Phi Delta Kappan*, *67*, 194–198.

(1986). Inside Intelligence. *American Scientist*, *74*, 137–143.

(1988). A Three-Facet Model of Creativity. In R. J. Sternberg (Ed.), *The Nature of Creativity: Contemporary Psychological Perspectives* (pp. 125–147). Cambridge: Cambridge University Press.

(1997). Managerial Intelligence: Why IQ Isn't Enough. *Journal of Management*, *23*(3), 463–475.

(1998). A Balance Theory of Wisdom. *Review of General Psychology*, *2*, 347–365.

(2001a). Why Schools Should Teach for Wisdom: The Balance Theory of Wisdom in Educational Settings. *Educational Psychologist*, *36*(4), 227–245.

(2001b). Wisdom and Education. *Perspectives in Education*, *19*(4), 1–16.

(2003). *Wisdom, Intelligence, and Creativity Synthesized*. Cambridge: Cambridge University Press.

(2005). WICS: A Model of Giftedness in Leadership. *Roeper Review*, *28*(1), 37–44.

(2007). A Systems Model of Leadership: WICS. *American Psychologist*, *62*(1), 34–42.

(2009). WICS: A New Model for Liberal Education. *Liberal Education*, *95*(4), 20–25.

(2010). *College Admissions for the 21st Century*. Cambridge, MA: Harvard University Press.

(2018). A Triangular Theory of Creativity. *Psychology of Aesthetics, Creativity, and the Arts*, *12*, 50–67.

(2018). Theories of Intelligence. In S. I. Pfeiffer, E. Shaunessy-Dedrick, and M. Foley-Nicpon (Eds.), *APA Handbooks in Psychology: APA Handbook of Giftedness and Talent* (p. 145–161). Washington, DC: American Psychological Association.

(2019). Why People Often Prefer Wise Guys to Guys Who Are Wise: An Augmented Balance Theory of the Production and Reception of Wisdom. In R. J. Sternberg and J. Glueck (Eds.), *The Cambridge Handbook of Wisdom* (pp. 162–181). Cambridge: Cambridge University Press.

(2020). The Augmented Theory of Successful Intelligence. In R. J. Sternberg and S. B. Kaufman (Eds.), *The Cambridge Handbook of Intelligence*, 2nd ed. Cambridge: Cambridge University Press.

(2021). *Adaptive Intelligence*. Cambridge: Cambridge University Press.

Sternberg, R. J., and Davidson, J. E. (1982). The Mind of the Puzzler. *Psychology Today*, *16*, 37–44.

Sternberg, R. J., and Kaufman, S. B. (Eds.) (2011). *The Cambridge Handbook of Intelligence*. Cambridge: Cambridge University Press.

Sternberg, R. J., and Jordan, J. (Eds.) (2005). *Handbook of Wisdom: Psychological Perspectives*. Cambridge: Cambridge University Press.

Sternberg, R. J., and Lubart, T. (1996). Investing in Creativity. *American Psychologist*, *51*, 677–688.

and The Rainbow Project Collaborators (2006). The Rainbow Project: Enhancing the SAT through Assessments of Analytical, Practical and Creative Skills. *Intelligence*, *34* (4), 321–350.

Sternberg, R. J., and Smith, C. (1985). Social Intelligence and Decoding Skills in Nonverbal Communication. *Social Cognition*, *2*, 168–192.

Thagard, P. (1984). Conceptual Combination and Scientific Discovery. In P. Asquith and P. Kitcher (Eds.), *PSA, 1*. East Lansing: Philosophy of Science Association.

Torrance, E. P. (1968). A Longitudinal Examination of the Fourth-Grade Slump in Creativity. *Gifted Child Quarterly*, *12*, 195–199.

Tourangeau, R., and Rips, L. (1991). Interpreting and Evaluating Metaphors. *Journal of Memory and Language*, *30*, 452–472.

van Aken, L., van der Heijden, P. T., Oomens, W., Kessels, R. P. C., and Egger, J. I. M. (2017). Predictive Value of Traditional Measures of Executive Function on Broad Abilities of the Cattell-Horn-Carroll Theory of Cognitive Abilities. *Assessment, 1,* 1–11.

Vartanian, O., Martindale, C., and Kwiatkowski, J. (2007). Creative Potential, Attention, and Speed of Information Processing. *Personality and Individual Differences, 43,* 1470–1480.

Viriyayudhakorn, K., Kunifuji, S., and Ogawa, M. (2011). A Comparison of Four Association Engines in Divergent Thinking Support Systems on Wikipedia. In *Knowledge, Information, and Creativity Support Systems* (pp. 226–237). Heidelberg: Springer-Berlin.

Visser, B. A., Ashton, M. C., and Vernon, P. A. (2006). Beyond *g*: Putting Multiple Intelligence Theory to the Test. *Intelligence, 34,* 487–502.

Wallach, M. A., and Kogan, N. (1965). *Modes of Thinking in Young Children: A Study of the Creativity-Intelligence Distinction.* New York: Holt, Rinehart & Winston.

Wallas, G. (1926). *The Art of Thought.* New York: Harcourt Brace and Company.

Ward, T. B. (1994). Structured Imagination: The Role of Conceptual Structure in Exemplar Generation. *Cognitive Psychology, 27,* 1–40.

  (2008). The Role of Domain Knowledge in Creative Generation. *Learning and Individual Differences, 18*(4), 363–366.

  (2015). Content, Collaboration and Creativity in Virtual Worlds. In G. Green and J. Kaufman (Eds.). *Video Games and Creativity.* San Diego: Academic Press.

  (2018). Creativity As a Continuum. In J. C. Kaufman and R. J. Sternberg (Eds.), *The Nature of Human Creativity* (pp. 335–350). Cambridge: Cambridge University Press.

Ward, T. B., Finke, R. A., and Smith, S. M. (1995). *Creativity and the Mind: Discovering the Genius Within.* New York: Plenum Press. https://doi.org/10.1007/978-1-4899-3330-0.

Ward, T. B., Saunders, K. N., and Dodds, R. A. (1999). Creative Cognition in Gifted Adolescents. *Roeper Review, 21,* 260–265.

Ward, T. B., and Sifonis, S. M. (1997). Task Demands and Generative Thinking: What Changes and What Remains the Same? *Journal of Creative Behavior, 31,* 245–259.

Walker, B. R., and Jackson, C. J. (2014). How the Five-Factor Model and Revised Reinforcement Sensitivity Theory Predict Divergent Thinking. *Personality and Individual Differences, 57,* 54–58.

Weisberg, R. W. (2006). *Creativity: Understanding Innovation in Problem Solving, Science, Invention, and the Arts.* New York: John Wiley & Sons.

White, J. H. (1978). *The American Railroad Passenger Car.* Baltimore: Johns Hopkins University Press.

Willis, J. O., Dumont, R., and Kaufman, A. S. (2011). Factor-Analytic Models of Intelligence. In R. J. Sternberg and S. B. Kaufman (Eds.), *The Cambridge Handbook of Intelligence* (pp. 44–45). Cambridge: Cambridge University Press.

Yang C., and Li, X. (2012). Research Progress in Extension Innovation Method and Its Applications. *Industrial Engineering Journal, 15,* 131–137.

Yi, X., Plucker, J. A., and Guo, J. (2015). Modeling Influences on Divergent Thinking and Artistic Creativity. *Thinking Skills and Creativity, 16,* 1662–1668. doi.org/10.1016/j.tsc.2015.02.002.

8 Cultural Perspectives on Creativity

TODD LUBART, VLAD P. GLĂVEANU, HERIE DE VRIES, ANA CAMARGO, AND MARTIN STORME

INTRODUCTION

Creativity – the ability to generate original productions that are meaningful in their context – is a culturally embedded phenomenon. It may involve a person or a group of people who create. The cultural context in which the creative act occurs (with its physical and social facets) has many levels, ranging from the family, school, and work-organizational settings to local community, regional, national, or transnational ones. **Culture**, as a social environment, can be defined as "an historically transmitted pattern of meanings visible and tangible in symbols. A system of conceptions is inherited and expressed in symbolic forms. These forms are the means by which men and women (or human beings) communicate, continue their culture, and develop their knowledge about and attitudes toward life" (Geertz, 1973, p. 89). In the GLOBE international research program, House and Javidan (2004, p. 15) defined culture as "shared motives, values, beliefs, identities, and interpretations or meanings of significant events that result from common experiences of members of collectives and are transmitted across age generations."

In this chapter, we start from the premise that the meaning of creativity and that of culture are intrinsically bound to each other (see Glăveanu, 2014). Creativity as a process uses "culturally-impregnated materials" (ideas, signs, objects, values, etc.) to create new and meaningful artifacts that contribute to culture itself (both the macro-culture of entire groups or nations, and the micro-culture of local actors and subcultures).

There are many facets of culture, apart from the national one; these include the regional, ethnic, religious and linguistic facets, gender, and generational facets, and with respect to organizations, the departmental, division and corporate facets (Valsiner, 2014). Given the variations within and between cultural contexts, an enhanced understanding of creativity may be gained by examining, in-depth, creative expression in a specific cultural setting, as well as comparing and contrasting creativity in different cultures. This chapter does not seek to provide a comprehensive review of all relevant studies on the topic. Rather, the goal is to raise key issues, highlight major trends, and provide illustrations of research findings. In this way, this chapter offers a complementary view to previous syntheses on creativity and culture (see Lubart, 1990, 1999; Ludwig, 1992; Niu and Sternberg, 2002; Rudowicz, 2003; Westwood and Low, 2003; Glăveanu, 2016).

In this chapter, two main cultural perspectives on creativity will be examined. First, the sociocultural psychology of creativity and its basic premises will be introduced and discussed. This approach is based on a view of interdependence between person and culture and studies creative action in its cultural context. Does "creativity," for instance, mean the same thing in different cultural settings? We highlight existing research based on people's conceptions of creativity, including implicit and explicit definitions of creativity, descriptions of creative people, and evaluations of creative productions. Second, we will present cross-cultural studies that make comparisons between the expression of creativity in two or more contexts. We will focus on the **individualism-collectivism** dimension, on which societies tend to vary. Are these **cultural dimensions** related to differences in creativity? In addition, we will present work on the impact of exposure to multiple cultures and the use of cultural tools – including modern technologies– as sources of creativity.

The Sociocultural Approach to Creativity

The basic premise of the sociocultural approach is that creativity doesn't happen "within the head" of isolated individuals but rather in the interaction between people, places, objects, and institutions. Creative action is, in this perspective, intrinsically social and cultural, given the fact that it is made possible by the use of signs (for instance, language) and tools (for example, technology). This view builds on the early works of people such as Lev Vygotsky (1930/1998), John Dewey (1934) and Mikhail Bakhtin (1929/1984).

Their views, however, did not make an impact on the psychology of creativity when it emerged as an area of scientific study in the mid-twentieth century. This is because the concerns of researchers after 1950 (see Guilford, 1950) had to do with the relation between creativity and intelligence, on the one hand, or between creativity and personality, on the other (Barron and Harrington, 1981). Only gradually, from the 1970s and 1980s onwards, the study of groups and society entered creativity research, mainly through the systemic thinking of Csikszentmihalyi (1988) and Gruber (2005), the historical analyses of Simonton (1975), and the social psychological approach of Amabile (1982). However, for as much as these new theories considered the social context of creativity, they did not provide an explicit understanding of culture. It is only in recent years that cultural and sociocultural psychologists started to focus on creativity (e.g., Glăveanu, Gillespie, and Valsiner, 2015) and developed frameworks that recognize it as simultaneously psychological and cultural.

Let's take a concrete example to demonstrate this: Easter egg decoration (see Figure 8.1). This might not be what most people think about when it comes to creativity, but it is the case that each decorated egg has unique features and the process of decoration involves mixing and matching a variety of existing patterns in new ways (for more details, see Glăveanu, 2013a). Undoubtably, all the "materials" craftswomen work with are cultural in nature. The motifs they place on the egg have symbolic meanings; for example, the net stands for the separation between good and evil, the star is a symbol of perfection and femininity, and the black color for the background (specific for the village where Glăveanu did his fieldwork) doesn't mean death or sadness but permanence and eternity. Moreover, the physical tools used – for example, melted wax and the wooden stick with a

Figure 8.1 Decorated
Romanian eggs.
Source: iStock/Getty Images Plus

metal pin at the end to apply the wax – are not invented by the decorator but are a legacy of previous generations. Whereas for many, Easter egg decoration, and other similar crafts, qualify as tradition rather than creativity, we need to remember that traditions are never static and that creative action, no matter the domain, builds on existing cultural traditions, tools, and symbols.

The sociocultural study of creativity makes us aware of the fact that, in every cultural context, creativity comes out of the interaction between various elements and cannot be reduced to the person of the creator or the object or idea being created. This system includes five elements (5 "A"s) and the relations between them: people doing the creating (actors), the people they collaborate with or address with their creativity (audiences), the processes they engage to create (actions), the outcomes they come to produce (artifacts), and the properties of the material environment they use to create (affordances) (see Glăveanu, 2013b, 2015).

Where exactly is culture in this model? In line with the sociocultural view, there is no distinct element called "culture." Instead, culture is considered to shape the ways in which the five "elements" interact with each other. The particular organization of the actors, audiences, actions, artifacts, and affordances reflects the cultural beliefs, values, and norms specific for a certain group, situation, or moment in time.

For example, the creative actions of a painter will depend on the specific audiences he or she is in dialogue with, and the material means at his/her disposal (and their affordances). Equally, the work of a scientist, for instance, is an act of communication directed at different audiences (e.g., peers, reviewers, inventors), generating new and meaningful artifacts (theories or objects), and building on the affordances of technology and of previous scientific discoveries. It is important to note that, in this paradigm, culture is not studied only at the national level or in terms of shared beliefs and values; it is embedded in language, objects, social relations, institutions, and the knowledge we each draw on to be creative.

Conceptions of Creativity in Cultural Context

The conception of creativity includes its definition as well as its different aspects or characteristics. For example, in psychology, Western researchers' definitions of creativity tend to focus on a capacity to produce work (ideas or productions of all kinds) that is both novel-original and adaptive or useful given the task or limitations of the situation. Do the same defining features hold across all cultural settings, both national and local? Needless to say, research needs to be conducted in the most unbiased way possible so that researchers from a Western cultural background do not see everything through their own perspective. In this respect, it was noted several times in Kaufman and Sternberg's *International Handbook of Creativity* (2006) that research on creativity in various parts of the world has often been dominated by Western paradigms.

Several methods allow conceptions of creativity to be examined for possible cultural differences. First, it is possible to ask people in different cultural settings to define creativity in their own culturally appropriate way. Second, people can name examples of "creativity" in their cultural context, and the common aspects can be examined. Third, people can specify the individual or social variables that characterize creative people or creative performance. Finally, people may be asked to judge a set of creative works. The way they evaluate creativity can provide insight into the criteria that they use implicitly.

One goal of research on conceptions of creativity is to define the concept. A second goal, as mentioned earlier, is to identify characteristics associated with creativity within and between cultural settings. These include, for example, the fields of endeavor in which creativity is valued in a certain culture, the categories of people who are expected to be creative, and the way that creative activities are organized.

Defining Features

Research evidence suggests that there may be some universal components of creativity. The most obvious one is the notion of novelty or originality. However, novelty is itself context-dependent. What is novel in one society may not be novel in another. Furthermore, the degree of novelty is relevant. As an extreme case, some authors have argued that a vast number of sentences uttered in everyday conversations are novel combinations of words. In this view, nearly everyone engages in some creative activity every day (Chomsky, 1972; D'Agostino, 1984). However, for others, this kind of novelty is not sufficient and would be disregarded. Thus, it is possible to distinguish the issue of what is novel (content) from how much novelty has been expressed (degree). The degree of novelty leads to an important definitional issue concerning the fundamental nature of the novelty. Is the conceptual model one of a break with the past, a radical, categorically new and different idea? Or, rather, is the model one of progressive improvement, modification, and adaptation (see Puccio and Chimento, 2001)? In this second case, the cutoff for deciding that an idea or other form of production is creative will be less strict. It has been suggested that a high level of novelty, with a conceptual break, may be the underlying view in some cultures, in particular, Western ones, and the more gradual concept of continuing levels of novelty, working off of an existing idea, may characterize other cultures, perhaps Eastern-oriental ones (see Niu and Sternberg, 2006). For example, Li (1997) compared Chinese ink-brush painting and modern Western painting, suggesting that creative Chinese painting introduces novelty while respecting a set of basic visual features, whereas Western painting favors work that can move in a new direction on any aspect that the artist chooses. Different processes of creating may be associated with these kinds of novelty. Thus, there seems to be a general reference to novelty across cultural definitions of creativity, but the meaning of this novelty, and the way to achieve it, may vary substantially.

The second main definitional component of creativity that seems to be cross-culturally recognized is adaptive value. The term "value" is used here to cover the notions of usefulness, constraint satisfaction, adaptiveness, appropriateness, effectiveness, and relevance within the context in which the novelty is generated. It is clear that, across various domains of endeavor, the relative weight of novelty versus adaptive value can vary. For example, in the artistic field, novelty is perhaps more highly valued than adaptiveness, whereas in engineering, the trend may be inverted. If "usefulness" is highly valued in a cultural context, the adaptiveness component of creativity will have a relative importance with respect to the novelty component (see, for example, Paletz and Peng, 2008).

Finally, the notion of adaptive value has another facet, which is the societal utility of the creative act. This trend appears most clearly in studies of creativity in Asian and African settings; creativity involves novelty that contributes positively to society (Niu and Kaufman, 2005; Mpofu et al., 2006; also see Niu, 2019). For example, in Kenya, creative storytelling, according to Gacheru et al. (1999), should be both imaginative and provide an ethical message.[1] Some debate on novel thinking and productions, such as inventions for evil purposes (the dark side of creativity; Cropley et al., 2010), may not necessarily be classified as creative acts in all cultures because they lack moral validity, such as creating a new bomb, a new virus, or planning a crime.

A few studies conducted across national cultures have examined if there were differences in creativity ratings of productions, such as drawings, evaluated by judges from different cultures. Some studies compared judges in the United States and China (Niu and Sternberg, 2001; Chen et al., 2002; Rostan, Pariser, and Gruber, 2002; Niu, 2019). For example, Chen et al. (2002) had American and Chinese college students make drawings based on geometric figures (triangle, rectangle, circle). These drawings were evaluated by American and Chinese undergraduate judges, who had not produced drawings and weren't informed of the origin of each drawing. The overall correlation between the judges from different cultures was .97, indicating a nearly perfect level of inter-judge agreement on the relative creativity of the productions. Indeed, it can be argued that these studies optimized the conditions for cross-cultural agreement because the tasks used relatively neutral stimuli, drawings, familiar in

---

[1] See for example, Aghan Odero Agan's work as a modern Kenyan storyteller, www.youtube.com/watch?v=eTDzJn_iUB4

(a)

Figure 8.2 Drawing (a) and (b), from adolescents in Benin.
Source: C.-R. Anoumou (2019)

(b)

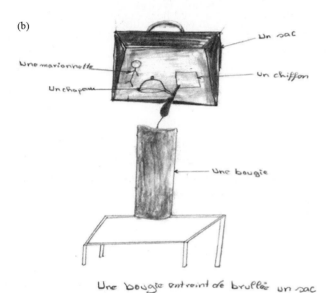

both cultures; moreover, judges were from relatively similar groups (university students) and were blind to the cultural origin of each production.

In Figure 8.2A and B, this kind of study is illustrated with productions from Benin, a West African country. Adolescents, in response to EPoC measures of creative potential (Lubart, Besançon, and Barbot, 2013), produced drawings based on a set of photos of objects (a candle, hat, marionette, bag, etc.) (Anoumou, Lubart, and Bourgeois, 2019). Judges from Benin and France each rated the drawings and there was good intercultural agreement on creativity. In Figure 8.2A, a typical drawing showing an average level of creative thinking is depicted, whereas in Figure 8.2B, a more original idea is presented, in which the candle leads to setting the carrying bag on fire, and the bag contains several other objects.

Product versus Process Orientation

The creative act, or **creative process**, refers to the sequence of actions, including mental events that lead to the production. Some cultures, particularly modern Western cultures, focus on the result of the creative process, with little attention to the way that the creator achieved the outcome. This view can be contrasted with an Eastern perspective, in which the key to creativity is the process more than the result. The creative process is cyclic, nonlinear, and enlightenment-oriented. It involves connecting to a larger reality, such as reconfiguring or rediscovering existing elements. In this way, respecting traditions is not alien to creating, because the creative act involves finding new interpretations of existing elements and giving new breath to old ideas and practices. Along this line, Westwood and Low (2003) cited the examples of creativity from a Hindu perspective, in which traditional truths are revealed in a new way, and classic Chinese visual art, in which a well-known topic represented with a certain style is explored in a new way.

Gender Differences

As Ludwig (1992) noted, various gender-related differences can be observed for creativity as we look across cultures. In certain traditional societies, men may show their creativity in woodcraft, sculpture, and medicinal-healing practices, whereas women may express their creativity in basket weaving, making clothing, embroidery, rugs, or pottery (see, for example, Shostak, 1993; Oral, 2006). In some cultures, one gender group may be allowed access to fields involving creative work, with the other gender group denied access. Kim (2007) argued that Asian cultures based on Confucianism have long fostered inequality between men and women, with a woman traditionally being expected to show high levels of obedience, which is not contributive to creative work. Of course, creative work is not inherently gender-typed; recent trends suggest that gender-related organization of creativity may be decreasing given the numerous changes in modern societies.

Individual or Collective Forms

In some cultural contexts, the individual creator is the focus of attention, whereas in other cultures, creativity is mainly a collective act, often situated at the group level (Lubart, 1999). For example, a contrast can be made in the musical domain between a focus on creative composition being driven by individual composers or by musical groups. In traditional Balinese society, Colligan (1983) observed that musical creativity is an essentially collective task accomplished by musical groups rather than by individual musicians, as in jazz. Sawyer (2006) described another example of habitual collective (dyadic) creativity in traditional societies, in which a shaman, based on a vision from a possession state, would work with a carver to realize a spiritual mask for ceremonial use. The position that a culture adopts on the individualistic nature of creativity is hypothesized to be related to the individualism-collectivism dimension of cultural variation, which will be described in more detail later in this chapter.

Domains

Several authors have observed that some cultures channel creativity into certain domains more than others (Lubart, 1990, 1999; Ludwig, 1992). Creativity may, for example, be recognized, valued, and promoted in the visual arts or technical inventions more than in religious or political spheres (Mpofu et al., 2006). For instance, it has been noted that Islamic societies appear to foster artistic creativity, in particular, in non-representational styles (such as geometric designs, decorative works, calligraphy), as well as in verbal creativity in domains such as poetry, literary compositions, storytelling, and folk songs (Ludwig, 1992, Khaleefa et al, 1996; Mpofu et al., 2006; Oral, 2006). Other reports indicate that, in Turkey, scientific and technological creativity are highly valued. In Latin America, there is emphasis on creativity in business and advertising (Rudowicz, 2003).

In this respect, a cross-cultural study showed that the process differs across cultural contexts. Güss et al. (2017) compared artists in Russia, Cuba, and Germany, and found, based on interviews, that different steps of the creative process varied in these cultures. For example, emotional frustration was a typical part of the creative process in Germany and Russia, but not in Cuba. The cognitive and motivational parts of the process differed as well: Cuban artists saw themselves typically as working within and in the middle of society, whereas for German and Russian artists, this was rare, and isolation from society was the norm.

Big-C, little-c

The distinction between eminent cases of creativity, Big-C creativity, and everyday acts of creativity, little-c creativity, can be examined across cultures. In some cultural settings, everyone can be creative. In others, it is viewed as an exclusive ability, reserved for a few exceptional people.

It seems that numerous Western societies recognize everyday creativity but highlight and glorify the eminent cases of creativity, such as Albert Einstein, Marie Curie, Johann Sebastian Bach, Leonardo da Vinci, and Sylvia Plath. Montuori and Purser (1995) raised the possibility of the "Lone Genius Myth"; cultures that focus on eminent cases of creativity tend to highlight the individual characteristics of these special people, reducing the perceived contribution of their environment. This tendency was hypothesized to be related to a culture's position on the individualism-collectivism dimension, which is presented in the next section.

In contrast, according to some reports in other cultures, everyone is naturally creative in all activities of life, such that the question itself of nominating creative people is odd and often meets with no response. For example, the !Kung San are a tribal group living in the Kalahari Desert, who engage in creative activities such as bead-weaving, storytelling, and music performance. When Shostak (1993) asked who were the most creative people, respondents would often list everyone engaged in the activity. Mpofu et al. (2006) reported on a study with people from Arab and sub-Saharan Africa, representing twenty-eight linguistic groups. They found that a concept of creativity was often expressed as a commonplace ability intertwined with resourcefulness, intelligence, wisdom, talent, originality, and inventiveness. In their sample, more than two-thirds of the sub-Saharan and Arab Africans described themselves as involved in creative activities in their daily life. On the extreme side of little-c creativity, the possibility of creativity at the personal level, in creative acts of self-development that yield no tangible production, can be mentioned. This personal creativity, a form of self-actualization or individual self-development, is valued in some cultures more than others (see Kaufman and Beghetto, 2013; Karwowski and Kaufman, 2017).

The Cross-Cultural Approach to Creativity

Cross-cultural research describes variations of human behaviors, similarities and differences between cultures, as well as the impact of culture on behavior (Berry et al., 2002). It starts from different scientific principles, however, than those of sociocultural-oriented colleagues (Shweder, 1990; Cole, 1996).

Culture Influences the Amount of Creativity

The issue of whether one culture fosters creativity more than another has often been raised. This question concerns both the quantity of creative production in a given culture and the quality or greatness of the productions. Simonton (1999, 2019), using the **historiometric approach**, has greatly contributed to comparisons of creativity within and across cultural centers during long historical periods. During times of political turmoil, war, and ideological diversity, for example, creativity was found to be impacted; for instance, technological inventions were favored. Comparisons between contemporary cultures in terms of creative production has been attempted, typically using samples from two different cultures, such as students from United States and from China. In these studies, the participants complete the same experimental creative thinking task and their productions are compared. These productions may be responses to divergent thinking tests, drawings, collages, or other kinds of work. There are some important methodological issues, such as the appropriateness of the "creativity" task in each culture as a valid measure of creativity.

Several studies have shown that one cultural group outperforms another (such as American vs. Chinese student comparisons; Ng, 2001). The next step is to investigate why these differences were observed. In some cases, there may be several other variables, which confound and can explain results, instead of the "culture" variable. For example, it is important that the two contrasting cultural groups do not differ in age, socioeconomic status, education level, access to technology, and other variables. If these potential confounds are controlled, the remaining differences observed stem, it is argued, from cultural characteristics. As a start, the creativity task may be more meaningful and culturally appropriate to one group compared to another. Imagine a divergent thinking task concerning everything you could do with a coconut. This task is perhaps very meaningful for children in the Philippines where coconuts are plentiful compared to Inuit children who have no experience with them.

Some studies comparing creative performance in Westerners (notably people from the United States) with Easterners (Asians in Japan, Hong Kong, Taiwan, and Singapore) have found results favoring samples from the United States (for examples of studies using divergent thinking tests, see Saeki, Fan, and Van Dusen, 2001; Kharkhurin and Samadpour Motalleebi, 2008). Niu and Sternberg (2001) compared artistic creativity in American (Yale University) and Chinese (Peking University) students using collage-making and alien-drawing tasks. The productions were evaluated by American and Chinese graduate students in psychology. The results indicated that the American students received higher scores on creativity than Chinese students, according to both American and Chinese judges (who were blind to the cultural origin of each drawing). Needless to say, the findings are not always in favor of US samples. In studies showing an advantage for a Chinese sample, the argument that the task taps a specific domain enhanced by a particular kind of education in the culture showing good results is typically evoked (Niu and Sternberg, 2002, 2003).

In terms of the psychological bases of cultural effects, a few main cultural value dimensions have guided cross-cultural studies in past decades (Hofstede, 1980; Schwartz, 1994, 1999; Triandis, 1994). For example, using Schwartz's framework, employee creativity in Israel and India related to the cultural value of "conformity" (negatively) and "achievement" (positively) (Cohen and Erlich, 2015). The dimensions proposed by Hofstede (1980, 2011) in his landmark study of people working at IBM across the world are among the most known and researched: **individualism-collectivism**, **power distance** (high and low), **masculinity-femininity**, **uncertainty avoidance** (high and low), **long-term versus short-term orientation**, and **indulgence versus restraint**. Work related to creativity has centered on individualism-collectivism, uncertainty avoidance, and power distance (Hofstede, 2001; Rank et al, 2004). Individualism-collectivism characterizes the strength and cohesion of bonds between people, with people looking after themselves and immediate families in individualist societies and looking after the larger societal unit to which they belong in collectivist societies. **Power distance** refers to the extent to which power and authority are expected and accepted to be distributed (un)equally in a society. Uncertainty avoidance concerns the extent to which people experience stresses, or are uncomfortable concerning the unknown future, and feel threatened by uncertain, unknown, and ambiguous situations.

In general, strong collectivism, high levels of uncertainty avoidance, and high power distance are negatively related to national levels of inventiveness (Hofstede, 2001). In a study of national rates of innovation in thirty-three countries, societies with low uncertainty avoidance, low power distance, and high individualism showed relatively more patents per capita (Shane, 1992; 1993). An acceptance of uncertainty (low uncertainty avoidance) may foster tolerance for risk and change. Individualism is associated with autonomy, independence (defining one's self as unique from the group), and freedom. The meta-analysis conducted by Taras, Kirkman, and Steel (2010) on the literature on the relationships between Hofstede's dimensions and indicators of innovation found that innovation is negatively correlated with uncertainty avoidance ($r = -0.41$) and positively with individualism ($r = 0.65$).

Using the Global Innovation Index (GII), there was also a strong negative relation with power distance, positive relation with individualism, and no correlation with uncertainty avoidance (Rinne, Steel, and Fairweather, 2012). Ng (2003) proposed a model in which cultural individualism-collectivism influences the self-construal of an individual, as independent or interdependent on others, and this self-concept in turn influences creativity and conformity tendencies. Lack of power distance, characteristic of non-hierarchical societies, fosters enhanced interactions and communication between people at different status levels, such as superiors and subordinates. Finally, hierarchical societies do not tend to embrace change because of the potential redistribution of power that might go against vested interests.

The main hypothesis is that cultures showing the creativity-compatible profile on certain dimensions (individualism, etc.) will favor the development and expression of creativity. People from these cultures should show higher performance on laboratory creativity tasks, more creative productions (e.g., more patents for inventions), and greater levels of creativity (e.g., Nobel prize winners). It is worth noting as well that phases of creative and innovative processes may relate differentially to these cultural dimensions. For example, low power distance, individualism, and low uncertainty avoidance may foster idea generation but hinder idea implementation. Hofstede (1991, 2001) suggested collecting ideas in certain cultural contexts (e.g., weak uncertainty avoidance, with tolerance for deviant ideas and unpredictable situations) and refining them in others (strong uncertainty avoidance, sense of detail and precision).

Some recent studies have started to examine additional cultural dimensions. For example, Everdingen and Maars (2003) investigated the adoption of innovation in different cultural contexts, finding that countries with a high level of uncertainty avoidance and a low level of long-term orientation, such as Mediterranean countries, were found to be slower when adopting innovations compared with northern European countries. Shane, Venkkataraman, and MacMillan (1995) examined national culture and preferences for innovation-championing strategies in 30 countries, with 1,228 professionals from 4 different industries. Innovation champions are those who promote the new ideas and help to overcome resistance to these ideas in organizational contexts. In this study, innovation was defined as any idea that is new to an organization (administrative, technological, product, process, etc.). Questionnaires were used to measure the perceived effectiveness of various innovation championing strategies. The results show that the cultural value of high uncertainty avoidance is related to preferences for idea champions to work within existing organizational rules and procedures to promote the ideas. For the culturally high power distance contexts, effective innovation champions focus on gaining the approval of important authority figures, whereas in low power distance contexts, innovation champions can seek to build a broad base of people who see value in an innovation. Finally, the cultural value of collectivism was associated with a strategy of getting people from different organizational departments to see the benefits of an innovation and thereby build consensus for the new idea.

Another aspect of cultures is their level of tightness-looseness, which refers to the degree that social norms are endorsed (Gelfand et al., 2011). In tight cultures, individuals show a strong respect of social norms and rules and strictly punish deviant behavior; in loose cultures, individuals display a greater flexibility toward enforcement of social norms and rules and tolerate deviant behavior. Chua, Roth, and Lemoine (2015) investigated the dynamic impact of cultural tightness on the tendency of creators to engage and succeed in creativity tasks. To examine this question, the authors used the data from a crowdsourcing platform, on which companies propose creative contests to generate ideas for marketing purposes. Individuals from all over the world can participate in contests that are proposed by companies. With the data from this platform, it is possible to assess the cultural characteristics of the countries of the company that start the contest, the individuals who choose to engage in the contest, and the individuals who win the contest. Chua et al. (2015) found that creativity engagement and success depend on the cultural tightness of the countries of the creator, of the receptor, and on the cultural distance between the creator's and the receptor's countries. More specifically, individuals from tight cultures are less likely to engage and succeed in creative tasks that are foreign and culturally distant. Also, the greater the distance between the countries, the stronger the negative impact of cultural tightness; in addition, in countries with a tight culture, foreign entrants are less likely to encounter creative success. For immediate benefits, it seems that countries with tight cultures should therefore look for creative potential in their own population as their audience is more likely to find the ideas of such persons more creative.

Cultural Issues: Multiculturalism and Technology

In the end, both sociocultural and cross-cultural approaches make distinct contributions to our understanding of creativity as a contextual, situated phenomenon. Sociocultural research considers culture as an integral part of creativity (and, inversely, creativity as the "engine" of cultural growth and development) and pays particular attention to how the meaning of creativity and its practice are co-constructed in local cultural settings. Cross-cultural investigations consider the influence of culture on creative production through its impact on value orientations and their clustering at national and supra-national levels. Both point to the importance of integrating multiple cultural elements within creative acts and, as such, they are interested by how multicultural experiences might shape creativity. It is not only language, for instance, that differs across cultural contexts, but also the tools available for creators to do their work. The rise of new technologies, an essential part of today's global culture, is of interest as it may impact and shape creativity.

Multicultural Experiences

A line of research has been developing in recent decades concerning the influence of exposure to several cultures. This work concerns effects of short-term stays in a foreign culture, as well as long-term exposure to a multicultural society, living near to contrasting cultural centers, or living in a bilingual or multilingual context. Multicultural experiences may involve time spent living abroad, interactions with people from diverse nationalities, ethnic groups, exposure to foreign languages, immigration experiences, and exposure to other cultures via educational experiences. In general, the basic hypothesis is that exposure to multiple cultures and/or multiple languages is beneficial for creativity. This exposure enhances knowledge and provides contrasts with typical modes of thought and action that help people overcome their cultural habits. Multicultural experiences may foster openness to new ideas. Multicultural experience can provide exposure and knowledge concerning diverse ideas, allow multiple interpretations of the same object, "destabilize" routine knowledge structures, promote a tendency to seek information from unfamiliar sources, and foster syntheses of diverse ideas (Leung et al., 2008).

The earliest studies focused on potential advantages of bilingualism for creativity, generally using divergent thinking tests in which participants have to generate as many original ideas as possible in a given time (see Ricciardelli, 1992; Simonton, 2008). In a recent example of this kind of research using a divergent-thinking test and a structured imagination test, Kharkhurin (2009) compared Farsi-English bilinguals living in the United Arab Emirates and Farsi monolinguals living in Iran. Bilingualism was related to higher originality scores for the divergent thinking test and the tendency to break away from standard category properties in the structured-imagination task. In another study, Russian-English bilingual immigrants showed enhanced performance compared to English monolingual native speakers, with effects of age of bilingual acquisition and exposure time to the new culture (Kharkhurin, 2008).

Of course, these studies illustrate a few of the potential complications with studies of bilingual populations: bilinguals may live in a completely different cultural context than monolinguals, they may be part of a subculture within a larger cultural context, and they may be immigrants who integrated a new cultural context. Furthermore, they may be part of a minority group. Studies that used a bicultural population have shown that the degree to which an individual identifies with both cultures has an effect on creativity. Biculturals who identified as biculturally blended (biculturals that identify with two cultures in equal measure) generated ideas that were more original in a divergent thinking task, compared to those that identified more with one culture over the other (Saad et al., 2012). There are a number of potential confounds (such as minority status), leading the "pure" effect of bilingualism to be hard to isolate. Additionally, there are different perspectives concerning the degrees and types of bilingualism such as high- and low-proficiency bilingualism (Lambert, 1981; Hommel et al., 2011).

Using bilingual participants can be tricky; the language used in tasks can affect participants' fluency score (which corresponds to the total number of ideas generated) and originality score on divergent thinking tasks (Kharkhurin and Altarriba, 2016). Furthermore, when comparing similar bilingual populations, it is important to keep the sociocultural contexts of the different study populations in mind (Kharkhurin, 2010). Once confounds associated with bilingualism are taken into account, to the extent that they can be controlled, bilingualism is hypothesized to facilitate creativity due to the specific "double coding" of concepts in memory, with each language providing nuances of the same concept. Another facilitative effect of bilingualism is enhanced mental flexibility, which perhaps develops as bilinguals need to move from one language to another (language switching) in their daily life (see Simonton, 2008 for a review of this literature). Supporting this idea, among early bilinguals, higher rates of everyday language switches were positively associated with performance in creative tasks (Dijksterhuis and Meurs, 2006; Soveri et al., 2011). The extent to which bilinguals switch languages in daily life is positively related to the number and originality of ideas found in verbal and graphical divergent thinking tasks (Karkhurin and Wei, 2015). The effect of habitual language switching on creativity is even stronger when bilinguals are required to switch languages during a divergent-thinking task (Storme et al., 2017). In addition to effects of exposure to multiple languages, research on societies' geopolitical situation, generally using data on creative output of societies over centuries, have shown that societies located near contrasting cultural centers, or at the crossroads of cultural exchange, tend to show higher creative output (Simonton, 1984). Data also show that societies characterized by political fragmentation (such as multiple political entities composing the society, multiple political parties) tend to have higher rates of professionally-related creative activity (Simonton, 1984; 1999). A historical ethno-psychological approach suggests that exposure to multiple sources of power is beneficial, allowing an expanded worldview, and less conformity pressure (see Therivel, 1995).

Some recent studies have focused directly on multicultural exposure showing benefits for creativity (Leung et al., 2008). For example, in one experimental study, people who saw simultaneously stimuli from two cultures (American and Chinese) wrote more creative stories than those exposed to stimuli from only one culture. These same participants, tested one week later, showed a continuing effect of the multicultural experience on creativity. In other studies, positive links were found between creative idea generation, using tasks such as generating unconventional gift ideas and a questionnaire of multicultural life experiences. Other research found that executives' foreign work experiences were predictive of the level of innovation of firms (Godart et al., 2015); in particular, the depth of the executives' multicultural experience – the amount of time that an individual spent in foreign countries – is the most predictive of firms' creativity.

In a series of studies with university students, participants who recalled multicultural experiences before completing a creativity task were more creative than those who recalled an experience within their own culture (Maddux, Adam, and Galinsky, 2010). In a different study, participants who reflected on the reasons behind the existence of cultural differences were also more creative (compared to a group that considered reasons explaining within-culture differences).

Two perspectives on why multicultural experiences and creativity are related can be distinguished. The first one – the spreading activation perspective (Mednick, 1962) – assumes that multicultural experiences lead to an expansion of connections in semantic networks that leads in turn to unconventional associations and greater originality in divergent thinking. The second perspective emphasizes the effect of multicultural experiences on cognitive functioning and conflict resolution skills (e.g., Leung and Chiu, 2010). According to this perspective, being exposed to multiple cultures fosters the ability to combine and integrate competing perspectives on the same object – an ability referred to as "integrative complexity" (Suedfeld, Tetlock, and Streufert, 1992), which is positively associated to creativity (e.g., Tadmor, Tetlock, and Peng, 2009). Empirical research supports this reasoning. For example, Çelik, Storme, and Forthmann (2016) found a positive relationship between the amount of value conflict – that is, the extent to which a social environment is characterized by disputes and debates between individuals about core values – in an individual's environment and his/her level of divergent thinking in highly diverse environments. This finding suggests that multicultural experiences benefit creativity when individuals engage actively in cultural confrontation.

Most research on multicultural experience concerns adult populations. In children, there is relatively little research to date on identity, migration, and acculturation processes relating to creativity. In a recent study, instead of the general positive correlation of multicultural experience and creativity, a contrasting result was found. Children's scientific creativity was impacted negatively if their parents or they themselves were born in another country than the one where they were going to school (de Vries and Lubart, 2019). Specifically, the originality and convergence of concepts of scientific creativity were significantly negatively related to the number of family members who were born in a foreign country. A study concerning young adolescents in Taiwan from mono- and bicultural families, on the other hand, found that children from bicultural families (children's mothers born in Taiwan) scored higher on divergent thinking in fluency, originality, and flexibility on a Chinese version of the Torrance test (Wu et al., 1999). According to the authors, there were, however, multiple factors involved, such as socioeconomic differences between the groups and interactive effects involving culture and personality (the trait of extraversion). This illustrates the need for greater understanding of the way that multiculturalism impacts creativity during childhood.

Technological Culture and Its Impact on Creativity

It is clear that, over the past few decades, advances in technology and science have greatly altered the world in which we live. Only thirty years ago, floppy disks, boom boxes, and visits to physical libraries and corporate meetings were all common practice. Today, having access to cloud storage, vast amounts of real-time information, virtual teams and meetings, and online libraries increase the realm of possibilities in a way that has become a new culture in itself. The COVID-19 pandemic has accelerated this trend. Yet the effects of technology on creativity have only just begun to be studied in fields including education and business. Enterprise mobile applications have been found to increase perceived job performance, which, in turn, increases perceived job creativity among employees, managers, and senior executives (Chung, Lee, and Choi, 2015). The way online teams collaborate and, more specifically, the different characteristics of their communication (frequency, decentralization, reactivity) influence the teams' creativity; notably their idea generation and product outcomes (Gaggioli et al., 2015; Karakaya and Demirkan, 2015).

Recent work has reflected on the current and future impact that technology has on creativity (Burkhardt and Lubart, 2010; Sporton, 2015; Zagalo and Branco, 2015; Glaveanu et al., 2019). For example, word-processing programs, compared with handwritten composition of literary texts, may dramatically influence the literary creative process. Playing computer games may develop certain skills (such as visual tracking ability and speed) and promote a reward system within the game that is a cultural model for longer-term motivations (see Green and Kaufman, 2015). There are several ways in which computers may impact creators' work, ranging from providing support (e.g., a helper that reminds people to take a break, check work for banality, etc.) to computers as full-fledged partners in the creative process, generating new content that a person may integrate or rework (Lubart, 2005).

The point here is the cultural impact of technological tools on the human creative process may be important. In this regard, virtual reality environments offer a new cultural space in which people act and eventually "create." Multiple-user virtual environments (MUVE), such as Second Life, provide rich virtual environments in which people represented by their avatars interact.[2] In some recent work, we examined the impact of these MUVE on creative performance and found effects of the "physical" attributes of these work spaces and the characteristics of the avatars, which may allow individuals to "escape" their traditional culturally determined roles and patterns of behavior (Ward and Sonneborn, 2009; Guegan, Nelson, and Lubart, 2017; Bourgeois et al., 2020).

CONCLUSION

Culture is omnipresent, and for this very reason, its impact is often underestimated. Culture provides the bedrock, the deep psychological structure in which all human activity occurs. For complex activities with social facets, such as creativity, the importance of understanding the influence of culture is particularly important. Culture influences both the production of "creative" work and its reception, recognition, and diffusion. Culture influences the who, what, and why of creativity; it influences the way that creativity is expressed and the degree to which it is expressed. In this chapter, we examined findings from two different approaches (sociocultural and cross-cultural) and several cultural contexts to illustrate the different ways in which culture shapes creativity. First, we argued that culture influences the definition and conceptual boundaries of creativity, although there is some evidence for similarities across cultures on key components of creativity. Second, we presented research on basic cultural dimensions on which societies vary and explored the implications for creativity. Third, we

---

[2] www.secondlife.com

discussed exposure to several cultures, multiculturalism, and of the use of technology, with research suggesting a positive impact on creativity, given the right circumstances.

Our Research Contribution

As an example of research on creativity and culture, we highlight a study of the structure of creative ability across cultures (Storme et al., 2017). Whether creativity is a general or a domain-specific ability is an important question in psychology. For example, if someone is able to invent creative stories, will he or she then also be able to make creative drawings, or do these two domains require a different form of creativity? From a methodological point of view, answering the question of the domain-specificity of creativity means looking at the correlations between performance in different tasks (e.g., verbal tasks vs. graphical tasks). The stronger the correlations between tasks, the more creativity can be considered as a general ability. In this research, our objective was to investigate whether the strength of the correlations between tasks depends on the cultural context in which one lives. We used the EPoC battery (Evaluation of Creative Potential; Lubart, Besanàçon, and Barbot, 2013) and the WKCT (Wallach and Kogan's (1965) Creative Thinking Test) to assess the verbal and graphic creative potential of children living in Paris and Hong Kong. In each location, there were monocultural children (i.e., French children living in Paris, Chinese children living in Hong Kong) and multicultural groups (i.e., French children living in Hong Kong, Chinese children living in Paris). Our findings revealed that the cultural context in which children live has an impact on the strength of the correlations between the different creativity tasks. For example, the two figural/graphical divergent thinking subtests (WKCT and EPoC) were significantly more strongly correlated among Chinese children living in France than among Chinese children living in China. This study has important methodological implications; it suggests that it is easier to generalize the results found in one creativity task to other creativity tasks in some cultural contexts more than in others. This illustrates some of the challenges of creativity assessment, especially when used to compare cultures.

Critical/Creative Thinking Questions

1. Is every creative act culturally bound?
2. How does the meaning of "being creative" vary across cultures?
3. Are some cultures more creative than others?
4. Generate several hypotheses about the impact of a technologically rich culture on creativity.

5. Indicate three potential biases in cross-cultural research on creativity that limit the conclusions about multicultural exposure as a source of stimulation for creative thinking.

GLOSSARY

creative process: The sequence of actions, including mental events, that lead to an original, meaningful production.

creativity: The ability to generate original productions that are meaningful in their context.

culture: "An historically transmitted pattern of meanings visible and tangible in symbols. A system of conception is inherited and expressed in symbolic forms" (Geertz, 1973, p. 89); a system of "shared motives, values, beliefs, identities, and interpretations or meanings of significant events that result from common experiences of members of collectives and are transmitted across age generations" (House and Javidan, 2004).

cultural dimension: A continuum on which cultures can be compared.

historiometric approach: The application of statistical quantitative analyses to historical data.

individualism-collectivism: The degree of integration of social groups within a society and their level of interdependence. In individualistic societies, individuals tend to be independent and achieving personal goals is encouraged. In collectivist societies, there is a strong sense of interdependence and collective interests are prioritized over individual goals.

indulgence versus restraint: A society's level of control toward the fulfillment of desires and impulses. Indulgence reflects the encouragement of free gratification and the pursuit of fun activities. Restraint depicts the suppression of gratification through norms and regulations.

long-term versus short-term orientation: A society's inclination to conceive short- or long-term goals and decisions, influenced by the past or the future. Long-term orientation reflects a culture's value of norms and traditions and inclination to strive for long-term growth and success based on past experiences. Short-term orientation highlights the value of change, and short-term actions based on the possibility of future success.

masculinity-femininity: Oftentimes referred to as "tough vs. tender" culture, refers to a preference for assertive-related behavior compared to more neutral and "tender" behaviors. Masculine cultures are inclined to value assertiveness, achievement, and competition. Feminine cultures are said to value consensus seeking, cooperation, modesty, and quality of life.

power distance: The degree of power distribution and inequality that is tolerated. National cultures with a high power distance tolerate differences in power and the existence of hierarchy. Low power distance cultures favor equal distribution of power among individuals and decentralized structures.

uncertainty avoidance: A culture's tolerance of uncertainty and ambiguity. High uncertainty avoidance reflects low tolerance for risk taking, uncertainty, and ambiguity. Low uncertainty avoidance indicates high tolerance for risk taking, uncertain, and ambiguous behavior.

REFERENCES

Amabile, T. M. (1982). The Social Psychology of Creativity: A Consensual Assessment Technique. *Journal of Personality and Social Psychology, 43*, 997–1013.

Anoumou, C.-R., Lubart, T., and Bourgeois-Bougrine, S. (2019). Teachers' Perceptions of Creativity: Implicit Conceptions of Creativity in West Africa. *International Journal of Creativity and Problem Solving*, *29*(2), 17–32.

Bakhtin, M. (1929/1984). *Problems in Dostoevsky's Poetics*. Edited and translated by Caryl Emerson. Minnesota: University of Minnesota Press.

Barron, F., and Harrington, D. (1981). Creativity, Intelligence, and Personality. *Annual Review of Psychology*, *32*, 439–476.

Basadur, M., Pringle, P., and Kirkland, D. (2002). Crossing Cultures: Training Effects on the Divergent Thinking Attitudes of Spanish-Speaking South American Managers. *Creativity Research Journal*, *14*(3–4), 395–408.

Bourgeois-Bougrine, S., Richard, P., Burkhardt, J. M., Frantz, B., and Lubart, T. (2020). The Expression of Users' Creative Potential in Virtual and Real Environments: An Exploratory Study. *Creativity Research Journal*, *32*(1), 55–65.

Burkhardt, J.-M., and Lubart, T. (2010). Creativity in the Age of Emerging Technology. *Creativity and Innovation Management*, *19*, 160–166.

Çelik, P., Storme, M., and Forthmann, B. (2016). A New Perspective on the Link between Multiculturalism and Creativity: The Relationship between Core Value Diversity and Divergent Thinking. *Learning and Individual Differences*, *52*, 188–196.

Chan, S. K.-C., Bond, M. H., Spencer-Oatey, H. and Rojo-Laurilla, M. (2004). Culture and Rapport Promotion in Service Encounters: Protecting the Ties That Bind. *Journal of Asian Pacific Communication*, 14 (2), 245–60.

Chang, J. H., Hsu, C. C., Shih, N. H., and Chen, H. C. (2014). Multicultural Families and Creative Children. *Journal of Cross-Cultural Psychology*, *45*(8), 1288–1296.

Chen, C., Kasof, J. Himsel, A. J., Greenberger, E., Dong, Q., and Xue, G. (2002). Creativity in Drawings of Geometric Shapes: A Cross-Cultural Examination with the Consensual Assessment Technique. *Journal of Cross-Cultural Psychology*, *33*, 171–187.

Cheung, F. M., van de Vijver, F. J., and Leong, F. T. (2011). Toward a New Approach to the Study of Personality in Culture. *American Psychologist*, *66*(7), 593.

Chomsky, N. (1972). *Language and Mind*, 2nd ed. New York: Harcourt Brace Jovanovich.

Chua, R. Y., Roth, Y., and Lemoine, J. F. (2015). The Impact of Culture on Creativity: How Cultural Tightness and Cultural Distance Affect Global Innovation Crowdsourcing Work. *Administrative Science Quarterly*, *60*(2), 189–227.

Cohen, A., and Erlich, S. (2015). Individual Values, Psychological Contracts, and Innovative Work Behavior: A Comparison between Employees from Israel and India. *Business Creativity and the Creative Economy*, *1*(1), 61–80.

Cole, M., and Wertsch, J. V. (1996). Beyond the Individual-Social Antinomy in Discussions of Piaget and Vygotsky. *Human development*, *39*(5), 250–256.

Colligan, J. (1983). Musical Creativity and Social Rules in Four Cultures. *Creative Child and Adult Quarterly*, *8*(1), 39–47

Cropley, D. H., Cropley, A. J., Kaufman, J. C., and Runco, M. A. (Eds.). (2010). *The Dark Side of Creativity*. Cambridge: Cambridge University Press.

Csikszentmihalyi, M. (1988). Society, Culture, and Person: A Systems View of Creativity. In R. Sternberg (Ed.), *The Nature of Creativity: Contemporary Psychological Perspectives* (pp. 325–339). Cambridge: Cambridge University Press.

D'Agostino, F. (1984). Chomsky on Creativity. *Synthese*, *58*, 85–117.

de Vries, H., Lubart, T. (2019). Scientific Creativity: Divergent and Convergent Thinking and the Impact of Culture. *Journal of Creative Behavior*. *53*(2), 145–155.

Dewey, J. (1934). *Art As Experience*. New York: Penguin.

Dijksterhuis, A., and Meurs, T. (2006). Where Creativity Resides: The Generative Power of Unconscious Thought. *Consciousness and Cognition*, *15*(1), 135–146.

Gacheru, M., Opiyo, M., Smutny, J. F. (1999). Children's Creative Thinking in Kenya. *Childhood Education*, *75*(6), 346–349.

Gaggioli, A., Mazzoni, E., Milani, L., and Riva, G. (2015). The Creative Link: Investigating the Relationship between Social Network Indices, Creative Performance and Flow in Blended Teams. *Computers in Human Behavior*, *42*, 157–166. doi:10.1016/j.chb.2013.12.003.

Geertz, C. (1973). *The Interpretation of Cultures*. New York: Basic Books.

Gelfand, M. J., Raver, J. L., Nishii, L., Leslie, L. M., Lun, J., Lim, B. C., and Aycan, Z. (2011). Differences between Tight and Loose Cultures: A 33-Nation Study. *Science*, *332*(6033), 1100–1104.

Glăveanu, V. P. (2013a). Creativity and Folk Art: A Study of Creative Action in Traditional Craft. *Psychology of Aesthetics, Creativity, and the Arts*, *7*(2), 140–154.

(2013b). Rewriting the Language of Creativity: The Five A's Framework. *Review of General Psychology*, *17*(1), 69–81.

(2014). *Thinking through Creativity and Culture: An Integrated Model*. New Brunswick: Transaction Publishers.

(2015). On Units of Analysis and Creativity Theory: Towards a 'Molecular' Perspective. *Journal for the Theory of Social Behaviour*, *45*(3), 311–330.

(Ed.) (2016). *The Palgrave Handbook of Creativity and Culture Research*. London: Palgrave.

Glăveanu, V. P., Gillespie, A., and Valsiner, J. (Eds.). (2015). *Rethinking Creativity: Perspectives from Cultural Psychology*. London: Routledge.

Glăveanu, V. P., and Lubart, T. (2014). Decentring the Creative Self: How Others Make Creativity Possible in Creative Professional Fields. *Creativity and Innovation Management*, *23*(1), 29–43.

Glăveanu, V. P., Ness, I. J., Wasson, B., and Lubart, T. (2019). Sociocultural Perspectives on Creativity, Learning, and Technology. In C. A. Mullen (Ed.), *Creativity under Duress in Education?* (pp. 63–82). Cham: Springer.

Godart, F. C., Maddux, W. W., Shipilov, A. V., and Galinsky, A. D. (2015). Fashion with a Foreign Flair: Professional Experiences Abroad Facilitate the Creative Innovations of Organizations. *Academy of Management Journal*, *58*(1), 195–220.

Green, G. P., and Kaufman, J. C. (Eds.) (2015). *Video Games and Creativity*. New York: Elsevier.

Gruber, H. (2005). The Creative Person As a Whole: The Evolving Systems Approach to the Study of Creative Work. In E. Gruber and K. Bödeker (Eds.), *Creativity, Psychology and the History of Science* (pp. 35–104). Dordrecht: Springer.

Guegan, J., Nelson, J., and Lubart, T. (2017). The Relationship Between Contextual Cues in Virtual Environments and Creative Processes. *Cyberpsychology, Behavior, and Social Networking*, *20*(3), 202–206. doi.org/10.1089/cyber.2016.0503.

Guilford, J. P. (1950). Creativity. *American Psychologist*, *5*, 444–454.

Güss, C. D., Tuason, M. T., Göltenboth, N., and Mironova, A. (2017). Creativity Through the Eyes of Professional Artists in Cuba, Germany, and Russia. *Journal of Cross-Cultural Psychology*. doi:0022022117730817.

Hofstede, G. (1980) *Culture's Consequences: International Differences in Work-Related Values*. Beverly Hills: Sage.

(2001). *Culture's Consequences: Comparing Values, Behaviors, Institutions and Organizations across Nations*. Thousand Oaks: Sage.

(2011). Dimensionalizing Cultures: The Hofstede Model in Context. *Online Readings in Psychology and Culture*, *2*(1), 8.

Hofstede, G., and Jan, H. G. (1991). *Cultures and Organizations: Software of the Mind.* London: McGaw-Hill.

House, R. J., Hanges, P. J., Javidan, M., Dorfman, P. W., and Gupta, V. (Eds.). (2004). *Culture, Leadership and Organizations: The GLOBE Study of 62 Societies.* Thousand Oaks: Sage.

House, R. J., and Javidan, M. (2004). Overview of GLOBE. In R. J. House, P. J. Hanges, M. Javian, P. Dorfman, and V. Gupta (Eds.), *Leadership, Culture and Organizations: The GLOBE Study of 62 Societies* (pp. 9–28). Thousand Oaks: Sage

Jahoda, G. (1993). *Crossroads between Culture and Mind: Continuities and Change in Theories of Human Nature.* Cambridge, MA: Harvard University Press.

Karakaya, A. F., and Demirkan, H. (2015). Collaborative Digital Environments to Enhance the Creativity of Designers. *Computers in Human Behavior*, *42*, 176–186. doi:10.1016/j. chb.2014.03.029.

Karwowski, M., and Kaufman, J. C. (2017). *The Creative Self: Effect of Beliefs, Self-Efficacy, Mindset, and Identity.* San Diego: Elsevier Academic Press.

Kaufman, J. C., and Baer, J. (2004). The Amusement Park Theoretical (APT) Model of Creativity. *The International Journal of Creativity and Problem Solving*, *14*(2), 15–25.

Kaufman, J. C., and Beghetto, R. A. (2013). Do People Recognize the Four Cs? Examining Layperson Conceptions of Creativity. *Psychology of Aesthetics, Creativity, and the Arts*, *7*(3), 229–236.

Kaufman, J. C., and Sternberg, R. J. (2006). *The International Handbook of Creativity.* New York: Cambridge University Press.

Khaleeefa, O. H., Erdos, G., and Ashria, I. H. (1996). Creativity in an Indigenous Afro-Arab Islamic Culture: The Case of Sudan. *Journal of Creative Behavior*, *30*, 268–283.

Kharkhurin, A. V. (2008). The Effects of Linguistic Proficiency, Age of Second Language Acquisition, and Length of Exposure to a New Cultural Environment on Bilinguals' Divergent Thinking. *Bilingualism: Language and Cognition. 11*(2), 225–243.

(2009). The Role of Bilingualism in Creative Performance on Divergent Thinking and Invented Aliens Creativity Tests. *Journal of Creative Behavior*, *43*(1), 59–71.

(2010). Sociocultural Differences in the Relationship between Bilingualism and Creative Potential. *Journal of Cross-Cultural Psychology*, *41*(5–6), 776–783. doi:10.1177/0022022110361777.

Kharkhurin, A. V., and Altarriba, J. (2016). The Effect of Mood Induction and Language of Testing on Bilingual Creativity. *Bilingualism: Language and Cognition*, *19*(5), 1079–1094. doi:10.1017/S1366728915000528.

Kharkhurin, A. V., and Motalleebi, S. N. S. (2008). The Impact of Culture on the Creative Potential of American, Russian an Iranian College Students. *Creativity Research Journal*, *20*(4), 404–411.

Kharkhurin, A. V., and Wei, L. (2015). The Role of Code-Switching in Bilingual Creativity. *International Journal of Bilingual Education and Bilingualism*, *18*(2), 153–169.

Kim, K. H. (2007). Exploring the Interactions between Asian Culture (Confucianism) and Creativity. *Journal of Creative Behavior*, *41*(1), 28–53.

Lambert, W. E. (1981). Bilingualism and Language Acquisition. *Annals of the New York Academy of Sciences*, *379*(1), 9–22.

Leung, A. K., and Chiu, C.-Y. (2010). Multicultural Experience, Idea Receptiveness, and Creativity. *Journal of Cross-Cultural Psychology*, 41, 723–741.

Leung, A. K., Maddux, W. W., Galinsky, A. D., and Chiu, C. (2008). Multicultural Experience Enhances Creativity. *American Psychologist*, *63*(3), 169–181.

Li, J. (1997). Creativity in Horizontal and Vertical Domains. *Creativity Research Journal, 10*(2–3), 107–132.

Lubart, T. I. (1990). Creativity and Cross-Cultural Variation, *International Journal of Psychology, 25* (1), 39–59.

(1999). Creativity across Cultures. In R. J. Sternberg (Ed.) *The Cambridge Handbook of Creativity* (pp. 339–350). New York: Cambridge University Press.

(2005). How Can Computers Be Partners in the Creative Process? *International Journal of Human Computer Studies, 63*(4–5), 366–369.

Lubart, T., Besançon, M., and Barbot, B. (2013). *Evaluation du Potentiel Créatif (EPoC) [Evaluation of Potential for Creativity]*, Paris: Hogrefe.

Lubart, T., Zenasni, F., and Barbot, B. (2013). Creative Potential and Its Measurement. *International Journal of Talent Development and Creativity, 1*(2), 41–51.

Ludwig, A. M. (1992). Culture and Creativity. *American Journal of Psychotherapy, 46*(3), 454–469.

Maddux, W. W., Adam, H., and Galinsky, A. D. (2010). When in Rome . . . Learn Why the Romans Do What They Do: How Multicultural Learning Experiences Facilitate Creativity. *Personality and Social Psychology Bulletin, 36*(6), 731–741. doi:10.1177/0146167210367786.

Mednick, S. (1962). The Associative Basis of the Creative Process. *Psychological Review, 69*(3), 220–232.

Montuori, A., and Purser, R. E. (1995). Deconstructing the Lone Genius Myth: Toward a Contextual View of Creativity. *Journal of Humanistic Psychology, 35*(3), 69–111.

Mpofu, E., Myambo, K., Mogaji, A. A., Mashego, T.-A., and Khaleefa, O. H. (2006). African Perspectives on Creativity. In J. C. Kaufman and R. J. Sternberg (Eds.), *The International Handbook of Creativity* (pp. 456–489). New York: Cambridge University Press.

Niu, W. (2019). Eastern–Western Views of Creativity. J. Kaufman and R. J. Sternberg (Eds.), *The Cambridge Handbook of Creativity*, 448–461, New York: Cambridge University Press.

Niu, W., and Kaufman, J. C. (2005) Creativity in Troubled Times: Factors Associated with Recognitions of Chinese Literary Creativity in the 20th Century. *Journal of Creative Behavior, 39*(1), 57–67.

Niu, W., and Sternberg, R. J. (2001). Cultural Influences on Artistic Creativity and Its Evaluation. *International Journal of Psychology, 36*(4), 225–241.

(2002). Contemporary Studies on the Concept of Creativity: The East and the West. *Journal of Creative Behavior, 36*, 269–288.

(2003). Societal and School Influence on Students' Creativity. *Psychology in the Schools, 40*, 103–114.

(2006). The Philosophical Roots of Western and Eastern Conceptions of Creativity. *Journal of Theoretical and Philosophical Psychology, 26*(1–2), 18.

Ng, A. K. (2001). *Why Asians Are Less Creative Than Westerners*. Singapore: Pearson Education.

(2003). A Cultural Model of Creative and Conforming Behavior. *Creativity Research Journal, 15* (2–3), 223–233.

Oral, G. (2006). Creativity in Turkey and Turkish-Speaking Countries. In J. C. Kaufman and R. J. Sternberg (Eds.), *The International Handbook of Creativity* (pp. 337–373). New York: Cambridge University Press.

Paletz, S. B. F., and Peng, K. (2008). Implicit Theories of Creativity across Cultures: Novelty and Appropriateness in Two Product Domains. *Journal of Cross-Cultural Psychology, 39*(3), 286–302.

Puccio, G., and Chimento, M. D. (2001). Implicit Theories of Creativity: Laypersons' Perceptions of the Creativity of Adaptors and Innovators. *Perceptual and Motor Skills, 92*, 675–681.

Rank, J., Pace, V. L., and Frese, M. (2004). Three Avenues for Future Research on Creativity, Innovation, and Initiative. *Applied Psychology: An International Review*, *53*(4), 518–528.

Ricciardelli, L. A. (1992). Creativity and Bilingualism. *Journal of Creative Behavior*, *26*, 242–254.

Rinne, T., Steel, G. D., and Fairweather, J. (2012). Hofstede and Shane Revisited: The Role of Power Distance and Individualism in National-Level Innovation Success. *Cross-Cultural Research*, *46*(2), 91–108.

Rostan, S. M., Pariser, D., and Gruber, H. E. (2002). A Cross-Cultural Study of the Development of Artistic Talent, Creativity and Giftedness. *High Ability Studies*, *13*(2), 125–155.

Rudowicz, E. (2003). Creativity and Culture: A Two-Way Interaction. *Scandinavian Journal of Educational Research*, *47*(3), 273–290.

Rudowicz, E., and Hui, A. (1998). Hong Kong People's Views of Creativity. *Gifted Education International*, *13*(2), 159–174.

Saad, C. S., Damian, R. I., Benet-Martínez, V., Moons, W. G., and Robins, R. W. (2013). Multiculturalism and Creativity: Effects of Cultural Context, Bicultural Identity, and Ideational Fluency. *Social Psychological and Personality Science*, *4*(3), 369–375. doi:10.1177/1948550612456560.

Saeki, N., Fan, X., and Dusen, L. (2001). A Comparative Study of Creative Thinking of American and Japanese College Students. *The Journal of Creative Behavior*, *35*(1), 24–36.

Sawyer, R. K. (2006). *Explaining Creativity: The Science of Human Innovation*. New York: Oxford University Press.

Schwartz, S. H. (1994). Are There Universal Aspects in the Structure and Contents of Human Values? *Journal of Social Issues*, *50*(4), 19–45.

(1999). A Theory of Cultural Values and Some Implications for Work. *Applied Psychology*, *48*, 23–47.

Shane, S. (1992). Why Do Some Societies Invent More Than Others? *Journal of Business Venturing*, *7*(1), 29–47.

(1993). Cultural Influences on National Rates of Innovation. *Journal of Business Venturing*, *8*(1), 59–73.

Shane, S., Venkataraman, S., and MacMillan, I. (1995). Cultural Differences in Innovation Championing Strategies. *Journal of Management*, *21*(5), 931–952.

Shostak, M. (1993). The Creative Individual in the World of the !Kung San. In S. Lavie, K. Narrayan, and R. Ronaldo (Eds.), *Creativity/Anthropology* (pp. 54–69). Ithaca: Cornell University Press.

Simonton, D. K. (1975). Sociocultural Context of Individual Creativity: A Transhistorical Time-Series Analysis. *Journal of Personality and Social Psychology*, *32*(6), 1119–1133.

(1984). *Genius, Creativity and Leadership*. Cambridge, MA: Harvard University Press.

(1999). Creativity from a Historiometric Perspective. In R. J. Sternberg (Ed.), *The Cambridge Handbook of Creativity*. (pp. 116–133). New York: Cambridge University Press.

(2008). Bilingualism and Creativity. In J. Altarriba and R. R. Heredia (Eds.), *An Introduction to Bilingualism: Principles and Processes* (pp. 147–166). Mahwah: Lawrence Erlbaum Associates.

(2019). The Sociocultural Context of Exceptional Creativity: Historiometric Studies. In I. Lebuda and V. P. Glăveanu (Eds.), *The Palgrave Handbook of Social Creativity Research* (pp. 177–189). New York: Palgrave Macmillan.

Soveri, A., Rodriguez-Fornells, A., and Laine, M. (2011). Is There a Relationship between Language Switching and Executive Functions in Bilingualism? Introducing a Within-Group Analysis Approach. *Frontiers in Psychology*, *138*, 1–8.

Sporton, G. (2015). *Digital Creativity: Something from Nothing*. New York: Palgrave Macmillan.

Storme, M., Celik, P., Camargo, A., Forthmann, B., Holling, H., and Lubart, T. (2017). The Effect of Forced Language Switching during Divergent Thinking: A Study on Bilinguals' Originality of Ideas. *Frontiers in Psychology*, *8*, 2086.

Storme, M., Lubart, T., Myszkowski, N., Cheung, P. C., Tong, T., and Lau, S. (2017). A Cross-Cultural Study of Task Specificity in Creativity. *The Journal of Creative Behavior*, *51*(3), 263–274.

Suedfeld, P., Tetlock, P. E., and Streufert, S. (1992). *Conceptual/Integrative Complexity* (pp. 393–400). New York: Cambridge University Press.

Tadmor, C. T., Tetlock, P. E., and Peng, K. (2009). Acculturation Strategies and Integrative Complexity the Cognitive Implications of Biculturalism. *Journal of Cross-Cultural Psychology*, 40(1), 105–139.

Taras, V., Kirkman, B. L., and Steel, P. (2010). Examining the Impact of Culture's Consequences: A Three-Decade, Multilevel, Meta-Analytic Review of Hofstede's Cultural Value Dimensions. *Journal of Applied Psychology*, *95*(3), 405–439.

Therivel, W. A. (1995). Long-Term Effect of Power on Creativity. *Creativity Research Journal*, *8*(2), 173–192.

Triandis, H. T. (1994). *Culture and Social Behaviour*. New York: McGraw-Hill.

Triandis, H. C. (2007). *Culture and Psychology: A History of the Study of Their Relationship*. New York: Guilford Press.

Torrance, E. P. (1974). *Torrance Tests of Creativity Thinking*. Lexington: Personnel Press.

Wu, C.-C., Chen, F.-Y., Kuo, C.-H., Lin, W.-W., Liu, S.-H., and Chen, Y.-H. (1999). *The Newly Developed Creative Thinking Test: A Research Report for the Ministry of Education's Six-Year Student Counseling Program*. Taipei: Foundation for Scholarly Exchange.

Valsiner, J. (2014). *An Invitation to Cultural Psychology*. London: Sage.

Van Everdingen, Y. M., and Waarts, E. (2003). The Effect of National Culture on the Adoption of Innovations. *Marketing Letters*, *14*(3), 217–232.

Vygotsky, L. S. (1930/1998). Imagination and Creativity in Childhood. *Soviet Psychology*, *28*(10), 84–96.

Wallach, M. A., and Kogan, N. (1965). *Modes of Thinking in Young Children*. Oxford: Holt, Rinehart & Winston.

Ward, T. B., and Sonneborn, M. S. (2009).Creative Expression in Virtual Worlds: Imitation, Imagination, and Individualized Collaboration. *Psychology of Aesthetics, Creativity, and the Arts*, *3*(4), 211–221.

Westwood, R., and Low, D. R. (2003). The Multicultural Muse: Culture, Creativity and Innovation. *International Journal of Cross Cultural Management*, *3*(2), 235–259.

Wursten, H., and Jacobs, C. (2013). *The Impact of Culture on Education*. Helsinki: The Hofstede Centre, Itim International.

Zagalo, N., and Branco, P. (Eds.). (2015). *Creativity in the Digital Age*. London: Springer-Verlag.

9 Personality, Emotions, and Creativity

JESSICA HOFFMANN, ZORANA IVCEVIC, AND GREGORY FEIST

INTRODUCTION

Emotions are fuel for creativity: from inspiration to do something creative, to determination for follow-through, and enjoyment of the finished product. Moreover, if emotions are fuel for creativity, we will demonstrate how certain personality traits, such as **openness to experience**, are akin to turbocharging the engine, lowering the threshold for creative thought and creative behavior. Emotion-related personality traits – tolerance of ambiguities and risks inherent in doing something new – are at the core of one's willingness to make the decision to do something creative. Steve Jobs, for example, was famously willing to go on with plans for the iPad in spite of popular wisdom that people would not be interested in the device (Buchanan, 2013). Finally, we will propose that people need not be at the mercy of their personality nor emotional state, but rather can channel their personal experience into creativity through their ability to recognize, understand, and regulate emotions effectively.

We organize this chapter into three major sections, beginning with the intersection of personality and creativity, then we discuss the role of emotion states during creative acts, and conclude with the role of a person's emotion skills in helping transform creative potential into creative achievement. Throughout, we will reference **personality traits** (unique ways of thinking, feeling, and acting, relatively stable through time and across situations), **emotions** (a person's immediate physiological and psychological response to a thought or event), **feelings** (the subjective experience of an emotion), **moods** (a more generalized mental state that tends to be less intense and more diffuse than an emotion), and **affect** (another word for feeling, defined by two dimensions: **valence** – how pleasant or unpleasant the feeling is, and **arousal** – the energy or activation level experienced in the body). We have provided the definitions here; however, the distinctions among these terms is not rigid and scientists often times use them flexibly (e.g., the distinction between emotion and mood can be blurry and these terms are at times used interchangeably).

The Creative Personality

The topic of the creative personality has a long history. Almost every major personality theorist of the twentieth century developed a theory of the creative person, from Sigmund Freud to Carl Rogers, Abraham Maslow, and even B. F. Skinner. Modern research on the

The work on this chapter was funded in part through a collaboration with the Botin Foundation, Santander, Spain (*Emotions, Creativity and the Arts* grant; Principal investigators: Zorana Ivcevic and Marc Brackett).

creative person began in earnest in 1950 with J. P. Guilford's (1950) American Psychological Association (APA) presidential address and the establishment of the University of California's Institute of Personality Assessment and Research (IPAR) under the direction of Donald MacKinnon. Other IPAR researchers included Frank Barron, Harrison Gough, Ravenna Helson, Richard Crutchfield, and Wallace Hall. Often using extensive, "live-in" assessments, researchers studied the personalities of creative scientists, writers, architects, mathematicians, and graduate students over the course of three days of intensive testing in their laboratories.

In 2010, Gregory Feist put forth the **functional model of creative personality,** which states that personality traits, such as openness to experience, can increase a person's likelihood for creative thought and creative behavior. The model describes the manner by which our genetics influence how our brains are structured and how they function, which in turn affects our personality traits, and these traits affect various aspects of creativity. It is possible to distinguish four kinds of personality traits, depending on their function – how we typically think (**cognitive traits**), how we interact with others (**social traits**), how we typically feel and what motivates us (**motivational-affective traits**), and traits related to mental health (clinical traits). These personality traits in turn impact our tendency toward thinking and behaving creatively; specifically, personality traits predict what type of work people choose and how creative they aspire or are willing to be, how often they work on something creative, how creative is their work, and how much they achieve in the creative work. We will go through each layer of the model in more detail below.

Evolutionary and Genetic Influences on Creativity and Personality

Creativity is one of the trademark traits, if not the trademark trait, of the human species, but why? Darwin and Wallace's theory of natural selection states that traits that serve some adaptive purpose for survival get selected over generations and become more common in a species, or even create a new species (Darwin and Wallace, 1858). Could this be the case for tendencies toward creative thought and creative behavior? Less well known is another idea by Darwin called sexual selection, which posits that members of the same sex compete for mating opportunities and the opposite sex finds certain competitively successful traits and qualities to be attractive. Over generations, these attractive traits also become more common and characteristic of a species. Geoffrey Miller (2000), for instance, put forth the most comprehensive theory describing how sexual-selection processes are behind the evolution of human creativity. Research supports that wit, intelligence, charm, and creativity are attractive qualities in a potential mate. Feist (2001), however, argued for a finer distinction: Natural selection pressures have shaped applied forms of creativity (technology, science, engineering), whereas sexual selection pressures have shaped ornamental forms of creativity (art, music, dance, writing). Research evidence is consistent with this theory, with ornamental-aesthetic creative behaviors rated as more sexually appealing than applied-technical creative behaviors (Kaufman et al., 2016a), and findings showing that successful male creative artists have more sexual partners than less successful ones (Clegg, Miell, and Nettle, 2011).

Twin and adoption research has also been used to look at how much of creative behavior can be attributed to genetics. By comparing the creative achievement between monozygotic twins (identical) who share 100 percent of the same DNA, and dizygotic (fraternal) twins who share 50 percent of the same DNA just like any other sibling pairs, and by comparing the creative achievement of adopted children compared to biological children in the same home, researchers can tease apart the role of genetics from environmental factors in creativity. Such studies have concluded that creative achievement has a sizable genetic component (Nichols, 1978; Hur, Jeong, and Piffer, 2014; Piffer and Hur, 2014; Velázquez, Segal, and Horowitz, 2015; Barbot and Eff, 2019).

Brain Structures and Processes

There is no single brain region where creativity occurs, as many different processes are at play during creativity. **Idea generation**, or the act of producing many solutions to a given problem, involves wider, defocused thinking that allows for broad scanning of knowledge and memories. In contrast, **idea evaluation**, or the act of judging the value of ideas, involves cognitive control, focused attention, and critical thinking. Research suggests that the brain structures and pathways associated with idea generation and idea evaluation are distinct (Martindale, 1999; Jung et al., 2013; Chen et al., 2014) and that different personality traits are associated with each of the two processes (Fürst, Ghisletta, and Lubart, 2016).

There is research that connects brain activity, personality, and creativity. For instance, research into the association between cortical arousal, extraversion, and creative thought shows that extraverted people who produced highly original ideas while solving a creative idea generation task showed the lowest levels of cortical arousal, compared with introverted individuals, who produced less original ideas (Fink and Neubauer, 2008). Moreover, in two separate studies, Beaty et al. (2014) found that the more efficient the brain's default mode network was (i.e., a set of interacting brain regions active when the brain is at wakeful rest, such as during daydreaming or mind-wandering), the higher the person's personality trait of openness to experience, thus showing an important biological component to openness to experience.

Cognitive Personality Traits

Cognitive personality traits refer to how people typically process information, solve problems, and respond to new situations. Chief among the cognitive personality traits related to creativity is openness to experience, the disposition to explore, be curious, and enjoy novel experiences (Ivcevic and Mayer, 2009; Martinsen, 2011; Kaufman, 2013; Chang et al., 2014; Agnoli et al., 2015; Ivcevic and Brackett, 2015; Chen, 2016; Karwowski and Lebuda, 2016; Kaufman et al., 2016b; Tan et al., 2016). Open people tend to be more imaginative and curious and consequently more creative (Feist, 1998). And yet, even this relationship between openness and creativity is a complex one. Openness to experiences has two major components: openness and intellect. Research shows that the openness component is strongly associated with artistic creativity, while the intellect component is most strongly associated with scientific creativity (Kaufman et al., 2016b).

One cognitive trait narrower than openness to experiences that is a hallmark of creative thought and achievement is **cognitive flexibility.** This trait involves fluidly switching and moving between different categories or ideas or coming up with many distinct categories of ideas. It can be viewed both as a cognitive ability and a personality trait related to openness to experiences. After intensive observations of creative individuals in many domains of work, Frank Barron (1963) wrote that creative people can flexibly switch between many cognitive and personality states due to their greater "ego-strength." More recent experimental research supports this view as well, demonstrating that creative idea generation is associated both with controlled and flexible thinking (Zabelina and Robinson, 2010; Baas et al., 2013).

Social Personality Traits

The behaviors and attitudes that concern one's relationships with other people, such as questioning what authority figures say (**nonconformity**), being comfortable around strangers and large groups of people (**extraversion**), being warm and accommodating toward others (**agreeableness**), and believing one is better or worse than others (dominance, confidence, and arrogance), are largely referred to as **social personality traits.** After openness to experience, one component of extraversion (confidence-assertiveness) is the personality trait with the strongest association to creativity (Feist, 1998). However, the other component of extraversion (sociability-gregariousness) is generally not related to creativity. In fact, there is evidence that in some creative domains (e.g., science, literature, art, poetry, and musical composition), creative people are more introverted and socially withdrawn than sociable and outgoing (Feist, 1999). Agreeableness is also generally not related to creativity, though nonconformity is one component of low agreeableness.

Creativity, at its core, involves defiance, either of oneself, the crowd, or the Zeitgeist (Sternberg, 2018), and risk-taking is an essential component of defiance (Urban, 2003; Amabile and Pratt, 2016; Sternberg, 2018). In particular, social or reputational risk is present whenever a person makes an unconventional choice (from selecting an unusual hairstyle to proposing an alternative theory in astrophysics). Diverging from conventional ideas or behaviors is associated with uncertainty as people consider possible negative social consequences of being different. People have to weigh whether it is worth doing something creative or if the risk of negative reactions (ridicule, anger) by teachers, mentors, or colleagues is too great. Pfeffer and Sutton (2000) identified fear about one's status as the basis for the "knowledge-doing gap" in organizations; low social risk-taking inhibits sharing new and original ideas and implementing innovations.

Motivational-Affective Personality Traits

Motivational-affective traits energize our behavior; they refer to a person's desire to persist and be successful in activities. Terms that describe a person's motivational traits include descriptors such as persistent, driven, ambitious, and impulsive. Indeed, research shows that many creative artists, businesspeople, and scientists are driven, ambitious, and persistent (Amabile, 1996; Batey and Furnham, 2006; Ceci and Kumar, 2016). If those who have a desire to produce works that leave a mark on the world are to succeed, they also need to be driven, focused, and ambitious. They are not the kind of people who give up easily in the face of hindrances and roadblocks.

Engaging in a creative activity because of the pleasure and challenge that it poses is known as **intrinsic motivation** (e.g., Amabile, 1996). Intrinsic motivation predicts how often people work on creative activities and how creative their work is; for example, the number of hours per week art students work on their art, how many artworks they make, and their commitment to art and potential as an artist, as rated by their instructor (Amabile et al., 1994). With well-known creators, studies show that enjoyment is a driver of their persistence to continue creating (Csikszentmihalyi, 1996), and studies of those working in research and development suggest that intrinsic motivation may come from (in part) their supervisor's support for creativity and their own belief that they are capable of success. Intrinsic motivation in turn predicts willingness to take risks and predicts supervisor ratings of employees' creativity at work (Dewett, 2007).

Beyond intrinsic motivation, **passion** indicates a strong emotional desire and commitment to an activity that is important to one's identity (Fredricks, Alfeld, and Eccles, 2010; Cardon et al., 2013; Moeller et al., 2017). The person's passion can be described as what they desire to do, commit to doing, and persist in doing. In studies of adolescents, many of the activities about which students reported feeling passionate were creative in nature (music, drama, art; Fredricks et al., 2010; Moeller et al., 2017). In a study of experienced entrepreneurs, passion predicted not only creativity, but persistence (Cardon et al., 2013).

Clinical Traits

Personality traits that are associated with vulnerabilities for mental disorders can be considered clinical traits, even though by themselves they do not offer clinical diagnoses (Bienvenu et al., 2004; Zimbarg et al., 2016). Trait hypomania, for example, is a clinical trait characterized by very high energy levels and a tendency to have many and racing ideas. Similar to trait levels of positive affect, trait hypomania can broaden one's thinking, which under some circumstances can lead to more creative thought by making people more willing to take risks and by coming up with unusual thoughts or associations (Fredrickson, 2001; Lloyd-Evans, Batey, and Furnham, 2006; Feist, 2012; Rogaten and Moneta, 2015). Trait hypomania is related to one component of creative thinking, namely, idea-generation, as well as self-perceptions of creativity, engagement in creative activities, and high creative achievement (Eckblad and Chapman, 1986; Schuldberg, 1990; Furnham et al., 2008; von

Stumm, Chung, and Furnham, 2011). It is worth noting, however, that it might be the case that clinical traits, like hypomania, make originality more likely and are less relevant to meaningfulness or usefulness criteria for creativity.

Another clinical trait related to creativity is **schizotypy**, which consists of four core parts: (1) unusual experiences (i.e., hallucinatory and/or magical thinking), (2) cognitive disorganization (i.e., tangential, poorly organized thinking, or derailed thinking), (3) introvertive anhedonia (i.e., lack of enjoyment), and (4) impulsive nonconformity (i.e., unstable mood, disregard for social conventions and norms; Mason, Claridge, and Jackson, 1995). More specifically, these four components can be divided into "positive schizotypy," made up of the unusual experiences and impulsive nonconformity components, and "negative schizotypy," made up of the cognitive disorganization and introvertive anhedonia components. In a meta-analysis of forty-five articles, some features of schizotypy are more conducive to creativity than others, with positive schizotypy being more likely to facilitate creativity than negative schizotypy. In other words, while magical ideation, odd beliefs, and unusual perceptual experiences may help with "thinking outside the box," and nonconformity may lead to an absence of self-censorship, negative symptoms such as social isolation or limited affect are less helpful (Acar and Sen, 2013).

The association between schizotypy and creativity may be universal and a result of sexual selection. There is cross-cultural evidence that the association between creativity and schizotypy exists in both Asian and European cultures (Batey and Furnham, 2008; Landgraf et al., 2015; Wang et al., 2017). Furthermore, Beaussart, Kaufman, and Kaufman (2012) present evidence that the schizotypy-creativity relationship may be a sexually selected trait, in that it is associated with short-term mating success in men. Finally, people high in schizotypy show less brain activity in areas associated with impulse control while solving a creative problem (Park, Kirk, and Waldie, 2015). As such, research on schizotypy illustrates multiple aspects of the functional model of creative personality, including both its biological and cultural foundations and how they can facilitate creativity.

One way to think about the association between clinical traits and creativity is to consider a "shared vulnerability" model (Carson, 2019) represented as a Venn diagram with two overlapping circles, one representing Creativity and one representing Psychopathology, with Creative Genius in the middle. Protective factors – characteristics associated with a lower likelihood of psychopathology, or those that decrease the negative impact of a risk factor – are included in the Creativity circle (e.g., high IQ, working memory skills, cognitive flexibility). Meanwhile, risk factors are listed in the Psychopathology circle (e.g., low IQ, working memory deficits, perseveration). In the overlapping portion of the circles are shared vulnerabilities, including the tendency to notice and pay attention to that which is new (novelty salience) or seemingly extraneous or irrelevant (cognitive disinhibition) and hyperconnectivity. Although this model has been specifically formulated to explain creativity of creative genius – famous creators who have achieved at exceptionally high levels – some research suggests that the shared vulnerability is relevant for other creative individuals (Akinola and Mendes, 2008).

Considerations

One consideration is that while a long-standing assumption exists that genetics influence brain processes, and the brain structures and functions affect personality and creativity, it may also be true that creative behavior influences personality, or that personality influences brain activity. Indeed, there is evidence that personality differences can lead to differences in brain activity. For example, a longitudinal study provides evidence that being high in the personality trait of openness to experience can buffer against the loss of gray matter in the right parietal lobe of the brain (Taki et al., 2013). This was true regardless of age, gender, and brain size. Creative thought and behavior can also influence personality, insofar as they shape experience, and therefore may epigenetically affect the way that certain genes are expressed as a person develops (Simonton, 1999).

A second consideration is that there is an implicit assumption in much of creativity research that creativity is benign or benevolent; that is, creativity is a force for good and positive change or contribution. This assumption is visible in many creativity measures, such as when people are asked to create new inventions, write short stories, or creative humorous captions. However, not all creativity is oriented toward positive goals (Cropley et al., 2010). Cropley, Kaufman, and Cropley (2008) defined the term **malevolent creativity** – behavior that is original and useful toward a goal of harming others. Malevolent creativity can be related to the **dark triad** of traits – people who have subclinical levels of narcissism, a manipulative personality (Machiavellianism), and subclinical levels of psychopathy (Paulhus and Williams, 2002). The dark triad traits are associated with tendencies toward self-promotion, deception, emotional coldness, aggression, and unethical behavior.

Some research reports positive associations between creative thinking and the dark triad (narcissism, psychopathy, and Machiavellianism). That is, lying, cheating, being narcissistic and manipulative can involve creative ways of thinking and behaving, and research has supported that more creative thinking and behaving are linked with these traits. For example, those high on self-reported creativity and creative humor also score high on self-reported narcissism (Jonason, Richardson, and Potter, 2015). Others have found that it is especially the elements of lying, cheating, and deception (components of psychopathy) that correlate with remote (creative) associations (Beaussart, Andrews, and Kaufman, 2013; Gino and Wiltermuth, 2014). Gino and Wiltermuth (2014), in a series of experiments, demonstrated that holding prior differences in creative ability constant, those who cheated the most had the most creative associations and that, when participants were given the opportunity to lie about how well they had done on tasks in the lab, dishonesty led to increased creative ideas. Moreover, they also found that it was the act of breaking rules and thus feeling subsequently less restricted by them that accounted for the relationship between deception and creative thinking. Similarly, but more drastically, Cropley (Cropley and Cropley, 2013; Cropley et al., 2008) and Eisenman (1999) have argued and shown that novelty and creative problem solving can be used for serious harmful social outcomes, such as criminal behavior or terrorism.

These findings are consistent with a classic finding in the literature on personality and creativity showing that creative people doubt, question, and even flaunt social norms and rules (Feist, 1993, 1998; Galang et al., 2016). Gino and Ariely (2012) also conducted a series of quasi-experiments in which people with creative personalities were more prone to deception and cheating and people primed to think creatively were more likely to behave dishonestly when given the opportunity.

Emotions and Creativity

When examining the role of emotions in creativity, we must first define the scope of this relationship. Figure 9.1 depicts a model illustrating the interaction between emotion and creativity. On the level of the creative person(ality), we can think about the emotion-related personality traits of the individual (such as those described by motivational-affective traits

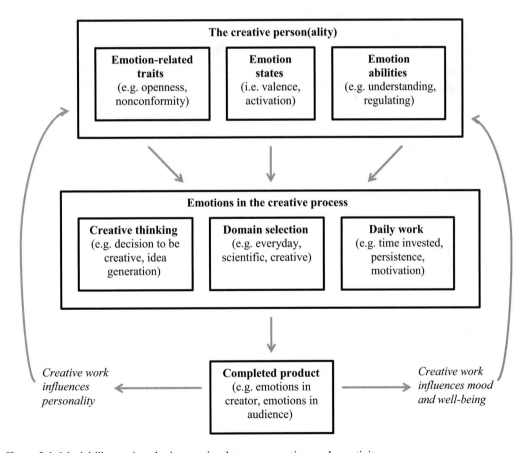

Figure 9.1 Model illustrating the interaction between emotion and creativity.

and some clinical traits discussed in the section above), a person's decision to be creative, their choice and interest in creative domains, and how often they engage in creative activities. On the level of the creative process, we can explore both **emotion states** – relatively short-lived emotional experiences, and **emotion abilities** – capacities for thinking and reasoning about and with emotions (Mayer, Roberts, and Barsade, 2008). Finally, on the level of creative products, we recognize that creators experience emotions as a result of their creative work (e.g., satisfaction and pride after completing a symphony) and that their creative product elicits emotions in their audience (e.g., amusement, wonder, interest, disgust). As we discussed the role of personality traits in creativity, we already addressed emotion-related traits and their relationship with creativity. Here, we focus on the role of emotion states and emotion abilities in relation to creative process and creative products.

Emotion States in the Creative Process

Emotions affect the whole creative process, from motivating creative work, through idea generation, to working through obstacles and persisting toward actualization of creative ideas. The dominant line of research has examined the effects of pleasant and unpleasant emotion states – relatively short emotional experiences – on idea generation and insight. These studies used the experimental procedure of mood induction; participants would be put in a specific mood (the mood was induced in them) by showing them video clips, making them think they received social approval or rejection, or giving them small gifts. Then, participants would be given a creative thinking task, such as thinking of unusual uses for a brick or a tin can or considering how to improve education in their academic departments. After more than three decades of research, evidence has accumulated that positive, activating emotion states (e.g., being happy) enhance performance on tests of creative thinking (Baas, De Dreu, and Nijstad, 2008; Feist, 2012).

However, interviews with eminent creators and studies of professionally creative people show that a wide range of both pleasant and unpleasant emotions are present in the creative process. Artists, designers, composers, screenwriters, and scientists all describe experiencing anxiety and frustration at the vagueness of their initial ideas, joy during inspiration, but also pain or anguish in the often long process of taking an idea and making it a reality (Botella et al., 2013; Glăveanu et al., 2013; Bourgeois-Bougrine et al., 2014). Indeed, some research supports the role of negative emotions for idea generation. For example, in an interview study, professional adults described that moderate levels of anger benefit creative idea generation by correcting errors and stimulating new ideas (Yang and Hung, 2015). Akinola and Mendes (2008) found that negative mood induced through social rejection resulted in greater creativity on a collage-making task, particularly for those who have higher vulnerability as measured by an adrenal steroid linked to depression.

Support for the role of negative emotions in the creative process is also available from momentary assessments of emotion in everyday life. In a thirteen-day diary study, Conner and Silvia (2015) asked young adults to complete a positive and negative emotion scale, as well as to rate how creative they were each day (defined as coming up with novel or original ideas, expressing oneself in an original way, or engaging in artistic activities). As in previous research, those who reported more positive affect, especially high activation positive affect, rated their days as being more creative than those who reported less positive affect. Also, high activation negative affect (feeling angry, hostile, and irritable) was associated with higher creativity. In another study, college students completed online surveys three times a day over ten days, reporting on their current mood and their creative process engagement (whether they were working on problem identification, information processing, and idea generation; To et al., 2012). Both positive and negative activated emotion states were associated with higher creative engagement, and positive and negative deactivating moods were associated with less creative engagement. Furthermore, activating negative moods at one time point were associated with more creative engagement at the next survey time point.

Studies showing benefits of both positive and negative emotions on creativity have added complexity to how creativity and emotions are linked. Kaufmann and Vosburg (2002) raised a question about the effect of time on creativity tasks when they found that those in a positive mood performed best early on, while those in the control (neutral) and negative mood conditions performed best later in the task. Other research examined the role of how the creativity task is framed. Friedman, Förster, and Denzler (2007) found that participants induced to experience a positive mood produced more ideas when the task was framed as fun and those in negative moods produced more ideas when the task was framed as serious. Studies of stress have also showed that the kind of stressor makes a difference. Social-evaluative stressors show an upside-down U-shaped relationship with creativity, with low to medium-level of stress associated with higher creative thinking compared to no stress or high stress (Byron, Khazanchi, and Nazarian, 2010). However, stress caused by something uncontrollable is increasingly detrimental to creative thinking in a linear fashion (more stress, less creative thinking). Furthermore, for those high in trait anxiety, stressors decreased creativity; for those low in trait anxiety, stressors increased creativity.

Two models speak to the role of emotion states in creative thinking. The **feelings-as-information** model describes moods as a source of information that can be used to direct thinking (Clore, Schwarz, and Conway, 1994; Schwarz, 2012). Unpleasant moods signal that there is a problem to solve and dissatisfaction signals the need to persist to improve the situation. Thus, distress (e.g., job dissatisfaction, budget shortages) can serve as motivation for creative thinking (Anderson, De Dreu, and Nijstad, 2004). By contrast, pleasant moods signal successful performance and indicate that effort can be reduced, which sometimes can be premature (Zhou and George, 2001; George and Zhou, 2002). This signaling value of positive emotions (all is good, no need for further action) can explain declining benefits of positive moods on creative thinking with longer time spent on task (Baas et al., 2008).

The **dual pathway model** was specifically formulated to address the role of emotions in creative thinking; it integrates existing research by positing that activating moods, whether positive or negative, should enhance creativity, albeit through different paths (De Dreu, Baas, and Nijstad, 2008). Positive activating moods benefit creativity by enhancing cognitive flexibility, while negative activating moods enhance perseverance (De Dreu et al., 2008; To et al., 2012). This model accounts for both the effect of framing discussed previously, with regard to seeing an event as fun or serious, and the findings that both positive and negative moods can enhance creativity, particularly when creativity is defined to include performance on longer-term tasks where persistence comes into play.

Emotion States and the Creative Product

Not only do emotions impact creative thinking and behavior, but creative behavior also affects a creator's emotional state. For example, Amabile et al. (2005) showed that positive affect predicted creativity at work and also found that people described positive affect as a consequence of creativity (including positive emotions such as joy, pride, satisfaction, and relief). Artists describe feeling a mix of satisfaction and exhaustion when they complete a work, and scientists describe feeling satisfaction and pride, but also anxiety about presenting their work (Glăveanu et al., 2013). Even simply working on idea generation thinking tasks increases positive mood (while tasks that require one correct answer increase negative mood; Chermahini and Hommel, 2012). Creative activities such as water coloring, writing poetry, and dance are commonly used as therapeutic strategies to decrease negative affect and distress in clinical patients (Slayton, D'Archer, and Kaplan, 2010).

Conner, DeYoung, and Silvia (2016) found that creative behavior on a given day led to more positive affect (especially activating emotions like being energetic or excited) and flourishing on the next day. This was true regardless of the level of creativity on the second day. However, the authors did not find that positive affect on one day predicted creativity the following day; therefore, the effect of creative behavior on mood is thought to be more than simply a positive mood-creative activity upward spiral. Rather, a large study across five countries and four languages found that working on creative tasks led to an increase in positive emotions due to an increase in feelings of autonomy (i.e., freedom to express ideas and opinions; Bujacz et al., 2016).

Creative products also have emotional effects on their audience. Tinio (2013) describes the process by which a person views art and depicts how this process mirrors (in reverse order) the process by which the art was created. Viewers begin by perceiving surface features of an artwork, then move through intermediate, memory-based processing, and end finding underlying meaning and personal relevance. Art viewing can elicit a range of emotions in the viewer well beyond positive emotions (Silvia, 2009), including confusion or surprise (knowledge-based emotions), anger, disgust, and contempt (hostile emotions), and pride, shame, or embarrassment (self-conscious emotions). Emotions are also elicited by consumer products. Horn and Salvendy (2009) found that positive affect predicts willingness to purchase innovative consumer products.

Emotion Abilities and Creativity

As research on a wide range of emotions in the creative process accumulates, the question becomes: *What do creators do with these emotions?* Emotions don't just happen to us; rather, we can to a substantial extent influence them. Although research in this area is still relatively sparse, support for the importance of abilities to use and regulate emotions is emerging from studies of children at play (Hoffmann and Russ, 2012) to professionals at work (Parke, Seo, and Sherf, 2015). **Emotion abilities** are one's capacity to process information about emotions and solve problems involving emotions. **Emotional intelligence** is the most studied emotion ability and it includes accurately reading nonverbal cues from others, being able to use emotions to enhance thinking, problem-solving, and decision-making, understanding the causes and consequences of different emotions, and **regulating emotions** for specific goals (Izard et al., 2007; Mayer et al., 2008; Tamir, 2016).

Using emotions involves taking one's emotional state into consideration when prioritizing or directing thinking, choosing tasks that will benefit from a given emotion state, and purposefully putting ourselves in particular emotion states to help some aspect of thinking and problem-solving (Mayer and Salovey, 1997; Mayer et al., 2008). For example, people can use their emotions as information to help them notice a problem (e.g., I am feeling angry, there must be something unfair that happened), recognize that more effort is needed (e.g., I am feeling disappointed, I need to do more work on this), or mark that they have succeeded (Martin et al., 1993; Schwarz, 2012).

Interviews with creators show that emotions often direct their thinking, particularly when observations lead to inspiration. For instance, composers, artists, and writers describe using emotionally rich observations of their environments – places, smells, interactions – to tell a convincing story (Glăveanu et al., 2013). Similarly, designers describe turning frustration and anxiety experienced when problems arise into the drive toward finding solutions (Sas and Zhang, 2010). Huy (2002) found that managers also used emotions to create commitment among employees for innovation projects. Other examples of using emotions are when leaders choose to strategically share positive emotions to inspire original thinking or to encourage persistence toward challenging goals (George, 2000; Vallerand et al., 2003), as well as when entrepreneurs convey passion about a creative idea to potential investors (Cardon, Sudek, and Mitteness, 2009).

Beyond using the emotion one is already experiencing, people can intentionally put themselves in an emotion state that can be useful for the task they face. In one study, people were told they would be completing either a task requiring precise analytic thinking or one requiring creative and imaginative thinking. When given a choice of happy or sad music before starting the task, people tended to choose music that would put them in a mood most helpful to the task; those expecting to work on a creative task chose happy music, and those expecting to work on an analytic task chose sad music (Cohen and Andrade, 2004). People also sometimes choose to generate emotions congruent with their traits to help them do better on creative thinking tasks. In a series of experiments, college students higher on neuroticism (trait characterized by sad and anxious emotions) chose to recall worrisome (as opposed to happy) memories when facing a creativity task and thus create a more negative activated mood. Moreover, it worked: when those higher on neuroticism were induced to feel worried, they performed better on a creative idea generation task (alternate uses for a brick) and produced more creative designs (cabin of a commercial airplane; Leung et al., 2014).

In addition to using emotions to help thinking and problem solving, regulating emotions is an important emotion ability. Emotion regulation is the ability to influence the course of one's emotions in ways that can help reach a certain goal. This can include preventing or reducing an unwanted emotion (e.g. stage anxiety), as well as initiating, maintaining or enhancing a wanted emotion states (e.g., making oneself more confident before a presentation). To be effective, emotion regulation has to be based on understanding consequences of potential reactions in emotion-laden situations, knowledge of what actions tend to be helpful for particular goals, and an ability to evaluate what actions would be most beneficial in specific situations (Mayer et al., 2008).

The idea that emotion regulation is important for creativity is not a new one. Freud (1925/1958) described how regulating potentially overwhelming emotions can lead to creativity through the defense mechanism of sublimation, the channeling of socially inappropriate impulses and emotions into socially desirable behavior, such as when aggression is expressed through art. Research has demonstrated this theoretical effect, such as in an experiment in which those participants who were asked to suppress anger produced sculptures, poems, and cartoon captions rated as more creative than control participants (Kim, Zeppenfeld, and Cohen, 2013). Developmental research also shows that successful emotion regulation as reported by parents and elementary school children predicts both children's imagination in pretend play and their performance on creative idea generation tests (Hoffmann and Russ, 2012). Interviews with designers vividly illustrate emotion regulation in their creative work (Sas and Zhang, 2010). Designers describe the deliberate nature of purposefully maintaining positive moods for as long as needed, how to change emotions like frustration into persistence, and finding a balance between relaxation and stimulation.

Emotion regulation in itself can enhance creative thinking. For instance, some research shows that a shift from a negative to positive mood is a better predictor of creativity than a shift from a neutral to positive mood (Bledow, Rosing, and Frese, 2013). Those professionals in creative positions whose moods shifted from negative to positive (from the morning to the afternoon), rated their days as more creative than those whose moods did not shift. Similarly, psychology graduate students who were induced to feel a negative and then a positive mood showed higher flexibility and originality on a creativity task. The negative to positive change offers an opportunity to access information available from both the negative and the positive mood perspectives; negative moods provide information about possible limitations and pitfalls and positive moods provide remote associations helpful in generating creative ideas.

Beyond emotion regulation allowing a person to experience more positive emotions, Ivcevic and Brackett (2015) identified another way that emotion regulation influences creativity. In high school students, emotion regulation ability affected creativity by increasing persistence and passion. This effect was observed in those with medium or high levels of openness to experience but not those low in openness, suggesting that emotion regulation helps transform creative potential (personality tendency toward imagination and originality) into creative behavior by enabling individuals to maintain interest and effort.

Future Directions

Where should we go from here? The models that connect personality traits, emotion states, emotion abilities, and creative thinking and achievement are complex, and to examine them we need sophisticated lines of research. For example, we should examine how the same emotion states differentially impact separate steps of the creative process (e.g., positive, activating emotions for idea generation, but skepticism and dissatisfaction during editing or refinement). We must further expand our understanding of the interplay of creative behavior and the creative personality to include the dark side of creativity and the bidirectional nature of a person's genetics, personality traits, and creative behavior. We caution that the same predictors, such as emotion states, traits, or abilities, can have different effects depending on the individuals being studied (college students vs. professionals), the outcomes being examined (creative idea generation on brief laboratory tasks vs. creativity of products that took weeks or months to complete), as well as the domains of creativity (poetry vs. physics).

There is great value in experimental research, but creativity tasks in such research are short out of necessity, which limits the kinds of creative outcomes that can be studied (quick thinking vs. making real life creative products) and the validity of those studies for making conclusions about everyday creative behavior in school or work. For example, how does a creator follow-through from a creative inspiration to a Broadway play years later? What contexts, personality traits, and life experiences allow a child who builds with blocks to develop a creative identity and pursue a career in architecture?

Several technological innovations make it possible to open the black box of what happens during the creative process. For example, there are portable sensors that can provide information about arousal levels while people work on a creative task. (Poh, Swenson, and Picard, 2009). As this technology has been used to study group problem-solving (Chikersal et al., 2017), it can be applied to the study of creativity in real-life settings. Furthermore, there is increasing evidence for the validity of software that identifies facial expressions characteristics of a set of specific emotions (Bernin et al., 2017). This technology can be used to analyze facial expressions of emotion during the creative process and as an effect of creative activity and products.

Finally, future research should systematically examine the role of abilities to use emotions to aid thinking and abilities to understand and regulate emotions in the creative process. Such research explicitly acknowledges individual agency in relation to emotions – people are able to influence the course of their emotions and mobilize them in the service of their goals (Tamir, 2016). As an emerging area of work, this research should include multiple methods, from interviews with creators to studies using ability tests and informant-reports of ability and experience sampling studies that can capture the use and regulation of emotions as they unfold in creative work. Many questions about emotion abilities await answers, from their role in motivating creativity to regulating emotions in the service of creative goals.

Our Research Contribution

Dr. Jessica Hoffmann became interested in the benefits of creative self-expression after experiencing the benefits of play therapy for her own anxiety as a young child. She currently serves as Director of Adolescent Initiatives at the Yale Center for Emotional Intelligence, leading two main initiatives: RULER for High Schools and inspirED. Both focus on the intersection of emotional intelligence, creative problem solving, and the power of school-based, preventative mental health approaches. Jessica has collaborated with colleagues from Italy, Spain, and Mexico, and published in journals including *Emotion, Creativity Research Journal* and the *Journal of Cross-Cultural Psychology.*

Dr. Zorana Ivcevic got interested in studying creativity as an undergraduate when she read a description by a great creativity scholar Frank Barron (1963) that creative individuals are "occasionally crazier, yet adamantly saner" than the general population. She ended up studying that question, as well as the role of emotional intelligence abilities in creativity. Most research on creativity and emotions studied emotions that are imposed on people. Dr. Ivcevic asks a different question: How do people use and manage emotions outside the laboratory where we have a certain level of agency over our emotions. She has published on the relationship between emotional intelligence and emotional creativity, the process of self-regulation for creativity, and how managing emotions can help transform creative potential into recognizable creativity.

Gregory Feist is widely published in the psychology of creativity, personality of creative people, the psychology of science, and the development of scientific talent. One major focus of his is establishing the psychology of science as an independent study of science, along the lines of the history, philosophy, and sociology of science. His major effort toward this end was the book *Psychology of Science and the Origins of the Scientific Mind* (2006, Yale University Press).

Critical/Creative Thinking Questions

1. How might the personality trait of openness to experience (which includes openness to varied ideas, feelings, actions, aesthetics, and values) help or hurt an artist during different parts of the creative process? (e.g., deciding to do something new, persisting when challenged, or selling their work to an audience)?
2. What anecdotal evidence could you use to explain how unpleasant feelings (e.g., sadness, loneliness, anger etc.) might help an artist to be more creative? How could unpleasant feelings help a scientist or a designer?

3. How does the ability to regulate emotions help or hurt the creative process? Start with people's decision to share a creative idea, their idea generation and evaluation process, and while actually working on the creative project.

4. Give an example of how a person might use an emotion as inspiration for a creative behavior.

5. What cognitive, social, motivational-affective, and clinical traits might make it more likely that one makes a decision to share their creative ideas with others at school or work?

GLOSSARY

affect: A feeling state varying along two dimensions: valence and arousal.

agreeableness: A personality trait describing a tendency to be compassionate and polite, warm toward others, trustworthy, altruistic, honest, modest, and cooperative.

arousal: The energy or activation level experienced in the body.

cognitive flexibility: The ability to fluidly switch between different categories or ideas, or come up with many distinct categories of ideas.

cognitive personality traits: How people habitually process information, solve problems, and respond to new situations (e.g., curiosity).

dark triad of traits: A constellation of three traits: subclinical levels of narcissism, a manipulative personality (Machiavellianism), and subclinical levels of psychopathy, resulting in tendencies toward self-promotion, deception, emotional coldness, aggression, and unethical behavior.

dual pathway model: A theory that posits that activating moods, whether positive or negative, should enhance creativity, albeit through different paths, with positive activating moods benefiting creativity by enhancing cognitive flexibility, while negative activating moods enhance perseverance.

emotion: The immediate physiological and psychological response to a thought or event.

emotion abilities: Capacities for thinking and reasoning about and with emotions.

emotional intelligence: Ability to accurately perceive emotions in oneself and others, use emotions to help thinking and problem solving, understand likely causes and consequences of emotions, and regulate emotions.

emotion states: Relatively short-lived emotional experiences.

extraversion: The trait of being confident and assertive, as well as sociable and outgoing.

feelings: The subjective experience and conscious awareness of an emotion.

feelings-as-information model: A theory that proposes feelings as a source of information about what is going on in people's environment (e.g., happiness signals success).

functional model of creative personality: A theory that describes how biological and personality traits of a person function to lower the threshold for creative behavior.

idea evaluation: The act of judging the value or quality of ideas.

idea generation: The act of producing many solutions to a given problem.

intrinsic motivation: The drive to do an activity because of the pleasure and challenge of the activity rather than for some external reason (e.g., rewards such as grades or money).

malevolent creativity: Behavior that is original and useful but has the intent to harm others.

mood: A general mental state, less intense than an emotion, occurring over hours, days, or weeks.

motivational-affective traits: Traits that deal with a person's emotions and motivation, directing and energizing behavior (e.g., intrinsic motivation).

nonconformity: A personality trait associated with the behaviors and attitudes of questioning what authority figures say.

openness to experience: A trait of being curious and intellectual, as well as open to new experiences and interested in aesthetic experiences.

passion: A strong emotional desire and commitment to an activity that is important to one's identity.

personality traits: Characteristic patterns of thinking, feeling, and behaving that are relatively stable through time and across situations.

regulating emotions: The ability to manage one's emotions including preventing or reducing unwanted feelings, as well as initiating, maintaining, or enhancing wanted feelings.

schizotypy: A clinical trait defined as consisting of four core traits that exist on a continuum in the general population: (1) unusual experiences, (2) cognitive disorganization, (3) introvertive anhedonia, and (4) impulsive nonconformity.

social personality traits: Traits that concern one's relationships with other people (e.g., nonconformity).

using emotions: The ability to take one's emotional state into consideration when prioritizing or directing thinking; to choose tasks that will benefit from a particular emotional state, and to purposefully generate emotions that will enhance thinking or problem-solving.

valence: A term used when describing the relative pleasantness or unpleasantness of a feeling.

REFERENCES

Acar, S., and Sen, S. (2013). A Multilevel Meta-Analysis of the Relationship between Creativity and Schizotypy. *Psychology of Aesthetics, Creativity, and the Arts*, 7(3), 214. doi.org/10.1037/a0031975.

Agnoli, S., Franchin, L., Rubaltelli, E., and Corazza, G. E. (2015). An Eye-Tracking Analysis of Irrelevance Processing As Moderator of Openness and Creative Performance. *Creativity Research Journal*, 27(2), 125–132. doi.org/10.1080/10400419.2015.1030304.

Akinola, M., and Mendes, W. B. (2008). The Dark Side of Creativity: Biological Vulnerability and Negative Emotions Lead to Greater Artistic Creativity. *Personality and Social Psychology Bulletin*, 34(12), 1677–1686. doi.org/10.1177/0146167208323933.

Amabile, T. M. (1996). *Creativity in Context: Update to the Social Psychology of Creativity*. Boulder: Westview Press.

Amabile, T. M., Barsade, S. G., Mueller, J. S., and Staw, B. M. (2005). Affect and Creativity at Work. *Administrative Science Quarterly*, 50(2), 367–403. doi.org/10.2189/asqu.2005.50.3.367.

Amabile, T. M., Hill, K. G., Hennessey, B. A., and Tighe, E. M. (1994). The Work Preference Inventory: Assessing Intrinsic and Extrinsic Motivational Orientations. *Journal of Personality and Social Psychology*, 66(5), 950–967.

Amabile, T. M., and Pratt, M. G. (2016). The Dynamic Componential Model of Creativity and Innovation in Organizations: Making Progress, Making Meaning. *Research in Organizational Behavior*, 36, 157–183. doi.org/10.1016/j.riob.2016.10.001.

Anderson, N., De Dreu, C. K., and Nijstad, B. A. (2004). The Routinization of Innovation Research: A Constructively Critical Review of the State-of-the-Science. *Journal of Organizational Behavior*, 25(2), 147–173. doi.org/10.1002/job.236.

Baas, M., De Dreu, C. K., and Nijstad, B. A. (2008). A Meta-Analysis of 25 Years of Mood-Creativity Research: Hedonic Tone, Activation, or Regulatory Focus? *Psychological Bulletin*, *134*(6), 779. doi.org/10.1037/a0012815.

Baas, M., Roskes, M., Sligte, D., Nijstad, B. A., and De Dreu, C. K. (2013). Personality and Creativity: The Dual Pathway to Creativity Model and a Research Agenda. *Social and Personality Psychology Compass*, *7*(10), 732–748. doi.org/10.1111/spc3.12062.

Barbot, B., and Eff, H. (2019). The Genetic Basis of Creativity: A Multivariate Approach. In J. C. Kaufman and R. J. Sternberg (Eds.), *The Cambridge Handbook of Creativity* (pp. 132–147). New York: Cambridge University Press.

Barron, F. (1963). *Creativity and Psychological Health*. Oxford: Van Nostrand.

Batey, M., and Furnham, A. (2006). Creativity, Intelligence, and Personality: A Critical Review of the Scattered Literature. *Genetic, Social, and General Psychology Monographs*, *132*(4), 355–429.

(2008). The Relationship between Measures of Creativity and Schizotypy. *Personality and Individual Differences*, *45*(8), 816–821.

Beaty, R. E., Benedek, M., Wilkins, R. W., Jauk, E., Fink, A., Silvia, P. J., and Neubauer, A. C. (2014). Creativity and the Default Network: A Functional Connectivity analysis of the Creative Brain at Rest. *Neuropsychologia*, *64*, 92–98. doi.org/10.1016/j.neuropsychologia.2014.09.019.

Beaussart, M. L., Andrews, C. J., and Kaufman, J. C. (2013). Creative Liars: The Relationship between Creativity and Integrity. *Thinking Skills and Creativity*, *9*(2010), 129–134. doi.org/10.1016/j.tsc.2012.10.003.

Beaussart, M. L., Kaufman, S. B., and Kaufman, J. C. (2012). Creative Activity, Personality, Mental Illness, and Short-Term Mating Success. *The Journal of Creative Behavior*, *46*(3), 151–167. doi.org/10.1002/jocb.11.

Bernin, A., Müller, L., Ghose, S., von Luck, K., Grecos, C., Wang, Q., and Vogt, F. (2017). Towards More Robust Automatic Facial Expression Recognition in Smart Environments. In *Proceedings of the 10th International Conference on Pervasive Technologies Related to Assistive Environments* (pp. 37–44). doi.org/10.1145/3056540.3056546.

Bienvenu, O. J., Samuels, J. F., Costa, P. T., Reti, I. M., Eaton, W. W., and Nestadt, G. (2004). Anxiety and Depressive Disorders and the Five-Factor Model of Personality: A Higher- and Lower-Order Personality Trait Investigation in a Community Sample. *Depression and Anxiety*, *20*(2), 92–97. doi.org/10.1002/da.20026.

Bledow, R., Rosing, K., and Frese, M. (2013). A Dynamic Perspective on Affect and Creativity. *Academy of Management Journal*, *56*(2), 432–450. doi.org/10.5465/amj.2010.0894.

Botella, M., Gläveanu, V., Zenasni, F., Storme, M., Myszkowski, N., Wolff, M., and Lubart, T. (2013). How Artists Create: Creative Process and Multivariate Factors. *Learning and Individual Differences*, *26*, 161–170. doi.org/10.1016/j.lindif.2013.02.008.

Bourgeois-Bougrine, S., Glaveanu, V., Botella, M., Guillou, K., De Biasi, P. M., and Lubart, T. (2014). The Creativity Maze: Exploring Creativity in Screenplay Writing. *Psychology of Aesthetics, Creativity, and the Arts*, *8*(4), 384. doi.org/10.1037/a0037839.

Buchanan, M. (2013). "How Steve Jobs Made the iPad Succeed When All Other Tablets Failed." *Wired*, November 2. www.wired.com/2013/11/one-ipad-to-rule-themall-all-those-who-dream-big-are-not-lost/.

Bujacz, A., Dunne, S., Fink, D., Gatej, A. R., Karlsson, E., Ruberti, V., and Wronska, M. K. (2016). Why Do We Enjoy Creative Tasks? Results from a Multigroup Randomized Controlled Study. *Thinking Skills and Creativity*, *19*, 188–197. doi.org/10.1016/j.tsc.2015.11.002.

Byron, K., Khazanchi, S., and Nazarian, D. (2010). The Relationship between Stressors and Creativity: A Meta-Analysis Examining Competing Theoretical Models. *Journal of Applied Psychology*, *95*(1), 201. doi.org/10.1037/a0017868.

Cardon, M. S., Gregoire, D. A., Stevens, C. E., and Patel, P. C. (2013). Measuring Entrepreneurial Passion: Conceptual Foundations and Scale Validation. *Journal of Business Venturing*, *28*(3), 373–396. doi.org/10.1016/j.jbusvent.2012.03.003.

Cardon, M. S., Sudek, R., and Mitteness, C. (2009). The Impact of Perceived Entrepreneurial Passion on Angel Investing. *Frontiers of Entrepreneurship Research*, *29*(2), 1. http://digitalknowledge .babson.edu/fer/vol29/iss2/1.

Carson, S. H. (2019). *Creativity and Mental Illness*. In J. Kaufman and R. Sternberg (Eds.), *The Cambridge Handbook of Creativity* (pp. 296–318). New York: Cambridge University Press.

Chang, C. C., Wang, J. H., Liang, C. T., and Liang, C. (2014). Curvilinear Effects of Openness and Agreeableness on the Imaginative Capability of Student Designers. *Thinking Skills and Creativity*, *14*, 68–75. doi.org/10.1016/j.tsc.2014.09.001.

Ceci, M. W., and Kumar, V. K. (2016). A Correlational Study of Creativity, Happiness, Motivation, and Stress from Creative Pursuits. *Journal of Happiness Studies*, *17*(2), 609–626. doi.org/10.1007/ s10902–015-9615-y.

Chen, B. (2016). Conscientiousness and Everyday Creativity among Chinese Undergraduate Students. *Personality and Individual Differences*, *102*, 56–59.

Chen, Q., Yang, W., Li, W., Wei, D., Li, H., Lei, Q., and Qiu, J. (2014). Association of Creative Achievement with Cognitive Flexibility by a Combined Voxel-Based Morphometry and Resting-State Functional Connectivity Study. *Neuroimage*, *102*(Part 2), 474–483. doi.org/10.1016/j .neuroimage.2014.08.008.

Chermahini, S. A., and Hommel, B. (2012). Creative Mood Swings: Divergent and Convergent Thinking Affect Mood in Opposite Ways. *Psychological Research*, *76*(5), 634–640. doi.org/10 .1007/s00426–011-0358-z.

Chikersal, P., Tomprou, M., Kim, Y. J., Woolley, A. W., and Dabbish, L. (2017). Deep Structures of Collaboration: Physiological Correlates of Collective Intelligence and Group Satisfaction. In *Proceedings of the 2017 ACM Conference on Computer Supported Cooperative Work and Social Computing* (pp. 873–888). doi.org/10.1145/2998181.2998250.

Clegg, H., Miell, D., and Nettle, D. (2011). Status and Mating Success amongst Visual Artists. *Frontiers in Psychology*, *2*, 1–4. doi.org/10.1016/j.paid.2016.06.061.

Clore, G. L., Schwarz, N., and Conway, M. (1994). Affective Causes and Consequences of Social Information Processing. In R. S. Wyer and T. K. Srull (Eds.), *Handbook of Social Cognition*, 323–417.

Cohen, J. B., and Andrade, E. B. (2004). Affective Intuition and Task-Contingent Affect Regulation. *Journal of Consumer Research*, *31*(2), 358–367. doi.org/10.1086/422114.

Conner, T. S., and Silvia, P. J. (2015). Creative Days: A daily Diary Study of Emotion, Personality, and Everyday Creativity. *Psychology of Aesthetics, Creativity, and the Arts*, *9*(4), 463. doi.org/10 .1037/aca0000022.

Conner, T. S., DeYoung, C. G., and Silvia, P. J. (2016). Everyday Creative Activity As a Path to Flourishing. *The Journal of Positive Psychology*, *13*(2), 181–189. doi.org/10.1037/0022-3514.94.5 .739.

Cropley, D. H., and Cropley, A. J. (2013). *Creativity and Crime: A Psychological Analysis*. Cambridge: Cambridge University Press. doi-org/10.1017/CBO9781139176118.

Cropley, D. H., Cropley, A. J., Kaufman, J. C., and Runco, M. A. (2010). *The Dark Side of Creativity*. Cambridge: Cambridge University Press.

Cropley, D. H., Kaufman, J. C., and Cropley, A. J. (2008). Malevolent Creativity: A Functional Model of Creativity in Terrorism and Crime. *Creativity Research Journal, 20*(2), 105–115.

Csikszentmihalyi, M. (1996). *Flow and the Psychology of Discovery and Invention.* New York: HarperCollins.

Darwin, C. and Wallace, A. (1858) On the Tendency of Species to Form Varieties; and on the Perpetuation of Varieties and Species by Natural Means of Selection. *Journal of the Proceedings of the Linnean Society, Zoology, 3,* 45–62.

De Dreu, C. K., Baas, M., and Nijstad, B. A. (2008). Hedonic Tone and Activation Level in the Mood-Creativity Link: Toward a Dual Pathway to Creativity Model. *Journal of Personality and Social Psychology, 94*(5), 739. doi.org/10.1037/0022-3514.94.5.739.

Dewett, T. (2007). Linking Intrinsic Motivation, Risk Taking, and Employee Creativity in an R&D Environment. *R&D Management, 37*(3), 197–208. doi.org/10.1111/j.1467-9310.2007.00469.x.

Eckblad, M., and Chapman, L. J. (1986). Development and Validation of a Scale for Hypomanic Personality. *Journal of Abnormal Psychology, 95*(3), 214–222. doi.org/10.1037//0021-843x.95.3 .214.

Eisenman, R. (1999). Creative Prisoners: Do They exist? *Creativity Research Journal, 12*(3), 205–210.

Feist, G. J. (1993). A Structural Model of Scientific Eminence. *Psychological Science, 4*(6), 366–371. doi.org/10.1111/j.1467-9280.1993.tb00583.x.

(1998). A Meta-Analysis of Personality in Scientific and Artistic Creativity. *Personality and Social Psychology Review, 2*(4), 290–309. doi.org/10.1207/s15327957pspr0204_5.

(1999). *Autonomy and Independence: Encyclopedia of creativity,* vol. 1 (pp. 157–163). San Diego: Academic Press.

(2001). Natural and Sexual Selection in the Evolution of Creativity. *Bulletin of Psychology and the Arts, 2,* 11–16.

(2010). The Function of Personality in Creativity: The Nature and Nurture of the Creative Personality. In J. C. Kaufman and R. J. Sternberg (Eds.), *The Cambridge Handbook of Creativity* (pp. 113–130). New York: Cambridge University Press.

(2012). Affective States and Traits in Creativity. In M. Runco (Ed.), *The Creativity Research Handbook,* vol. 3 (pp. 61–102). New York: Hampton Press.

Fink, A., and Neubauer, A. C. (2008). Eysenck Meets Martindale: The Relationship between Extraversion and Originality from the Neuroscientific Perspective. *Personality and Individual Differences, 44*(1), 299–310. doi.org/10.1016/j.paid.08.010.

Friedman, R. S., Förster, J., and Denzler, M. (2007). Interactive Effects of Mood and Task Framing on Creative Generation. *Creativity Research Journal, 19*(2–3), 141–162. doi.org/10.1080/ 10400410701397206.

Fredricks, J. A., Alfeld, C., and Eccles, J. (2010). Developing and Fostering Passion in Academic and Nonacademic Domains. *Gifted Child Quarterly, 54*(1), 18–30. doi.org/10.1177/ 0016986209352683.

Fredrickson, B. L. (2001). The Role of Positive Emotions in Positive Psychology: The Broaden-and-Build Theory of Positive Emotions. *American Psychologist, 56*(3), 218–226.

Freud, S. (1958). *On Creativity and the Unconscious. Papers on Applied Psychoanalysis: Collected Works of Sigmund Freud.* New York: Harper (Originally published in 1925.)

Furnham, A., Batey, M., Anand, K., and Manfield, J. (2008). Personality, Hypomania, Intelligence and Creativity. *Personality and Individual Differences, 44*(5), 1060–1069. doi.org/10.1016/j.paid .2007.10.035.

Fürst, G., Ghisletta, P., and Lubart, T. (2016). Toward an Integrative Model of Creativity and Personality: Theoretical Suggestions and Preliminary Empirical Testing. *The Journal of Creative Behavior, 50*(2), 87–108. doi.org/10.1002/jocb.71.

Galang, A. J. R., Castelo, V. L. C., Santos III, L. C., Perlas, C. M. C., and Angeles, M. A. B. (2016). Investigating the Prosocial Psychopath Model of the Creative Personality: Evidence from Traits and Psychophysiology. *Personality and Individual Differences, 100*, 28–36. doi.org/10.1016/j.paid.2016.03.081.

George, J. M. (2000). Emotions and Leadership: The Role of Emotional Intelligence. *Human Relations, 53*(8), 1027–1055. doi.org/10.1037/0021-9010.86.3.513.

George, J. M., and Zhou, J. (2002). Understanding When Bad Moods Foster Creativity and Good Ones Don't: The Role of Context and Clarity of Feelings. *Journal of Applied Psychology, 87*(4), 687. doi.org/10.1037/0021–9010.86.3.513.

Gino, F., and Ariely, D. (2012). The Dark Side of Creativity: Original Thinkers Can Be More Dishonest. *Journal of Personality and Social Psychology, 102*(3), 445. doi.org/10.1037/a0026406.

Gino, F., and Wiltermuth, S. S. (2014). Evil genius? How Dishonesty Can Lead to Greater Creativity. *Psychological Science, 25*(4), 973–981. doi.org/10.1177/0956797614520714.

Glǎveanu, V., Lubart, T., Bonnardel, N., Botella, M., De Biaisi, P. M., Desainte-Catherine, M., Georgsdottir, and Zenasni, F. (2013). Creativity As Action: Findings from Five Creative Domains. *Frontiers in Psychology, 4*, 176. doi.org/10.3389/fpsyg.2013.00176.

Guilford, J. P. (1950). Creativity. *American Psychologist, 5*, 444–454.

Hoffmann, J., and Russ, S. (2012). Pretend Play, Creativity, and Emotion Regulation in Children. *Psychology of Aesthetics, Creativity, and the Arts, 6*(2), 175. doi.org/10.1037/a0026299.

Horn, D., and Salvendy, G. (2009). Measuring Consumer Perception of Product Creativity: Impact on Satisfaction and Purchasability. *Human Factors and Ergonomics in Manufacturing and Service Industries, 19*(3), 223–240. doi.org/10.1002/hfm.20150.

Hur, Y. M., Jeong, H. U., and Piffer, D. (2014). Shared Genetic and Environmental Influences on Self-Reported Creative Achievement in Art and Science. *Personality and Individual Differences, 68*, 18–22. doi.org/10.1016/j.paid.2014.03.041.

Huy, Q. N. (2002). Emotional Balancing of Organizational Continuity and Radical Change: The Contribution of Middle Managers. *Administrative Science Quarterly, 47*(1), 31–69. doi.org/10.2307/3094890.

Ivcevic, Z., and Brackett, M. A. (2015). Predicting Creativity: Interactive Effects of Openness to Experience and Emotion Regulation Ability. *Psychology of Aesthetics, Creativity, and the Arts, 9*(4), 480–487. doi.org/10.1037/a0039826.

Ivcevic, Z., and Mayer, J. D. (2009). Mapping Dimensions of Creativity in the Life-Space. *Creativity Research Journal, 21*(2–3), 152–165. doi.org/10.1080/10400410902855259.

Izard, C. E., Trentacosta, C. J., King, K. A., Morgan, J. K., and Diaz, M. (2007). Emotions, Emotionality, and Intelligence in the Development of Adaptive Behavior. In G. Matthews, M. Zeidner, and R. Roberts (Eds.), *The Science of Emotional Intelligence: Knowns and Unknowns* (pp. 127–150). Oxford: Oxford University Press.

Jonason, P. K., Richardson, E. N., and Potter, L. (2015). Self-Reported Creative Ability and the Dark Triad Traits: An Exploratory Study. *Psychology of Aesthetics, Creativity, and the Arts, 9*(4), 488–494. doi.org/10.1037/aca0000037.

Jung, R. E., Mead, B. S., Carrasco, J., and Flores, R. A. (2013). The Structure of Creative Cognition in the Human Brain. *Frontiers in Human Neuroscience, 7*, 1–13. doi.org/10.3389/fnhum.2013.00330.

Kapoor, H. (2015). The Creative Side of the Dark Triad. *Creativity Research Journal, 27*(1), 58–67. doi.org/10.1080/10400419.2014.961775.

Karwowski, M., and Lebuda, I. (2016). The Big Five, the Huge Two, and Creative Self-Beliefs: A Meta-Analysis. *Psychology of Aesthetics, Creativity, and the Arts, 10*(2), 214–232. doi.org/10.1037/aca0000035.

Kaufman, S. B. (2013). Opening up Openness to Experience: A Four-Factor Model and Relations to Creative Achievement in the Arts and Sciences. *The Journal of Creative Behavior, 47*(4), 233–255. doi.org/10.1002/jocb.33.

Kaufman, S. B., Kozbelt, A., Silvia, P., Kaufman, J. C., Ramesh, S., and Feist, G. J. (2016a). Who Finds Bill Gates Sexy? Creative Mate Preferences as a Function of Cognitive Ability, Personality, and Creative Achievement. *The Journal of Creative Behavior, 48*, 1–19. doi.org/10/1002/jocb.33.

Kaufman, S. B., Quilty, L. C., Grazioplene, R. G., Hirsh, J. B., Gray, J. R., Peterson, J. B., and DeYoung, C. G. (2016b). Openness to Experience and Intellect Differentially Predict Creative Achievement in the Arts and Sciences. *Journal of Personality, 84*(2), 248–258. doi.org/10.1111/jopy.12156.

Kaufmann, G., and Vosburg, S. K. (2002). The Effects of Mood on Early and Late Idea Production. *Creativity Research Journal, 14*(3–4), 317–330. doi.org/10.1207/S15326934CRJ1434_3.

Kim, E., Zeppenfeld, V., and Cohen, D. (2013). Sublimation, Culture, and Creativity. *Journal of Personality and Social Psychology, 105*(4), 639. doi.org/10.1037/a0033487.

Landgraf, S., Ilinykh, A., Haller, C. S., Shemelina, O., Cropley, D., von Treskow, I., and van der Meer, E. (2015). Culture Makes the Differences: The "Creativity-Schizotypy" Association Varies between Germans and Russians. *The International Journal of Creativity and Problem Solving, 25*(1), 35–61.

Leung, A. K. Y., Liou, S., Qiu, L., Kwan, L. Y. Y., Chiu, C. Y., and Yong, J. C. (2014). The Role of Instrumental Emotion Regulation in the Emotions-Creativity Link: How Worries Render Individuals with High Neuroticism More Creative. *Emotion, 14*(5), 846. doi.org/10.1037/a0036965.

Lloyd-Evans, R., Batey, M., and Furnham, A. (2006). Bipolar Disorder and Creativity: Investigating a Possible Link. *Advances in Psychology Research, 40*, 111–142.

Martin, L. L., Ward, D. W., Achee, J. W., and Wyer, R. S. (1993). Mood As Input: People Have to Interpret the Motivational Implications of Their Moods. *Journal of Personality and Social Psychology, 64*(3), 317. doi.org/10.1037/0022-3514.64.3.317.

Martindale, C. (1999). Biological Bases of Creativity. In R. Sternberg (Ed.), *The Cambridge Handbook of Creativity* (pp. 137–152). Cambridge: Cambridge University Press.

Martinsen, Ø. L. (2011). The Creative Personality: A Synthesis and Development of the Creative Person Profile. *Creativity Research Journal, 23*(3), 185–202. doi/org/10.1080/10400419.2011/595656.

Mason, O., Claridge, G., and Jackson, M. (1995). New Scales for the Assessment of Schizotypy. *Personality and Individual Differences, 18*(1), 7–13.

Mayer, J. D., Roberts, R. D., and Barsade, S. G. (2008). Human Abilities: Emotional Intelligence. *Annual Review of Psychology, 59*, 507–536. doi.org/10.1146/annurev.psych.59.103006.093646.

Mayer, J. D. and Salovey, P. (1997). What Is Emotional Intelligence? In P. Salovey and D. Sluyter (Eds.), *Emotional Development and Emotional Intelligence: Educational Implications* (pp. 3–31). New York: Basic Books.

Miller, G. F. (2000). *The Mating Mind: How Sexual Choice Shaped the Evolution of Human Nature.* New York: Doubleday.

Moeller, J., Dietrich, J., Eccles, J. S., and Schneider, B. (2017). Passionate Experiences in Adolescence: Situational Variability and Long-Term Stability. *Journal of Research on Adolescence, 27*(2), 344–361. doi.org/10.1111/jora.12297.

Nichols, R. C. (1978). Twin Studies of Ability, Personality and Interests. *Homo, 29*(3), 158–173.

Park, H. R., Kirk, I. J., and Waldie, K. E. (2015). Neural Correlates of Creative Thinking and Schizotypy. *Neuropsychologia, 73*, 94–107. doi.org/10.1016/j.neuropsychologia.2015.05.007.

Parke, M. R., Seo, M. G., and Sherf, E. N. (2015). Regulating and Facilitating: The Role of Emotional Intelligence in Maintaining and Using Positive Affect for Creativity. *Journal of Applied Psychology, 100*(3), 917. doi.org/10.1037/a0038452.

Paulhus, D. L., and Williams, K. M. (2002). The Dark Triad of Personality: Narcissism, Machiavellianism, and Psychopathy. *Journal of Research in Personality, 36*(6), 556–563. doi.org/10.1016/S0092–6566(02)00505-6.

Pfeffer, J., and Sutton, R. I. (2000). *The Knowing-Doing Gap: How Smart Companies Turn Knowledge into Action*. Cambridge, MA: Harvard Business School Press.

Piffer, D., and Hur, Y. M. (2014). Heritability of Creative Achievement. *Creativity Research Journal, 26*(2), 151–157. doi.org/10.1080/10400419.2014.901068.

Poh, M. Z., Swenson, N. C., and Picard, R. W. (2009). Comfortable Sensor Wristband for Ambulatory Assessment of Electrodermal Activity. In *1st Biennial Conference of the Society for Ambulatory Assessment* (pp. 25–28). http://alumni.media.mit.edu/~zher/papers/Poh-etal-SAA-2009.pdf.

Rogaten, J., and Moneta, G. B. (2015). Use of Creative Cognition and Positive Affect in Studying: Evidence of a Reciprocal Relationship. *Creativity Research Journal, 27*(2), 225–231. doi.org/10.1080/10400419.2015.1030312.

Sas, C., and Zhang, C. (2010). Do Emotions Matter in Creative Design? In *Proceedings of the 8th ACM Conference on Designing Interactive Systems, Aarhus Denmark*. www.researchgate.net/profile/Corina_Sas/publication/221441540_Do_emotions_matter_in_creative_design/links/5509564e0cf27e990e0e546d.pdf.

Schuldberg, D. (1990). Schizotypal and Hypomanic Traits, Creativity, and Psychological Health. *Creativity Research Journal, 3*(3), 218–230. doi.org/10.1080/10400419009534354.

Schwarz, N. (2012). Feelings-As-Information Theory. *Handbook of Theories of Social Psychology*, 1:289–308.

Silvia, P. J. (2009). Looking Past Pleasure: Anger, Confusion, Disgust, Pride, Surprise, and Other Unusual Aesthetic Emotions. *Psychology of Aesthetics, Creativity, and the Arts, 3*(1), 48. doi.org/10.1037/a0014632.

Simonton, D. K. (1999). Talent and Its Development: An Emergenic and Epigenetic Model. *Psychological Review, 106*, 435–457.

Slayton, S. C., D'Archer, J., and Kaplan, F. (2010). Outcome Studies on the Efficacy of Art Therapy: A Review of Findings. *Art Therapy, 27*(3), 108–118. doi.org/10.1080/07421656.2010.10129660.

Sternberg, R. J. (2018). A Triangular Theory of Creativity. *Psychology of Aesthetics, Creativity, and the Arts, 12*(1), 50. dx.doi.org/10.1037/aca0000095.

Taki, Y., Thyreau, B., Kinomura, S., Sato, K., Goto, R., Wu, K., and Fukuda, H. (2013). A Longitudinal Study of the Relationship between Personality Traits and the Annual Rate of Volume Changes in Regional Gray Matter in Healthy Adults. *Human Brain Mapping, 34*(12), 3347–3353. doi.org/10.1002/hbm.22145.

Tamir, M. (2016). Why Do People Regulate Their Emotions? A Taxonomy of Motives in Emotion Regulation. *Personality and Social Psychology Review, 20*(3), 199–222. doi.org/10.1177/10888683155586325.

Tan, C. S., Lau, X. S., Kung, Y. T., and Kailsan, R. A. L. (2019). Openness to Experience Enhances Creativity: The Mediating Role of Intrinsic Motivation and the Creative Process Engagement. *The Journal of Creative Behavior*, *53*(1), 109–119. doi.org/10.1002/jocb.170.

Tinio, P. P. (2013). From Artistic Creation to Aesthetic Reception: The Mirror Model of Art. *Psychology of Aesthetics, Creativity, and the Arts*, *7*(3), 265–275. doi.org/10.1037/a0030872.

To, M. L., Fisher, C. D., Ashkanasy, N. M., and Rowe, P. A. (2012). Within-Person Relationships between Mood and Creativity. *Journal of Applied Psychology*, *97*(3), 599. doi.org/10.1037/a0026097.

Urban, K. K. (2003). Toward a Componential Model of Creativity. In D. Ambrose, L. M. Cohen, and A. J. Tannenbaum (Eds.), *Creative Intelligence: Toward Theoretic Integration* (pp. 81–112). Cresskill: Hampton Press.

Vallerand, R. J., Blanchard, C., Mageau, G. A., Koestner, R., Ratelle, C., Léonard, M., and Marsolais, J. (2003). Les passions de l'ame: On Obsessive and Harmonious Passion. *Journal of Personality and Social Psychology*, *85*(4), 756. doi.org/10.1037/0022-3514.85.4.756.

Velázquez, J. A., Segal, N. L., and Horwitz, B. N. (2015). Genetic and Environmental Influences on Applied Creativity: A Reared-Apart Twin Study. *Personality and Individual Differences*, *75*, 141–146. doi.org/10.1016/j.paid.2014.11.014.

Von Stumm, S., Chung, A., and Furnham, A. (2011). Creative Ability, Creative Ideation and Latent Classes of Creative Achievement: What Is the Role of Personality?. *Psychology of Aesthetics, Creativity, and the Arts*, *5*(2), 107–114. doi.org/10.1037/a0020499.

Wang, M. Z., Chen, W., Zhang, C., and Deng, X. L. (2017). Personality Types and Scholarly Creativity in Undergraduate Students: The Mediating Roles of Creative Styles. *Personality and Individual Differences*, *105*, 170–174. doi.org/10.1080/10400419.2017.1302777.

Yang, J. S., and Hung, H. V. (2015). Emotions As Constraining and Facilitating Factors for Creativity: Companionate Love and Anger. *Creativity and Innovation Management*, *24*(2), 217–230.

Zabelina, D. L., and Robinson, M. D. (2010). Creativity As Flexible Cognitive Control. *Psychology of Aesthetics, Creativity, and the Arts*, *4*(3), 136–143. doi.org/10.1037/a0017379.

Zhou, J., and George, J. M. (2001). When Job Dissatisfaction Leads to Creativity: Encouraging the Expression of Voice. *Academy of Management Journal*, *44*(4), 682–696. doi.org/10.2307/3069410.

Zimbarg, R. E., Mineka, S., Bobova, L., Craske, M. G., Vrshek-Schallhorn, S., Griffith, J. W., and Anand, D. (2016). Testing a Hierarchical Model of Neuroticism and Its Cognitive Facets: Latent Structure and Prospective Prediction of First Onsets of Anxiety and Unipolar Mood Disorders during 3 Years in Late Adolescence. *Clinical Psychological Science*, *4*(5) 805–824. doi.org/10.1177/2167702615618162.

10   Motivation and Creativity

BETH A. HENNESSEY

INTRODUCTION

The study of psychology is highly complex. In many areas of investigation, the more we learn, the more we realize just how much we don't yet understand. Two especially ephemeral phenomena that have received a great deal of research attention are task motivation and **creativity** of performance (defined as a novel and useful solution to a problem or other open-ended task). Researchers and theorists have explored questions of motivation since the mid-1800s. And as far back as Plato (circa 400 BC), there have been discussions about the need for creativity and ways to foster its development. During the nineteenth century, one popular theory was that creativity was closely tied to madness. By the time of World War II, theorists had come to explore creativity from an aesthetic point of view. Shortly thereafter, the launching of Sputnik in the 1950s prompted a seismic change to the perspective of many researchers. Attention shifted to the physical sciences and engineering, and creativity came to be seen as a means for keeping up with international competition. This competitive theme is still alive and well today. Creativity researchers now devote much of their investigative efforts to business. Earlier work in this area concentrated primarily on the invention of new products, while more contemporary studies have tended to focus on **creative management** – techniques designed to boost innovation with an emphasis on how best to promote employees' productivity and effectiveness. Along these same lines, a smaller group of investigators now concentrate on questions of how to promote creativity in the schools. In both the workplace and the classroom, theorists have come to understand that creative performance is very much tied to motivational orientation.

Creativity and Motivation

Motivation is powerful. Motivational orientation determines the boundary between what we are capable of doing and what we will actually do in any given situation. Without the right kind of motivation, we are unlikely to play with ideas, take risks, or feel at all comfortable with the possibility of failure. Without the right kind of motivation, creativity is nearly impossible. Researchers and theorists have long appreciated this association between aspects of performance, including creativity of performance, and motivational orientation. As early as 1913, the great educational philosopher and theorist John Dewey identified the link between student interest or curiosity and effort expended in the classroom. Another early investigation to establish the connection between motivation and performance focused on the effects of expected reward on preschoolers' motivation for using magic markers (Lepper, Greene, and Nisbett, 1973). In this study, children who contracted with experimenters to make a drawing in order to receive a Good Player Award spent significantly less time using markers during subsequent free-time periods than did their peers who had been randomly assigned to either a no reward or an unexpected reward condition; and in addition, products produced under expected reward conditions were judged to be of significantly lower quality than products made by the unexpected reward or control, no reward, groups.

Early investigations such as this "magic marker study" did not target creativity of performance per se, but researchers soon moved on to explicitly investigate the interplay between motivational orientation and creativity. Hundreds of empirical studies of the impact of promised reward have been carried out. And, in addition, a number of meta-analyses have also been reported. **Meta-analysis** is a statistical procedure that allows for the aggregation of data across multiple empirical investigations. Researchers employing this technique must include any and all studies they can find that target a specific research question. There is no picking and choosing. In some cases, all studies entered into the analysis are assumed to be equally important. In other cases, researchers employ statistical procedures that allow them to weigh more heavily studies incorporating high numbers of participants and/or particularly careful methodologies. A calculation of **effect size** (or treatment effect, e.g., the impact of expected reward on **intrinsic motivation** and/or creativity) is then carried out for each investigation entering into the meta-analysis. These individual values are then aggregated to determine an effect size across studies. Findings that are largely consistent from one study to the next will result in a relatively large combined effect size. Importantly, effect size calculations go beyond an indication of whether study results are significant or whether they could be explained by chance. Effect size estimates indicate whether the phenomenon in question has real-world significance. In other words, in this context, effect size estimates answer the question of whether a teacher or an employer could see the effects of promised reward on performance with their "naked eyes."

Up until fairly recently, it was believed by many that the overall message was crystal clear. The expectation of a reward could be expected to undermine both intrinsic task interest and creativity of performance. In fact, the promise of a reward was not the only killer of task interest and creativity to be identified by researchers. A variety of performance incentives, including expected evaluation, time limits, and competition, have also been shown to have deleterious effects (Amabile, 1988, 1996; Hennessey and Amabile, 1998; Hennessey, 2003, 2010, 2015b). Over time, however, experimental paradigms, most especially reward contingencies, have become increasingly complex. Any fruitful area of experimental investigation must show this kind of progression. The research process is far from stagnant. Earlier simplistic models and educated explanations, often termed hypotheses, which served researchers well as they embarked on groundbreaking paths of inquiry come to be replaced with more sophisticated approaches informed by the findings reported in an ever-expanding literature. New potentially influential variables come to be incorporated into theories and investigative paradigms, while other variables originally thought to be of importance are dropped. Study participants are selected to include a wider diversity of individuals and, over time, this tweaking of initial research questions and models leads to the generation and systematic testing of new, far more nuanced, hypotheses.

This generative process of model building and hypothesis generation is crucial to the investigative process. First comes an educated guess, a **hypothesis** or hunch about some phenomenon. Researchers then proceed to test this hypothesis, and when a sufficient number of investigations have all led to the same general conclusion (e.g., intrinsic motivation is conducive to creativity and the introduction of extrinsic incentives will reduce intrinsic motivation and creativity), the next step is to build a **model** that captures this mechanism or process underlying human behavior. Models guide researchers and theorists in a number of important ways. They help to organize and frame findings across a multiplicity of studies and suggest avenues for further investigation (allowing researchers to ask, "What would happen if . . .").

It is now clear that, contrary to hypotheses proposed in the 1970s and 1980s, the imposition of a reward or other extrinsic constraint cannot be expected to impact everyone in the same negative way. In one paper, Wiechman and Gurland (2009) reported that personality differences appear to influence the effect of extrinsic rewards on intrinsic motivation. Researchers have also investigated how gender (Chen and Zhao, 2013), socioeconomic status (Dai et al., 2012), and differences in intrinsic and extrinsic motivational orientations impact creativity of performance. Some investigations have also contrasted trait (relatively stable across time and place) and state (changeable and influenced by environmental factors) and intrinsic and extrinsic motivational orientations (e.g., Moneta, 2012). Still other investigators have explored individual differences in confidence (Cho and Lyn, 2011), psychological empowerment (Zhang and Bartol, 2010), creative self-beliefs (Putwain, Kearsley, and Symes, 2012), developmental dispositions (Upadhyay and Dalal, 2013), optimism (Icekson, Roskes, and Moran, 2014), and other aspects of cognitive style, such as the ways in which a promised reward is construed (Friedman, 2009; Malik, Butt, and Choi, 2015).

Over time, there have also appeared investigations and theoretical pieces challenging the notion that rewards (and other extrinsic constraints such as evaluation) should ever be framed as detrimental to intrinsic task motivation and creative performance. This debate first surfaced in the mid-1990s, prompting researchers from within and outside the behavioral-psychology tradition to publish a series of opposing commentaries, sharp critiques, and acrimonious replies (see Eisenberger and Cameron, 1996, 1998; Hennessey and Amabile, 1998; Lepper, 1998). Researchers and theorists tend to feel strongly about their work and do not always take kindly to opposing views. Researchers have now learned that rewards conveying competence information (indications that the individual is performing well) may not impact intrinsic motivation (and creativity of performance) in the same way as rewards that are promised and delivered with the sole intention of controlling behavior.

Many of the discrepancies in the literature focused on the impact of expected reward (and other extrinsic constraints) can, in fact, be explained by the choices researchers make as to how best to **operationalize** creativity and motivation. In other words, investigators must decide how they will quantify and measure these ephemeral constructs and how they will know creativity or intrinsic/extrinsic motivation when they see it. What are needed are experimental tasks that truly tap creativity by offering many, if not infinite, paths to completion and no one "right" or "best" solution. In addition, it only makes sense to expect an undermining of intrinsic motivation when the task to be completed is initially intrinsically interesting. Innate levels of interest in the target creativity task constitute one crucial distinction between many of the empirical studies showing negative versus positive effects of reward on task motivation and quality of performance. Overall, in the words of George (2007): "Rather than assume that intrinsic motivation underlies creativity, researchers need to tackle this theoretical linkage more directly and in more depth" (p. 445).

An Exploration of Intrinsic and Extrinsic Motivation

Intrinsic motivation is most often operationalized in the literature as the motivation to approach a task out of sheer interest in the activity itself and excitement about the challenges that lay ahead. When fueled by intrinsic motivation, people perceive that their involvement is free of strong external control: they get the sense that they are playing rather than working (e.g., West, Hoff, and Carlsson, 2013). The solution to a problem or the eventual outcome of a project may not be at all obvious; but deep down inside, the individual is fueled by the conviction that they have the requisite skills necessary to get the job done. **Extrinsic motivation**, on the other hand, is the motivation to do something for some external goal, some incentive outside of the task itself, such as an impending evaluation or the promise of a reward.

In situations where creativity is the goal, intrinsic motivation has frequently been shown to be preferable to extrinsic motivation. And, in fact, intrinsic motivation has been linked to a variety of other learning and performance benefits as well, including increased levels of cognitive flexibility (McGraw 1978; Amabile et al., 1994) and superior long-term retention of information (Conti, Amabile, and Pollak, 1995). In fact, these benefits of intrinsic motivation that have been demonstrated for adults also appear to apply to students in elementary and secondary school classrooms. Studies focused on this younger group have repeatedly demonstrated intrinsic motivation to be preferable to extrinsic motivation (Grolnick, Ryan, and Deci, 1991; Guay and Vallerand, 1997). Children who are intrinsically motivated toward an activity are more likely to undertake that activity voluntarily, and they are also more likely to learn complex material effectively (see Deci and Ryan, 1985b). More recent classroom-based fieldwork also shows that students who approach new learning material with intrinsic goals engage more deeply and persist longer (Vansteenkiste, Lens, and Deci, 2006). Generally speaking, extrinsic motivation has consistently been shown to lead to better performance only on tasks requiring rote recitation, precise performance under strong time pressure, and the completion of familiar, repetitive procedures. An intrinsically motivated state, characterized by deeply focused attention, enhanced cognitive functioning, and increased and persistent activity, leads to deeper, more long-lasting learning and better problem-solving on open-ended tasks (McGraw and McCullers, 1979). In fact, a large number of related investigations have demonstrated that when individuals approach new concepts with high levels of curiosity and interest, information is better learned and remembered (Hidi, 1990; Flink, Boggiano, and Main, 1992; Lepper and Cordova, 1992; Tobias, 1994).

Importantly, intrinsic motivation promotes far more than cognitive function, memory, and persistence. Motivational orientation also helps to determine the kinds of activities that individuals will choose to pursue in the first place. When given a choice of open-ended problems requiring a creative solution, extrinsically motivated students tended to opt for the easiest possible tasks (Condry and Chambers, 1978; Pittman, Emery, and Boggiano, 1982). Intrinsically motivated persons are more likely to take risks and explore solutions to questions or problems that represent for them an appropriate level of difficulty and challenge.

Motivational Mechanisms

Given the many empirical demonstrations of the role played by intrinsic motivation in the selection of tasks, perseverance at those tasks, and deeply focused attention, it makes sense that intrinsic motivation would be especially conducive to creativity. As summarized by Amabile's **intrinsic motivation principle of creativity** outlined previously, earlier conceptualizations of the relation between intrinsic and extrinsic motivation tended to rely on an essentially hydraulic, either-or conceptualization. As extrinsic incentives increased, intrinsic motivation and the likelihood of ensuing creativity were thought to inevitably decrease.

But can extrinsic constraints be expected to consistently kill intrinsic task motivation and creativity of performance? Or must this now decades-old principle be modified to "fit" more recent data? In the past decade or so, the position taken by many researchers and theorists on this issue, including Amabile herself, has become far more nuanced. The focus has shifted from a fairly simplistic attempt to distinguish between intrinsic and extrinsic motivational orientations or to define intrinsically motivated behaviors as those that occur in the absence of extrinsic motivators toward efforts to capture distinctly different forms (and impacts) of extrinsic motivation. Toward this end, Amabile and colleagues have long worked to develop a **componential model** (Amabile, 1988; Amabile and Pratt, 2017) depicting both the internal and external determinants of motivational orientation. In fact, a review of the literature reveals that Amabile's original 1988 componential model was one of the first theories of creativity and innovation to attempt a comprehensive exploration of both individual and environmental factors impacting creative behavior and the many ways these two forces are intertwined. More recently, Amabile and Pratt (2017) presented significant revisions to this model focusing especially on individual-level psychological processes that have emerged as powerful influences. These individual processes include a sort of "progress loop" whereby a sense of engaging in meaningful work increases intrinsic motivation, which increases

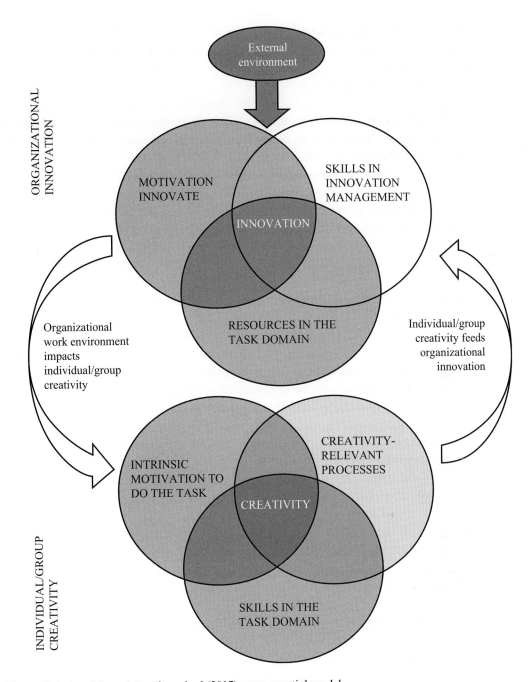

Figure 10.1 Amabile and Pratt's revised (2017) componential model.

Source: www.semanticscholar.org/paper/The-dynamic-componential-model-of-creativity-and-in-Amabile-Pratt/
384e5576914abf53c62b0eba0d4acd7482d84e00/figure/1

creative work, which increases organizational innovation (see Figure 10.1). In many ways, this looping idea fits well with the concept of **motivational synergy**, where extrinsic motivation can under certain specific circumstances combine with intrinsic motivation to promote the creative process.

Mindful of these new insights, in 1996, Amabile published a reworking of the intrinsic motivation principle. Although many extrinsic motivators in the workplace and other environments often appear to undermine intrinsic motivation and creativity, some may not. If rewards or other motivators are presented in a controlling fashion, leading people to feel that they are being bribed or dictated to, the undermining effects are likely to occur. However, if rewards confirm people's competence (for example, by recognizing the value of their contributions), or enable them to become more deeply involved in work they are excited about (for example, by giving them more resources to do that work effectively), intrinsic motivation and creativity might actually be enhanced (see Deci, Koestner, and Ryan, 2001; Friedman, 2009; Yoon et al., 2015). A recent meta-analysis carried out by Cerasoli, Nicklin, and Ford (2014) corroborated this view with the finding that intrinsic motivation and extrinsic incentives, most notably rewards, are not necessarily antagonistic.

A series of three related "immunization" studies (Hennessey, Amabile, and Martinage, 1989; Hennessey and Zbikowski, 1993) demonstrated just this sort of dynamic. Elementary school students given intrinsic motivation training as to how they might keep extrinsic constraints such as the promise of reward in perspective, subsequently showed significantly higher levels of intrinsic task motivation than did children randomly assigned to a control/no-training condition. Moreover, the creativity of products produced by children who had received training and were promised a reward for their task participation was higher than that of any other design group. In fact, these study findings are in keeping with a growing body of data collected across all age groups from laboratory experiments (Amabile, Hennessey, and Grossman, 1986), and non-experimental studies (Amabile, Phillips, and Collins, 1994; Amabile et al., 1994; Amabile and Kramer, 2011; Baer, 2012; Zhu, Gardner, and Chen, 2016) demonstrating how, under certain circumstances, extrinsic motivation can play a facilitative role in the creative process.

In one prototypical study, targeting amateur musicians, Eisenberg and Thompson (2011) found that musical improvisations were judged as more creative under competitive rather than non-competitive conditions. Here too, motivational patterns revealed effects that could not be explained by a simple additive process. Musicians randomly assigned to a competition condition were found to be both more intrinsically motivated than their peers in the no-competition condition and more stressed. Moreover, the musicians who were competing against one another also produced more creative improvisations than their peers in the non-competition group (see also Vansteenkiste and Deci [2003] for somewhat similar study findings). How is it possible that placement in a competitive situation could simultaneously lead to both higher levels of stress and increased levels of creativity and intrinsic motivation? What might be the cognitive mechanism(s) behind this effect?

Self-Perception Underpinnings – Self-Determination Theory

Many theorists would argue that it is important to explore the role played by self-perception processes in determining motivational orientation (and creativity of performance). Early investigations revealed that, in situations where both a plausible intrinsic and extrinsic explanation for our actions are available, each of us tends to dismiss the internal cause in favor of the external cause. Social psychologists variously referred to this process as "discounting" (Kelly 1973) or "over-justification," a formulation derived from the attribution theories of Bem (1972), Kelley (1973), and deCharms (1968). Subsequent research efforts supplemented these discounting and overjustification models with cognitive evaluation theory or CET (Deci 1975; Deci, Cascio, and Krussel, 1975; Deci and Ryan, 1985a) in an attempt to more fully explain the relation between extrinsic and intrinsic motivation with a focus on how external consequences affect internal motivational orientation. And building on this work, Deci and Ryan offered a conceptual refinement of the CET model in the form of **self-determination theory** (SDT) (Deci and Ryan 1985a, 1985b, 1996, 2000, 2008a, 2008b; Ryan and Deci, 2017).

SDT focuses on innate psychological needs and the degree to which individuals are able to satisfy these basic needs as they pursue and attain their valued goals. Integrating a variety of literatures, this model offers a synthesis of what for many years had been a conglomeration of related but distinct motivational approaches (including considerations of intrinsic motivation and internalization). SDT operationalizes extrinsic motivation as a construct far more complex than the simple absence of intrinsic motivation. Focusing on causality orientations, or characteristic ways that each of us develops for understanding and orienting to inputs, Deci and Ryan have hypothesized that individuals vary in the degree to which they exhibit three orientations: "autonomy," "control," and "impersonal." These same researchers then have gone on to argue that these individual differences have important implications for a variety of motivationally involved processes, including creative performance.

Within this SDT framework, extrinsic motivation (termed "controlled motivation" by Deci and Ryan) and intrinsic motivation (termed "autonomous motivation") are viewed as the anchors of a highly complex and multilayered continuum. Across time and situational context, individuals are seen to differ in the ways they perceive environmental constraints and their reactions to them. Some persons, in fact, come to internalize environmental controls and behavioral regulations and believe they follow these rules as a result of free will rather than because limits and expectations have been externally imposed. In yet another demonstration of the ways in which theorizing and model building are generative and evolutionary processes, this focus on the process of internalization has now shifted the attention of many researchers and theorists away from the intrinsic/extrinsic motivation distinction and toward a new dichotomy that emphasizes the fundamental differences between autonomous and controlled motivation. Importantly, autonomous motivation does not always signal that persons are acting entirely independently. Instead, this motivational orientation stems from a need to act with choice and volition – with a sense of psychological freedom and ownership of one's own behaviors (Deci and Ryan, 2000; Ryan and Deci, 2017). In addition to the need for autonomy, the SDT framework also underscores two other basic psychological needs: competence and relatedness (Deci and Ryan, 2000). Individuals acting with competence feel a sense of mastery over their environment and a confidence about developing new skills. The need for relatedness, on the other hand, revolves around the need to feel connected to at least a few others – to love and care for them and to feel their love and care in return.

Since its inception, self-determination theory has enjoyed a great deal of attention in the empirical research literature. Investigators all over the world have attempted to address questions and criticisms concerning the cross-cultural generalizability of SDT, with perhaps the bulk of these studies targeting students at the elementary, middle, and high school levels. Jang et al. (2009) tested the SDT prediction that high school students in collectively oriented South Korea would benefit from classroom experiences of autonomy support and psychological need satisfaction. Across four studies, findings supported the theory's cross-cultural generalizability. Similarly, a series of three studies involving elementary and secondary school students and carried out by Roth et al. in 2006 lent strong support to the relative autonomy continuum proposed by SDT. In 2009, Deci himself teamed up with colleagues Ma and Zhou to show that the SDT framework captured well the motivational orientation of children attending rural Chinese schools (Zhou, Ma, and Deci, 2009).

While these and other study results like them are informative, generally speaking, the outcomes of investigations applying the SDT perspective to issues of academic motivation and school achievement have been somewhat mixed. While self-determination does, in fact, appear to explain motivational and performance outcomes in some situations, some theorists argue that the model is insufficient.

Can SDT Explain It All, or Are There Two Different Types of Intrinsic Motivation?

Given the extensive literature demonstrating the negative impact of expected reward on motivational orientation and qualitative aspects of performance, including creativity, the grading process is an area of continued theoretical controversy. In many respects, the grading system commonly employed across a variety of academic contexts is a ubiquitous real-world example of the use of extrinsic constraints to motivate behavior. Study results as to the efficacy of the grading system are mixed. Importantly, the receipt of an "A" on a report card is a distinctly different kind of reward than the opportunity to play with an instant camera (the reward offered in an early foundational study conducted by Amabile et al. [1986]). The bulk of the theoretical and empirical work on the effects of reward cited earlier in this chapter, from Lepper, Greene, and Nisbett's (1973) seminal work on down, focused on so-called task-contingent rewards: rewards promised and delivered to those who complete an activity without regard to the quality of their performance. This type of reward contingency has repeatedly been found to undermine intrinsic task interest and creativity of performance. But a grade on a report card is performance-contingent. Moreover, the receipt of an "A," or other performance-contingent reward, signals to the recipient that they have been deemed competent, maybe even gifted.

Proponents of what is termed general interest theory (GIT) (e.g., Eisenberger, Pierce, and Cameron, 1999; Jovanovic and Matejecic, 2014) argue that the receipt of a high grade or other performance-contingent reward for an initially interesting task is most likely to increase subsequent task intrinsic motivation if the reward is informational and serves to satisfy the need for competence. Yet advocates of self-determination theory might contend that the pressure to obtain the reward of a high grade will undermine a student's need for autonomy, thereby decreasing intrinsic task motivation.

Overall, empirical studies involving situations in which the receipt of reward is contingent on quality of task performance have yielded mixed results. Performance-contingent rewards have been variously found to have either no appreciable impact or even a positive impact on task interest and qualitative aspects of performance. Could it be that the construct termed intrinsic motivation is better conceptualized as two (or more) distinctly different types of motivation – one focused on more immediate reactions to the task that is accomplished and the other focused on more long-term, continuing task motivation and willingness to persist once the initial task is ended (e.g., Cameron et al., 2005)?

Pulfrey, Darnon, and Butera (2013), in fact, demonstrated the usefulness of this distinction in an investigation of the impact of grades on middle school students' intrinsic motivation. Cooper and Jayatilaka (2006) also underscored the need for theorists to consider a third type of motivation beyond the dichotomous intrinsic/extrinsic distinction, but their findings call for a consideration of what they term "obligation motivation." According to this formulation, obligation motivation results from extrinsic rewards that are not predicated on task performance but are instead tied to feelings of obligation to mandates such as the need to do one's best in school. Additionally, yet another group of investigators (e.g., Gilson and Madjar, 2011) found that intrinsic motivation is associated mainly with the production of radical ideas, while extrinsic motivation is linked more closely with the generation of ideas that are solution-driven and developed on the basis of concrete practices.

Muddying the conceptual waters even further are some especially complex findings emerging from studies focused on organizational creativity and the performance of employees charged with making innovations in product design and marketing. Intrinsic motivation can have both positive and negative outcomes in the workplace (see Grant and Shin [2012] for a review). How are researchers and theorists to make sense of these various research outcomes? In a 2016 meta-analysis of studies investigating motivational mechanisms of employee creativity, Liu, Jiang, Shalley, Keem, and Zhou underscored the need for a more fine-grained examination of motivation and creativity. Research findings reported by Yoon et al. (2015) typify the complexities of this relation. Their investigation examined the effects of tangible and intangible creativity-contingent rewards on employee creativity. In seemingly direct opposition to SDT or intrinsic motivation principle predictions, tangible rewards for creativity were negatively related to extrinsic task motivation; while employee creativity was positively related to extrinsic motivation but not to intrinsic motivation. In an attempt to frame and explain their own study findings regarding creativity in the workplace, Yoon et al. (2015) made the point that investigations carried out in a real-world business setting, outside the highly controlled and often artificial laboratory environment, are subject to a whole host of influences, many of which go unrecognized by researchers and study participants alike. Clearly, more work needs to be done in this area if researchers are to fully appreciate the complexities of the workplace. Individual differences in workers' perceptions of and affective response to their corporate culture and the degree of fairness exhibited there are but two of the factors that may serve to mediate or moderate the impact of rewards and other extrinsic constraints on motivational orientation and creativity of performance.

The Role of Affect

The management of knowledge workers necessitates the building of a community of employees who have satisfying "inner work lives" marked by predominantly positive emotions, a favorable view of their company, their work, and their colleagues, as well as strong intrinsic motivation. These are the conclusions taken from a large and especially comprehensive longitudinal research program carried out in a variety of corporate settings (Amabile and Kramer, 2011). These data and others like them consistently show a strong relation between positive affect, intrinsic motivation, and creativity. The undermining of intrinsic interest and the potential for creative breakthroughs may result as much from emotion or affect as it does from thoughts or cognitive analysis (see Hennessey, 2010). It is no accident that contemporary views of intrinsic motivation frequently include an affective component. In fact, the influential work of Csikszentmihalyi and colleagues (e.g., Nakamura and Csikszentmihalyi, 2003; Csikszentmihalyi, Abuhamdeh, and Nakamura, 2005) has brought to light the elation that can result from the kind of deep task involvement often termed "flow" or "optimal experience."

Recent explorations of the potential link between affect and creative performance have revealed that, under certain circumstances, negative affect can sometimes lead to *increases* in creativity (e.g., Kaufman and Vosburg, 1997; Kaufmann, 2003). Just as studies of the interplay between intrinsic and extrinsic motivation have become far more nuanced, so too have investigations into the role played by affect begun to take a variety of directions. George and Zhou (George and Zhou, 2007; George, 2011) developed a "dual-tuning" model illustrating how positive and negative moods can interact in supportive settings to influence employee creativity. More specifically, these researchers found that when supervisors provided a supportive context for creativity and positive mood was high, negative mood had a strong, positive relation to creativity. Workers' creativity was, in fact, highest when the context was supportive and both positive and negative moods were high. Building on this perspective, Bledow, Rosing, and Frese (2013) reported data showing what they termed an "affective shift," whereby a highly creative outcome results when an individual experiences an episode of negative affect followed by a decrease in negative affect and an increase in positive affect.

The Role of Culture: A Final Overarching Consideration

Throughout the literature exploring the intersection between motivation and creativity and across a number of the empirical investigations reviewed here, perhaps most especially investigations of the business world, researchers have focused on study participants living, learning, and working in non-Western environments. Yet curiously, only occasionally have theorists and researchers addressed the possibility that the relation between motivational orientation and creativity in one cultural context may be distinctly different from the relation in another. While some researchers have talked of "supportive motivational milieus," corporate or classroom "climates," or the complex social systems found within large organizations, until recently, at least, few investigators have asked how the culture into which we are born impacts our creative development and performance. Importantly, however, as explained by Csikszentmihalyi (1999), the creative act is as much a product of social and cultural influences as it is cognitive or psychological. Creativity must be seen and studied as a highly contextualized phenomenon. In fact, most everything we think we understand about creativity and the creative process is socio-culturally dependent.

One psychological area of investigation that has been shown to be directly tied to both motivational orientation and cultural influence focuses on individual differences in self-construal. There are a number of significant differences between Eastern and Western perspectives on the self, and nowhere are these differences more striking than in cross-cultural comparisons of assumptions about control. In the East, emphasis tends to be placed on forces of control imposed by the environment to which the individual is expected to adapt. Asians are thought to exercise, on average, what Ng (2001) terms "secondary control," shaping their internal needs and desires in order to maximize the goodness of fit with existing reality. In the West, people are expected to rise above externally imposed constraints and even to alter their environment so as to better meet their own needs as well as the needs of others. In this cultural context, it is the individual who needs to feel primary control. As summarized by Ng (2001), Asian societies tend to place more value on extrinsic motivation, while Western societies value intrinsic motivation. A thorough delineation of the social and cultural context in which creativity flourishes (or fails to flourish) is essential to any investigation of the psychology of creativity. Researchers must determine how study participants view their situation – their status and their role in the creative process. Do they feel comfortable exploring their creative potential, and do they approach experimental tasks or projects at school and in the workplace with a strong and primarily individualistic sense of purpose? Or are they instead willing to "take a back seat" and to defer to the other members of the group? Are they looking for consensus? Are they driven by a fundamental need to feel autonomous and in control of their situation or are they content to look within themselves for evidence of that control? And finally, do they feel capable of and excited about coming up with a creative idea or approach to a problem, or has their lack of experience with such open-ended situations left them uncertain and unwilling to explore the possibilities?

These are just some of the questions, some of the considerations, that must be addressed by investigators and theorists exploring the motivation-creativity connection across cultures. The impact of culture cannot be overstated, especially perhaps when it comes to the individual's interactions with others. It is quite likely that classrooms and workplaces spread across the globe are characterized by distinctly different sets of social-cognitive dynamics – cultural and subcultural differences in self-construal as well as important differences in the relationships between students and their teachers or employees and their managers, which, in turn, might make for distinctly different relations between the imposition of extrinsic constraints, task motivation, and creativity of performance. A small but growing group of researchers is now pursuing these issues. Hennessey (2015a, 2017) offered a systems perspective of creative performance integrating not only individual differences in experience, skill, and motivational orientation but also considerations of classroom or workplace culture as well as overall culturally determined attitudes, practices, and norms. Chiu and Kwan (2010) also proposed a systems or process model of creativity that explores the role of culture at each stage of knowledge creation, providing data to show that culture can affect creative outcomes through its effects on a variety of social and psychological processes.

In sum, it would appear that there is more than one motivational path to creativity, and cultural norms may have much to do with which path is chosen. For decades, investigators who focused on the interface between motivation and creativity concentrated on Western, often American, workplaces and classrooms; and findings from study to study were remarkably consistent. The imposition of extrinsic constraints such as the promise of a reward or the expectation or evaluation were thought to universally undermine intrinsic motivation and creativity. Either-or hydraulic models leaving no room for nuance and based on just two alternatives served the research community well. The proposition that as extrinsic motivation increases intrinsic motivation (and creativity) are bound to decrease was a good place to start. But in recent years, investigators have come to discover considerable variability across individuals as well as variability in motivational orientation and creative performance tied to differences in cultural contexts. Researchers and theoreticians must be ever vigilant to keep cultural biases, most especially Western biases, and simplistic assumptions from affecting their work. Similarly, schools and companies setting out to stimulate creativity and innovation must guard against a one-size-fits-all application of research findings to their own particular context. Studies carried out in one nation may have little, if anything, to say about how best to structure the workplace or classroom environment in another part of the world. Factors that support intrinsic motivation and creativity in one culture may have no important effect, or even a negative effect, on the creative performance of individuals or groups in another culture. And even persons who are all living and learning in the same cultural context are likely to exhibit important and complex individual differences. The research and applied, practical challenges are many.

Motivation and creativity are complicated. But investigators and theorists will continue to persevere, mindful that it is creativity that moves civilization forward. Now, perhaps more than ever, it is essential that we learn how to better harness creative potential if we are to even begin to tackle the many medical, economic, global-political, and environmental challenges placed before us.

My Research Contribution

After teaching at the elementary level, I returned to graduate school to find answers to the question of how best to set up classroom routines that are optimally conducive to students' intrinsic motivation and creativity. I have published numerous papers documenting how the imposition of extrinsic constraints such as expected reward and evaluation can kill student motivation and creativity. I am especially proud of my work attempting to immunize students against the negative effects of extrinsic constraints, reasoning that if we can't change the way classroom routines are constructed, maybe we can change how students respond to the rewards and the evaluations used to control them (see Hennessey, Amabile, and Martinage, 1989; Hennessey and Zbikowski, 1993).

Another of my contributions involves the study and refinement of the consensual assessment technique (CAT) (Hennessey, Mueller, and Amabile, 2020). The question of how best to measure and compare the creativity of study participants has long challenged researchers. The CAT specifies that judges be recruited to assess the relative creativity of tangible products produced in the "real world" or in the context of experimentally controlled studies. These judges are not trained in any way, nor do they have the opportunity to confer with one another. Instead, using five- or seven-point scales, they individually rate the creativity (and often the technical goodness and aesthetic appeal) of products such as collages, haiku poems, and cartoon captions. Despite the fact that there is no training involved, levels of reliability (agreement) as to the relative creativity of products are amazingly high. Although creativity may be difficult to define, it is something that we can recognize and agree on. The CAT has served investigators especially well and is now considered the "gold standard" of creativity assessment procedures (Baer and McKool, 2014). In fact, most of the empirical studies cited in this chapter relied on consensual assessment.

Right now, my recent theorizing about the intersections of culture, creativity, and motivation is the work that most excites me. Traditionally, research in this area has focused on Western European study participants. It is my goal to expand this research lens to include persons from a wide variety of cultural and economic backgrounds (see Hennessey, 2017).

Critical/Creative Thinking Questions

1. As a researcher, how would you set out to define and measure creativity? Are you satisfied with the approach taken by the consensual assessment technique (CAT) and the assertion that the best measure of the creativity of a work of art, a theory, a research proposal, or any other artifact is the combined assessment of experts in that field? What are other ways that creativity might be operationalized and measured?
2. If you were a classroom teacher or a manager in a business setting, how much emphasis and energy would you devote to the promotion of creativity? How important is it to develop students' and employees' creativity? Can you see any downsides to some of the factors shown to nurture creativity?
3. Do you believe that the many research investigations and theories outlined in this chapter have important real-world significance, or are constructs like creativity and motivation, not to mention the interaction between them, far too complex to quantify or manipulate?
4. A careful reading of this chapter reveals just how much models and theories morph over time. Once steadfast principles (e.g., extrinsic motivation is detrimental to creativity) become increasingly more nuanced and refined. In other words, theorizing and model building are very much iterative pursuits. Research is far from a stagnant process. Each new finding poses far more questions than it does answers. Where do you see creativity investigations moving in the future? What are, in your view, some of the most important areas to be explored?
5. What is the role of culture in the creative process? Do you believe that the internal and external (environmental) determinants of creative outcomes are pretty much universal worldwide? Or would you expect that the intersection between motivational orientation and creative performance varies considerably from culture to culture? Why or why not? Elaborate on your thinking here.

GLOSSARY

componential model: Any model attempting to integrate a variety of factors, influences, components of a phenomenon or process. In the case of creativity, the componential model strives to combine an examination of internal and external influences on creative performance.

creative management: Techniques designed to boost innovation with an emphasis on how best to promote employees' productivity and effectiveness.

creativity: Creativity as demonstrated/operationalized by a novel and useful solution to a problem or some other open-ended task.

effect size: A mathematical calculation of a study's treatment effect, for example, the impact of expected reward on intrinsic motivation and/or creativity. Importantly, effect size calculations go beyond an indication of whether study results are statistically significant or whether they could be explained by chance. Effect size estimates indicate whether the phenomenon in question has real-world significance. In studies of reward effects on motivation and creativity, they answer the question of whether a teacher or an employer could see the effects of promised reward on performance or task motivation with their "naked eyes."

extrinsic motivation: The motivation to engage in a task for some reason beyond interest in or excitement about the task itself, such as the promise of a reward or the expectation of a grade.

hypothesis: An educated guess or hunch about some phenomenon or relationship between phenomena (e.g., intrinsic motivation is conducive to creativity and extrinsic motivation is most often detrimental).

intrinsic motivation: The motivation to engage in a task for the sheer pleasure and enjoyment of the task itself.

intrinsic motivation principle of creativity: Intrinsic motivation, the motivation to engage in a task for the sheer pleasure and enjoyment of the task itself, is conducive to **creativity** while **extrinsic motivation**, the motivation to engage in a task for some outside reason such as the promise of a reward or the expectation of a grade, is almost always detrimental.

meta-analysis: A statistical procedure that allows for the aggregation of data across multiple empirical investigations.

model: A representation of an idea, a process, or a system that is used to describe and explain phenomena that cannot be experienced directly. Models guide researchers and theorists in a number of important ways. They help to organize and frame findings across a multiplicity of studies and suggest avenues for further investigation (allowing researchers to ask, "What would happen if . . .").

motivational synergy: Where extrinsic motivation can under certain specific circumstances combine with intrinsic motivation to promote the creative process.

operationalize: Investigators must decide how they will quantify and measure ephemeral constructs such as creativity or intrinsic and extrinsic motivation. When they operationalize these constructs, they specify how they will recognize and measure these variables when they see them.

self-determination theory: A theory that focuses on innate psychological needs and the degree to which individuals are able to satisfy these basic needs as they pursue and attain their valued goals. Integrating a variety of literatures, this model offers a synthesis of what for many years had been a conglomeration of related but distinct motivational approaches (including considerations of the need to feel competent, autonomous, and connected to others).

REFERENCES

Amabile, T. M. (1988). A Model of Creativity and Innovation in Organizations. In B. S. Cummings (Ed.), *Research in Organizational Behavior* (pp. 123–167). Greenwich: JAI Press.

(1996). *Creativity in Context*. Boulder: Westview.

Amabile, T. M., Hennessey, B. A., and Grossman, B. (1986). Social Influences on Creativity: The Effects of Contracted-for Reward. *Journal of Personality and Social Psychology*, *50*, 14–23.

Amabile, T. M., Hill, K., Hennessey, B. A., and Tighe, E. (1994). The Work Preference Inventory: Assessing Intrinsic and Extrinsic Motivational Orientations. *Journal of Personality and Social Psychology*, *66*, 950–967.

Amabile, T. M., Kramer, S. J. (2011). *The Progress Principle: Using Small Wins to Ignite Joy, Engagement, and Creativity at Work*. Cambridge, MA: Harvard Business Review Press.

Amabile, T. M., Phillips, E., and Collins, M. A. (1994). Person and Environment in Talent Development: The Case of Creativity. In N. Colangelo, S. Assouline, and D. Ambronson (Eds.), *Talent Development* (pp. 265–280). Dayton: Ohio Psychology Press.

Amabile, T. M., and Pratt, M. G. (2017). The Dynamic Componential Model of Creativity and Innovation in Organizations: Making Progress, Making Meaning. *Research in Organizational Behavior*, *37*, 157–183.

Baer, M. (2012). Putting Creativity to Work: The Implementation of Creative Ideas in Organizations. *Academy of Management Journal*, *55*, 1102–1119.

Baer, J. and McKool, S. S. (2014). The Gold Standard for Assessing Creativity. *International Journal of Quality Assurance in Engineering and Technology Education*, *3*, 81–93.

Bem, D. (1972). Self-Perception Theory. In L. Berkowitz (Ed.), *Advances in Experimental Social Psychology*, vol. 6 (pp. 1–62). New York: Academic Press.

Bledow, R., Rosing, K., and Frese, M. (2013). A Dynamic Perspective on Affect and Creativity. *Academy of Management Journal*, *56*, 432–450.

Cameron, J., Pierce, W. D., Banko, K. M., and Gear, A. (2005). Achievement-Based Rewards and Intrinsic Motivation: A Test of Cognitive Mediators. *Journal of Educational Psychology*, *97*, 641–655.

Chen, Y., and Zhao, Q. (2013). Gender Differences in Business Faculty's Research Motivation. *Journal of Education for Business*, *88*, 314–324.

Cerasoli, C. P., Nicklin, J. M., and Ford, M. T. (2014). Intrinsic Motivation and Extrinsic Incentives Jointly Predict Performance: A 40-Year Meta-Analysis. *Psychological Bulletin*, *140*, 980–1008.

Chiu, C.-Y., and Kwan, L. Y.-Y. (2010). Culture and Creativity: A Process Model. *Management and Organization Review*, *6*, 447–461.

Cho, S., and Lin, C.-Y. (2011). Influence of Family Processes, Motivation, and Beliefs about Intelligence on Creative Problem Solving of Scientifically Talented Individuals. *Roeper Review*, *33*, 46–58.

Condry, J., and Chambers, J. (1978). Intrinsic Motivation and the Process of Learning. In M. R. Lepper and D. Greene (Eds.), *The Hidden Costs of Reward* (pp. 61–84). Hillsdale: Lawrence Earlbaum.

Conti, R., Amabile, T. A., and Pollack, S. (1995). The Positive Impact of Creative Activity: Effects of Creative Task Engagement and Motivational Focus on College Students' Learning. *Personality and Social Psychology Bulletin*, *21*, 1107–1116.

Cooper, R. B., and Jayatilaka, B. (2006). Group Creativity: The Effects of Extrinsic, Intrinsic, and Obligation Motivations. *Creativity Research Journal*, *18*, 153–172.

Csikszentmihalyi, M. (1999). A Systems Perspective on Creativity. In R. Sternberg (Ed.), *Handbook of Creativity* (pp. 313–335). Cambridge: Cambridge University Press.

Cskiszentmihalyi, M., Abuhamdeh, S., and Nakamura, J. (2005). Flow. In A. J. Elliot and C. S. Dweck (Eds.), *Handbook of Competence and Motivation* (pp. 598–608). New York: Guilford Publications.

Dai, D. Y., Tan, X., Marathe, D., Valtchea, A., and Pruzek, R. M. (2012). Influences of Social and Educational Environments on Creativity during Adolescence: Does SES Matter? *Creativity Research Journal*, *24*, 191–199.

deCharms, R. (1968). *Personal Causation*. New York: Academic Press.

Deci, E. L. (1975). *Intrinsic Motivation*. New York: Plenum.

Deci, E. L., Cascio, W. F., and Krussel, J. (1975). Cognitive Evaluation Theory and Some Comments on the Calder and Staw Critique. *Journal of Personality and Social Psychology*, *31*, 81–85.

Deci, E. L., Koestner, R., and Ryan, R. M. (2001). Extrinsic Rewards and Intrinsic Motivation in Education: Reconsidered Once Again. *Review of Educational Research*, *71*, 1–27.

Deci, E. L., and Ryan, R. M. (1985a). The General Causality Orientations Scale: Self-Determination in Personality. *Journal of Personality and Social Psychology*, *19*, 109–134.

(1985b). *Intrinsic Motivation and Self-Determination in Human Behavior*. New York: Plenum.

(1996). *Why We Do What We Do: Understanding Self-Motivation*. New York: Penguin.

(2000). The What and Why of Goal Pursuits: Human Needs and the Self-Determination of Behavior. *Psychological Inquiry*, *11*, 227–268.

(2008a). Facilitating Optimal Motivation and Psychological Well-Being across Life's Domains. *Canadian Psychology*, *49*, 14–23.

(2008b). Self-Determination Theory: A Macrotheory of Human Motivation, Development, and Health. *Canadian Psychology*, *49*, 182–185.

Dewey, J. (1913). *Interest and Effort in Education*. Boston: Houghton Mifflin.

Eisenberg, J., and Thompson W. F. (2011). The Effects of Competition on Improvisers' Motivation, Stress, and Creative Performance. *Creativity Research Journal*, *23*, 129–136.

Eisenberger, R., and Cameron, J. (1996). Detrimental Effects of Reward: Reality or Myth? *American Psychologist*, *51*, 1153–1166.

(1998). Reward, Intrinsic Interest, and Creativity: New Findings. *American Psychologist*, *53*, 676–679.

Eisenberger, R., Pierce, W. D., and Cameron, J. (1999). Effects of Reward on Intrinsic Motivation – Negative, Neutral, and Positive: Comment on Deci, Koestner, and Ryan. *Psychological Bulletin*, *125*, 677–691.

Flink, C., Boggiano, A. K., and Main, D. S. (1992). Children's Achievement-Related Behaviors: The Role of Extrinsic and Intrinsic Motivational Orientations. In A. K. Boggiano and T. S. Pittman (Eds.), *Achievement and Motivation: A Social-Developmental Perspective* (pp. 189–214). New York: Cambridge University Press.

Friedman, R. S. (2009). Reinvestigating the Effects of Promised Reward on Creativity. *Creativity Research Journal*, *21*, 258–264.

George, J. M. (2007). Creativity in Organizations. *Academy of Management Annals*, *1*, 439–477.

(2011). Dual Tuning: A Minimum Condition for Understanding Affect in Organizations? *Organizational Psychology Review*, *1*, 147–164.

George, J. M., and Zhou, J. (2007). Dual Tuning in a Supportive Context: Joint Contributions of Positive Mood, Negative Mood, and Supervisory Behaviors to Employee Creativity. *Academy of Management Journal*, *50*, 605–622.

Gilson, L. L., and Madjar, N. (2011). Radical and Incremental Creativity: Antecedents and Processes. *Psychology of Aesthetics, Creativity, and the Arts*, *5*, 21–28.

Grant, A. M. and Shin, J. (2012). Work Motivation: Directing, Energizing, and Maintaining Effort (and Research). In R. M. Ryan (Ed.), *Oxford Handbook of Motivation* (pp. 505–519). New York: Oxford University Press.

Grolnick, W. S., Ryan, R. M. and Deci, E. L. (1991). Inner Resources for School Achievement: Motivational Mediators of Children's Perceptions of Their Parents. *Journal of Educational Psychology*, *83*, 508–517.

Guay, F., and Vallerand, R. J. (1997). Social Context, Students' Motivation, and Academic Achievement: Towards a Process Model. *Social Psychology of Education*, *1*, 211–233.

Hennessey, B. A. (2003). The Social Psychology of Creativity. *Scandinavian Journal of Educational Research*, *47*, 253–271.

(2010). The Creativity – Motivation Connection. In J. C. Kaufman and R. J. Sternberg (Eds.), *The Cambridge Handbook of Creativity* (pp. 342–365). New York: Cambridge University Press.

(2015a). Creative Behavior, Motivation, Environment and Culture: The Building of a Systems Model. *Journal of Creative Behavior*, *49*, 194–2010.

(2015b). Reward, Task Motivation, Creativity and Teaching: Towards a Cross-Cultural Examination. *Teachers College Record, 117*, 1–28.

(2017). Taking a Systems View of Creativity: On the Right Path toward Understanding. *The Journal of Creative Behavior, 51*, 341–344.

Hennessey, B. A., and Amabile, T. M. (1998). Reward, Intrinsic Motivation, and Creativity. *American Psychologist, 53*, 674–675.

Hennessey, B. A., Amabile, T. M., and Martinage, M. (1989). Immunizing Children against the Negative Effects of Reward. *Contemporary Educational Psychology, 14*, 212–227.

Hennessey, B. A., Mueller, J. S. and Amabile, T. M. (2020). Consensual Assessment. In M. A. Runco and S. Pritzker (Eds.), *Encyclopedia of Creativity*, 3rd ed. (pp. 199–205). New York: Elsevier.

Hennessey, B. A., and Zbikowski, S. M. (1993). Immunizing Children against the Negative Effects of Reward: A Further Examination of Intrinsic Motivation Training Techniques. *Creativity Research Journal, 6*, 297–307.

Hidi, S. (1990). Interest and Its Contribution As a Mental Resource for Learning. *Review of Educational Research, 60*, 549–571.

Icekson, T., Roskes, M., and Moran, S. (2014). Effects of Optimism on Creativity under Approach and Avoidance Motivation. *Frontiers in Human Neuroscience, 8*, 105. doi.org/10.3389/fnhum.2014.00105.

Jang, H., Reeve, J., Ryan, R. M., and Kim, A. (2009). Can Self-Determination Theory Explain What Underlies the Productive Satisfying Learning Experiences of Collectivistically Oriented Korean Students? *Journal of Educational Psychology, 101*, 644–661.

Jovanovic, D., and Matejevic, M. (2014). Relationship between Rewards and Intrinsic Motivation for Learning – Researches Review. *Procedia – Social and Behavioral Sciences, 149*, 456–460.

Kaufmann, G. (2003). Expanding the Mood–Creativity Equation. *Creativity Research Journal, 15*, 131–135.

Kaufmann, G., and Vosburg, S. K. (1997). "Paradoxical" Mood Effects on Creative Problem-Solving. *Cognition and Emotion, 11*, 151–170.

Kelley, H. (1973). The Processes of Causal Attribution. *American Psychologist, 28*, 107–128.

Lepper, M. R. (1998). A Whole Much Less Than the Sum of Its Parts: A Comment on Eisenberger and Cameron. *American Psychologist, 53*, 675–676.

Lepper, M. R., and Cordova, D. T. (1992). A Desire to Be Taught: Instructional Consequences of Intrinsic Motivation. *Motivation and Emotion, 16*, 187–208.

Lepper, M. R., Greene, D., and Nisbett, R. E. (1973). Undermining Children's Intrinsic Interest with Extrinsic Tewards: A Test of the Overjustification Hypothesis. *Journal of Personality and Social Psychology, 28*, 129–137.

Liu, D., Jiang, K., Shalley, C. E., Keem, S., and Zhou, J. (2016). Motivational Mechanisms of Employee Creativity: A Meta-Analytic Examination and Theoretical Extension of the Creativity Literature. *Organizational Behavior and Human Decision Processes, 137*, 236–263.

Malik, M. A. R., Butt, A. N., and Choi, J. N. (2015). Rewards and Employee Creative Performance: Moderating Effects of Creative Self-Efficacy, Reward Importance, and Locus of Control. *Journal of Organizational Behavior, 36*, 59–74.

McGraw, K. O. (1978). The Detrimental Effects of Reward on Performance: A Literature Review and a Prediction Model. In M. R. Lepper and D. Greene (Eds.), *The Hidden Costs of Reward* (pp. 33–60). Hillsdale: Erlbaum.

McGraw, K. O., and McCullers, J. (1979). Evidence of a Detrimental Effect of Extrinsic Incentives on Breaking a Mental Set. *Journal of Experimental Social Psychology, 15*, 285–294.

Moneta, G. (2012). Opportunity for Creativity in the Job As a Moderator of the Relation between Trait Intrinsic Motivation and Flow in Work. *Motivation and Emotion, 36,* 491–503.

Nakamura, J., and Csikszentmihalyi, M. (2003). The Motivational Sources of Creativity As Viewed from the Paradigm of Positive Psychology. In L. G. Aspinwall and U. M. Staudinger (Eds.), *A Psychology of Human Strengths: Fundamental Questions and Future Directions for a Positive Psychology* (pp. 257–269). Washington, DC: American Psychological Association.

Ng, A. K. (2001). *Why Asians Are Less Creative Than Westerners.* Singapore: Prentice-Hall.

Pittman, T. S., Emery, J., and Boggiano, A. K. (1982). Intrinsic and Extrinsic Motivational Orientations: Reward-Induced Changes in Preference for Complexity. *Journal of Personality and Social Psychology, 42,* 789–797.

Pulfrey, C., Darnon, C., and Butera, F. (2013). Autonomy and Task Performance: Explaining the Impact of Grades on Intrinsic Motivation. *Journal of Educational Psychology, 105,* 39–57.

Putwain, D. W., Kearsley, R., and Symes, W. (2012). Do Creativity Self-Beliefs Predict Literacy Achievement and Motivation? *Learning and Individual Differences, 22,* 370–374.

Ryan, R. M., and Deci, E. L. (2017). *Self-Determination Theory: Basic Psychological Needs in Motivation, Development and Wellness.* New York: Guilford.

Roth, G., Assor, A., Kanat-Maymon, Y., and Kaplan, H. (2006). Assessing the Experience of Autonomy in New Cultures and Contexts. *Motivation and Emotion, 30,* 365–376.

Tobias, S. (1994). Interest, Prior Knowledge and Learning. *Review of Educational Research, 64,* 37–54.

Upadhyay, D. K., and Dalal, A. K. (2013). Growing up As a Creative Musician: The Role of Psychosocial Dispositions and Environment. *Psychological Studies, 58,* 427–436.

Vansteenkiste, M., and Deci, E. L. (2003). Competitively Contingent Rewards and Intrinsic Motivation: Can Losers Remain Motivated? *Motivation and Emotion, 27,* 273–299.

Vansteenkiste, M., Lens, W., and Deci, E. L. (2006). Intrinsic versus Extrinsic Goal Contents in Self-Determination Theory: Another Look at the Quality of Academic Motivation. *Educational Psychologist, 4,* 19–31.

Wiechman, B. M., and Gurland, S. T. (2009). What Happens during the Free-Choice Period? Evidence of a Polarizing Effect of Extrinsic Rewards on Intrinsic Motivation. *Journal of Research in Personality, 43,* 716–719.

West, S., Hoff, E., and Carlsson, I. (2013). Playing at Work: Professionals' Conceptions of the Functions of Play on Organizational Creativity. *The International Journal of Creativity and Problem Solving, 23,* 5–23.

Yoon, H. J., Sung, S. Y., Choi, J. N., Lee, K., and Kim, S. (2015). Tangible and Intangible Rewards and Employee Creativity: The Mediating Role of Situational Extrinsic Motivation. *Creativity Research Journal, 27,* 383–393.

Zhang, X., and Bartol, K. M. (2010). Linking Empowering Leadership and Employee Creativity: The Influence of Psychological Empowerment, Intrinsic Motivation, and Creative Process Engagement. *Academy of Management Journal, 53,* 107–128.

Zhou, M., Ma, W. J., and Deci, E. L. (2009). The Importance of Autonomy for Rural Chinese Children's Motivation for Learning. *Learning and Individual Differences, 19,* 492–498.

Zhu, Y.-Q., Gardner, D. G., and Chen, H.-G. (2016). Relationships between Work Team Climate, Individual Motivation, and Creativity. *Journal of Management.* doi:10.1177/0149206316638161.

11 Creativity and Mental Health

SHELLEY CARSON, ELLEN YANG, AND MARIE FORGEARD

INTRODUCTION

Creativity is defined as the ability to generate ideas or products that are both original and in some way useful or adaptive (Barron, 1969). At the highest level, creative ideas, processes, and products have benefited humanity by helping us to survive and adapt to a changing environment (Richards, 1990). At a more personal level, creative work in the arts, music, literature, science, technology, and medicine has reduced suffering, improved daily living, and enriched our mental and physical experience of the world. Research demonstrates that simply engaging in creative activity can provide physical and mental health benefits as well (Cohen, 2006; Eschleman et al., 2014; Conner, DeYoung, and Silvia, 2016). Yet, despite these abundant benefits of creative work, the notion that there is a relationship between creativity and mental illness – the "mad genius" concept – is widespread. If creativity is so beneficial, can it also be related to increased risk for mental illness?

The "mad genius" controversy is one of the most contentious disagreements in modern creativity research, with researchers on one side arguing that there is a large body of biographical evidence and **empirical** research supporting a relationship between creativity and mental illness (e.g., Andreasen, 2008; Simonton, 2010), while the other side argues that the empirical research is flawed and the relationship is a myth (e.g., Schlesinger, 2009, 2014; Sawyer, 2012).

In this chapter, we will look at some evidence for both sides of this debate, as well as the latest attempts to explain the findings. We will also look at how important creativity is for mental health and healing.

Creativity and Mental Illness: Historical Precedents

Since the time of the ancient Greeks, writers have speculated on a connection between creativity and certain types of mental illness. Plato, for example, remarked that poets, philosophers, and dramatists had a tendency to suffer from "divine madness" (Plato, 360 BC), while Aristotle asked why all those who have become eminent in philosophy, poetry, or the arts tended to be melancholic (Aristotle, 1984). These appear to be the first historical references to a tendency for creative individuals to suffer from mania and depression respectively.

It was, however, the writers and artists of the Romantic era who solidified the concept of the mad genius. The romantics applauded (and perhaps adopted) signs of mental illness as a proud badge of affliction that separated them from dreaded normality (Becker, 2014) and considered the most creative work to be accomplished at the border between sanity and insanity.

Early evidence for the creativity/mental illness connection, then, consisted of observations and examples from the lives of creative luminaries. Indeed, biographical reports of the lives of creative individuals, such as William Blake, Robert Schumann, Vincent van Gogh, Virginia Woolf, William Faulkner, Ernest Hemingway, and Sylvia Plath, as well as of contemporary creatives, including Robin Williams, Carrie Fisher, and Amy Winehouse, provide additional biographical evidence for a creativity/mental illness connection. However, the World Health Organization estimates that 450 million people worldwide suffer from mental disorders (World Health Organization, 2013). Therefore, even if rates of mental illness were actually *lower* among highly creative individuals than in the general population, there would still be a great many individuals (perhaps millions) who are both creative and have mental disorders (Carson, 2014a). If a genuine connection between creativity and **psychopathology** existed, it would need to be supported by empirical evidence, not merely by observations and examples.

Creativity and Mental Illness: Empirical Evidence for a Connection

During the mid-twentieth century, three studies were conducted that influenced later research. First, Adele Juda (1949) found that the majority of the 294 German-speaking artists and scientists in her research study were "normal" (not "insane"), although she also noted that "the geniuses and their families show a much higher incidence of psychosis and psychoneurosis than the average population" (p. 307). Second, a study by Heston (1966) reported that the adopted-away children of mothers with schizophrenia were more likely to hold creative jobs and have colorful lives than were the adopted-away offspring of mothers without schizophrenia. And finally, Karlsson (1970) found that males in Iceland born between 1881 and 1910 who had a relative with psychosis were almost three times as likely to be registered in *Who's Who* for excellence in a creative field as those without a relative with psychosis.

These findings sparked new research, beginning in the late 1980s, into the possible connection of mental disorder and high creative achievement. The disorders most often investigated included mood disorders (depression and bipolar disorder) and **schizophrenia-spectrum** disorders. However, substance abuse disorders, and more recently, attention deficit disorders (ADHD) have also been associated with enhanced levels of creativity.

Creativity and Mental Illness: Research Methods

Modern research on the topic of creativity and psychopathology has employed a number of different methods, including the following:

- **case studies**: These studies follow single individuals over a span of time and examine creativity and psychopathology trends.
- **historiometric studies**: These studies perform quantitative analyses on historical biographical data to determine trends concerning creativity and mental illness.
- **clinical studies**: These studies examine persons diagnosed with psychiatric disorder relative to those in a control group and test them on a variety of creativity measures.
- **psychometric studies**: These studies compare creative to non-creative groups on a variety of measures of psychopathology symptoms.
- **meta-analytic studies**: These studies compile the results of data from a number of independent studies on the topic of creativity and various disorders in order to determine overall trends.
- **brain imaging studies**: These studies examine commonalities between the brains of creative individuals and the brains of those with mental disorders.
- **molecular genetics studies**: These studies examine specific genetic variants that are found to be shared among disordered and creative subjects.

Creativity and Mood Disorders

Several studies have been influential in suggesting that risk for mood disorders may be elevated among highly creative individuals. Andreasen (1987), using a case study format, found that authors of the prestigious Iowa Writers Workshop were four times more likely to suffer from bipolar disorder than matched controls, and that 80 percent of the writers reported suffering from a mood disorder. Jamison (1989) also used case studies to examine mood disorders and found an unusually high percentage of mood disorders (38 percent), and specifically bipolar disorder (6.4 percent), in award-winning writers and artists in the United Kingdom. Finally, Ludwig (1994) reported that rates of both depression (56 percent) and mania (19 percent) were higher in a group of 59 female writers in the University of Kentucky National Women Writer's Conference than those of controls matched for age and education. However, these studies have been cited for methodological flaws. For example, critics of the creativity/psychopathology connection point out that Andreasen selected all the writers and control subjects, as well as conducting all the psychiatric interviews herself, in her 1987 study, which could lead to unconscious bias on the part of the researcher. Jamison's (1989) study did not include a control group, and, again she selected all the subjects herself, which could have led to a bias in selecting those with signs of mood disorder (Schlesinger, 2009, 2014; Sawyer, 2012).

Several studies have also examined mood disorders and creativity from a historiometric perspective, utilizing biographical information to assess mental disorders in creative luminaries. Ludwig (1992, 1995), using biographical data, analyzed psychiatric symptoms in over 1,000 deceased individuals in 19 different professions and reported that persons in creative professions had significantly higher rates of mood disorders than those from other professions. Additional historiometric studies have found high rates of mood disorders in abstract expressionist painters (Schildkraut, Hirshfeld, and Murphy, 1994), jazz musicians (Wills, 2003), female poets (Kaufman, 2001), and male creators (Post, 1994). Again, these historiometric studies have not gone without criticism. While the Ludwig (1992, 1995) study has been cited for diagnosing mental disorders too broadly (Sawyer, 2012), historiometric studies in general have been criticized for making diagnoses based primarily on anecdotal accounts that may represent a personal agenda of the biographer of the famous person in question (Schlesinger, 2012).

In the two largest studies of creativity and mental illness, Kyaga et al. (2011, 2013) examined creative professions and psychopathology status listed in Swedish population registries. These studies found that Swedish citizens in artistic occupations had higher rates of bipolar disorder than those in non-creative professions, while writers had higher rates of unipolar depression (as well as other forms of psychopathology) than non-writers. Family members of those diagnosed with bipolar disorder were more likely to be in creative professions than those who did not have a psychiatric family history. Critics, however, have also found fault with these studies, claiming that having a creative profession is not an adequate measure of creativity. Many artists or writers are not necessarily more creative than people who have chosen another profession, such as sales or medicine (Sawyer, 2014).

Examining a clinical sample, Richards et al. (1988) studied creativity across the bipolar spectrum and found that subjects who had a less severe form of the illness (**cyclothymia**), as well as family members of subjects who had bipolar disorder, had greater creative accomplishments and interests than either control subjects or the subjects with full-blown bipolar disorder themselves. The results of the Richards et al. (1988) study suggest that milder forms of mood disorder or a family risk for disorder may enhance creativity, while full-blown bipolar disorder may be detrimental to creativity. This **inverted "U" hypothesis** of creativity and psychopathology (Richards et al., 1988) is supported by additional studies that have found **hypomania** (a subclinical measure of bipolar tendencies) to be associated with higher creativity scores (e.g., Vellante et al., 2011; Zabelina, Condon, and Beeman, 2014).

Finally, a meta-analysis of twenty-eight studies found a positive and significant relationship between bipolar disorder and creativity (Baas et al., 2016).

Creativity and Schizophrenia-Spectrum Disorders

Biographers have long noted psychotic and odd or eccentric behavior in a number of creative individuals. The visionary poet and artist William Blake described having hallucinations since childhood, believing that many of his poems and paintings were given to him by spirits or demons (Galvin, 2004). And Nikola Tesla, the scientist credited with developing alternating electrical current, became convinced that he was telecommunicating with Martians (Tesla, 1901). However, biographers also point out that even when creative luminaries suffer from psychotic episodes, they do not produce quality creative work during actual psychotic states (e.g., Nasar, 1998). Indeed, most studies have not found higher rates of schizophrenia in creative persons, but studies *have* found higher rates of schizophrenia in the families of creative persons than in controls (e.g., Heston, 1966; Karlsson, 1970). In their Swedish population study, Kyaga et al. (2011), found that the siblings of people with schizophrenia were more likely than the norm to hold creative positions. These findings suggest that inheriting part, but not all, of the schizophrenia **genotype** may be beneficial to creativity.

Both relatives of people with schizophrenia and people who score high on divergent thinking measures of creativity are also more likely to display traits of **schizotypal personality** or **schizotypy** (Claridge, 1997). Schizotypy is part of the schizophrenia spectrum. While persons who are high in schizotypy are not necessarily mentally disordered, they may display odd behaviors and beliefs, and they may appear eccentric. A number of past studies found that creative subjects had higher schizotypal personality scores than less creative subjects (e.g., Schuldberg et al., 1988; Poreh, Whitman, and Ross, 1994; Cox and Leon, 1999; Green and Williams, 1999).

Further, a certain type of schizotypy, called positive schizotypy or **psychosis-proneness**, has been found to be elevated in studies of artists and poets (e.g., O'Reilly, Dunbar, and Bentall, 2001; Burch et al., 2006; Nettle, 2006). Psychosis-proneness includes unusual perceptual experiences (e.g., hearing voice-like noises in the wind) and magical thinking (e.g., paranormal beliefs) (Mason and Claridge, 2006). A meta-analysis of forty-five studies showed a significant positive relationship between positive schizotypy and creativity (Acar and Sen, 2013).

As with mood disorders, there is some evidence for an "inverted U" relationship between creativity and the schizophrenia spectrum. Kinney et al. (2000–2001) found that schizophrenia-spectrum traits tend to run in families and that creativity levels were higher in subjects who had two or more positive schizotypal traits than in subjects with either no schizotypal traits or with full-blown schizophrenia.

Creativity and Alcoholism

Alcohol has been noted as a method of summoning the muse since the time of the ancient Greeks. In his drama *The Knights*, Aristophanes (424 BC) has the character of Demosthenes utter, "Come, bring hither quick a flagon of wine, that I may soak my brain and get an ingenious idea." Modern research on creativity and alcoholism points to a higher rate of alcoholism in creative groups, especially creative writers, than in the general population. While the National Comorbidity Survey Replication Study estimates the lifetime risk for alcoholism in the United States at 5.4 percent (Kessler et al., 2005), 30 percent of the writers from Andreasen's (1987) Iowa Writers Workshop study suffered from alcoholism, and 14 percent of the writers, composers, and artists from Post's (1994) biographical review of famous men were alcoholic. In Ludwig's (1992; 1995) study of over 1,000 deceased individuals in 19 different professions, alcoholism was increased in all the creative professions, ranging from 22 percent in artists to 37 percent in fiction writers. Finally, Dardis (1989) noted that of the eight American novelists who had won the Nobel Prize for Literature before 1990, five were confirmed alcoholics.

Experimental studies indicate that low-to-moderate doses of alcohol can improve certain aspects of creativity (Norlander, 1999; Jarosz, Colflesh, and Wiley, 2012), particularly in the insight or idea generation phase of the creative process. This beneficial effect of alcohol may be due to its ability to disinhibit – or turn down the volume on – executive control centers of the brain, allowing more stimuli to enter into conscious awareness for creative combination (Carson, 2014b). As with other disorders, there is evidence for an "inverted U" association between alcoholism and creativity. Moderate drink may aid creativity (e.g., Jarosz et al., 2012), but full-blown alcoholism is harmful for creative efforts.

Creativity and ADHD

Attention deficit hyperactivity disorder (ADHD) has a shorter history than other disorders that have been associated with creativity. Nevertheless, signs of attention deficit or hyperactivity have been attributed to creative luminaries throughout history. According to Cramond (1995), these include Thomas Jefferson, Robert Frost, and Frank Lloyd Wright. A growing number of studies have reported increased scores on divergent thinking task measures of creativity in children or adolescents with ADHD (Shaw and Brown, 1991; Cramond, 1994; Abraham et al., 2006; Fugate, Zentall, and Gentry, 2013; Gonzalez-Carpio, Serrano, and Nieto, 2017). Studies also point to higher levels of ADHD symptoms in creative or gifted children (Healey and Rucklidge, 2006; Fugate et al., 2013). Adults diagnosed with ADHD score higher than non-ADHD controls on both cognitive (White and Shaw, 2006, 2011) and real-world creative accomplishments (White and Shaw, 2011). And Kyaga et al. (2013) found higher rates of ADHD in members of the writing profession than in non-writers in the Swedish population.

In support of the "inverted U" hypothesis of creativity and psychopathology, a recent meta-analysis of ADHD and creativity indicated that, at the level of everyday creativity, full-blown ADHD may be detrimental (Paek, Abdulla, and Cramond, 2016). Healey and Rucklidge (2006) also report that in a group of highly creative children, 40 percent had higher scores on a measure of ADHD symptoms but none of these gifted children met full criteria for an actual ADHD diagnosis.

ADHD is associated with a pattern of mind wandering, as opposed to purposefully controlled thought (Seli et al., 2015). Mind wandering has been shown to be important to the creative process, with several studies linking this state to an increase in creative problem solving (Tan et al., 2015; Zedelius and Schooler, 2015). Mind wandering is linked to activation of specific regions of the brain known as the **default mode network**, which brings us to some of the neuroscience that has examined the creativity/mental illness connection.

Creativity and Brain Imaging Associations with Mental Illness

Brain imaging studies have also found some evidence for a connection between creativity and certain types of psychopathology. In general, when people are engaged in a cognitive task, the **executive network** of the brain (associated with deliberate, consciously directed thinking) becomes active, while the default mode network (associated with mind wandering) becomes deactivated. Activation of the two networks is more or less mutually exclusive (Buckner, Andrews-Hanna, and Schacter, 2008). However, several brain imaging studies have found that in highly creative people, part of the default mode network remains active during cognitive tasks (Takeuchi et al., 2011; Fink et al., 2014), a pattern similar to that found in patients with schizophrenia (Whitfield-Gabrieli et al., 2009) and those who score high on a measure of schizotypy (Fink et al., 2014). These studies suggest that both highly creative people and those who are prone to psychosis may have difficulty inhibiting cognitive activity that isn't relevant to the task performance.

A PET scan study found that high divergent thinkers had unusual dopamine D2 receptor densities in a certain region of the brain, similar to the pattern found in patients with schizophrenia (de Manzano et al., 2010). The authors speculate that this pattern is associated with abnormal sensory gating, allowing more sensory information to flow into the brain for processing.

One of the interesting conclusions of these brain imaging studies is that the brain markers common to creativity and mental illness seem to include failures to appropriately inhibit the contents of conscious awareness. These characteristics could increase the risk for mental illness but could also improve creativity by increasing the number of elements individuals could combine to form novel or original ideas.

Creativity and Genetic Variations Associated with Mental Illness

Creativity appears to be influenced by multiple genetic variations (Kozbelt et al., 2014), as do the types of mental illness associated with creativity (Purcell et al., 2009). If there is a connection between creativity and mental illness, then we would expect to find an overlap in some of these genetic variants. Researchers have indeed reported such overlaps.

Kéri (2009) examined a variant in the neuregulin 1 gene (NRG1) that has been linked to increased risk for psychosis and found that it was also linked to creative achievement in individuals with high intellectual and academic achievement. Reuter et al. (2006) found that a variant in the dopamine D2 receptor gene was linked to certain forms of creativity, and this variant has also been associated with schizophrenia and addiction (Noble, 2000; Golimbet et al., 2003). An allele of the D4 dopamine receptor gene, implicated in novelty-seeking, has been associated with both creativity and ADHD (Takeuchi et al., 2015).

Imagination is considered a main component of creativity. Crespi et al. (2016) measured thirty-three common genetic variants associated with risk for schizophrenia in a large sample of non-disordered university students and found that higher genetic risk for schizophrenia predicted better scores on a measure of imagination. In a series of large genome-wide association studies (GWAS) using Icelandic, Danish, and Swedish population samples, Power et al. (2015) found higher risk scores for both schizophrenia and bipolar disorder were associated with measures of creativity, including membership in an artistic society, a creative profession, or high creative achievement scores.

We are just beginning to understand the genetic underpinnings of human behavior. However, research findings suggest that there is a genetic connection between creativity and certain forms of mental disorder, even if the specific nature of that connection has yet to be unraveled.

Creativity and Mental Illness: Reviewing the Evidence

The evidence summarized in this chapter indicates that there is a large and growing body of research investigating the interface between creativity and different forms of mental illness, including mood disorders (especially bipolar disorder), schizophrenia-spectrum traits or disorders (especially schizotypy or psychosis-proneness), alcoholism, and, more recently, ADHD. However, it is also the case that there is an inverted "U" relationship between creativity and psychopathology, with milder or subclinical versions, rather than more severe forms of disorder, providing creative benefit. In the same vein, first-degree relatives of severely mentally ill people, who may have inherited some but not the entire genotype for a mental disorder, may get the bulk of the creative advantage. Studies do not support the idea that all – or even most – highly creative individuals suffer from mental illness but that they merely have a somewhat greater risk for disorder than the general population. Finally, critics have found fault with much of the research in this field. They have brought attention to legitimate methodological problems of some of the work and believe that the connection between creativity and madness has been overhyped (e.g., Schlesinger, 2009; Sawyer, 2012). However, given so much evidence from such a large variety of scientific approaches, the conclusion is that some form of connection between high levels of creativity and a risk for certain types of mental disorder exists (Simonton, 2014). Next, we discuss possible explanations for this connection.

Explanatory Models of the Creativity/Mental Illness Connection

Several sociocultural theories have been proposed to account for the higher risk of certain forms of psychopathology among highly creative individuals (e.g., Richards, 1990; Becker, 2014). First, the *cultural expectation model*, suggests that creative people may either purposely or unconsciously exhibit symptoms of mental illness to enhance their creative persona because the "mad genius" stereotype is engrained in our cultural expectations. Second, the *social drift model*, suggests that people with mental illness tend to drift away from standard nine-to-five occupations that generally require rule-based behaviors, and in turn drift toward creative professions such as writing, art, or music that are more lenient toward unconventional lifestyles (Ludwig, 1995). A third sociocultural theory, the *labeling model*, suggests that labeling a creative person as mentally ill may be a method of silencing innovative ideas that threaten the status quo (e.g., Brower, 1999).

Sociocultural theories likely explain a portion of the overlap between creativity and psychopathology. However, many studies show heritability patterns of creativity and psychopathology (e.g., Heston, 1966; Karlsson, 1970; Jamison, 1993; Kyaga et al., 2013), underlying brain similarities of creativity and psychopathology (e.g., de Manzano et al., 2010), and common genetic alterations of creativity and mental illness (e.g., Kéri, 2009), suggesting that there may be an underlying biological relationship.

Looking at the evidence from a biological perspective, Baas et al. (2016) presented a model of creativity and psychopathology based on behavioral approach and avoidance systems. Their model suggests that creativity is positively associated with disorders of the approach system (including bipolar disorder, positive schizotypy, and ADHD). Note that the approach system relies on the neurotransmitter dopamine, and dopamine plays a central role in bipolar disorder, schizophrenia, and ADHD (Baas et al., 2016), as well as alcoholism (Volkow et al., 2013). Dopamine has also been implicated in many studies of creative functioning (e.g., Reuter et al., 2006; de Manzano et al., 2010; Zabelina et al., 2016). However, dopamine is likely not the entire story underlying the connection between creativity and risk for mental illness, or a greater percentage of people with mental illness would be making their mark creatively.

A final model, the **shared vulnerability model**, suggests that psychopathology and creativity may share genetic components that are expressed as either mental illness or creativity depending upon the presence of other protective or risk factors (Carson, 2011). This model, also referred to as the shared neurocognitive vulnerability model of creativity and psychopathology, suggests an explanation for why highly creative individuals are at greater risk for psychopathology than the general population. It also explains why not all highly creative individuals have mental illness and why not all individuals with mental illness are unusually creative. Additionally, it may explain the increased levels of creativity in first-degree relatives of individuals with serious mental illness (e.g., Heston, 1966; Karlsson, 1970; Kyaga et al., 2013). Finally, it may explain why certain mental disorders remain in the gene pool despite their obvious negative consequences for humanity and the lower incidence of reproduction among those who suffer from them. The shared vulnerability model suggests that some aspects of the genotype of these disorders may deliver a positive advantage for the species by increasing creativity when coupled with protective factors, thus improving human adaptability.

The Shared Vulnerability Model of Creativity and Psychopathology

The disorders that have been associated with creativity are both heritable and **polygenetic**, meaning that they include contributions from multiple genes (Whitfield et al., 1998; Berrettini, 2000). Further, these disorders may indeed have some genetic underpinnings in common with each other (e.g., Sharp et al., 2014). Although inheriting the entire genotype for a disorder may put a person at risk for illness, inheriting a portion of that genotype may lead to cognitive effects that are beneficial, especially when this portion is combined with certain protective factors. For example, one such cognitive effect is entry into an altered brain state that allows access to material that is normally filtered from conscious awareness. This altered brain state could be associated with psychosis in full-blown mental illness, but when combined with protective factors such as high IQ, this state could provide a pathway through expanded *doors of perception* (Huxley, 1954), and promote experiences of creative insight.

A predisposition to mental disorder may allow a creative person to process ideas in an unusual way to solve creative tasks (Carson, 2014a). A number of biographical accounts of the creative process (see Ghiselin, 1952) include descriptions of creative ideas that arose from unknown sources and were experienced in a manner somewhat similar to delusional "thought insertion." For example, Nobel Prize winner (and diagnosed schizophrenia patient) John Forbes Nash said that his creative mathematical breakthroughs and his delusions about outer space aliens giving him commands "came to me in the same way" (Nasar, 1998, p. 11). It seems possible, as the genome-wide studies suggest (Power et al., 2015), that some part of the genetic risk for psychotic disorders is contributing to the experience of creative insights.

Although shared vulnerabilities allow the person access to material normally unavailable in consciousness, protective factors may provide the means to process and manipulate that material to form original and adaptive ideas and products rather than becoming overwhelmed by the excess stimuli. The shared vulnerability model is fluid and will continue to expand as our knowledge of brain function and gene interactions increases.

Components of the Shared Vulnerability Model

The original shared vulnerability model (see Figure 11.1) proposed several mechanisms associated with **psychopathology** that could enhance creativity (Carson, 2011), including:

- **cognitive disinhibition**: A condition, associated with schizophrenia, schizotypal personality, and psychosis-proneness, where irrelevant or extraneous information that is normally outside of conscious awareness is not filtered out.

(cont.)

- **novelty-seeking**: A condition that may provide motivation to pursue novel or original tasks but which is also associated with alcohol use, addiction, and bipolar disorder.
- **neural hyperconnectivity**: A condition of unusual patterns of neural connections that may lead to unusual associations or odd combinations of preexisting information. Such patterns have been found in people with schizophrenia, bipolar disorder, schizotypal personality, and ADHD.

These vulnerability factors, when combined with protective factors, can improve creative outcomes even while increasing risk for mental disorder. Protective factors in the model include:

- **high IQ**: This allows the individual to process and manipulate, rather than be overwhelmed by, additional stimuli and connections accessed through shared vulnerability factors (Carson, Peterson, and Higgins, 2003).
- **high working memory capacity**: This allows the individual to hold information in mind, to process it, and to manipulate it.
- **cognitive flexibility**: This allows the person to change perspectives and also to disengage from common problem solutions to find less common solutions.

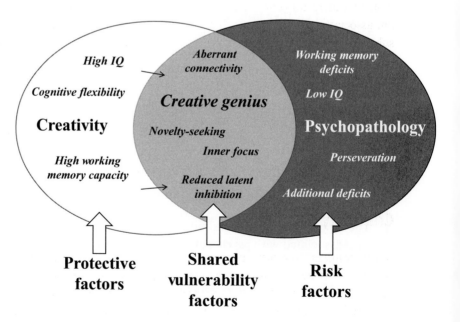

Figure 11.1 The shared neurocognitive vulnerability model of creativity and psychopathology.

Creativity and Psychopathology: The Paradox Explained

We began by noting the paradox of creativity, mental illness, and mental health. On the one hand, creativity is a crucially important human trait. Creative activity, at least the everyday variety (Conner et al., 2016), is associated with positive mental health. On the other hand, we have seen quite a large body of evidence (although certainly some of it is criticized for methodological reasons) for increased risk of mental illness in high-level creative achievers. Simonton (2014) has labeled this the "mad genius paradox." He suggests that, across the spectrum of creative accomplishment, creativity is related to positive mental health. However, as the level of creative achievement increases, the risk for mental illness also increases, with the greatest risk for mental disorder carried by those at the highest end of the creative achievement distribution. This theory fits well with the shared vulnerability model. Individuals who have protective factors but lack the shared vulnerability factors represent the large group who contribute to everyday forms of human creativity. However, that smaller group of creators with shared vulnerability factors *and* protective factors may not only be at greater risk for psychopathology but may also be in a position to make the most original and outstanding creative contributions, taking creativity from the realm of everyday magic to that of genius.

Despite some methodological flaws, the bulk of evidence – from anecdotal accounts to brain imaging and molecular genetic research – suggests that, at the highest levels of creative achievement, there may an increased risk for certain disorders, especially bipolar disorder, psychosis-proneness (schizotypy), alcohol dependence, and ADHD. The evidence also suggests that there is a genetic component to both creativity and the forms of mental disorder that are associated with creative achievement. The evidence further suggests that milder, perhaps subclinical, versions of these disorders are more beneficial to creativity than are full-blown versions of disorder. However, even though the evidence points to an increased risk for these disorders among highly creative individuals, it is just that – an increased risk. The research does not suggest that all, or even a majority, of those who achieve high levels of creative accomplishment experience mental illness; the majority of highly creative people do not, though perhaps they may display some subclinical traits of the disorders in question. A shared vulnerability model appears to account for the current data in this field. We now turn to how creative work can be used as a pathway to health and healing.

Creativity and Healing

Many eminent creators have anecdotally described the therapeutic effects of engaging in creative activities during which they came up with potentially novel and useful ideas or products (Sternberg and Lubart, 1999). These include writers Virginia Woolf, Graham Greene, and Anne Sexton, as well as painters Vincent Van Gogh, Paul Klee, and Frida Kahlo, and composers, such as Mozart and Duke Ellington, among many others (Van Gogh, 1889; Caramagno, 1992; Sandblom, 1997; Carson, 2012).

Two Artists on the Healing Power of the Arts

Dutch impressionist painter **Vincent Van Gogh** spent a year receiving treatment at Saint-Paul Asylum in Saint-Rémy-de-Provence, South of France, from May 1889 to May 1890. Though the exact nature and causes of Van Gogh's difficulties are still debated (e.g., Arnold, 2004), what is not is the severity of his symptoms, which included mood difficulties and psychosis and ended in the artist taking his own life in July 1890 at the age of 37. While in Saint-Rémy-de-Provence, most of the art Van Gogh created was inspired by the grounds of the asylum and the view from his window. In September 1889, Van Gogh writes to his brother Theo about the therapeutic benefits he experienced while painting:

Yesterday I began to work a little again – on a thing that I see from my window – a field of yellow stubble that they are ploughing, the contrast of the violet-tinted ploughed earth with the strips of yellow stubble, background of hills. Work distracts me infinitely better than anything else, and if I could once really throw myself into it with all my energy possibly that would be the best remedy. (Van Gogh, 1889, paras 4–5)

The life of acclaimed English writer **Virginia Woolf** was marked by severe mental health difficulties likely resulting from bipolar disorder, for which no effective treatment besides the "rest cure" existed (Caramagno, 1992). Woolf experienced her first manic episode at the age of 13, soon after the death of her mother, and continued to experience significant symptoms throughout her life despite her artistic productivity (Koutsantoni, 2012). In her diary, the writer noted the beneficial effect that writing exerted on her mental state:

Odd how the creative power at once brings the whole universe to order. I can see the day whole, proportioned – even after a long flutter of the brain such as I've had this morning[;] it must be a physical, moral, mental necessity, like setting the engine off. (Woolf, 1934/2003, p. 213)

In parallel with these anecdotal reports, clinicians also noticed that some individuals receiving treatment for severe psychiatric difficulties were highly motivated and inspired by creative projects. Soon after World War I, German psychiatrist Hans Prinzhorn built a well-known collection of art created by individuals hospitalized in Heidelberg for psychiatric reasons. A published book on this collection became a best seller, and the art of the mentally ill, judged to have a raw and pristine creative quality, inspired that of twentieth-century expressionist artists throughout Europe (Thys, Sabbe, and De Hert, 2012). Building on this example as a potential source of strength and opportunity for self-expression, clinical treatment programs now typically offer patients opportunities to engage in artistic activities using various modalities (e.g., visual arts, music, drama, dance, or play, among others) (Malchiodi, 2012).

Earlier in the chapter, we explored several models explaining the relationship between creativity and psychopathology, focusing on the shared vulnerability model. However, one additional explanation that we introduce here is the *healing* hypothesis, which suggests that people who are suffering from symptoms of mental disorder are compelled to engage in creative activities specifically because they may bring relief and improve well-being (Richards, 2007; Forgeard and Elstein, 2014). This hypothesis might apply to individuals who turn to various creative art forms after their symptoms emerge.

The Usefulness of Art Therapy

How much empirical evidence exists to support the claim that creative activities and behaviors have the capacity to heal suffering? In a recent report, researchers for the World Health Organization reviewed over 3,000 studies of the effects of the arts on health and well-being. This report concluded that participation in the arts (broadly defined to include visual arts, music, dance, film, theater, and literature) has a role in prevention of mental illness, such as depression, as well as in treatment of mental illness from mild symptoms of anxiety to symptoms of severe conditions such as major depression, PTSD, and psychosis (Fancourt and Finn, 2019). Much of the research addressing this claim has been carried out in the discipline of art therapy. We review here evidence pertaining to the use of the visual arts (though, as noted above, many other modalities exist and have also been studied scientifically).

Art therapy by definition provides individuals with a space to potentially come up with novel and meaningful ways of expressing themselves. Art therapists typically are Master's level clinicians with specialized training and credentials (although other clinicians may use art in their work, they do not practice art therapy). Art therapy is often (but not always) offered as an **adjunctive** intervention, meaning that it is typically not the primary therapy offered for a specific condition (such as depression). There is wide variation in the approach to art therapy depending upon the training of the clinician (Malchiodi, 2012); however, the goals of all art therapists are the same: "[enrich] the lives of individuals, families, and communities through active art-making, creative process, applied psychological theory, and human experience within a psychotherapeutic relationship" (American Art Therapy Association, 2017, para. 1).

Interventions using visual arts activities have documented that art therapy may be beneficial for a range of problems and populations. Reviews of **efficacy studies** (which compare a therapy or other intervention to a control condition) have found that, overall, art therapy interventions lead to significantly greater improvements in outcomes than control conditions, but these differences tend to be small across studies (e.g., Maujean, Pepping, and Kendall, 2014). For example, Kopytin and Lebedev (2013) found that war veterans with stress-related disorders who engaged in a four-week art therapy intervention experienced greater relief in depressive symptoms than veterans in a control group (among other outcomes). Similarly, Haeyen et al. (2018) found that adults with personality disorders who took part in a ten-week art therapy intervention experienced larger improvements in symptoms and in adaptive functioning than a control group. Other studies, including non-randomized or uncontrolled trials, also provide important information suggesting that art therapy is effective in real-world clinical settings for a wide range of problems including mood symptoms, psychosis, trauma-related symptoms, or dementia, among other difficulties (Slayton, D'Archer, and Kaplan, 2010).

Although evidence pertaining to the benefits of art therapy is growing, not all studies have found that art therapy leads to a reduction in symptoms of mental disorder (e.g., Crawford et al., 2012). The existence of mixed findings highlights the need to further investigate the circumstances under which art therapy is effective and the best methods to test outcomes of interventions that utilize creative modalities (Holttum and Huet, 2014).

How Do Creative Activities Heal?

A large and growing body of evidence suggests that artistic activities can be therapeutic, but the presence of mixed results compels researchers to determine when these activities are or are not useful. It is important to understand the psychological processes explaining when and why the generation of novel and useful ideas or products appears beneficial. We discuss here three specific benefits of creative activity: the role of changes in affect, increases in self-efficacy, and opportunities for **meaning-making**.

Affect. Perhaps the best-studied of these processes is the degree to which creative activities may directly influence positive and negative affect. A body of experimental research using healthy populations has shown that artistic activities enhance short-term mood and can help counteract the effects of negative **mood inductions**. By manipulating instructions (e.g., asking participants to draw in order to vent negative emotions vs. to distract oneself), these studies have also shown that creating to distract oneself is especially effective and might account for therapeutic effects, standing in contrast with the psychodynamic idea of **catharsis** or venting of negative emotions (Drake and Winner 2012, 2013; Drake and Hodge, 2015).

More recently, studies using the **experience sampling method** (ESM) to assess creativity and affect in everyday life contexts have also shown that creative behavior enhances well-being and positive affect. In these studies, participants are asked to respond to multiple short surveys every day using a mobile device (Cotter and Silvia, 2019). Researchers are then able to look at associations between variables at each time point, as well as dynamic relationships between variables from one time point to the next. Importantly, variables are not measured in the laboratory but in everyday life contexts, maximizing the research's **ecological validity**. Using this method, Conner and Silvia (2015) found that daily reports of self-perceived creativity were associated with positive emotions such as happiness and excitement. This was especially true for participants high in **openness to experience**, a personality trait that is associated with intellectual curiosity and imagination, and is one of the best predictors of creative achievement (Feist, 1998). Importantly, openness to experience also predicts more adaptive affective responses to stress (McCrae and Sutin, 2009). Thus, being open and curious about new perspectives, a tendency associated with creativity, may help with stress regulation by preventing **maladaptive** suppression or avoidance-based coping strategies (Williams et al., 2009).

Creative and general self-efficacy. General **self-efficacy** is defined as the degree to which individuals perceive that they can control events in their lives and take action to solve problems (Bandura, 1997). It is related to resilience and positive mental health (Chorpita, Brown, and Barlow, 2016). Canadian adults who participated in a single-session art program supervised by an art therapist increased significantly on a measure of self-efficacy (Kaimal et al., 2017). In another study, senior adults taking part in a six-week song-writing program also showed significant increases in general self-efficacy (Bergner and Carson, in preparation). Creative self-efficacy, which is defined as the subjective belief that one is able to come up with novel and useful (i.e., creative) ideas, products, or behaviors, is also associated with well-being and adaptive personality functioning (Beghetto, 2006; Karwowski and Lebuda, 2016). In a recent study, students' sense of creative self-efficacy related to indices of psychological adjustment during some types of extracurricular activities (e.g., athletic, prosocial) (Forgeard and Benson, 2017). Creative self-efficacy is especially interesting because it is directly linked to the core process hypothesized to be responsible for healing – that is, the capacity to engage in creative thinking and/or behavior.

Meaning-making and growth following adversity. Creative activities may also be particularly well suited to help participants make meaning out of difficult experiences. Whenever we experience stressful events, we need to integrate new information about this experience into our beliefs about ourselves, others, and the world. Highly adverse events, in particular, may force individuals to reconsider assumptions or beliefs they previously took for granted about themselves and their lives and to engage in deliberate cognitive processing to make meaning out of past experiences (Janoff-Bulman, 2006; Cann et al., 2011). As a result, some people report not just being able to understand and make meaning of difficult experiences but also growing from them. The positive changes people report following experiences of **adversity** have been described in the psychological literature as the phenomenon of **posttraumatic growth** (Tedeschi and Calhoun, 2004). People tend to report five main types of growth following adversity. These include improved interpersonal relationships, new possibilities for one's life, enhanced feelings of personal strengths, heightened appreciation for life, and renewed spirituality (Tedeschi and Calhoun, 1996). Creativity may enhance this phenomenon (Zausner, 1998). One study showed that for a group of participants suffering from cancer, taking part in an arts program was associated with increases in self-reported posttraumatic growth (Garland et al., 2007). Another study found that when asked to think about the most impactful stressful event they had ever experienced, participants in an online sample who reported higher levels of distress associated with the event also reported larger self-perceived increases in creativity (Forgeard, 2013). Most recently, a study of Israeli adults (64 percent of whom had been exposed to war as civilians) showed that exposure to a greater number of **traumatic events** related to higher creative self-efficacy, emotional creativity, and divergent thinking (Orkibi and Ram-Vlasov, 2019). Additional forms of creative work may enhance meaning-making. For example, writing memoirs and other forms of expressive writing can help individuals find coherence in past events and better understand them (Kaufman, 2018). Further research is needed to better understand the role played by creativity in coping with the effects of adversity.

Other general processes. The role of other general processes is important to note, although research on their role is relatively scarce. For example, several authors have noted that creative artistic activities lend themselves particularly well to practicing **mindfulness** (Monti et al., 2006; Clark, 2016), by providing a fertile space to pay "attention in a particular way: on purpose, in the present moment, and nonjudgmentally" (Kabat-Zinn, 2013, p. 4). By focusing on one's experience while creating an original product, participants may learn to better manage internal experiences (Chambers, Gullone, and Allen, 2009).

Another process worth investigating when creative activities are conducted in a social setting (i.e., with a facilitator/clinician, or in a group setting) is the opportunity to promote feelings of **social connectedness.** Group-based creative activities may help decrease feelings of isolation, provide opportunities for people to share their experiences with others, and elicit opportunities to offer/receive help (e.g., Johnson and Sullivan-Marx, 2006; Levine-Madori, 2013). In general, much more research is needed in order to understand how creative behavior affects psychological adjustment processes. Such research can help maximize the benefits of creative activities by determining what needs to happen during the creative process for people to experience therapeutic effects.

CONCLUSION

The large and growing body of research pertaining to creativity and mental health suggests that, overall, creativity is related to positive mental health. How can we reach this conclusion when we began by demonstrating that people who have contributed high levels of creative achievement throughout their lives may be at a somewhat greater risk than the general population for certain types of mental illness, including mood disorders, psychosis-proneness (schizotypy), alcohol dependence, and ADHD? First, the evidence suggests that either milder versions of these disorders or being a relative of someone with these disorders is more beneficial to creative production than having a full-blown disorder. This research indicates some genes (but not all) that are associated with mental illness may be helpful to creativity, as suggested in the shared vulnerability model of creativity and psychopathology. Next, we saw that many creative luminaries may have turned to their creative work for relief from mental illness symptoms, and, further, that creative activity in the form of art, music, writing, or dance therapies, has been shown to be effective in helping to heal the symptoms of several types of mental illness. We then explored the mechanisms of action that may explain how creative work heals. These mechanisms included: increasing positive affect, improving self-efficacy, helping individuals find meaning in adverse life events, developing mindfulness, and promoting social connections.

Research on the relationship between creativity and psychopathology, as well as research on the relationship between creativity and healing, is ongoing. As we learn more about how creativity and both mental illness and mental health are exhibited in the human brain, we will hopefully be able to design interventions to increase protective factors in those individuals who have shared vulnerability factors, thereby increasing their chances of making original and creative contributions and decreasing their chances of suffering from full-blown mental illness. Creativity has been and continues to be our pathway to survival, adaptation, and a life of rich and full experience. Continuing research into the mechanisms of creative thought, associated with both mental illness and mental health, will inform our journey on that pathway and help us better understand the road to well-being for all who strive to be their creative best.

Our Research Contribution

We see our major research contribution in this chapter as the shared vulnerability model of creativity and psychopathology, first presented by Dr. Shelley Carson in a 2011 issue of the *Canadian Journal of Psychiatry*. This model suggests that highly creative persons and persons with certain forms of mental illness may share one or more cognitive vulnerability factors (for instance, high levels of cognitive disinhibition, high levels of novelty-seeking, or unusual patterns of neural connectivity). These shared vulnerability factors may serve to either enhance creativity or act as a further risk for mental illness, depending upon the presence or absence of other cognitive protective factors (for example, high IQ, high capacity of working memory, or high level of cognitive flexibility). The model explains why highly creative people may be at greater risk for certain types of psychopathology. The types of psychopathology identified thus far include mood disorders (in particular, bipolar disorder), schizophrenia-spectrum disorders, alcoholism, and ADHD. The model also provides an explanation for why *all* creative people do not display psychopathology and why all people with psychopathology are not highly creative. Finally, the model also helps explain why the identified forms of mental illness have not been selected out of the human gene pool despite being detrimental to human beings. It may be that portions of the genome of these disorders are valuable to our species and, when combined with other protective factors, and may elevate creative abilities that benefit humanity.

Critical/Creative Thinking Questions

1. After reading the chapter, do you believe that creativity is associated more strongly with mental illness or mental health? Can you list the evidence for your answer?
2. Some critics of the "mad genius" hypothesis believe that by promoting research that indicates a connection between creativity and psychopathology, investigators may be romanticizing illnesses like bipolar disorder and alcoholism. This may inadvertently encourage creative individuals to refrain from seeking treatment or to stop their current

treatment. What effects do you think the mad genius debate might have on artists/writers/ musicians or other individuals who are currently working in creative fields?

3. According to this chapter, some creative individuals have used alcohol for cognitive disinhibition purposes, allowing more information to flow unfiltered into their conscious awareness. However, too much alcohol is ultimately harmful for creativity (and for health). Can you think of other healthier methods to achieve a state of cognitive disinhibition? (Monks can do it. So can long-distance runners.)

4. What do you think are some of the challenges that researchers may face when they try to test the efficacy or effectiveness of art therapy, in comparison to testing other treatments? What are some unique aspects of creative activities that could make them challenging to study?

5. Do you trust people's anecdotal reports that creative activities help them heal or grow from adversity? Why or why not? Are there any reasons why people may have difficulty reporting accurately on the benefits of creative activities?

6. Do you think the benefits of creative activities are specific to each **modality** (e.g., visual arts, music, writing, etc.), or do you think that these activities all share a common active ingredient that makes them all therapeutic?

7. Many people do not perceive themselves as creative (whether this is accurate or not). Do you think creative activities are helpful for anyone regardless of creative abilities or self-perceptions of creativity? Why or why not?

GLOSSARY

adjunctive: Added to something else as a supplement.

adversity: Difficulties, misfortune; term used to describe negative life events.

affect: Any experience of feeling or emotion.

catharsis: The venting of negative emotions.

cognitive disinhibition: A condition in which a person is unable to filter out irrelevant or extraneous information.

cyclothymia: A mild form of bipolar disorder where a person experiences elevated or hypomanic moods alternating over time with depressive symptoms.

default mode network: Network in the brain that is active when your mind is wandering or when you are recalling autobiographical material.

ecological validity: The degree to which findings from a study may generalize to phenomena of interest in the real world.

efficacy studies: Empirical studies that examine whether a specific treatment or approach works when compared to outcomes in a placebo control group.

empirical: Based on scientific observation rather than theory, logic, or opinion.

executive network: Network in the brain that is active when you are engaged in a goal-directed task.

experience sampling method: A method of gathering data in real time; participants report on their thoughts, feelings, behaviors either at scheduled times or in response to a prompt using a diary or a mobile device.

genotype: The genetic makeup or collection of genes responsible for specific genetic traits of an individual.

historiometric studies: Studies that perform quantitative analyses on historical biographical data to determine trends concerning a specific topic.

hypomania: A mild form of mania marked by elevated mood, high energy, and feelings of high self-esteem.

inverted "U" hypothesis: The theory that a little mental illness is helpful to creativity but full-blown mental illness may be detrimental to creativity (Richards et al., 1989).

maladaptive: Detrimental, counterproductive, or otherwise interfering with optimal functioning.

meaning-making: The process of how people construe, understand, or make sense of life events, relationships, and the self.

meta-analytic studies: Studies aggregating the results of analyses from several independent studies on a specific topic in order to determine overall trends.

mindfulness: "Paying attention in a particular way: on purpose, in the present moment, and nonjudgmentally" (Kabat-Zinn, 2013, p. 4); awareness of one's internal states and surroundings.

modality: The way or mode in which something exists or is done.

molecular genetics studies: Studies that examine specific variants of genes that are found to be shared among the subjects being researched.

mood inductions: Laboratory procedures that produce reliable changes in mood (often using music or film clips) so that the effects of various interventions on mood can then be studied.

openness to experience: A personality trait reflecting individuals' "ability and tendency to seek, detect, comprehend, utilize, and appreciate complex patterns of information, both sensory and abstract" (DeYoung, 2014, p. 2)

polygenetic: A trait or condition that is influenced by multiple genes.

posttraumatic growth: Positive psychological changes experienced following adversity.

psychometric studies: Studies that compare groups of individuals on a variety of measures to determine psychological or behavioral differences between the groups.

psychopathology: Scientific study of mental disorders.

psychosis: A severe condition where a person loses touch with reality. It is usually characterized by hallucinations and delusions.

psychosis-proneness: A condition in which a person displays schizotypal traits (the term is generally interchangeable with schizotypy).

schizophrenia-spectrum: This refers to the spectrum of disorders and traits ranging from full-blown schizophrenia on the severe end to odd, eccentric (but not disordered) behavior on the more normal end of the spectrum. It includes brief psychotic disorder, schizotypal personality disorder, and non-disordered schizotypy.

schizotypal personality: A set of personality traits characterized by unusual perceptual experiences, magical thinking, mild paranoia, and asocial behavior.

schizotypy: The range of schizotypal traits found across the schizophrenia-spectrum. People who are very high in schizotypy may qualify for a diagnosis of schizophrenia or another spectrum disorder, while people who are in the midrange may be high-functioning but have schizotypal personality characteristics.

self-efficacy: The degree to which individuals perceive that they can control events in their lives and take action to solve problems.

sensory gating: The automatic process through which the brain filters out unnecessary environmental stimuli coming in from the sensory organs. This prevents an overload of irrelevant information for processing in higher brain centers.

shared vulnerability model: A model explaining the relationship between creativity and psychopathology that suggests highly creative individuals may display certain genetic factors that may enhance creativity but may also act as risk factors for psychopathology. These "shared vulnerability factors" will tend to be expressed as either creativity or psychopathology depending upon the presence of certain cognitive protective factors.

social connectedness: The degree to which a person feels close to others.

traumatic event: An event in which a person is either directly or indirectly exposed to actual or threatened death, injury, or sexual violence (American Psychiatric Association, 2013).

REFERENCES

Abraham, A., Windmann, S., Siefen, R., Daum, I., and Güntürkün, 0. (2006). Creative Thinking in Adolescents with Attention Deficit Hyperactivity Disorder (ADHD). *Child Neuropsychology*, *12*(2), 111–123.

Acar, S., and Sen, S. (2013). A Multilevel Meta-Analysis of the Relationship between Creativity and Schizotypy. *Psychology of Aesthetics, Creativity, and the Arts*, *7*, 214–228.

American Art Therapy Association. (2017). *History and Background.* www.arttherapy.org/aata-history-background.html.

Andreasen, N. C. (1987). Creativity and Mental illness: Prevalence Rates in Writers and Their First-Degree Relatives. *American Journal of Psychiatry*, *144*, 1288–1292.

(2008). The Relationship between Creativity and Mood Disorders. *Dialogues in Clinical Neuroscience*, *10*, 251–255.

Aristophanes. (424 BC). *The Knights.* http://classics.mit.edu/Aristophanes/knights.pl.txt.

Aristotle. (1984). Problems. In J. Barnes (Ed.), *The Complete Works of Aristotle*, vol. 2 (pp. 1319–1527). Princeton: Princeton University Press.

Arnold, W. N. (2004). The Illness of Vincent van Gogh. *Journal of the History of the Neurosciences*, *13*, 22–43.

Baas, M., Nijstad, B. A., Boot, N. C., and De Dreu, C. K. W. (2016). Mad Genius Revisited: Vulnerability to Psychopathology, Biobehavioral Approach-Avoidance, and Creativity. *Psychological Bulletin*, *142*(6), 668–692.

Bandura, A. (1997). *Self-Efficacy: The Exercise of Control.* New York: Freeman.

Barron, F. (1955). The Disposition toward Originality. *Journal of Abnormal and Social Psychology*, *51*, 478–485.

Becker, G. (2014) A Socio-Historical Overview of the Creativity-Pathology Connection: From Antiquity to Contemporary Times. In J. Kaufman (Ed.), *Creativity and Mental Illness*. Cambridge: Cambridge University Press, pp. 3–24.

Beghetto, R. A. (2006). Creative Self-Efficacy: Correlates in Middle and Secondary Students. *Creativity Research Journal*, *18*, 447–457.

Bergner, R., and Carson, S. H. (in preparation). *Sing a New song: Community Songwriting and Singing to Enhance the Quality of Life and Health of Older Adults.*

Berrettini, W. H. (2000). Susceptibility Loci for Bipolar Disorder: Overlap with Inherited Vulnerability to Schizophrenia. *Biological Psychiatry*, *47*, 245–251.

Buckner, R. L., Andrews-Hanna, J. R., and Schacter, D. L. (2008). The Brain's Default Network: Anatomy, Function, and Relevance to Disease. *Annals of the New York Academy of Science*, 1124, 1–38.

Burch, G. St. J., Pavelis, C., Hemsley, D. R., and Corr, P. J. (2006). Schizotypy and Creativity in Visual Artists. *British Journal of Psychology*, 97, 177–190.

Cann, A., Calhoun, L. G., Tedeschi, R. G., Triplett, K. N., Vishnevsky, T., and Lindstrom, C. M. (2011). Assessing Posttraumatic Cognitive Processes: The Event Related Rumination Inventory. *Anxiety, Stress, and Coping*, 24, 137–156.

Caramagno, T. C. (1992). *The Flight of the Mind: Virginia Woolf's Art and Manic-Depressive Illness*. Los Angeles: University of California Press.

Carson, S. H. (2010). *Your Creative Brain: Seven Steps to Maximize Imagination, Productivity, and Innovation in Your Life*. San Francisco: Jossey-Bass.

(2011). Creativity and Psychopathology: A Genetic Shared-Vulnerability Model. *Canadian Journal of Psychiatry*, 56, 144–153.

(2014a). Leveraging the "Mad Genius" Debate: Why We Need a Neuroscience of Creativity and Psychopathology. *Frontiers in Human Neuroscience*, 8, Article 771.

(2014b). Cognitive Disinhibition, Creativity, and Psychopathology. In D. K. Simonton (Ed.), *The Wiley Handbook of Genius* (pp. 198–221). Oxford: Wiley.

Carson, S. H, Peterson, J. B., and Higgins, D. M. (2003). Decreased Latent Inhibition Is Associated with Increased Creative Achievement in High-Functioning Individuals. *Journal of Personality and Social Psychology*, 85, 499–506.

Chambers, R., Gullone, E., and Allen, N. B. (2009). Mindful Emotion Regulation: An Integrative Review. *Clinical Psychology Review*, 29, 560–572.

Chorpita, B. F., Brown, T. A., and Barlow, D. H. (2016). Perceived Control As a Mediator of Family Environment in Etiological Models of Childhood Anxiety. *Behavior Therapy*, 29, 457–476.

Claridge, G. (Ed.). (1997). *Schizotypy: Implications for Illness and Health*. New York: Oxford University Press.

Clark, S. M. (2016). *DBT-Informed Art Therapy: Mindfulness, Cognitive Behavior Therapy, and the Creative Process*. Philadelphia: Jessica Kingsley Publishers.

Cohen, G. D. (2006). Research on Creativity and Aging: The Positive Impact of the Arts on Health and Illness. *Generations*, 30(1), 7–15.

Conner, T. S., and Silvia, P. J. (2015). Creative Days: A Daily Diary Study of Emotion, Personality, and Everyday Creativity. *Psychology of Aesthetics, Creativity, and the Arts*, 9, 463–470.

Conner, T. S., DeYoung, C. G., and Silvia, P. J. (2016). Everyday Creative Activity As a Path to Flourishing, *Journal of Positive Psychology*, doi:10.1080/17439760.2016.1257049.

Cotter, K. N., and Silvia, P. J. (2019). Ecological Assessment in Research on Aesthetics, Creativity, and the Arts: Basic Concepts, Common Questions, and Gentle Warnings. *Psychology of Aesthetics, Creativity, and the Arts*, 13(2), 211–217.

Cox, A. J. and Leon, J. L. (1999). Negative Schizotypal Traits in the Relation of Creativity to Psychopathology. *Creativity Research Journal*, 12, 25–36.

Cramond, B. (1994). "The Relationship between Attention Deficit Hyperactivity Disorder and Creativity." Paper presented at the annual meeting of the American Educational Research Association, April 4–8, 1994. New Orleans, LA.

(1995). *The Coincidence of Attention Deficit Hyperactivity Disorder and Creativity*. Storrs: The National Research Center on the Gifted and Talented. http://nrcgt.uconn.edu/research-based_resources/cramond/.

Crawford, M. J., Killaspy, H., Barnes, T. R., Barrett, B., Byford, S., Clayton, K., and Waller, D. (2012). Group Art Therapy As an Adjunctive Treatment for People with Schizophrenia: Multicentre Pragmatic Randomised Controlled Trial. *BMJ*, *344*, e846.

Crespi B., Leach E., Dinsdale N., Mokkonen M., Hurd P. (2016). Imagination in Human Social Cognition, Autism, and Psychotic-Affective Conditions. *Cognition*, *150*, 181–199.

Dardis, T. (1989). *The Thirsty Muse: Alcohol and the American Writer*. New York: Tichnor and Fields.

de Manzano, O., Cervenka, S., Karbanov, A., Farde, L., and Ullén, F. (2010). Thinking Outside a Less Intact Box: Thalamic Dopamine d2 Receptor Densities Are Negatively Related to Psychometric Creativity in Healthy Individuals. *PLoS One*, *5*, e10670.

Drake, J. E., and Hodge, A. (2015). Drawing versus writing: The Role of Preference in Regulating Short-Term Affect. *Art Therapy*, *32*(1), 27–33.

Drake, J. E., and Winner, E. (2012). Confronting Sadness through Art-Making: Distraction Is More Beneficial Than Venting. *Psychology of Aesthetics, Creativity, and the Arts*, *6*, 255–261.

   (2013). How Children Use Drawing to Regulate Their Emotions. *Cognition and Emotion*, *27*, 512–520.

Eschleman, K. J., Madsen, J., Alarcon, G., and Barelka, B. (2014). Benefiting from Creative Activity: The Positive Relationships between Creative Activity, Recovery Experiences, and Performance-Related Outcomes *Journal of Occupational and Organizational Psychology*, *87*(3), 579–598.

Fancourt, D., and Finn, S. (2019). *Health Evidence Network Synthesis Report #67: What Is the Evidence on the Role of the Arts in Improving Health and Well-Being?* Copenhagen: World Health Organization.

Feist, G. J. (1998). A Meta-Analysis of Personality in Scientific and Artistic Creativity. *Personality and Social Psychology Review*, *2*, 290–309.

Fink, A., Weber, B., Koschutnig, K., Benedek, M., Reishofer, G., Ebner, F. et al. (2014). Creativity and Schizotypy from the Neuroscience Perspective. *Cognitive, Affective, and Behavioral Neuroscience*, *14*, 378–387.

Forgeard, M. J. C. (2013). Finding Benefits after Adversity: The Relationship between Self-Reported Posttraumatic Growth and Creativity. *Psychology of Aesthetics, Creativity, and the Arts*, *7*, 245–264.

Forgeard, M. J. C., and Benson, L. (2017). Extracurricular Involvement and Psychological Adjustment in the Transition from Adolescence to Emerging Adulthood: The Role of Mastery and Creative Self-Efficacy. *Applied Developmental Science*, *23*(1), 41–58.

Forgeard, M. J. C., and Elstein, J. G. (2014). Advancing the Clinical Science of Creativity. *Frontiers in Psychology*, 5, Article 216.

Fugate, C. M., Zentall, S. S., and Gentry, M. (2013). Creativity and Working Memory in Gifted Students with and without Characteristics of Attention Deficit Hyperactive Disorder: Lifting the Mask. *Gifted Child Quarterly*, *57*(4), 234–246.

Galvin, R. (2004). William Blake: Visions and Verses. *Humanities*, *25*, 16–20.

Garland, S. N., Carlson, L. E., Cook, S., Lansdell, L., and Speca, M. (2007). A Non-Randomized Comparison of Mindfulness-Based Stress Reduction and Healing Arts Programs for Facilitating Post-Traumatic Growth and Spirituality in Cancer Outpatients. *Supportive Care in Cancer*, *15*, 949–961.

Gonzalez-Carpio, G., Serrano, J. P., and Nieto. N. (2017). Creativity in Children with Attention Deficit Hyperactivity Disorder (ADHD). *Psychology*, *8*, 319–334.

Ghiselin, B. (1952). *The Creative Process*. Berkeley: University of California Press.

Golimbet, V. E., Aksenova, M. G., Nosikov, V. V., Orlova, V. A., and Kaleda, V. G. (2003). Analysis of the Linkage of the Taq1A and Taq1B Loci of the Dopamine D2 Receptor Gene with Schizophrenia in Patients and Their Siblings. *Neuroscience and Behavioral Physiology, 33*, 223–225.

Green, M. J., and Williams, L. M. (1999). Schizotypy and Creativity As Effects of Reduced Cognitive Inhibition. *Personality and Individual Differences, 27*, 263–276.

Haeyen, S., van Hooren, S., van der Veld, W., and Hutschemaekers, G. (2018). Efficacy of Art Therapy in Individuals with Personality Disorders Cluster B/C: A Randomized Controlled Trial. *Journal of Personality Disorders, 32*, 527–542.

Healey, D., and Rucklidge, J. J. (2006) An Investigation into the Relationship Among ADHD Symptomatology, Creativity, and Neuropsychological Functioning in Children. *Child Neuropsychology, 12*, 421–438.

Heston, L. L. (1966). Psychiatric Disorders in Foster Home Reared Children of Schizophrenic Mothers. *British Journal of Psychiatry, 112*, 819–825.

Holttum, S., and Huet, V. (2014). The MATISSE Trial – a critique: Does Art Therapy Really Have Nothing to Offer People with a Diagnosis of Schizophrenia? *SAGE Open, 4*, 1–11.

Huxley, Aldous (1954). *The Doors of Perception*. New York: Harper and Brothers.

Jamison, K. R. (1989). Mood Disorders and Patterns of Creativity in British Writers and Artists. *Psychiatry, 52*, 125–134.

(1993). *Touched with Fire*. New York: Free Press.

Jarosz, A. F., Colflesh, G. J. F., Wiley, J. (2012). Uncorking the Muse: Alcohol Intoxication Facilitates Creative Problem Solving. *Consciousness and Cognition, 21*, 487–493.

Johnson, C. M., and Sullivan-Marx, E. M. (2006). Art Therapy: Using the Creative Process for Healing and Hope among African American Older Adults. *Geriatric Nursing, 27*, 309–316.

Juda, A. (1949). The Relationship between Highest Mental Capacity and Psychic Abnormalities. *American Journal of Psychiatry, 106*, 296–307.

Kabat-Zinn, J. (2013). *Full Catastrophe Living: Using the Wisdom of Your Body and Mind to Face Stress, Pain, and Illness*, rev. ed. New York: Bantam.

Kaimal, G., Mensinger, J. L., Drass, J. M., and Dieterich-Hartwell, R. M. (2017). Art Therapist-Facilitated Open Studio versus Coloring: Differences in Outcomes of Affect, Stress, Creative Agency, and Self-Efficacy. *Canadian Art Therapy Association Journal, 30*, 56–68.

Kaufman J. C. (2001). The Sylvia Plath Effect: Mental Illness in Eminent Creative Writers. *The Journal of Creative Behavior, 35*, 37–50.

(2018). Finding Meaning with Creativity in the Past, Present, and Future. *Perspectives on Psychological Science, 13*(6), 734–749.

Karlsson, J. L. (1970). Genetic Association of Giftedness and Creativity with Schizophrenia. *Hereditas, 66*, 177–182.

Kéri, S. (2009). Genes for Psychosis and Creativity: A Promoter Polymorphism of the Neuregulin 1 Gene Is Related to Creativity in People with High Intellectual Achievement. *Psychological Science, 20*, 1070–1073.

Kessler, R. C., Berglund, P., Demler, O., Jin, R., Merikangas, K. R., and Walters, E. E. (2005). Lifetime Prevalence and Age-of-Onset Distribution of *DSM-IV* Disorders in the National Comorbidity Survey Replication. *Archives of General Psychiatry, 62*, 593–602.

Kinney, D. K., Richards, R., Lowing, P. A., LeBlanc, D., Zimbalist, M. E., and Harlan, P. (2000–2001). Creativity in Offspring of Schizophrenic and Control Parents: An Adoption Study. *Creativity Research Journal, 13*, 17–25.

Kopytin, A., and Lebedev, A. (2013). Humor, Self-Attitude, Emotions, and Cognitions in Group Art Therapy with War Veterans. *Art Therapy*, *30*, 20–29.

Koutsantoni, K. (2012). Manic Depression in Literature: The Case of Virginia Woolf. *Medical humanities*, *38*, 7–14.

Kozbelt, A., Kaufman, S., Walder, D., Ospina, L., and Kim, J. (2014). The Evolutionary Genetics of the Creativity-Psychosis Connection. In J. Kaufman (Ed.), *Creativity and Mental illness* (pp. 102–132). Cambridge: Cambridge University Press.

Kyaga, S., Landén, M., Boman, M., Hultman, C. M., Langström, N., and Lichtenstein, P. (2013). Mental Illness, Suicide and Creativity: 40-Year Prospective Total Population Study. *Journal of Psychiatric Research*, *47*, 83–90.

Kyaga, S., Lichtenstein, P., Boman, M., Hultman, C., Langstrom, N., and Landen, M. (2011). Creativity and Mental Disorder: Family Study of 300,000 People with Severe Mental Disorder. *British Journal of Psychiatry*, *199*, 373–379.

Levine-Madori, L. (2013). Utilizing a Thematic Approach to Art Therapy with Seniors: Enhancing Cognitive Abilities and Social Interactions. In P. Howie, S. Prasad, and J. Kristel (Eds.), *Using Art Therapy with Diverse Populations: Crossing Cultures and Abilities* (pp. 317–327). Philadelphia: Jessica Kingsley.

Ludwig A. (1992). Creative Achievement and Psychopathology: Comparison among Professions. *American Journal of Psychotherapy*, *46*, 330–354.

(1994). Mental Illness and Creative Activity in Female Writers. *American Journal of Psychiatry*, *151*, 1650–1656.

(1995). *The Price of Greatness: Resolving the Creativity and Madness Controversy*. New York: Guilford Press.

Malchiodi, C. A. (Ed.). (2012). *The Handbook of Art Therapy*, 2nd ed. New York: Guilford.

Mason, O. and Claridge, G. (2006). The Oxford-Liverpool Inventory of Feelings and Experiences (O-LIFE): Further Description and Extended Norms. *Schizophrenia Research*, *82*, 203–211.

Maujean, A., Pepping, C. A., and Kendall, E. (2014). A Systematic Review of Randomized Controlled Studies of Art Therapy. *Art Therapy*, *31*, 37–44.

McCrae, R. R., and Sutin, A. R. (2009). Openness to Experience. In M. R. Leary and R. H. Hoyle (Eds.), *Handbook of Individual Differences in Social Behavior* (pp. 257–273). New York: Guilford.

Monti, D. A., Peterson, C., Kunkel, E. J. S., Hauck, W. W., Pequignot, E., Rhodes, L., and Brainard, G. C. (2006). A Randomized, Controlled Trial of Mindfulness-Based Art Therapy (MBAT) for Women with Cancer. *Psycho-Oncology*, *15*, 363–373.

Nasar, S. (1998). *A Beautiful Mind: The Life of Mathematical Genius and Nobel Laureate John Nash*. New York: Simon & Schuster.

Nettle, D. (2006). Schizotypy and Mental Health amongst Poets, Visual Artists, and Mathematicians. *Journal of Research in Personality*, *40*, 876–890.

Noble, E. P. (2000). Addiction and Its Reward Process through Polymorphisms of the D2 Dopamine Receptor Gene: A Review. *European Psychiatry*, *15*, 79–89.

Norlander, T. (1999). Inebriation and Inspiration? A Review of the Research on Alcohol and Creativity. *Journal of Creative Behavior*, *33*, 22–44.

O'Reilly, T., Dunbar, R., and Bentall, R. (2001). Schizotypy and Creativity: An Evolutionary Connection. *Personality and Individual Differences*, *31*, 1067–1078.

Orkibi, H., and Ram-Vlasov, N. (2019). Linking Trauma to Posttraumatic Growth and Mental Health through Emotional and Cognitive Creativity. *Psychology of Aesthetics, Creativity, and the Arts*, 13, 416–430.

Paek, S. H., Abdulla, A. M., and Cramond, B. (2016). A Meta-Analysis of the Relationship between Three Common Psychopathologies – ADHD, Anxiety, and Depression – and Indicators of little-c Creativity. *Gifted Child Quarterly*, *60*, 117–133.

Plato. (360 BC) *Phaedrus*. MIT Internet Classics. http://classics.mit.edu/Plato/phaedrus.html.

Post, F. (1994). Creativity and Psychopathology: A Study of 291 World-Famous Men. *British Journal of Psychiatry*, *165*, 22–34.

Power, R. A., Steinberg, S., Bjornsdottir, G., Rietveld, C. A., Abdellaoui, A. Nivard, M., and Stefanson, K. (2015). Polygenic Risk Scores for Schizophrenia and Bipolar Disorder Predict Creativity. *Nature Neuroscience*, *18*(7), 953–955.

Purcell S. M, Wray N. R, Stone J. L, Visscher P. M, O'Donovan M. C. et al. (2009) Common Polygenic Variation Contributes to Risk of Schizophrenia and Bipolar Disorder. *Nature*, *460*, 748–752.

Reuter, M., Roth, S., Holve, K. and Henning, J. (2006) Identification of First Genes for Creativity: A Pilot Study. *Brain Research*, *1069*, 190–197.

Richards, R. R. (1990): Everyday Creativity, Eminent Creativity, and Health: "Afterview" for CRJ Issues on Creativity and Health. *Creativity Research Journal*, *3*, 300–326.

(2007). *Everyday Creativity and New Views of Human Nature*. Washington, DC: American Psychological Association.

Richards, R. R., Kinney, D. K., Lunde, I., Benet, M., and Merzel, A. P. C. (1988). Creativity in Manic-Depressives, Cyclothymes, Their Normal Relatives, and Control Subjects. *Journal of Abnormal Psychology*, *97*, 281–288.

Sandblom, P. (1997). *Creativity and Disease: How Illness Affects Literature, Art and Music*. New York: Marion Boyars.

Sawyer, R. K. (2012). *Explaining Creativity: The Science of Human Innovation*, 2nd ed. New York: Oxford University Press.

(2014). "Creativity and Mental illness: Is There a Link?" Blog post, January 23, 2014. www.huffingtonpost.com/dr-r-keith-sawyer/creativity-and-mental-ill_b_2059806.html.

Schildkraut, J. J., Hirshfeld, A. J., and Murphy, J. M. (1994). Mind and Mood in Modern Art II: Depressive Disorders, Spirituality, and Early Deaths in the Abstract Expressionists of the New York School. *American Journal of Psychiatry*, *151*, 482–488.

Schlesinger, J. (2009). Creative Mythconceptions: A Closer Look at the Evidence for the "Mad Genius" Hypothesis. *Psychology of Aesthetics, Creativity, and the Arts*, *3*(2), 62–72.

(2014). Building Connections on Sand: The Cautionary Chapter. In J. C. Kaufman (Ed.), *Creativity and Mental Illness* (pp. 60–75). Cambridge: Cambridge University Press.

Sharp, S. I., McQuillin, A., Marks, M., Hunt, S. P., Stanford, S. C., Lydall, G. J., and Gurling, H. M. D. (2014). Genetic Association of the Tachykinin Receptor 1 TACR1 Gene in Bipolar Disorder, Attention Deficit Hyperactivity Disorder and the Alcohol Dependence Syndrome. *American Journal of Medical Genetics, Part B*, *165B*, 373–380.

Shaw, G. A., and Brown, G. (1991). Laterality, Implicit Memory and Attention Disorder. *Educational Studies*, *17*(1), 15–23.

Simonton, D. K. (2010). So You *Want* to Become a Creative Genius? You *Must* Be Crazy! In D. Cropley, J. Kaufman, A. Cropley, and M. Runco (Eds.), *The Dark Side of Creativity* (pp. 218–234). New York: Cambridge University Press.

(2014). The Mad-Genius Paradox: Can Creative People Be More Mentally Healthy But Highly Creative People More Mentally Ill? *Perspectives on Psychological Science, 9*, 470–480.

Slayton, S. C., D'Archer, J., and Kaplan, F. (2010). Outcome Studies on the Efficacy of Art Therapy: A Review of Findings. *Art Therapy: Journal of the American Art Therapy Association, 27*, 108–119.

Sternberg, R. J., and Lubart, T. I. (1999). The Concept of Creativity: Prospects and Paradigms. In R. J. Sternberg (Ed.), *Handbook of Creativity* (pp. 3–15). Cambridge: Cambridge University Press.

Takeuchi, H., Taki, Y., Hashizume, H., Sassa, Y., Nagase, T., Nouchi, R., and Kawashima, R. (2011). Failing to Deactivate: The Association between Brain Activity during a Working Memory Task and Creativity. *NeuroImage, 55*(2), 681–687.

Takeuchi, H., Tomita, H., Taki, Y., Kikuchi, Y., Ono, C., Yu, Z., and Kawashima, R. (2015). Cognitive and Neural Correlates of the 5-Repeat Allele of the Dopamine D4 Receptor Gene in a Population Lacking the 7-Repeat Allele. *NeuroImage, 110*, 124–135.

Tedeschi, R. G., and Calhoun, L. G. (1996). The Posttraumatic Growth Inventory: Measuring the Positive Legacy of Trauma. *Journal of Traumatic Stress, 9*, 455–471.

(2004). Posttraumatic Growth: Conceptual Foundations and Empirical Evidence. *Psychological Inquiry, 15*, 1–18.

Tesla, N. (1901). Talking with the Planets. *Collier's Weekly, 26* (February 9, 2001), 4–5.

Thys, E., Sabbe, B., and De Hert, M. (2013). Creativity and Psychiatric Illness: The Search for a Missing Link – an Historical Context for Current Research. *Psychopathology, 46*(3), 136–144.

Van Gogh, V. (1889). *Letter to Theo.* http://vangoghletters.org/vg/letters/let798/letter.html.

Vellante, M., Zucca, G., Preti, A., Sisti, D., Rocchi, M. B., Akiskal, K. K. et al. (2011). Creativity and Affective Temperaments in Non-Clinical Professional Artists: An Empirical Psychometric Investigation. *Journal of Affective Disorders, 135*, 28–36.

Volkow, N. D., Tomasi, D., Wang, G. J., Telang, F., Fowler, J. S., and Wong, C. T. (2013) Predominance of D2 Receptors in Mediating Dopamine's Effects in Brain Metabolism: Effects of Alcoholism. *Journal of Neuroscience, 33*, 4527–4535.

Whitfield, J. B., Nightingale, B. N., O'Brien, M. E., Heath, A. C., Birley, A. J., and Martin, N. G. (1998). Molecular Biology of Alcohol Dependence, a Complex Polygenic Disorder. *Clinical Chemistry and Laboratory Medicine, 36*, 633–636.

White, H. A., and Shah, P. (2011). Creative Style and Achievement in Adults with Attention-Deficit/Hyperactivity Disorder. *Personality and Individual Differences, 50*, 673–677.

White, H., and Shah, P. (2006). Uninhibited Imaginations: Creativity in Adults with Attention Deficit Hyperactivity Disorder. *Personality and Individual Differences, 40*, 1121–1131.

Whitfield-Gabrieli, S., Thermenos, H. W., Milanovic, S., Tsuang, M. T., Faraone, S. V., McCarley, and Seidman, L. J. (2009). Hyperactivity and Hyperconnectivity of the Default Network in Schizophrenia and in First-Degree Relatives of Persons with Schizophrenia. *Proceedings of the National Academy of Science USA, 106*, 1279–1284.

Williams, P. G., Rau, H. K., Cribbet, M. R., and Gunn, H. E. (2009). Openness to Experience and Stress Regulation. *Journal of Research in Personality, 43*, 777–784.

Wills, G. I. (2003). Forty Lives in the Bebop Business: Mental Health in a Group of Eminent Jazz Musicians. *British Journal of Psychiatry, 183*, 255–259.

Woolf, V. (1934/2003). Friday, July 27th 1934. In L. Woolf (Ed.), *A Writer's Diary* (p. 213). Orlando: Harcourt.

World Health Organization (2013). *The World Health Report 2013: Research for Universal Health Coverage.* Geneva: WHO.

Zabelina, D. L., Colzato, L., Beeman, M., and Hommel, B. (2016). Dopamine and the Creative Mind: Individual Differences in Creativity Are Predicted by Interactions between Dopamine Genes DAT and COMT. *PLoS One*, *11*(1), e0146768.

Zabelina, D. L., Condon, D., and Beeman, M. (2014). Do Dimensional Psychopathology Measures Relate to Divergent Thinking or Creative Achievement? *Frontiers in Psychology*, *5*, 1–11.

Zausner, T. (1998). When Walls Become Doorways: Creativity, Chaos Theory, and Physical Illness. *Creativity Research Journal*, *11*, 21–28.

12 Creativity in K–12 Schools

RONALD A. BEGHETTO

INTRODUCTION

Do schools support or suppress creativity? Almost everyone has an opinion about this question. These opinions are informed, in part, from our prior schooling experiences as well as representations of school in the media and internet. Consider Sir Ken Robinson's wildly popular and influential TED talk, "Do schools kill creativity?" People who have watched this talk may come away with the impression that schools kill, or at least suppress, creativity. What do you think?

The purpose of this chapter is to explore the question of whether schools support or suppress creativity and highlight how addressing this question is much more nuanced than a simple "yes" or "no" answer. Prior to doing so, it is first important to recognize that student learning is the primary goal of K–12 schools (i.e., schools that serve students in kindergarten through 12th grade). Anything that is viewed as competing with that goal, even something that seems potentially beneficial (such as creativity), likely will be viewed as secondary or ancillary to the primary goal of supporting student learning.

Even though academic learning typically represents the primary goal of school, there have been a long line of educators and creativity researchers who have recognized and demonstrated that creativity can complement academic learning. Creativity researchers have, for instance, documented a positive albeit modest relationship between measures of creativity and academic learning (Gadja, Karwowksi, and Beghetto, 2016). Creativity researchers have also demonstrated that academic learning environments can serve as an important context for helping students simultaneously develop their academic learning of subject matter and their creative potential (Beghetto, 2016a). School-based creativity is therefore not only possible but probable in conditions where educators recognize and actively work to support the complimentary relationship between creativity and academic learning. Indeed, **school-based creativity** can be defined as *different ways of meeting predetermined teaching and learning goals or criteria*.

This definition has its basis in commonly agreed upon definitions of creativity (Plucker, Beghetto, and Dow, 2004; Runco and Jaeger, 2012), which define creativity as a combination of originality (e.g., doing things differently) and usefulness (e.g., meeting task constraints). This definition is important because it highlights how school-based creativity can

This chapter is based on the previously published chapter R. A. Beghetto (2019). Creativity in Classrooms. In J. C. Kaufman and R. J. Sternberg (Eds.), *The Cambridge Handbook of Creativity*, 2nd ed. New York: Cambridge University Press.

complement student learning by still focusing on meeting the primary academic goals of schooling; but the definition broadens the focus to include new and different ways of doing so. Equipped with this definition, the question of whether schools support or suppress creativity is less about a simple "yes" or "no" answer and instead focuses on where, how, and under what conditions might teachers and students be creative in schools.

Where Can Teachers and Students Be Creative?

Although creative expression can occur in almost any context, following the definition of school-based creativity presented earlier, classrooms represent the context that is most relevant for understanding creative expression in schools. This is because classrooms are environments designed to support academic learning and school-based creativity as it pertains to meeting academic learning goals in new and different ways. Consequently, classrooms will serve as the primary setting of interest in this chapter, while recognizing that other settings in schools also offer opportunities for students and teachers to be creative (e.g., lunchroom, gymnasium, auditorium, and outdoor spaces). In order to understand how and under what conditions creative expression can occur in classrooms, it is important to take some time to consider the unique features of classrooms and how these features might constrain or enhance creative expression.

Let us first consider how the features of classrooms can constrain creative expression. You likely are quite familiar with classrooms, but if you stop and think about the typical K–12 classroom setting in the United States, then you will soon realize that they are unique and somewhat constraining environments. Classrooms tend to be relatively small spaces (approximately 900 square feet; Abramson, 2015), which tend to house a relatively large group of people (twenty-five students and one teacher; NCES, 2013) over a long duration of time (approximately 13,000 hours over 12 years of schooling; Jackson, 1990). Students typically are grouped together in K–12 classrooms by age and generally are required to do much the same thing, in the same way, and at the same time as each other. Also, even though students are often seated in close proximity to each other, they often are required to work quietly and individually (e.g., "No talking," "Keep your eyes on your own paper"). Moreover, students typically are required to solve problems that have already been solved and work on tasks that tend to have one correct or expected way of completing them. In this way, sameness tends to be privileged in classrooms (Glăveanu and Beghetto, 2016).

Classrooms also serve as sites of continuous monitoring and assessment of students and teachers. Teachers continually monitor whether students are meeting expectations. One of the most persistently documented ways this monitoring of expectations occurs is during classroom discussions. Typically, classroom talk follows a repeating, three-part **IRE pattern** of Initiate, Respond, and Evaluate (Mehan, 1979). More specifically, teachers *initiate* discussions by asking students questions and looking for an expected answer, students then *respond* by trying to provide that expected response, and teachers quickly *evaluate* whether those responses match what they expected to hear and how they expected to hear it

(Beghetto, 2013). This IRE pattern of talk is so commonly associated with school that even young children playing school often follow the pattern (Cazden, 2001).

The monitoring of expected patterns of behavior is so widespread in school that the **prototypical formula for school success** can be thought of as doing what is expected and doing it how it is expected (Beghetto, 2018a). In some cases, continual monitoring and assessment is informal (e.g., "Pay attention," "Who can tell me the names of the main characters of this story?"); in other cases, it occurs in formal exams, tests, and performance expectations. In many cases, students are required to demonstrate their ability to meet expectations without the assistance of others and without the assistance of supports that would otherwise be readily available in any other setting (e.g., talking to other people, calculators, online instructional videos, internet searches, and so on). Students are not the only ones undergoing monitoring and assessment in schools. Teachers and educational leaders also undergo continual formal and informal assessment of their ability to meet expectations in expected ways by district administrators, colleagues, students, external stakeholders, and even themselves (Ingersoll, 2003; Smaller, 2015).

Understanding these unique and constraining features of classrooms provides an important backdrop to understanding why teachers and students may not be willing to demonstrate creative thought and behavior in classrooms. Indeed, depending on the situation and context, doing so may be viewed as too risky, particularly if they are being evaluated for not only meeting expectations but meeting those expectations in expected ways. This continual monitoring and ongoing evaluation of meeting expectations can stifle creative expression in classrooms (see also Amabile, 2006; Hennessey, 2017).

Even with these somewhat unique features and constraints, students and teachers can still develop and express their creativity in classrooms. Indeed, creativity can and often does thrive in constraints (Stokes, 2006, 2010). There are at least two key requirements to be met in order for this to happen. The first is that the typical expectations of meeting expectations need to be broadened to include allowing students and teachers to meet expectations in different and even unexpected ways. The second is that teachers and students need to know how to be creative in classroom contexts and be willing to take the risks necessary for creative expression. The remainder of this chapter explores how and under what conditions teachers and students can be creative in classroom contexts.

How Can Teachers and Students Can Be Creative?

When it comes to creativity in schools and classrooms, there are two major ways that teachers and students can be creative. The first is creative teaching and the second is creative learning. Table 12.1 summarizes these different ways teachers and students can be creative, including the requirements and opportunities for these forms of creative expression.

As displayed in Table 12.1, creative teaching and learning represent the primary ways in which teachers and students can develop and express their creativity in schools and classrooms. In the sections that follow, I elaborate on the summary provided in Table 12.1,

Table 12.1 Different ways teachers and students can be creative in schools and classrooms

Types of creative expression	Brief description	Requirements	Opportunities
Creative teaching	Creative teaching takes one of three forms: teaching *about* creativity, teaching *for* creativity, and teaching *with* creativity.	Teachers need to believe that they can teach creatively in their classrooms, know what it means to be a creative teacher, and be willing to assume that role.	Because creative teaching in schools involves infusing creativity and creative content into existing academic curricula, there are numerous opportunities for creative teaching.
Teaching about creativity	Helping students learn what creativity is (and is not), how it develops in and across different activities and subject areas, and the role creativity plays in learning and life.	Understanding of the field of creativity studies and incorporation of examples and activities that highlight creative expression in specific subject areas.	Teaching about creativity can occur in most any subject area by incorporating biographies, case studies, and examples of creative work in the subject area.
Teaching for creativity	Developing students' creative potential into creative achievement.	Understanding of strategies and approaches for infusing creative learning activities and experiences in the existing curriculum.	Numerous opportunities for students' creative expression in the curriculum, ranging from encouraging students to develop their own ways of doing things to projects that enable students to identify their own problems to solve and their own ways of solving them.
Teaching with creativity	Teaching academic subject matter in a creative fashion.	Knowledge of what is being taught coupled with attributes of creative behavior (e.g., openness, sensible risk-taking, possibility thinking).	Teachers can teach most any subject area in a creative away. This involves being willing to explore unexpected moments that emerge during a lesson and establishing openings for creative expression.

Table 12.1 (cont.)

Types of creative expression	Brief description	Requirements	Opportunities
Creative learning	The combination of individual and socio-cultural processes that result in new and personally meaningful understandings for oneself and others.	A classroom environment that allows for students to develop, share, and engage with different ways of understanding subject matter.	Creative learning can occur in most any subject area.
Creativity-in-learning	Focuses on the creative process involved in how individual students develop their understanding of new academic subject matter.	Students need opportunities and support to engage with academic subject matter in ways that promote a new and personally meaningful understanding.	Creativity-in-learning can occur in any subject area and with almost any topic as long as the concepts or experiences being presented are sufficiently novel to the students.
Learning-in-creativity	Focuses on having students share and test out their new and meaningful understandings with those of their teachers and peers.	Students need opportunities to share and test out their new and personally meaningful understandings with others. Teachers and peers need to be willing to engage with unexpected or different ideas, insights and understandings.	Learning-in-creativity can occur in situations where teachers have the time and willingness to explore different perspectives (i.e., not feeling too pressured to cover topics and quickly move on) and students have the confidence, willingness, and understanding of when it might be most beneficial to share their unique perspectives.

starting with various forms creative teaching can take and the challenges and opportunities that come with each of these forms of creative expression.

Creative Teaching

Creative teaching can take one of three forms (Beghetto, 2017): *teaching about creativity*, *teaching for creativity*, and *teaching with creativity*. **Teaching about creativity** refers to helping students learn what creativity is (and is not), how it develops in and across different activities and subject areas, and the role creativity plays in learning and life.

Teachers who teach about creativity will, of course, need to have a deep understanding of creativity, based on the work from the field of creativity studies. Knowledge of the field of creativity studies, however, is just a starting point. Given that K–12 teaching has a primary goal of promoting academic learning, teachers likely will not have the time or curricular space to teach a separate "creativity class." Rather, they will need to be able to find ways to blend creativity content within their regular academic subject matter teaching. Doing so can be challenging (Lassig, 2012), but it is possible to take a *both/and* approach (Beghetto, 2013) and infuse information about creativity in the teaching of core academic subject matter (e.g., Beghetto, Kaufman, and Baer, 2015; Renzulli, 2017).

One way teachers can take this both/and approach is to incorporate examples and models of creativity in their teaching. Root-Bernstein and Root-Bernstein (2016), for example, describe how teachers can go beyond simply teaching the "what" of academic topics and also explore the creative work of people in those subject areas, including the *who, how, when, why*, and *where* of that work. Teachers can also include mini-biographies of people doing creative work, relevant examples from various news and media sources, and even have their students develop "biographies of ideas" (Clapp, 2016) to develop an understanding of how creative ideas and innovations occur in and across academic subject areas. Teachers and students can invite and virtually interview professionals and experts (from poets to plumbers) to discuss examples of how creativity and learning play a role in their professional work (Beghetto, 2013).

Finally, and somewhat ironically, it is of course possible for a teacher to teach about creativity in very uncreative ways. When creativity becomes the subject or an integrated aspect of the subject being taught, it is still possible to be taught in traditional ways such as lectures and learning activities that simply require that students memorize and reproduce what they have learned about creativity. Consequently, it is also important for teachers who plan to teach about creativity to also understand how they might also teach about creativity more creatively (Simonton, 2012).

Teaching for creativity refers to efforts aimed at developing students' creative potential into creative achievement. Teaching for creativity in the context of K–12 classrooms is less about using general creative thinking activities (e.g., "Come up with 100 creative uses for a brick") and more about working with specific academic subject matter to cultivating students' potential to think creatively in the context of learning and real-world problems (e.g., "Come up with as many different ways of accurately solving this math problem" and "How might we come up with a creative way of addressing the problem of the bullying that goes on in the lunch room?").

Given that teachers have a lot of predetermined curriculum to cover and are working with large numbers of students, it is sometimes difficult to imagine how they might use curricular time to support students' creative ideas (Aljughaiman and Mowrer-Reynolds, 2005; Davies et al., 2012; Paek and Sumners, 2017). One promising direction for making room in their curriculum to support creative expression is called **lesson unplanning**. Lesson unplanning involves establishing openings in teachers' existing lessons and activities by replacing predetermined aspects of the curriculum with to-be-determined opportunities for students to share their own unique ideas and insights (Beghetto, 2018b).

A teacher could, for example, use lesson unplanning when assigning math practice problems to students. Rather than having students complete twelve math problems using one taught procedure, the teacher could have students complete six problems with the taught procedure and then spend time coming up with as many different ways as they can to solve one problem and share their different ways with other students in the class. Doing so can result in students generating multiple different ways of solving a problem, which can deepen their learning and creatively contribute to the learning of others (Niu and Zhou, 2017).

Teachers could also use as little as five minutes a day to engage students in identifying and solving problems that matter to them in their school, neighborhood, or surrounding community. Spending time on "five-minute projects" requires a small investment of time but over the course of a typical school year (180 days) can add up to meaningful opportunities for students to make creative contributions to their learning and lives.

Teaching for creativity in K–12 classrooms requires teachers to think differently about their curriculum and how they use curricular time. It also involves occasionally partnering with outside experts and community members. It also involves establishing a creativity supportive classroom environment that encourages students to productively work with uncertainty. The following is a brief overview of considerations for how teachers might teach for creativity (Schacter et al., 2006; Reeve, 2009; Davies et al., 2012; Beghetto, 2013, 2019; Beghetto and Kaufman, 2014; Hennessey, 2017; Sternberg, 2017), including:

- *Plan for and expect creative expression from students.* As mentioned, teachers can make openings in their lessons by replacing predetermined aspects of their lesson with opportunities to share their own unique ideas and insights. This includes establishing expectations for students to use what they are learning in creative ways as well as opportunities to identify their own problems to solve and their own ways of solving them. Doing so can be risky for both teachers and students, so it is important that teachers stress that even if ideas don't work out, students can still learn that such setbacks are part of the creative learning process.
- *Provide students with autonomy support.* In order for students to take the risks necessary for creative expression, they need to feel supported in sharing their own perspectives, making choices, and working through the consequences of those choices. When engaged in

creative learning, students can experience a range of emotions, including negative emotions. Part of supporting students' autonomy and learning involves acknowledging and accepting such emotions (e.g., "I can understand that you are extremely frustrated and angry that this didn't work out") rather than dismissing them (e.g., "Don't be upset. This is supposed to be fun"). Supporting autonomy still occurs in a context of clear expectations and guidance to help structure the uncertainty that students encounter.

- *Provide students with opportunities to view topics from different perspectives and engage in possibility thinking.* Given that school-based creativity involves meeting goals and expectations in new and different ways, it is important that students and teachers approach learning tasks and challenges from multiple perspectives. This includes challenging assumptions, asking "What if?" to explore new possibilities, being open to different perspectives, making the familiar unfamiliar, and imagining how the way things currently are experienced or understood could be experienced or understood in new and different ways.

- *Provide students with opportunities to view creativity and academic learning as means to other ends, rather than ends in themselves.* Typically, students are asked to learn academic subject matter as a means to its own end (e.g., "We will be learning how to write a persuasive argument this week so that you can write your own persuasive argument by the end of the week"). A creativity-supportive environment provides opportunities for students to experience using academic subject matter learning and their own creative ideas as a means to some other end ("You will be presenting your project idea to the Mayor's leadership team; you therefore need to know how to write and deliver a persuasive argument"). As mentioned, an example of this would be to provide students with opportunities to identify and creatively solve complex challenges in their schools, neighborhoods, and communities. Doing so allows students to realize that they are capable of working through ill-defined challenges and even of making a lasting, creative contribution that benefits others.

Teaching with creativity refers to teaching academic subject matter in a creative fashion. Teaching with creativity focuses on how teaching can be a creative action in itself. This is not to say that teaching with creativity has no impact on students. In fact, creativity scholars have described how teaching with creativity is tightly connected with teaching for student creativity (Jeffrey and Craft, 2004). One reason why teaching with creativity can impact student creativity is because when teachers demonstrate creative thinking and behavior, they are modeling and indirectly encouraging creative thought and behavior in their students (Lilly and Bramwell-Resjskind, 2004; Kaufman and Beghetto, 2013).

Like all forms of creative teaching, teaching with creativity requires that teachers have deep knowledge of what they are teaching. Teaching with creativity therefore involves teaching specific subject matter while at the same time approaching the act of teaching with openness, flexibility, sensible risk-taking, possibility thinking, and related attributes of creative behavior. This is often easier said than done (Simonton, 2012). Not only do aspiring teachers have limited exposure or experience with creative teaching (see Schacter et al., 2006), they may also come to believe that creative teaching takes more time and energy than more traditional approaches (Mullen, 2017). It is thereby not surprising that research exploring creative teaching practices has indicated that teaching with creativity may be difficult to maintain over the duration of an entire lesson (Gadja et al., 2017). Also, given that there are ever-persistent accountability pressures for K–12 teachers to ensure that their students perform well on standardized exams, teachers may feel little incentive to devote time and energy to teaching in more creative ways (Baer and Garrett, 2017).

One way that K–12 teachers can navigate these pressures and constraints is to recognize that they need not always be creative when they teach (Kaufman and Beghetto, 2013). Indeed, in many cases, teaching with creativity involves designing lessons and activities that provide occasional openings in the lesson for students to share their own creative ideas and perspectives. It also includes being willing to explore and navigate unexpected moments that emerge during a lesson (Aoki, 2005; Beghetto, 2013). Doing so is not about following wild ideas down a curricular rabbit hole, but rather being willing to listen carefully to students' unique perspectives while still keeping an eye toward the learning goals of a particular lesson. Teaching with creativity can thereby be thought of as a skillful blend between knowing when and how to improvise while still working within the academic constraints of the lesson or activity (Sawyer, 2004; Beghetto and Kaufman, 2011).

In some cases, this will involve spending additional time drawing out and exploring how an unexpected idea or turn in the lesson connects to what is being learned. In other cases, it will involve postponing the exploration of an idea for a later lesson or activity. In cases where teachers postpone the exploration of student ideas, it is important that the teacher actually returns to that idea, otherwise it will be experienced by students as a form of creative suppression or what has been called **killing ideas softly** (Beghetto, 2013). Killing ideas softly refers to gently, but still effectively dismissing and suppressing unexpected and potentially creative ideas (e.g., "That's a creative way of looking at it, but we need to get back on track").

Teachers should also be aware of how students are experiencing failures and setbacks and the messages they are receiving following such setbacks. Although it is true that failure, even painful failures, are part of the creative process, it is also true that students may experience creative mortification if they do not believe improvement is possible (Beghetto, 2014; Beghetto and Dilley, 2016).

Creative mortification refers to the indefinite suspension of a creative aspiration following a negative performance outcome. This seems to occur when students feel a combination of shame and a belief that they are not able to improve (Beghetto, 2014). A student who aspires to be a singer may stop pursuing singing following an embarrassing solo performance at a school recital if they are not prepared to take creative risks and to learn how to productively work through failures, even public and painfully embarrassing failures.

Teaching with creativity thereby also includes supporting students' creative identity development by modeling creative attitudes and frankly discussing the risks and setbacks that are often involved in creative work with their students. Doing so can go a long way in helping students hear and receive honest feedback about their current abilities in light of their goals and aspirations *and* the amount of sustained effort and deliberate practice necessary to improve upon their current creative abilities. In sum, teaching with creativity can be thought of as having the subject matter knowledge and willingness necessary to teach creatively and model creativity supportive attitudes for students.

Regardless of the form that creative teaching takes, it requires that teachers believe they can be creative in their classrooms (Paek and Sumners, 2017), understand what it means to be a creative teacher (Schacter et al., 2006; Davies et al., 2012), and be willing to assume their role as a creative teacher (Gralewski and Karwowski, 2016; Beghetto, 2019).

Creativity in Learning

Having discussed different ways that teachers can be creative, we can now turn our attention to how students can engage in creative learning. As discussed, supporting creativity in schools involves recognizing that creativity and learning can be compatible and interrelated goals (e.g., Sefton-Green et al., 2011; Littleton and Mercer, 2013; Beghetto, 2016). This recognition is perhaps best captured in the concept of creative learning.

Creative learning is defined as the combination of individual and socio-cultural processes that result in new and personally meaningful understandings for oneself and others (Beghetto, 2016; Beghetto and Schuh, in press). Creative learning has two components: creativity-in-learning and learning-in-creativity. **Creativity-in-learning** focuses on the creative process involved in how individual students develop their understanding of new academic subject matter. Whenever students encounter something new in their learning, they engage in a meaning-making process that involves attempting to make sense of the new information in light of what they already know. Not all forms of individual learning are creative learning. A student who, for instance, memorizes a new concept and is able to accurately identify that concept on a multiple-choice exam, but has not developed a personally meaningful understanding of that concept has not engaged in creative learning. Rather, the student has simply memorized a new concept. Only when students are able to develop a new and personally meaningful understanding of what they have been taught, can we say that they have engaged in creative learning.

Creativity-in-learning occurs at the subjective or mini-c level of creativity (Stein, 1953; Runco, 1996; Kaufman and Beghetto, 2009). **Mini-c creativity** refers to new and meaningful ideas, insights, and interpretations (Beghetto and Kaufman, 2007). Importantly, mini-c creativity need not be recognized as creative by others to still be considered creative by the person experiencing it. A student's mini-c insight about the role historical analysis can play in predicting future events can still be considered an example of creativity-in-learning, even if that insight is already known by that student's teacher and peers. In this way, individual creative learning has a subjective aspect to it but this not to say that anything goes when it comes to creative learning.

Creative learning, like all classroom learning, also has an evaluative aspect to it. Specifically, students' developing understanding is often checked to ensure that it is correct or at least fits with how ideas and concepts are understood by the teacher and a broader field of study. Consequently, a student's creative insight still needs to meet the academic criteria in order for it to be considered an example of creative learning.

When students share their unique understanding with others, creativity-in-learning can move into the second phase of creative learning called learning-in-creativity (Beghetto, 2016a). **Learning-in-creativity** refers to the creative contributions that students can make to the understanding of their teachers and peers. Learning-in-creativity can happen when a student shares a creative insight, interpretation, or perspective that is recognized as contributing to the learning and understanding of others. A student who shares a creative metaphor for understanding a scientific concept can support the understanding of others. In this case, the student's creative metaphor can be thought of as making a little-c creative contribution.

Little-c creative contributions refer to new and meaningful contributions that others recognize as creative. Little-c contributions are considered to be at the everyday level of creative expression, meaning that they may be viewed as creative in the context of a classroom, even if they are not recognized as creative by experts in a domain (Kaufman and Beghetto, 2009). An 8th grade student who shares a novel and mathematically accurate way of solving a story problem in math would be an example of a little-c creative contribution. Although a professional mathematician may view the insight as somewhat ordinary, in the context of the 8th grade math classroom, it can still be recognized as creative and beneficial to the learning of others.

In this way, creative learning can be thought of as occurring at two levels: the individual and social level. Consequently, supporting creative learning in schools requires that teachers and students need opportunities and support to engage with academic subject matter in ways that promote not only their ability to accurately demonstrate their understanding but also develop a personally meaningful understanding of that subject matter. They also need opportunities to share, test out, and receive supportive feedback on their understanding. Doing so no only helps ensure that they are developing an accurate understanding but also allows students to have the opportunity to make a creative contribution to others (Beghetto, 2016a).

Creative learning can be constrained or undermined in classroom settings that place too much focus on simply reproducing expected responses in expected ways. This can happen for a variety of reasons, even in classrooms where teachers might otherwise value creativity. When teachers feel overwhelmed by the amount of content they need to cover and the limited amount of time that they have to cover it, they may feel that spending any time on different ideas and perspectives would be too risky or disruptive (Kennedy, 2005; Beghetto, 2013).

Similarly, students who lack confidence in their ideas or do not see the value in behaving creatively may feel it is not worth the risk to share their unique perspectives and understanding with others. Indeed, valuing creativity and having a healthy sense of **creative confidence**, which refers to people's belief that they can successfully think and act in creative ways, seems to play an important role in transforming creative potential into creative achievement (Karwowski and Beghetto, 2019).

Even if students have a healthy sense of creative confidence and their teachers encourage creative expression, they may still run into roadblocks if they are not able to successfully "read the situation" and determine whether it might be beneficial to think and act creatively. Students need to know when it is beneficial to think and act creatively and when it is best to conform to expected ways of behaving. Even the most creativity supportive teacher would likely frown on a student taking creative license with safety procedures when conducting a potentially dangerous chemistry experiment.

The self and situational knowledge and awareness necessary to read a situation and determine whether creative behavior is worth the risk is called **creative metacognition** (Kaufman and Beghetto, 2013). Creative metacognition seems to play an important role in the development of creative competence as well as the development of a healthy creative identity. Consequently, teachers can play a key role in helping their students not only develop their creative confidence but also learn how and when it might be appropriate to think and act creatively in schools and classrooms.

One way of doing this is for the teacher to establish structured openings in their curriculum for students to think and act creatively. Such **creative openings**, which can be planned or emerge unexpectedly, provide students with opportunities to develop new insights, share and test out those insights, receive supportive feedback, and potentially contribute to the learning of others. These openings can occur in virtually any subject area, including topics that may be viewed as having little room for creative expression, such as mathematics (see Niu and Zhou, 2017) or in lessons that are designed to meet externally developed academic content standards (Beghetto, Kaufman, and Baer, 2015).

Opportunities for creative learning can range from small scale everyday academic lessons to learning experiences that are designed specifically to promote creative problem solving and creative expression beyond the walls of the classroom, such as design challenges and real-world problem solving projects (Hathcock and Dickerson, 2017; Renzulli, 2017; Saorín et al., 2017; Beghetto, 2018b). Whatever the scale, creative learning opportunities should occur in an otherwise supportive and structured environment so that students can receive the feedback and guidance they need to learn how to think and act creatively when it is beneficial to do so and also recognize when it might be best to conform to existing ways of thinking and acting.

CONCLUSION

This chapter opened with the question of: *Do schools support or suppress creativity?* Although some people may answer this question with an unequivocal "yes" or "no," the ideas presented in this chapter offer a more nuanced response to this question. Whether creativity is supported or suppressed in schools depends on a variety of factors, starting with whether creativity is viewed as being in competition with academic learning or whether it is viewed as being compatible.

As discussed, creativity is possible and likely in classroom settings where educators recognize and work to infuse creative opportunities within the context of academic learning. This is because school-based creativity is defined as meeting learning goals in new and different ways. Still, in order for creative expression to be supported in schools, it is important to also understand how the unique features of classroom environments can constrain creative expression both in terms of the physical and socio-psychological characteristics of classrooms.

Although it is true that students' and teachers' prototypical experiences in classrooms place real constraints on creative expression, it is still possible for creativity to occur in such settings in the form of creative teaching and creative learning. With respect to creative teaching, there are several ways that teachers can infuse creativity into instruction, including teaching about creativity, teaching for creativity, and teaching with creativity, or some combination thereof. Teachers, of course, need to believe that they can teach creatively, know what it means to be a creative teacher, and be willing to assume the role of a creative teacher.

When teachers approach teaching creatively, they, in turn, directly and indirectly support students' creative learning. One reason this happens is because teachers model creative behaviors to students. Another reason this happens is because creative teachers plan for and allow openings in their curriculum to learn in new, different, and personally meaningful ways. Indeed, creative learning is all about providing students with an opportunity to engage with and understand academic subject matter in new and different ways. This involves providing students with opportunities to share and test out their unique perspectives, receive feedback on those perspectives, and make alterations to those perspectives.

When students have an opportunity to engage in creative learning in and outside of the walls of the classroom, they have opportunities to develop their creative confidence, recognize the value of creativity, and develop an awareness of when to be creative and when not to be. Creative learning is also about providing students with opportunities to contribute to the learning and lives of others. It is in these ways that schools can support creative expression for students and teachers in and beyond the walls of schools and classrooms.

My Research Contribution

Professor Ronald Beghetto is an internationally recognized expert on creative thought and action in educational settings. Dr. Beghetto's work has contributed to understanding the role uncertainty plays in creativity, learning, instruction, and innovation; the relationship between creativity and academic learning; the development of more dynamic methods for studying creative expression in and beyond educational contexts; and how making principled changes to existing teaching, learning, and leadership practices can result in more creative, productive, and sustainable innovations.

He has also contributed to creativity theory, practice, and research with the development of the Four-C model of creativity with James C. Kaufman. The Four-C model provides a way of understanding different levels of creative magnitude and how creativity can develop from personally meaningful creative insights, ideas, and experiences (mini-c creativity) and can, with feedback, develop into everyday creative contributions recognized by others (little-c creativity). The model also describes how, with the development of domain specific expertise and deliberate practice, professional creative contributions can be made, which are recognized as creative and significant by experts in a field (Pro-c creativity) and how, in rare instances, legendary creative contributions can be made that stand the test of time and are recognized as having made profound and transformative impacts on fields of study, societies, and, occasionally, humanity itself (Big-C creativity).

Critical/Creative Thinking Questions

1. Having now read this chapter, how would you respond to someone who made the claim to you that schools "kill creativity"?
2. What has been your experience with creative support and creative suppression in schools? Have you ever witnessed or experienced the "killing of ideas softly" or "creative mortification"? What do you think schools could do better to support rather than suppress student and teacher creativity?
3. Recall your own experiences with current and prior teachers. Can you provide examples of whether and how your teachers approached teaching creatively? Do you feel there may be other ways that teachers can be creative in the classroom beyond the ways discussed in this chapter?
4. Can you think of some instances in your own prior learning experiences in school when you feel you engaged in creative learning and maybe even contributed

creatively to the learning of others? What factors seemed to support your creative learning?

5. In what ways have creative confidence and creative metacognition skills influenced your own willingness to think and act creatively in schools and classrooms? What other factors do you think are important in determining whether teachers and students would be willing to take the risks necessary for creative expression in classrooms?

GLOSSARY

creative confidence: People's belief that they can successfully think and act in creative ways.

creative learning: The combination of individual and socio-cultural processes that result in new and personally meaningful understandings for oneself and others.

creative metacognition: Personal and situational knowledge necessary to read the situation and weigh the potential costs against the potential benefits before taking creative action.

creative mortification: The indefinite suspension of a creative aspiration following a negative performance outcome.

creative openings: Planned or unexpected opportunities in the curriculum for students to develop creative insights, interpretations and ideas, share and test out those insights, and potentially contribute to the learning of others.

creative teaching: A term referring to one of three forms: teaching about creativity, teaching for creativity, and teaching with creativity.

creativity-in-learning: The creative process involved in how individual students develop their understanding of new academic subject matter.

IRE pattern: A common pattern of classroom discourse that refers to teachers Initiating known-answer questions, students attempting to Respond in expected ways, and teachers Evaluating whether students match those expectations.

killing ideas softly: Gently, but still effectively, dismissing and suppressing unexpected and potentially creative ideas.

learning-in-creativity: Having students share and test out their new and meaningful understandings with those of their teachers and peers.

lesson unplanning: The process of establishing creative openings in existing curricular experiences by replacing predetermined elements with to-be-determined elements.

little-c creative contributions: New and meaningful contributions, at the everyday or classroom level, that others recognize as creative.

mini-c creativity: New and meaningful ideas, insights, and interpretations.

prototypical formula for school success: Doing what is expected and doing it how it is expected to be done.

school-based creativity: Different ways of meeting predetermined teaching and learning goals or criteria.

teaching about creativity: Teaching students what creativity is (and is not), how it develops, and the role creativity plays in learning and life.

teaching for creativity: Developing students' creative potential into creative achievement.

teaching with creativity: Teaching academic subject matter in a creative fashion.

REFERENCES

Aljughaiman, A., and Mowrer-Reynolds, E. (2005). Teachers' Conceptions of Creativity and Creative Students. *Journal of Creative Behavior*, *39*, 17–34.

Amabile, T. M. (1996). *Creativity in Context: Update to the Social Psychology of Creativity*. Boulder: Westview.

Aoki, T. T. (2004). Spinning Inspirited Images. In W. F. Pinar and R. L. Irwin (Eds.), *Curriculum in a New Key: The Collected Works of Ted T. Aoki* (pp. 413–225). Mahwah: Lawrence Erlbaum Associates.

Baer, J., and Garrett, T. (2017). Accountability, the Common Core, and Creativity. In R. A. Beghetto and J. C. Kaufman (Eds.), *Nurturing Creativity in the Classroom*, 2nd ed. (pp. 45–66). New York: Cambridge University Press.

Beghetto, R. A. (2007). Ideational Code-Switching: Walking the Talk about Supporting Student Creativity in the Classroom. *Roeper Review*, *29*, 265–270.

(2013). *Killing Ideas Softly? The Promise and Perils of Creativity in the Classroom*. Charlotte: Information Age Publishing.

(2014). Creative Mortification: An Initial Exploration. *Psychology of Aesthetics, Creativity, and the Arts*, *8*, 266–276.

(2016). Creative Learning: A Fresh Look. *Journal of Cognitive Education and Psychology*, *15*, 6–23.

(2017). Creativity in Teaching. In J. C. Kaufman, J. Baer, and V. P. Glăveanu (Eds.), *The Cambridge Handbook of Creativity across Different Domains* (pp. 549–564). New York: Cambridge University Press.

(2018a). Taking Beautiful Risks in Education. *Educational Leadership*, *76*, 18–24.

(2018b). *What If? Building Students' Problem Solving Skills through Complex Challenges*. Alexandria: ASCD

(2019). *Beautiful Risks: Having the Courage to Teach and Learn with Creativity*. Lanham: Rowman and Littlefield

Beghetto, R. A., and Dilley, A. E. (2016). Creative Aspirations or Pipe dreams? Toward Understanding Creative Mortification in Children and Adolescents. *New Directions for Child and Adolescent Development*, *151*, 85–95.

Beghetto, R. A., and Kaufman, J. C. (2007). Toward a Broader Conception of Creativity: A Case for mini-c Creativity. *Psychology of Aesthetics, Creativity, and the Arts*, *1*, 73–79.

(2011). Teaching for Creativity with Disciplined Improvisation. In R. K. Sawyer (Ed.), *Structure and Improvisation in Creative Teaching* (94–109). Cambridge: Cambridge University Press.

(2014) Classroom Contexts for Creativity. *High Ability Studies*, *25*, 53–69.

Beghetto, R. A., Kaufman, J. C., and Baer, J. (2015). *Teaching for Creativity in the Common Core*. New York: Teachers College Press.

Beghetto, R. A., and Schuh, K. L. (in press). Exploring the Link between Imagination and Creativity: A Creative Learning Approach. In D. Preiss, D. Cosmelli, and Kaufman, J. C. (Eds.), *Mind Wandering and Creativity*. San Diego: Elsevier

Clapp, E. P. (2016). *Participatory Creativity: Introducing Access and Equity to the Creative Classroom*. New York: Routledge.

Cazden, C. B. (2001). *Classroom Discourse: The Language of Teaching and Learning*, 2nd ed. Portsmouth: Heinemann.

Davies, D., Jindal-Snape, D., Collier, C., Digby, R., Hay, P., and Howe, A. (2012). Creative Learning Environments in Education: A Systematic Literature Review. *Thinking Skills and Creativity*, *8*, 80–91.

Gajda, A., Beghetto, R. A., and Karwowski, M. (in press). Exploring Creative Learning in the Classroom: A Multi-Method Approach. *Thinking Skills and Creativity*, *24*, 250–267.

Gajda, A., Karwowski, M., and Beghetto, R. A. (2016). Creativity and School Achievement: A Meta-Analysis. *Journal of Educational Psychology*, *109*, 269–299.

Glăveanu, V., and Beghetto, R. A. (2016). The Difference That Makes a Creative Difference. In R. A. Beghetto and B. Sriraman (Eds.), *Creative Contradictions in Education: Cross-Disciplinary Paradoxes and Perspectives* (pp. 37–54). Switzerland: Springer

Gralewski, J., and Karawoski, M. (2016). Are Teachers' Implicit Theories of Creativity Related to the Recognition of Their Students' Creativity? *Journal of Creative Behavior*. doi:10.1002/jocb.140.

Hathcock, S. J., and Dickerson, D. (2017). Design-Based Challenges As a Means of Encouraging Creativity. In K. S. Taber, M. Sumida, and L. McClure. (Eds.), *Teaching Gifted Learners STEM Subjects* (pp. 198–209). New York: Routledge.

Hennessey, B. A. (2017). Intrinsic Motivation and Creativity in the Classroom: Have We Come Full Circle? In R. A. Beghetto and J. C. Kaufman (Eds.), *Nurturing Creativity in the Classroom*, 2nd ed. (227–264). New York: Cambridge University Press.

Ingersoll, R. M. (2003). *Who Controls Teachers' Work?: Power and Accountability in America's Schools*. Cambridge, MA: Harvard University Press.

Jackson, P. W. (1990). *Life in Classrooms*. New York: Teachers College Press.

Jeffrey, B., and Craft, A. (2004). Teaching Creatively and Teaching for Creativity: Distinctions and Relationships. *Educational Studies*, *30*, 77–87.

Karwowski, M., and Beghetto, R. A. (2019). Creative Behavior As Agentic Action. *Psychology of Aesthetics, Creativity, and the Arts*, *13*(4), 402–415.

Kaufman, J. C., and Beghetto, R. A. (2009). Beyond Big and Little: The Four C Model of Creativity. *Review of General Psychology*, *13*, 1–12.

(2013). In praise of Clark Kent: Creative Metacognition and the Importance of Teaching Kids When (Not) to Be Creative. *Roeper Review*, *35*, 155–165.

Kennedy, M. (2005). *Inside Teaching: How Classroom Life Undermines Reform*. Cambridge, MA: Harvard University Press.

Lassig, C. J. (2012) Creating Creative Classrooms. *The Australian Educational Leader*, *34*, 8–13.

Lilly, F. R., and Bramwell-Rejskind, G. (2004). The Dynamics of Creative Teaching. *Journal of Creative Behavior*, *38*, 102–124.

Littleton, K., and Mercer, N. (2013). *Interthinking: Putting Talk to Work*. London: Routledge.

Mehan, H. (1979). *Learning Lessons: Social Organization in the Classroom*. Cambridge, MA: Harvard University Press.

Mullen, C. A. (2017). *Creativity and Education in China: Paradox and Possibilities for an Era of Accountability*. Abingdon: Taylor and Francis.

National Center for Education Statistics (NCES). (2013). *2011–2012 Schools and Staffing Survey*, table 7. https://nces.ed.gov/surveys/sass/tables/sass1112_2013314_t1s_007.asp.

Niu, W., and Zhou, Z. (2017). Creativity in Mathematics Teaching: A Chinese Perspective (an Update). In R. A. Beghetto and J. C. Kaufman (Eds.), *Nurturing Creativity in the Classroom*, 2nd ed. (pp. 86–107). New York: Cambridge University Press.

Paek, S. H., and Sumners, S. E. (2017), The Indirect Effect of Teachers' Creative Mindsets on Teaching Creativity. *Journal of Creative Behavior*, doi:10.1002/jocb.180.

Plucker, J., Beghetto, R. A., and Dow, G. (2004). Why Isn't Creativity More Important to Educational Psychologists? Potential, Pitfalls, and Future Directions in Creativity Research. *Educational Psychologist*, *39*, 83–96.

Reeve, J. (2009). Why Teachers Adopt a Controlling Motivating Style toward Students and How They Can Become More Autonomy Supportive. *Educational Psychologist*, *44*, 159–175.

Renzulli, J. (2017). Developing Creativity across All Areas of the Curriculum. In R. A. Beghetto and J. C. Kaufman (Eds.), *Nurturing Creativity in the Classroom*, 2nd ed. (pp. 23–44). New York: Cambridge University Press.

Root-Bernstein, R., and Root-Bernstein, M. (2017). People, Passions, Problems: The Role of Creative Exemplars in Teaching for Creativity. In R. A. Beghetto and B. Sriraman (Eds.), *Creative Contradictions in Education* (pp. 143–180). Switzerland: Springer

Runco, M. A. (1996). Personal Creativity: Definition and Developmental Issues. *New Directions in Child Development*, *72*, 3–30.

Runco, M. A., and Jaeger, G. J. (2012). The Standard Definition of Creativity. *Creativity Research Journal*, *24*, 92–96.

Saorín, J. L., Melian-Díaz, D., Bonnet, A., Carrera, C. C., Meier, C., and De La Torre-Cantero, J. (2017). Makerspace Teaching-Learning Environment to Enhance Creative Competence in Engineering Students. *Thinking Skills and Creativity*, *23*, 188–198.

Sawyer, R. K. (2004). Creative Teaching: Collaborative Discussion As Disciplined Improvisation. *Educational Researcher*, *33*, 12–20.

Schacter, J., Thum, Y. M., and Zifkin, D. (2006). How Much Does Creative Teaching Enhance Elementary School Students' Achievement? *The Journal of Creative Behavior*, *40*, 47–72.

Sefton-Green, J., Thomson, P., Jones, K., and Bresler, L. (Eds.). (2011). *The Routledge International Handbook of Creative Learning*. London: Routledge.

Simonton, D. K. (2012). Teaching Creativity: Current Findings, Trends, and Controversies in the Psychology of Creativity. *Teaching of Psychology*, *39*, 217–222.

Smaller, H. (2015). The Teacher Disempowerment Debate: Historical Reflections on "Slender Autonomy". *Paedagogica Historica*, *51*, 136–151.

Stein, M. I. (1953). Creativity and Culture. *The Journal of Psychology*, *36*, 311–322.

Sternberg, R. J. (2017). Teaching for Creativity. In R. A. Beghetto and J. C. Kaufman (Eds.), *Nurturing Creativity in the Classroom*, 2nd ed. (pp. 394–414). New York: Cambridge University Press.

Stokes, P. D. (2006). *Creativity from Constraints: The Psychology of Breakthrough*. New York: Springer Publishing Company.

    (2010). Using Constraints to Develop Creativity in the Classroom. In R. A. Beghetto and J. C. Kaufman (Eds.), *Nurturing Creativity in the Classroom* (pp. 88–112). Cambridge: Cambridge University Press.

13 Improving Creativity in Organizational Settings
Applying Research on Creativity to Organizations
RONI REITER-PALMON, RYAN P. ROYSTON, AND KEVIN S. MITCHELL

INTRODUCTION

Creativity and innovation have been shown to be an important force in organizational performance and survival (Ford and Gioia, 1995; Dess and Picken, 2000; Shalley, Zhou, and Oldham, 2004; Mumford and Hunter, 2005; George, 2007). Changes in technology, globalization, and increased competition have all created an environment in which creativity and innovation are needed to handle situational demands, economic pressures, and frequent changes (Woodman, Sawyer, and Griffin, 1993; Mumford et al., 2002; Shalley et al., 2004; West et al., 2004). A recent survey by IBM (2010) indicated that addressing rapid changes and uncertainty are viewed as commonplace for managers, and therefore one of the most important skills for managers is that of creative thinking. Consequently, it is not surprising that organizational researchers have shown increased interest in understanding what improves creativity in organizations.

Creativity has typically been defined by focusing on the creative product. Specifically, creativity has been defined as the production of a "novel product, idea, or problem solution that is of value to the individual and/or the larger social group" (Hennessey and Amabile, 2010, p. 572). This means that creativity is viewed as a unique and useful solution to a problem facing the organization. From an organizational perspective, this focus on the product or outcome is important, as creative ideas that are not implemented are not beneficial for the organization. As a result, research and practice in the area of creativity and innovation within a business setting focus not only on developing creative ideas but also on the implementation of such ideas. For example, if asked to find a solution to lack of parking and the suggested idea is to build a parking garage on the moon – that would be an idea that is original, but cannot be implemented, and therefore not creative.

One important distinction that exists in the management and Industrial/Organizational Psychology literature is between creativity and innovation. Innovation has generally been defined as the implementation of creative ideas and solutions in an organization (West, 2002; Anderson, Potocnik, and Zhou, 2014). Anderson et al. (2014) define the relationship between creativity and innovation at work as the following:

the processes, outcomes, and products of attempts to develop and introduce new and improved ways of doing things. The creativity stage of this process refers to idea generation, and innovation refers to the subsequent stage of implementing ideas toward better procedures, practices, and key products. Creativity and innovation can occur at the level of the individual, work team, organization, or at more than one of these levels combined, but invariably result in identifiable benefits at one or more of these levels of analysis. (p. 2)

The definition proposed by Anderson et al. (2014) highlights a few issues. First, as noted, they differentiate between creativity and innovation. However, creativity here is defined as idea generation, in which potential solutions to a problem are generated, while no (or limited) attention is given to processes that occur prior to that such as **problem identification and construction**, in which a problem is first recognized, identified, and structured (Reiter-Palmon, 2018). Second, the focus here is on the outcome and the benefits that will result to the organization. This provides the framework for organizations to use to evaluate various approaches to improving creativity and innovation.

In addition, this definition makes it clear that creativity and innovation are viewed as complex and multifaceted phenomena that need to be studied across multiple levels, such as the individual, team or department, and organizational level (Mumford and Hunter, 2005; Reiter-Palmon, Herman, and Yammarino, 2008; Anderson et al., 2014). One important issue that arises from this issue of multiple levels is that the factors that facilitate creativity in one level may damage creativity at another level (Mumford and Hunter, 2005; Reiter-Palmon, de Vreede, and de Vreede, 2013). For example, while creative individuals tend to prefer to work independently, many creative projects require teamwork. These two issues, the need to understand creativity and innovation from a multi-level perspective and the notion that factors that are beneficial at one level may not be at another, will be covered within the sections below.

There are a number of ways in which organizations can facilitate creativity. At the individual level, creativity and innovation can be enhanced in two ways. First, organizations can choose individuals who are already creative, in other words, those individuals who have shown to be creative in the past, or have the potential to be creative based on a number of individual difference variables such as personality and motivation (Hunter, Cushenbery, and Friedrich, 2012). The selection for creativity can be based at the individual or team level (Hunter, Neely, and Gutworth, in press). Second, training for creativity has been viewed as another way organizations can improve creativity (Scott, Leritz, and Mumford, 2004). At the team and organizational level, several important contextual environmental factors have been suggested as ways to enhance creativity. One is a focus on team or organizational culture that facilitates creativity (Hunter et al., 2007). **Organizational culture** refers to the underlying beliefs, assumptions, values, and methods of interaction that influence the social and psychological environment within an organization. In the case of organizational creativity, culture may refer to how the organization values and encourages creativity. Another important issue is that of the rewards provided to creative individuals. Understanding the resources required for creative performance is also an important organizational factor. Finally, team composition, or who the team members are, and especially team diversity, can be used as a way to enhance creativity. Leaders play an important role across all of these aspects, at the individual, team, and organizational levels (Mumford and Hunter, 2005; Reiter-Palmon, Wigert, and de Vreede, 2011). It is not surprising that there is a significant amount of research focusing on ways in which leaders can enhance creativity, either directly or indirectly, through their effect on selection, training, culture, team diversity, rewards, and resources.

Selecting for Creativity

The Society for Industrial Organizational Psychologists (SIOP, 2003) defines **personnel selection** as any procedure or measure that is used to make employment-related decisions. These decisions can range from who to hire, who to promote, or who is included in specific training programs. At its core, the selection process should be able to differentiate applicants who will successfully perform the desired task versus those who may be unsuccessful (Polyhart, Schneider, and Schmitt, 2006). To this end, increasing creativity and innovation within an organization could be influenced by selecting for individuals that display creative skills and abilities. Selecting individuals, team members, and leaders for creative activities requires organizations to understand the predictors of creative performance, including how contextual factors influence these relationships.

Selecting Individuals and Teams

The effectiveness of creative teams is influenced by the characteristics of individual members. Some important characteristics relevant to individual-level creativity include cognitive ability, such as intelligence or creativity-specific processes such as **divergent thinking** or generating as many solutions or ideas as possible in response to a verbal or graphic prompt (Sternberg, 1997; Silvia, 2008). A common measure of divergent thinking is to provide as many uses as possible for a brick. To be effective at these creative processes, the individual must also possess knowledge and expertise in the field of interest (Vincent, Decker, and Mumford, 2002). In addition, personality factors such as openness (George and Zhou, 2001; Batey and Furnham, 2006), and intrinsic motivation (Amabile, 1996; Zhang, Zhang, and Song, 2015) have shown positive relationships with creative outcomes. **Openness to experience**, the Big-Five personality trait associated with being willing to try new things, imagination, curiosity, and being open-minded, has shown particular strength at predicting individual creativity (Feist, 1998; Furnham and Bachtiar, 2008; Hornberg and Reiter-Palmon, 2017; Patterson and Zibbarras, 2017). Other important individual differences for predicting creative performance include creative self-efficacy (Tierney and Farmer, 2002), mindsets of creativity (e.g., Karwowski, 2014; Hass, Katz-Buonincontro, and Reiter-Palmon, 2016), and creative personal identity (Karwowski, 2011). **Creative self-efficacy** is defined as one's confidence and views of their own capacity to be creative in their work and handling tasks that require creativity (Tierney and Farmer, 2002). **Creative mindsets** refer to how people view their own creativity as a characteristic as malleable, or something they can develop over time and with effort, or fixed, in which one's creativity is innate and cannot really be changed (Karwowski, 2014). Interestingly, it appears people may hold both views depending on what domain and level of creativity is being considered, as well as their creative experience (Karwowski, 2014; Karwowski, Royston, and Reiter-Palmon, 2019). **Creative personal identity** is defined as the importance that one places on creativity as an important aspect of themselves (Karwowski, 2016). Past research has shown the strength of each of these variables as predictors of creativity and has shown that each can be measured in a reliable and valid way. However, predicting individual creativity is complex and requires multiple assessments and components (e.g., Runco, 2004; Batey and Furnham, 2006; Furnham and Bachtiar, 2008; Hunter et al., 2012); therefore, a combination of well-established measures may provide better results than a single measure for creativity. In addition to using well-established measures of psychological constructs, **biographical inventory measures** allow organizations to identify individuals who are open to experience, willing to take risks, and proactively engage in creative efforts as demonstrated by past experience producing creative products (Malakate, Andriopoulos, and Gotsi, 2007). Beyond formal and well-established measures of creativity, organizations such as Amazon and Google have tried to identify creative individuals through other approaches such as nontraditional interview items that require flexible thinking and adaptive problem solving (Jaussi and Benson, 2012). However, there is little research on the validity of some of these nontraditional methods of identifying creativity.

Although selecting creative individuals into specific jobs and positions can have benefits to the organizations, it is also important to consider how this selection influences the team. Much of the work conducted in organizations, including creative work, is done in teams (Reiter-Palmon et al., 2011). When considering how creative individuals effectively work in a team environment, many other characteristics related to social interactions in addition to creativity should be considered during selection. Teams of creative individuals often benefit during creative problem solving due to obtaining multiple perspectives, increased knowledge, and more varied expertise. However, creative individuals also tend to be independent, competitive, critical, and introverted, which may increase the frequency of conflict with other team members (Feist 1998; Silvia et al., 2011). Placing too much emphasis on individual predictors of creativity during selection may not allow creative teams to fully benefit from each member's ability because of the danger of conflict in working relationships (Hunter and Cushenbery, 2015). Therefore, when focusing on selecting for team creativity, it is useful to also consider individual differences that promote teamwork, such as ability to appropriately handle conflict and communicate effectively (Salas, Sims, and Burke, 2005). Specifically, communication, information sharing, trust, psychological safety, and collaboration have been identified as important aspects of social interactions that increase creative work in teams (Reiter-Palmon et al., 2011). Individual difference characteristics can also have an effect on these social processes. For example, willingness to participate and collaborate with others are important individual characteristics that influence team creativity (Janssens and Brett, 2006). Participation refers to the level of effort that each team member will put forth in accomplishing team goals or tasks (Kahai, Sosik, and Avolio, 2003). Willingness to collaborate in creative teams is crucial because creative tasks are frequently unclear, complex, and require team members to rely on each other to complete work (Burke et al., 2006). When teams are composed of individuals who collaborate and participate, they tend to be better able to transform complex ideas into outcomes and products (De Dreu, Carsten, and West, 2001). When everyone on a team collaborates and cooperates, it increases creative performance because each person is able to elaborate and evaluate the ideas of others (Mathieuet et al., 2008).

In addition to the ability to work well in a team environment, another consideration is creating **interdisciplinary teams** composed of individuals with diverse knowledge, experience, and expertise, who work together toward a common goal. The use of interdisciplinary teams is a result of the rapid change and adaptation required to ensure organizational success and survival, as well as the complex problems that organizations face (Kozlowski and Bell, 2008; Rosen et al., 2011). Therefore, organizations must also consider the range and combination of knowledge and expertise of the team members. As a result, it is not enough to simply consider individual creativity during the selection process but to consider the context in which that individual will work and how the context will allow that individual to effectively demonstrate their creativity. As creative individuals must often work in groups, it is necessary to consider how well individuals work with others in social contexts.

An example in an organizational context that shows the importance of ensuring team members possess not only creative ability but also important team and social skills is that of Pixar's "Braintrust." This team was made up of individuals working within the organization and served as outside critics of movie projects and provided feedback that was unbiased by not being involved in a movie's production. They also provided help with creative problem solving. Ed Catmull, one of the co-founders of Pixar, was skilled at ensuring teams were made up of individuals who were not only highly creative but also worked together well. Catmull (2014) describes the environment of the Braintrust as one of psychological safety and shared trust. **Psychological safety** is a shared sense among all team members that the team environment is safe for sharing ideas, taking interpersonal risks, and a belief that the team will not reject or punish a team member for sharing ideas (Edmondson, 1999). Catmull recognized the importance of selecting creative individuals who would work well together in a team setting. For this reason, Steve Jobs, though another co-founder of Pixar, was not allowed to participate in the Braintrust because Catmull recognized that other group members would neither share ideas in his presence nor criticize his ideas even when they disagreed with him. Consequently, creative individuals working in team environments should not only be highly creative but be willing to collaborate and work interdependently with others to accomplish creative tasks.

As discussed, many predictors can be used when selecting creative individuals. Selecting individuals who are high in openness to experience, creative abilities, confidence in their creative abilities, and have experience in creative production allows organizations to ensure they are hiring individuals who can enhance the problem-solving effort. However, it is important to consider the context in which these individuals work. When working in team settings, it is important that individuals effectively collaborate, communicate, and cooperate with one another, as well as engage in appropriate task conflict to facilitate the creative effort.

Leadership and Selecting for Creative Leaders

Not only have we seen an increased focus on identifying individual- and team-level creativity, but companies are increasingly searching for leaders that can lead creative individuals and teams. Executives have pointed to the need for leaders to be creative, often crediting creativity and innovation as a key competitive edge in the marketplace (IBM, 2010). Many of the individual- and team-level predictors discussed above also apply when selecting leaders of creative teams, however, additional characteristics must be considered. Besides examining certain individual traits that are known to predict creativity (e.g., openness to new experiences), there are certain leadership skills and behaviors that have been shown to positively influence subordinates' creativity. These include manager support for creativity, creative expectations, and evaluation and implementation of creative ideas (Reiter-Palmon and Royston, 2017).

Managerial support and expectations are important factors that can positively influence employee creativity. When leaders support new ideas and promote a safe psychological space for employees to discuss original ideas, leaders may help increase those employees' creative performance (Carmeli, Reiter-Palmon, and Ziv, 2010). Borrowing from goal setting theory and expectation setting, we also know that when leaders expect their employees to perform more creatively, those employees generate more creative outcomes (Tierney and Farmer, 2004; Carmeli and Schaubroeck, 2007). This matching of expectation to outcome could be viewed as some form of a creative **Pygmalion effect**, in which higher expectations of creativity tend to lead to higher levels of creative performance. As we know that creativity can be positively impacted by leader behaviors of support and expectation of creative outcomes, we can gain valuable insight on how an organization selects creative leaders. A leader who creates a psychologically safe environment, is genuinely supportive of creative efforts, and sets expectations for employees to be creative is the leader an organization should consider for a creative role.

Moving from broad support and expectations, effective leaders of creative individuals and teams should assist the creative processes associated with creativity (Reiter-Palmon and Royston, 2017). Although much of the research on creative processes rests at the individual level, there has been work examining how leaders influence these processes to increase their employees' creativity. Leaders who support specific creative problem-solving processes (e.g., problem construction), tend to positively influence employee creative production (Redmond et al., 1993; Mumford et al, 2002). The logic here is that if a leader can better support and guide employees on the front end of structuring the problem, then those employees will more likely produce a novel solution. Moving toward the back end of the creative problem-solving process, leaders need to be proficient at evaluating the ideas generated by the team for quality and originality. Creative leaders supplement their employees' skills by weighing consequences and outcomes to assist in the best course of action that would ultimately lead to a creative outcome (Mumford, 1986; Mumford et al., 2007). Considering these findings from a selection perspective, organizations should strive to find those individuals who not only are generally supportive of creative endeavors but also display skills and abilities in assisting in specific creative problem-solving processes.

Personality and motivational factors also play a key role in selecting the best leaders for creativity. Openness to experience has been consistently shown to predict creative outcomes (Fiest, 1998; Hornberg and Reiter-Palmon, 2017). In regard to the other four factors of the Big Five, the relationships are not as clear; however, we propose that for leadership purposes, extraversion and conscientiousness most likely play a role in leader creativity and leading creative individuals and teams. Extraversion has been shown to be positively related to creative performance involving others (Hornberg and Reiter-Palmon, 2017). In terms of conscientiousness, when certain rules and procedures need to be followed, as in scientific domains, we see increased creativity (Feist, 1998). Leaders who are higher in openness, conscientiousness, and extraversion may show a relationship with increased creativity in their teams (Mitchell and Reiter-Palmon, in press).

One method by which organizations select and develop leaders is the use of **high-potential** programs for individuals who tend to show higher performance and more capacity to grow and succeed than their peers. These programs aim to identify and develop high-potential individuals for future roles within an organization (Silzer and Church, 2009; Church et al., 2015). These programs fill a dual role of selection and training and development. Whereas most high-potential programs do not focus on creative leaders as the target, the same principles apply. In a high-potential program, organizations could place potential creative leaders in situations where they are observed and evaluated for how that individual would build a workspace for their employees as well as how they respond to employees who produce creative products. These growth activities may also include observing how the leader supports specific creative problem-solving processes within the employees as well as the leader's ability to properly evaluate original ideas.

The selection of creative leaders, similar to creative individuals, can also include the use of assessments and measures of individual difference variables related to creativity. The challenge facing organizations is what makes the most sense for selecting creative leaders. From a predictor side, organizations need to consider the complexity of the selection system. **Assessment centers** are one traditional and effective technique for selecting leaders and involve using multiple job-related assessments and exercises to observe how job candidates perform in tasks that are part of the job. Using assessment centers allows organizations to evaluate the potential for both creative thinking as well as managing creative individuals and teams. Organizations should decide whether using a high-potential program makes sense (e.g., Silzer and Church, 2009), or whether they should emphasize what makes the most efficient selection process. Further, as is the case in selecting individuals for creative teams, simply selecting individuals based on leadership characteristics does not necessarily mean these leaders will be effective at facilitating creativity. Organizations may need to evaluate which characteristics are more important to select for, and possibly use training to help individuals develop the other important characteristics for their job.

In short, there are a variety of methods and measures that organizations can use in the selection process. However, it is important for any organization implementing processes to select for creativity to consider how contextual and individual differences interact. Personnel selection is only one way that creativity can be influenced in the organization. Training and development is a second major way that creativity can be influenced in organizational settings. While selection focuses on getting the creative people in the door or in the right positions, training and development focuses on building skills and abilities within the individuals, team members, and leaders already in the organization.

Can Creativity Be Developed?

As organizational leaders continue to recognize the importance and competitive advantage that employee creativity has in developing innovative products, they have sought ways to increase both individual and team creativity and innovation (Sternberg and Lubart, 1999). In addition to selecting the right people into jobs, training and development are another way for organizations to enhance the creative potential of its workforce (Montouri, 1992; Scott et al., 2004; Marlow et al., in press).

In a meta-analysis of the effectiveness of creativity training, Scott et al. (2004) found that training was linked to notable changes in divergent thinking, problem solving, creative-task performance, attitudes, and behaviors. Each of these aspects of creativity has been shown to be important to an organization's productivity, creativity climate, use of resources, and employee psychological well-being (e.g., Mumford and Gustafson, 1988; Amabile, 1996; Reiter-Palmon and Illies, 2004; Runco, 2004; Rasulzada and Dackert, 2009; Shalley, Gilson, and Blum, 2009).

Training that emphasizes the cognitive-processing activities that underlie creativity, such as problem identification, information gathering, conceptual combination, idea generation, idea evaluation, and implementation appear to be most effective at increasing creativity (Scott et al., 2004; Mumford, Hunter, and Byrne, 2009). Most effective creativity training programs also share a focus on **divergent thinking**, or generating as many solutions or ideas as possible in response to a verbal or graphic prompt, as a basis for instruction (Baer, 1996; Scott et al., 2004). These training programs can help individuals and teams to generate a greater number of ideas, which then increases the number of ideas that can be implemented by the team or organization (Birdi, 2007; Baruah and Paulus, 2008). Both idea generation and idea evaluation are typically desired outcomes for creativity training programs. However, Birdi (2007) found that while creativity training was indeed positively related to both idea generation and idea implementation, creativity training appeared to have a greater impact on idea generation. Further, Birdi (2007) found that environmental factors such as managerial support and **organizational climate** had a greater effect on idea implementation than creativity training. Therefore, despite the benefits of creativity training, organizations should ensure that environmental conditions encourage and allow employees to implement creative ideas in their jobs.

Teams can be trained in effective idea generation by following rules for effective brainstorming and learning effective ways to share information while avoiding **process loss** (Paulus and Brown, 2003). Process loss involves any actions, communication, or interactions that lead to less efficient problem solving in a group. Rules for brainstorming include generating as many ideas as possible, expressing any ideas that come to mind, sharing ideas without criticism or evaluation, and combining and building upon ideas to develop new ideas (Paulus and Brown, 2003; Baruah and Paulus, 2008). Teams can be trained in brainstorming rules, thus increasing the quality and quantity of ideas (Goldenberg, Larson, and Wiley, 2013; Litchfield, Fan, and Brown, 2013). Similarly, teams can be taught efficient ways to share information and make connections between the pieces of information shared (Baruah and Paulus, 2008). It has been suggested that effective idea generation may be hampered due to process loss, in which information is lost or restricted due to limits to the amount of time that each individual may share information (DeRosa, Smith, and Hantula, 2007). Process loss often occurs because individuals are not able to present their ideas while also listening to others, which results in a decreased amount of time for individuals to share ideas (Paulus et al., 2006). Training may focus on helping teams effectively share ideas without unnecessary discussion that prevents others from contributing, paying particular attention to shared ideas, encouraging each individual to share ideas to gain different perspectives, and making new connections with shared information (Dugosh et al., 2000; Paulus et al., 2006; Goldenberg et al., 2013).

Additionally, it is useful to train individuals to properly define problems and identify relevant information related to the problem. Basadur (2004) pointed out that people often are quick to move onto evaluating different solutions rather than gaining a complete understanding of the problem. Hasty evaluation and poor problem definition is problematic because individuals often narrow the problem too soon and may miss the overall goal or objective (Basadur, 2004). This problem can be increased in group settings when influential individuals such as the leader or a dominant personality steers the problem-solving process and other group members do not feel comfortable speaking up (Cronin and Weingart, 2007; Reiter-Palmon et al., 2011). Creativity training may focus on helping teams to pay attention to ideas presented by all group members, to encourage quiet group members to speak up, to question their own assumptions about how they approach the problem, and to actively engage in combining their own ideas with those of their teammates (Mobley, Doares, and Mumford, 1992; Mumford et al., 1997; Harvey, 2014).

Successful problem solving also requires teams and individuals to effectively evaluate and implement ideas. Idea evaluation includes assessing ideas against standards and determining whether any ideas from the generation phase should be implemented, revised, or rejected (Mumford, Lonergan, and Scott, 2002). Teams and individuals should be taught to integrate and combine information to develop a complete solution. Training in idea evaluation may include strategies for questioning assumptions, combining information and ideas together in new ways, and ensuring that each member has provided information on the problem (Harvey, 2014).

Creativity training may also take the form of teaching employees to work and produce within constraints or limitations. Organizational settings often present a series of challenges to effective creative problem solving, thus employees may benefit from training that teaches them strategies for identifying and working within constraints imposed by the workplace (Miron, Erez, and Naveh, 2004; Peterson et al., 2013). Constraints common to the workplace may include time pressures, availability of resources, individual skills or capacities, or the level of supervisory or team support for creativity (Li, 1997; Mandal, Thomas, and Antunes, 2009; Mueller and Kamdar, 2011). Peterson et al. (2013) suggested that providing training on working within constraints may also increase individual creative self-efficacy and motivation, which then increases creative problem solving-performance.

In addition to creativity training that emphasizes cognitive processes and working within the organizational environment, creativity training can focus on the individual by increasing positive attitudes toward creativity or increasing individual characteristics related to creativity, such as openness to experience, creative mindsets, or creative self-efficacy, which in turn increases their creative performance (Tierney and Farmer, 2002; Karwowski, 2014). Creative self-efficacy has received a great deal of attention as an individual characteristic that is associated with creative performance and can be increased through training (e.g., Tierney and Farmer, 2002, 2011; Karwowski, 2014, 2016). One way that organizations can increase individual confidence in their creative ability is training them to be confident in taking initiative to seek out or anticipate potential problems, changes, or opportunities (Basadur, 2004; Miron et al., 2004). Often, individuals wait for others, such as their leader, to identify problems (Basadur, 2004). However, when individuals are comfortable taking initiative and taking interpersonal risks, teams can benefit from gaining multiple perspectives and approaches to the problem (Jehn, 1995; Bradley et al., 2012).

In regard to increasing positive individual attitudes toward creativity and encouraging them to engage in training, one issue is determining how individual differences influence the effectiveness of the training. Individual differences such as motivation and creative self-efficacy may present challenges in employee engagement in the training (Kabanoff and Bottger, 1991; Jaussi and Benson, 2012). When training is offered as an optional opportunity, individuals who are already highly creative or intrinsically motivated often choose to engage in the program and therefore may not see significant changes in their own creativity because they already show high levels of creativity (Kabanoff and Bottger, 1991). Similarly, organizations may have difficulty making creativity training appealing to individuals who do not identify as creative individuals or those who not see creativity as being important to their everyday tasks (Jaussi, Randel, and Dionne, 2007). Therefore, organizations should carefully consider how to enhance the creative self-identity and motivation of individuals who do not strongly identify as a creative individual, while simultaneously providing opportunities for creative individuals to further enhance their creative abilities. Finally, creative mindsets, or viewing creativity as malleable and changeable and therefore trainable, or as fixed, and therefore not trainable, may also influence how much individuals benefit from training (Makel, 2009; Royston and Reiter-Palmon, 2016). Specifically, it is expected that those that view creativity as malleable, will be more likely to elect to participate in creativity training and also gain the most benefit from training (Royston and Reiter-Palmon, 2016).

Developing Creative Leaders

Similar to personnel selection, developing creative leaders builds from many of the individual- and team-level constructs discussed above. In a leadership sense, many of the training interventions involve instructing leaders on how they can best foster creativity within their workers and workspace.

Returning to our discussion on managerial support, it is important for leaders to support their employees' creative endeavors. When leaders are more supportive of employees engaging in creativity, those employees perform more creatively (e.g., Barnowe, 1975; Amabile et al., 2004). Soft-skills training could help a leader better understand how to foster more creative production by engaging in specific leadership behaviors. For example, leaders can be taught how to provide feedback in a way that is constructive and facilitates creativity, how to create an environment in which team members feel comfortable sharing ideas, and how to show support for creativity (Carmeli et al., 2010; Carmeli, Gelbard, and Reiter-Palmon, 2013).

In addition to supporting creativity, creative leaders must be able to recognize creative ideas and the products that come from them. As discussed above, trainings that focus on the cognitive processes underlying creativity appear to influence creative outcomes (Scott et al., 2004; Mumford et al., 2009). Training that helps leaders better understand the cognitive processes underlying team creativity should yield positive results that mimic the individual-level results. In addition, leaders have particular need for training geared toward ensuring that the team effectively identifies and elaborates on solutions (Gebert, Boerner, and Kearney, 2010). For this purpose, organizations should ensure that leaders are trained in standards used to judge the effectiveness of solutions and are adept at leading team problem-solving efforts (Reiter-Palmon et al., 2008; Hemlin and Olson, 2011).

Resource allocation may be another fruitful area for training leaders to be more innovative and refers to the assignment and distribution of available organizational resources to accomplish organizational goals. Leaders are perceived as the ones responsible for obtaining and distributing resources. Research has shown that both too few resources can lead to innovation (Kanter, 1985; Scott and Bruce, 1994; Ohly and Fritz, 2010) and that adequate resources can lead to innovation (Amabile et al., 1996; Sonenshein, 2014). In fact, resource availability may have a **curvilinear relationship** with innovation (Mumford and Hunter, 2005). A curvilinear relationship refers to a relationship between two variables in which as one variable increases, the other does as well to a certain point, after which as one increases, the other decreases. Therefore, having leaders trained in managing and allocating resources may lead to increased creativity in their employees. This notion of training leaders in **resource allocation** does have some traction. In an article by Henry Doss (2013), he argues that innovation leadership training fails because the company focuses on training to lead others rather than building and leading systems. Consequently, organizations should not only focus on training leaders how to lead a team of individuals but help them recognize and consider how the team interacts with the greater organization.

To this point we have discussed selecting and training individuals for creativity. Further, we have highlighted important considerations when an organization is selecting into a team or selecting a leader for a creative role, as well as training teams and leaders in creativity and innovation. We shift to a broader context now with a review of how organizational factors influence creativity and innovation.

Broader Organizational Interventions

As a result of the numerous benefits of creativity and innovation in the workplace, researchers and organizations alike have explored ways to enhance organizational creativity, including encouraging creativity through incentives, team diversity, shaping organizational climate, and resource allocation (Scott et al., 2004).

Team Diversity

Teams have been studied as a context in which individuals can thrive and be creative (Reiter-Palmon et al., 2013). Team composition, specifically the diversity of the team, has long been considered an important factor that should facilitate creativity (Woodman et al., 1993; Hulsheger, Anderson, and Salgado, 2009). As team composition may have far-reaching effects on organizational outcomes, organizations should pay special attention to the formation of teams. Early work in the area of team composition and creativity assumed that diversity in team composition would result in increased creative output of teams due to the diverse knowledge and experiences of the team members (Guzzo and Dickson, 1996; McLeod, Lobel, and Cox, 1996). However, more recent research now suggests that the impact of team diversity is much more complex (Hulshger et al., 2009; Reiter-Palmon et al., 2011). Research focusing on **demographic diversity**, that is, diversity based on age, gender, race, and the like has found mixed results in relation to creativity. For example, O'Reilly, Williams, and Barsade (1997) found that racial diversity had a moderate, positive influence on creativity and innovation; however, gender and tenure diversity had no effect, while Curseu (2010) found that team diversity (defined as gender, age, and national diversity combined) was moderately and positively related to the creativity of team output. On the other hand, Paletz et al. (2004) reported no differences in creativity between ethnically diverse and ethnically similar teams, and McLeod et al. (1996) found ethnic diversity to hinder team creativity. Choi (2007) found that groups diverse in terms of gender were less creative, whereas groups with age diversity were more creative. Finally, a meta-analysis indicated non-significant effects for the relationship between demographic diversity and team creativity and innovation (Hulsheger et al., 2009).

In an attempt to explain how diversity can sometimes be positively related to creativity and other times be negatively related to creativity, Li et al. (2017) evaluated the role of valuing diversity. Li et al. found that when teams were from different cultures, this was related to increased creativity, and even more so when teams viewed diversity as important.

Similarly, Homan et al. (2015) found that diversity training for teams increased creativity in teams composed of individuals from a variety of different nations, especially for teams that did not value diversity before the training. That is, training that was designed to facilitate understanding and acceptance of diversity improved creativity for diverse teams that did not hold these views prior to training. The results of these studies suggest that the relationship between creativity and demographic diversity may be more complex than initially thought. It is also possible that different variables (age vs. gender vs. ethnic diversity) will have different effects on creativity and innovation. In addition, perceptions about the role and importance of diversity for creativity may also shape the effect that team diversity has on creativity.

In contrast to demographic diversity, **functional diversity** or differences between people based on attributes that are relevant to job performance, such as diversity in education, function in the organization, and job relevant knowledge, skills, and abilities, appears to influence team creativity (Woodman et al., 1993; Milliken, Bartel, and Kurtzberg, 2003). Most research on functional diversity has found that teams comprising members from different and diverse functional backgrounds may outperform teams of individuals who all have similar backgrounds and experience in terms of creativity and innovation (Keller, 2001; Fay et al., 2006; Choi, 2007; Hulsheger et al., 2009). Richter et al. (2012) also suggested that functional diversity can serve as a way of gaining more extensive information for teams if teams are able to utilize this combined information. In their study utilizing 176 employees in 34 organizational research and development teams, they also found that functional diversity was related to creativity for employees with higher creative self-efficacy.

The results presented here suggest that demographic diversity may not be the most effective in facilitating creativity in teams, while functional diversity may be more beneficial. However, the relationships are complex and therefore just creating diverse teams may not be the solution for improving creativity. The first issue that organizations must address is how to create diverse teams and determine what it means when a team is diverse. Here we discussed two specific aspects, demographic diversity and functional diversity, but even within these, there are multiple dimensions. For example, a team can be diverse in terms of gender but not in terms of age, race, or culture. A team can be diverse in terms of educational background but not in terms of other specific abilities. In many cases, the call for diversity in teams results in a focus on demographic diversity without attention to functional diversity when organizations create teams. Given that demographic diversity may have minimal effects on creativity (Hulsheger et al., 2009), it may be more beneficial for organizations to focus on creating cross-functional or interdisciplinary teams. For example, organizations can create teams in which different departments in the organization are represented. Similarly, when selecting individuals to work in these teams, it is important to consider multiple ways in which the team can be diverse, including demographics, but also in terms of educational background and specific knowledge and skill.

The review of the literature also suggests that team diversity may not have a direct and linear relationship with creativity. Some of the research suggests that in order to benefit from the diversity that is present, individuals must value diversity and view it positively (Homan et al., 2015; Li et al., 2017). Others suggest that only when teams are able to overcome some of the difficulties inherent in diverse teams and capitalize on the diversity of information available, will creativity result (De Dreu et al., 2011; Reiter-Palmon et al., 2013). As noted by Homan et al. (2015), training may be one way in which teams and individuals within teams can learn to recognize the importance of diversity and accept diversity. All of these social processes can be trained and allow for improvement in team performance (Marlow et al., in press). Once teams overcome the social barriers that inhibit communication and information sharing and develop trust, teams and individuals can capitalize on the diversity of information offered by diverse teams.

Finally, leaders can have a profound effect on how teams react to diversity and whether teams can overcome the social process barriers inherent in diverse teams. There are a number of ways in which leaders can facilitate the development of effective social processes and acceptance and appreciation for diversity. Leaders can model appropriate social processes such as effective communication and information sharing, as well as acceptance and appreciation of diversity. In addition, leaders may provide opportunities for training to ease some of the difficulties that diverse teams may encounter, such as difficulties in communication, developing trust, and sharing information, as well as the potential for increased conflict. In addition, leaders can facilitate the creation of a culture of acceptance of diversity and open communication, which will be discussed next.

Organizational Climate

Organizational climate refers to how members of an organization experience the culture of an organization and is one of the most researched areas in the study of creativity and innovation in the workplace (Hunter et al., 2007). A number of theoretical frameworks have been suggested to understand the factors that contribute to a climate that facilitates creativity (Ekval, 1986; Anderson and West, 1988; Amabile and Conti, 1999). In a qualitative review of the climate for creativity literature, Hunter, Bedell, and Mumford (2005) found that most frameworks included common dimensions such as positive relationships with peers, support from top management, challenge, **autonomy** (the ability to choose and be in control over tasks and work behaviors), intellectual stimulation, and support for risk taking. Similarly, a meta-analysis conducted by Hunter et al. (2007) found overall that these climate dimensions were related to creative performance of individuals and teams in the organization. Further, the strongest climate dimensions were those related to having positive relationships, intellectual stimulation, and challenge. The importance of positive relationships is not surprising given the importance of social processes such as information sharing, communication, and trust for creativity and innovation. Intellectual stimulation and challenge speak to the importance of the cognitive factors. Together, these findings suggest that a work environment in which people are presented with meaningful and challenging work and that allows for the exchange of thoughts and ideas is critical for creativity.

In addition to effects on the individual, research suggests that having a supportive team is related to team creativity. Wang and Hong (2010) found that group support for creativity led to increased psychological safety, which in turn led to higher team creativity. Pirola-Merlo and Mann (2004) found that team climate affected team creativity indirectly through individuals' creativity. Similarly, Kessel, Kratzer, and Schultz (2012) found that high levels of psychological safety increased group knowledge sharing, which then led to higher team creativity and performance. Finally, Gilson and Shalley (2004) examined teams' engagement in creative processes and found that teams that were higher on engaging in creative processes also were more likely to have shared goals, valued participative problem solving, and had an overall team climate that was supportive of creativity. Although not exclusively evaluating team climate, in their meta-analysis, Hulsheger et al. (2009) found moderate to strong relationships between team creativity and team psychological safety, team support for innovation, and focus on creative tasks. Finally, top management support for innovation, another climate dimension, has also been linked to creativity and innovation (Damanpour and Schneider, 2006).

Leaders have long been viewed as important creators and transmitters of organizational climate (Schneider, Brief, and Guzzo, 1996; Amabile et al., 2004; Schein, 2010). Leaders can help in facilitating more effective discussions, creating positive team interactions that lead to increased trust and psychological safety, which in turn will lead to improved communication and information exchange within the team (Carmeli et al., 2013). Leaders to some extent control workflow, work assignment, and the degree of autonomy individual workers and the team have over the work, and as such can contribute the development of a climate of creativity as it relates to intellectual stimulation, challenge and autonomy. In addition, leaders can help employees find meaning in their work by ensuring that workers understand the importance of their contributions and how their work fits into the organizational vision and mission. In addition, the leaders at the top of the organization – the top management teams – can develop and shape a climate for creativity and innovation through the creation of a mission and vision as well as a strategy that focuses on creativity (Isaksen, 2007).

Rewards and Incentives

The effect of rewards on creativity has been debated for a number of years. Early work and theorizing by Amabile (1982, 1996) suggested that intrinsic motivation was important for creativity and innovation and that external motivation, including rewards, was harmful to creativity. However, in the last two decades, the negative relationship between creativity and external rewards has been questioned (Eisenberger and Rhoades, 2001). For example, Eisenberger and Cameron (1998) suggested that rewards offer individuals information about what the organization values and what is important and therefore should facilitate creativity. Malik, Butt, and Choi (2015) found that extrinsic rewards can influence intrinsic motivation and therefore will not always negatively impact creativity by introducing extrinsic motivation. Eisenberger and Armeli (1997) found that when rewards were large, they had a negative impact on creativity. A meta-analysis by Byron and Khazanchi (2012) found that rewards improved creativity when rewards depended on creative performance, when feedback regarding creative performance was provided, and when individuals are offered more control. This meta-analysis suggests that the relationship between rewards and creative performance can be positive, given certain circumstances. Adding to the complex nature of the relationship, a study by Caniels, De Stobbeleir, and De Clippeleer (2014) summarized twenty-two case studies of creative individuals in organizations and suggested that rewards may reduce **idea generation**, as external rewards are viewed as a form of pressure. However, extrinsic rewards were seen as encouraging the implementation of creative ideas. This study indicates that the stage of the process in which rewards are offered is also important.

In recent years, researchers and theorists have been moving away from an all-or-nothing approach to understanding the relationship between creativity and rewards. Rather, a more complex view has emerged, in which studies have focused on understanding the conditions that make external rewards effective in facilitating creativity (Malik and Butt, 2017). The results of these studies suggest that rewards can have a positive rather than negative influence on creativity but need to be managed carefully. Organizations hoping to use rewards to motivate employees to be creative must do so carefully so that intrinsic motivation is not hurt. Rewards should not be overly large, rewards should be provided for creative performance so that employees are clear on what is expected, and feedback about creative performance should be provided.

Resources

Another important organizational factor that can influence creativity is that of resources. Resources here refer not only to materials and funds but also to infrastructure and facilities, personnel (including having the right personnel), and time (Amabile and Griskiewicz, 1989). The development and implementation of new ideas is time-consuming and can be expensive in terms of personnel, material, and time. Therefore, the availability of resources is likely to influence creativity and innovation. Klein, Conn, and Sorra (2001) found that innovation was related to the availability of financial resources. Dougherty and Hardy (1996) studied product development teams and found that resource availability over the course of the product development effort was related to project success. It has been suggested that resource availability may facilitate creativity by allowing for experimentation, risk taking, and working on multiple promising projects simultaneously (Noriah and Gulati, 1996). Abundant resources also allow organizations to be better prepared for changes in the environment and respond to those more successfully (Pfeffer and Salancik, 2003). For example, a large coffee chain is more likely to try multiple new ideas for coffee flavors compared to the local coffee shop.

On the other hand, others have suggested that resource constraints or limitations may facilitate creativity as organizations needed to find creative ways to address problems while lacking resources (Hoegl, Gibbert, and Mazursky, 2008; Choi and Chang, 2009; Weiss, Hoegl, and Gibbert, 2011). Specifically because they lack the resources, these companies must respond creatively to market and external forces and do this quickly, or the organization will not survive (Hoegl et al., 2008). In addition, it has been suggested that while organizations that have resources available may be able to experiment and take risks, these organizations are reluctant to do so (George, 2005). In a series of four experimental studies, Scopelliti, Busacca, and Mazursky (2014) found that financial constraints led to the development of more creative products with fewer inputs and lower budget. Mehta and Zhu (2016) also found that resource scarcity resulted in less **functional fixedness**, or, in other words, when a person uses something beyond the way it has been traditionally used, which in turn resulted in greater creativity. For example, using a paper clip as a bookmark.

These contrasting findings have led to the suggestion that there is possibly a curvilinear, or "inverted U," relationship between constraints and creativity. The Goldilocks proposition, or the idea of having the "just right" level of constraints, suggests that too few constraints will result in the organization being not willing to develop and implement creative ideas or having too many ideas being developed, while too many constraints will result in the organization not being able to develop and implement creative ideas (Mumford and Hunter, 2005). For example, Graves and Lanowitz (1993) found that after a certain level, increased spending on R&D did lead to more new products. Noriah and Gulati (1996) also found this curvilinear relationship between resources and creativity. Medeiros, Partlow, and Mumford (2014), in an experimental study that manipulated the number of constraints participants encountered, found that too many constraints were not beneficial for creativity and that a moderate number of task constraints were particularly beneficial. It is therefore important for organizations to evaluate what resources are available to employees. On the one hand, too few resources may lead to difficulty in developing creative ideas, while, on the other hand, too many resources may result in the development of many ideas but ones of limited creativity. It is not clear at this point what the specific optimal level of appropriate resources and of what kind (money, equipment, personnel, and information) is needed.

CONCLUSION

In this chapter, we have provided an overview of the various ways in which organizations can improve creativity. Table 13.1 provides an overview and summary of the issues and recommendations for organizations. Following the theoretical and empirical work on creativity, these recommendations can be clustered around individual and contextual factors. Further, as creativity and innovation are complex issues, and reside at multiple levels, we recommend evaluating factors related to the individual, team, organization, and leadership. At the individual level, selection of people into the jobs and focusing on the appropriate attributes that would facilitate creativity and innovation has been discussed. The focus with selection is the identification of individual difference variables, such as openness to experience and creative ability, that would facilitate creativity for individual and teams. In addition, creativity can be facilitated through training. Aspects of individual difference and team functioning that are amenable to training should be trained and developed. While other aspects of individual differences that are more difficult to change and train, are best used for selection.

Table 13.1 Summary of recommendations for improving organizational creativity

Topic	Recommendation
Selecting for creative individuals	Use multiple types of measures as well as multiple constructs to select creative individuals
	Use well-established measures of constructs that have been shown to be related to creativity (e.g., openness to experience, creative self-efficacy) as predictors in the selection battery
	Use individual-level predictors of creativity along with consideration of other social and contextual factors, such as whether the individual will work as part of a team
Selecting for creative teams	Include measures of how well an individual works in team environments (e.g., willingness to collaborate and cooperate with others, ability to handle conflict well). Balance the use of predictors of creativity with predictors of effective teamwork.
Selecting for creative leaders	Select leaders of creative teams who demonstrate supportive behaviors that are supportive of creativity, such as support for new ideas and psychological safety.
	Select leaders based on their ability to successfully facilitate the creative process within the team, such as ability to provide guidance in generating ideas and evaluation of creative ideas.
	Consider using high-potential programs or assessment center tasks to measure and track leaders for positions where they will lead creative individuals.
Training creative individuals and teams	Use training focused on the cognitive processes that underlie the creative process (e.g., problem identification, idea generation, idea evaluation).
	Creativity training can also focus on improving attitudes toward creativity and increasing beliefs in one's own ability to be creative.
	Train teams on how to effectively brainstorm to improve idea generation and reduce process loss. For example, to pay attention to others' ideas, or combine ideas with the ideas of others.
	Train individuals and teams to work within limits on their resources, time, and skills.
Training creative leaders	Develop soft skills training focused on how managers can support their teams.
	Train leaders to understand the cognitive processes underlying creativity to better understand how to support each phase of the problem-solving effort.
	Train leaders to focus on how to identify, evaluate, and implement creative ideas.
	Provide training on ambidextrous leadership, or combining actions aimed at short-term exploitation of resources and longer-term resource exploration.
	Train leaders in effective resource distribution.
Broader organizational interventions	Create interdisciplinary and cross-functional teams which can provide the team with a variety of experience, knowledge, and skills that improve creativity.
	Train teams and leaders to value diversity.
	Create a culture of acceptance of diversity, model effective communication, promote an environment of psychological safety, and support for innovation.
	Select and train leaders that will help create an organizational culture that is conducive to creativity.
	Develop a culture of intellectual stimulation, challenge, and autonomy.
	Use appropriate rewards and incentives to facilitate creativity.
	Ensure that creative individuals and teams have the right level of resources.

From a contextual standpoint, issues relating to team diversity, organizational climate, and availability of resources have been suggested as important to organizational creativity and innovation. The team diversity literature suggests that the relationship between diversity and creativity and innovation is complex. Therefore, it is important to address this complexity if organizations choose to design diverse teams as a way to improve creativity. Specifically, it is important to consider multiple ways in which teams can be creative, with a particular focus on functional diversity. In addition, it is important to find ways to manage the possible negative impact of diversity on social processes, such as communication and trust, so that the positive effects of diversity may be manifested. Organizational climate is an important way in which organizations can facilitate creativity. Organizations should strive to establish a climate in which creativity and innovation are viewed as positive and beneficial and not as negative, provide support for innovation from all members (co-workers, supervisors, and top management), and allow for risk and failure without negative consequences. Creating such an organizational climate typically involves leaders setting the tone, being role models, and creating an environment in which individuals feel safe. Finally, resources, broadly defined, are critical for creativity and innovation. Research suggests that having just the right amount of resources, not too much and not too little, will support creativity and innovation, and it is up to the organization to identify which resources are critical and which are not.

Our Research Contribution

Roni Reiter-Palmon's research focuses on the cognitive processes of creativity, specifically those that occur early in the process (problem identification and construction) and late in the process (idea evaluation and idea choice). She studies these processes at the individual level, focusing on the factors that facilitate effective application of these processes. Additionally, she studies these processes at the team level. At the team level, our research focuses on how individual level processes get aggregated to a team level process and how social processes in teams (such as communication or psychological safety) influence the effectiveness of the processes and resulting creativity.

Critical/Creative Thinking Questions

1. In addition to using predictors of individual creativity, why is it important to consider other social and contextual factors when selecting creative individuals?
2. What challenges may emerge when leading teams of creative individuals? How might a leader effectively relieve some of these potential challenges?

3. When leading creative teams, what can leaders do to facilitate creativity in those they lead?

4. What may be effective methods of training individuals in creative thinking and processes?

5. Consider the role of diversity in team creativity. In what ways does diversity positively and negatively affect creativity?

6. What aspects of an organizational culture and climate appear to facilitate creativity?

7. How do rewards and incentives improve or hinder creativity?

GLOSSARY

assessment centers: A selection technique that involves using multiple job-related assessments and exercises to observe how job candidates perform in tasks that are part of the job.

autonomy: The ability to choose and be in control over tasks and work behaviors.

biographical inventory measures: Measures that allow identification of individuals who will perform well in a job position by assessing and collecting information on previous experience.

creative mindsets: Individual views people have in regard to their own creativity as a characteristic as malleable, or something they can develop over time and with effort, or fixed, in which one's creativity is innate and cannot really be changed. Current research shows that people may hold both mindsets at the same time, depending on experience, as well as domain and level of creativity being discussed.

creative personal identity: The importance that one places on creativity as an important aspect of themselves.

creative self-efficacy: One's confidence and views of their own capacity to be creative in their work and handling tasks that require creativity.

curvilinear relationship: A relationship between two variables in which as one variable increases, the other does as well to a certain point, after which as one increases, the other decreases.

demographic diversity: Team diversity based on age, gender, race, etc.

divergent thinking: Generating as many solutions or ideas as possible in response to a verbal or graphic prompt.

functional diversity: Diversity in attributes that are relevant to job performance, such as education, function in the organization, and job relevant knowledge, skills, and abilities.

functional fixedness: A cognitive bias that limits a person to use something strictly in the way it has been traditionally used.

high potential: Individuals who tend to show higher performance and more capacity to grow and succeed than peers.

idea generation: In the creative problem-solving process, this refers to when potential solutions to a problem are generated.

interdisciplinary teams: A group of individuals from several different fields, possessing different knowledge, experience, and expertise, who work together toward a common goal.

openness to experience: One of the Big-Five personality traits associated with being willing to try new things, imagination, curiosity, and being open-minded.

organizational climate: How members of an organization experience the culture of an organization.

organizational culture: The underlying beliefs, assumptions, values, and methods of interaction that influence the social and psychological environment within an organization.

personnel selection: Any procedure or test used to make employment- or promotion-related decisions.

problem identification and construction: In creative problem-solving, this refers to the cognitive process of first recognizing, identifying, and structuring a problem before generating ideas to solve the problem.

process loss: Any actions, communication, or interactions that lead to less efficient problem solving in a group.

psychological safety: A shared sense among all team members that the team environment is safe for sharing ideas, taking interpersonal risks, and a belief that the team will not reject or punish a team member for sharing ideas.

Pygmalion effect: The phenomenon observed when expectations of one's performance tends to affect one's actual performance. In the case of creative performance, individuals' creative performance tends to be influenced by supervisor expectations of creativity.

resource allocation: The assignment and distribution of available organizational resources to accomplish organizational goals.

REFERENCES

Amabile, T. M. (1982). The Social Psychology of Creativity: A Consensual Assessment Technique. *Journal of Personality and Social Psychology*, *43*, 997–1013. doi:10.1037/0022-3514.43.5.997.
(1996). *Creativity in Context*. New York: Westview.

Amabile, T. M., and Conti, R. (1999). Changes in the Work Environment for Creativity during Downsizing. *Academy of Management Journal*, *42*, 630–640. doi:10.2307/256984.

Amabile, T. M., Conti, R., Coon, H., Lazenby, J., and Herron, M. (1996). Assessing the Work Environment for Creativity. *The Academy of Management Journal*, *39*, 1154–1184. doi:10.2307/256995.

Amabile, T. M., and Gryskiewicz, N. (1989). The Creative Environment Scales: The Work Environment Inventory. *Creativity Research Journal*, *2*, 231–254.

Amabile, T. M., Schatzel, E. A., Moneta, G. B., and Kramer, S. J. (2004). Leader Behaviors and the Work Environment for Creativity: Perceived Leader Support. *The Leadership Quarterly*, *15*, 5–32. doi:10.1016/j.leaqua.2003.12.003.

Ancona, D. G., and Caldwell, D. F. (1992). Bridging the Boundary: External Activity and Performance in Organizational Teams. *Administrative Science Quarterly*, *37*, 634–665.

Anderson, N., De Dreu, C. K. W., and Nijstad, B. A. (2004). The Routinization of Innovation Research: A Constructively Critical Review of the State-of-the-Science. *Journal of Organizational Behavior*, *25*, 147–173. doi:10.1002/job.236.

Anderson, N., Potocnik, K., and Zhou, J. (2014). Innovation and Creativity in Organizations: A State-of-the-Science Review, Prospective Commentary, and Guiding Framework. *Journal of Management*, *40*, 1297–1333. doi:10.1177/0149206314527128.

Anderson, N. R., and West, M. A. (1998). Measuring Climate for Work Group Innovation: Development and Validation of the Team Climate Inventory. *Journal of Organizational Behavior*, *19*, 235–258. doi:10.1002/(SICI)1099-1379(199805)19:3<235::AID-JOB837>3.0.CO;2-C.

Baer, J. (1996). The Effects of Task-Specific Divergent-Thinking Training. *Creativity Research Journal*, *30*, 183–187. doi:10.1002/j.2162-6057.1996.tb00767.x.

Baer, M., Oldham, G. R., Jacobsohn, G. C., and Hollingshead, A. B. (2008). The Personality Composition of Teams and Creativity: The Moderating Role of Team Creative Confidence. *The Journal of Creative Behavior*, *42*, 255–282. doi:10.1002/j.2162-6057.2008.tb01299.x.

Barnowe, J. T. (1975). Leadership and Performance Outcomes in Research Organizations: The Supervisor of Scientists As a Source of Assistance. *Organizational Behavior and Human Performance*, *14*, 264–280. doi:10.1016/0030-5073(75)90029-X.

Baruah, J., and Paulus, P. B. (2008). Effects of Training on Idea Generation in Groups. *Small Group Research*, *39*(5), 523–541. doi:10.1177/1046496408320049.

Basadur, M. (2004). Leading Others to Think Innovatively Together: Creative Leadership. *The Leadership Quarterly*, *15*, 103–121. doi:10.1016/j.leaqua.2003.12.007.

Batey, M., and Furnham, A. (2006). Creativity, Intelligence, and Personality: A Critical Review of the Scattered Literature. *Genetic, Social, and General Psychology Monographs*, *132*(4), 355–429. doi:10.3200/MONO.132.4.355-430.

Birdi, K. (2007). A Lighthouse in the Desert? Evaluating the Effects of Creativity Training on Employee Innovation. *The Journal of Creative Behavior*, *41*(4), 249–270. doi:10.1002/j.2162-6057.2007.tb01073.x.

Bradley, B. H., Postlethwaite, B. E., Klotz, A. C., Hamdani, M. R., and Brown, K. G. (2012). Reaping the Benefits of Task Conflict in Teams: The Critical Role of Team Psychological Safety Climate. *Journal of Applied Psychology*, *97*, 151–158. doi:10.1037/a0024200.

Burke, C. S., Stagl, K. C., Klein, C., Goodwin, G. F., Salas, E., and Halpin, S. M. (2006). What Type of Leadership Behaviors Are Functional in Teams? A Meta-Analysis. *The Leadership Quarterly*, *17*(3), 288–307. doi:10.1016/j.leaqua.2006.02.007.

Buttner, E. H., Gryskiewicz, N., and Hidore, S. C. (1999). The Relationship between Styles of Creativity and Managerial Skills Assessment. *British Journal of Management*, *10*, 228–238. doi:10.1111/1467-8551.00129.

Byron, K., and Khazanchi, S. (2012). Rewards and Creative Performance: A Meta-Analytic Test of Theoretically Derived Hypotheses. *Psychological Bulletin*, *138*, 809–830. doi:10.1037/a0027652.

Caniels, M. C. J., De Stobbeleir, K., and De Clippeleer, I. (2014). The Antecedents of Creativity Revisited: A Process Perspective. *Creativity and Innovation Management*, *23*, 96–110. doi:10.1111/caim.12051.

Carmeli, A., Gelbard, R., and Reiter-Palmon, R. (2013). Leadership, Creative Problem-Solving Capacity, and Creative Performance: The Importance of Knowledge Sharing. *Human Resource Management*, *52*, 95–121. doi:10.1002/hrm.21514.

Carmeli, A., Reiter-Palmon, R., and Ziv, E. (2010). Inclusive Leadership and Employee Involvement in Creative Tasks in the Workplace: The Mediating Role of Psychological Safety. *Creativity Research Journal*, *22*, 250–260. doi:10.1080/10400419.2010.504654.

Carmeli, A., and Schaubroeck, J. (2007). The Influence of Leaders' and Other Referents' Normative Expectations on Individual Involvement in Creative Work. *The Leadership Quarterly*, *18*, 35–48. doi:10.1016/j.leaqua.2006.11.001.

Catmull, E. (2014). *Creativity, Inc.: Overcoming the Unseen Forces That Stand in the Way of True Inspiration*. New York: Random House.

Choi, J. N. (2007). Group Composition and Employee Creative Behavior in a Lorena Electronics Company: Distinct Effects of Relational Demography and Group Diversity. *Journal of Occupational and Organizational Psychology*, *80*, 213–234. doi:10.1348/096317906X110250.

Choi, J. N., and Chang, J. Y. (2009). Innovation Implementation in the Public Sector: An Integration of Institutional and Collective Dynamics. *Journal of Applied Psychology*, *94*, 245–253. doi:10.1037/a0012994.

Church, A. H., Rotolo, C., Ginther, N. M., and Levine, R. (2015). How Are Top Companies Designing and Managing Their High-Potential Programs? A Follow-up Talent Management Benchmark Study. *Consulting Psychology Journal: Practice and Research*, *67*, 17–47. doi:10.1037/cpb0000030.

Cronin, M. A., and Weingart, L. R. (2007). Representational Gaps, Information Processing, and Conflict in Functionally Diverse Teams. *The Academy of Management Review*, *32*(3), 761–773. doi:10.2307/20159333.

Curseu, P. L. (2010). Team Creativity in Web Site Design: An Empirical Test of a Systemic Model. *Creativity Research Journal*, *22*, 98–107. doi:10.1080/10400410903579635.

Damanpour, F., and Schneider, M. (2006). Phases of the Adoption of Innovation in Organizations: Effects of Environment, Organization and Top Managers. *British Journal of Management*, *17*, 215–236. doi:10.1111/j.1467-8551.2006.00498.x.

Dayan, M., Ozer, M., and Almazrouei, H. (2017). The Role of Functional and Demographic Diversity on New Product Creativity and the Moderating Impact of Project Uncertainty. *Industrial Marketing Management*, *61*, 144–154. doi:10.1016/j.indmarman.2016.04.016.

De Dreu, C. W., Carsten K. W., and West, M. A. (2001). Minority Dissent and Team Innovation: The Importance of Participation in Decision Making. *Journal of Applied Psychology*, *86*(6), 1191–1201. doi:10.1037/0021-9010.86.6.1191.

De Dreu, C. K. W., Nijstad, B. A., Bechtoldt, M. N., and Baas, M. (2011). Group Creativity and Innovation: A Motivated Information Processing Perspective. *Psychology of Aesthetics, Creativity, and the Arts*, *5*, 81–89. doi:0.1037/a0017986.

DeRosa, D. M., Smith, C. L., and Hantula, D. A. (2007). The Medium Matters: Mining the Long-Promised Merit of Group Interaction in Creative Idea Generation Tasks in a Meta-Analysis of the Electronic Group Brainstorming Literature. *Computers in Human Behavior*, *23*(3), 1549–1581. doi:10.1016/j.chb.2005.07.00.

Desivilya, H. S., Somech, A., and Lidgoster, H. (2010). Innovation and Conflict Management in Work Teams: The Effects of Team Identification and Task and Relationship Conflict. *Negotiation and Conflict Management Research*, *3*, 28–48. doi:10.1111/j.1750-4716.2009.00048.x.

Dess, G. G., and Picken, J. C. (2000). Changing Roles: Leadership in the 21st Century. *Organizational Dynamics*, *28*, 18–34. doi:10.1016/S0090-2616(00)88447-8.

Doss, H. (2013). Innovation: Five Keys to Educating the Next Generation of Leaders. *Forbes*. www.forbes.com/sites/henrydoss/2013/03/19/innovation-five-keys-to-educating-the-next-generation-of-leaders/#3ebab839b1a3.

Dougherty, D., and Hardy, C. (1996). Sustained Product Innovation in Large, Mature Organizations: Overcoming Innovation-to-Organization Problems. *The Academy of Management Journal*, *39*, 1120–1153. doi:10.2307/256994.

Dugosh, K. L., Paulus, P. B., Roland, E. J., and Yang, H. (2000). Cognitive Stimulation in Brainstorming. *Journal of Personality and Social Psychology*, *79*(5), 722–735. doi:10.1037/0022-3514.79.5.722.

Edmondson, A. C. (1999). Psychological Safety and Learning Behavior in Work Teams. *Administrative Science Quarterly*, *44*, 350–383. doi: 10.2307/2666999.

Eisenberger, R., and Cameron, J. (1998). Reward, Intrinsic Interest, and Creativity: New Findings. *American Psychologist*, *53*, 676–679. doi:10.1037/0003-066X.53.6.676.

Eisenberger, R., and Rhoades, L. (2001). Incremental Effects of Reward on Creativity. *Journal of Personality and Social Psychology*, *81*, 728–741. doi:10.1037//0022-3514.81.4.728.

Fay, D., Borrill, C., Amir, Z., Haward, R., and West, M. A. (2006). Getting the Most out of Multidisciplinary Teams: A Multi-Sample Study of Team Innovation in Health Care. *Journal of Occupational and Organizational Psychology*, *79*, 553–567. doi:10.1348/096317905X72128.

Feist, G. J. (1998). A Meta-Analysis of Personality in Scientific and Artistic Creativity. *Personality and Social Psychology Review*, *2*(4), 290–309. doi:10.1207/s15327957pspr0204_5.

Ford, C. M., and Gioia, D. A. (2000). *Creative Action in Organizations: Ivory Tower Visions and Real World Voices*. Thousand Oaks: Sage Publications.

Furnham, A., and Bachtiar, V. (2008). Personality and Intelligence As Predictors of Creativity. *Personality and Individual Differences*, *45*(7), 613–617. doi:10.1016/j.paid.2008.06.023.

Gebert, D., Boerner, S., and Kearney, E. (2010). Fostering Team Innovation: Why Is It Important to Combine Opposing Action Strategies? *Organization Science*, *21*, 593–608. doi:10.1287/orsc.1090.0485.

George, G. (2005). Slack Resources and the Performance of Privately Held Firms. *The Academy of Management Journal*, *48*, 661–676. doi:10.5465/AMJ.2005.17843944.

George, J. M. (2007). Creativity in Organizations. *The Academy of Management Annals*, *1*, 439–477. doi:10.1080/078559814.

George, J. M., and Zhou, J. (2001). When Openness to Experience and Conscientiousness Are Related to Creative Behaviour: An Interactional Approach. *Journal of Applied Psychology*, *86*, 513–524. doi:10.1037/0021-9010.86.3.513.

Gilson, L. L., and Shalley, C. E. (2004). A Little Creativity Goes a Long Way: An Examination of Teams' Engagement in Creative Processes. *Journal of Management*, *30*, 453–470. doi:10.1016/j.jm.2003.07.001.

Goldenberg, O., Larson, J. J., and Wiley, J. (2013). Goal Instructions, Response Format, and Idea Generation in Groups. *Small Group Research*, *44*(3), 227–256. doi:10.1177/1046496413486701.

Graves, S. B., and Langowitz, N. S. (1993). Innovative Productivity and Returns to Scale in the Pharmaceutical Industry. *Strategic Management Journal*, *14*, 593–605. doi:10.1002/smj.4250140803.

Guzzo, R. A., and Dickson, M. W. (1996). Teams in Organizations: Recent Research on Performance and Effectiveness. *Annual Review of Psychology*, *47*, 307–338. doi:10.1146/annurev.psych.47.1.307.

Harvey, S. (2014). Creative Synthesis: Exploring the Process of Extraordinary Group Creativity. *The Academy of Management Review*, *39*(3), 324–343. doi:10.5465/amr.2012.0224.

Hass, R. W., Katz-Buonincontro, J., and Reiter-Palmon, R. (2016). Disentangling Creative Mindsets from Creative Self-Efficacy and Creative Identity: Do People Hold Fixed and Growth Theories of creativity? *Psychology of Aesthetics, Creativity, and the Arts*, *10*, 436–446. doi:10.1037/aca0000081.

Hennessey, B. A., and Amabile, T. M. (2010). Creativity. *Annual Review of Psychology*, *61*, 569–598. doi:10.1146/annurev.psych.093008.100416.

Hoegl, M., Gibbert, M., and Mazursky, D. (2008). Financial Constraints in Innovation Projects: When Is Less More? *Research Policy*, *37*, 1382–1391. doi:10.1016/j.respol.2008.04.018.

Homan, A. C., Buengeler, C., Eckhoff, R. A., van Ginkel, W. P., and Voelpel, S. C. (2015). The Interplay of Diversity Training and Diversity Beliefs on Team Creativity in Nationality Diverse Teams. *Journal of Applied Psychology*, *100*, 456–467. doi:10.1037/apl0000013.

Hornberg, J., and Reiter-Palmon, R. (2017). Creativity and the Big Five Personality Traits: Is the Relationship Dependent on the Creativity Measure? In G. J. Feist, R. Reiter-Palmon, and J. C. Kaufman, *The Cambridge Handbook of Creativity and Personality Research* (pp. 275–293). Cambridge: Cambridge University Press.

Hulsheger, U. R., Anderson, N., and Salgado, J. F. (2009). Team-Level Predictors of Innovation at Work: A Comprehensive Meta-Analysis Spanning Three Decades of Research. *Journal of Applied Psychology*, *94*, 1128–1145. doi:10.1037/a0015978.

Hunter, S. T., and Cushenbery, L. (2015). Is Being a Jerk Necessary for Originality? Examining the Role of Disagreeableness in the Sharing and Utilization of Original Ideas. *Journal of Business and Psychology*, *30*, 621–639. doi:10.1007/s10869-014-9386-1.

Hunter, S. T., Bedell, K. E., and Mumford, M. D. (2007). Climate for Creativity: A Quantitative Review. *Creativity Research Journal*, *19*, 69–90. doi:10.1080/10400410709336883.

Hunter, S. T., Cushenbery, L., and Friedrich, T. (2012). Hiring an Innovative Workforce: A Necessary Yet Uniquely Challenging Endeavor. *Human Resource Management Review*. doi:10.1016/j.hrmr.2012.01.001.

Hunter, S. T., Neely, B. H., and Gutworth, M. B. (in press). Selection and Team Creativity: Meeting Unique Challenges through Diversity and Flexibility. In R. Reiter-Palmon (Ed.), *Team Creativity and Innovation*. New York: Oxford University Press.

IBM. (2010). *Capitalizing on Complexity*. www-935.ibm.com/services/c-suite/series-download.html.

Isaksen, S. G. (2007). The Climate for Transformation: Lessons for Leaders. *Creativity and Innovation Management*, *16*, 3–15. doi:10.1111/j.1467-8691.2007.00415.x.

Janssens, M., and Brett, J. M. (2006). Cultural Intelligence in Global Teams: A Fusion Model of Collaboration. *Group and Organization Management*, *31*, 124–153. doi:10.1177/1059601105275268.

Jaussi, K. S., and Benson, G. (2012). Careers of the Creatives: Creating and Managing the Canvas. In M. Mumford (Ed.), *Handbook of Organizational Creativity* (pp. 587–605). London: Elsevier/Academic Press.

Jaussi, K. S., Randel, A. E., and Dionne, S. D. (2007). I Am, I Think I can, and I Do: The Role of Personal Identity, Self-Efficacy and Cross-Application of Experiences in Creativity at Work. *Creativity Research Journal*, *19*(2–3), 247–258. doi:10.1080/10400410701397339.

Jehn, K. A. (1995). A Multimethod Examination of the Benefits and Detriments of Intragroup Conflict. *Administrative Science Quarterly*, *40*(2), 256–282. doi:10.2307/2393638.

Kabanoff, B., and Bottger, P. (1991). Effectiveness of Creativity Training and Its Relation to Selected Personality Factors. *Journal of Organizational Behavior*, *12*(3), 235–248. doi:10.1002/job.4030120306.

Kahai, S. S., Sosik, J. J., and Avolio, B. J. (2003). Effects of Leadership Style, Anonymity, and Rewards on Creativity-Relevant Processes and Outcomes in an Electronic Meeting System Context. *The Leadership Quarterly*, *14*(4–5), 499–524. doi:10.1016/S1048-9843(03)00049-3.

Kanter, R. (1985). Supporting Innovation and Venture Development in Established Companies. *Journal of Business Venturing*, *1*, 47–60. doi:10.1016/0883-9026(85)90006-0.

Karwowski, M. (2011). It Doesn't Hurt to Ask . . . But Sometimes It Hurts to Believe: Polish Students' Creative Self-Efficacy and Its Predictors. *Psychology of Aesthetics, Creativity, and the Arts*, *5*(2), 154–164. doi:10.1037/a0021427.

(2014). Creative Mindsets: Measurement, Correlates, Consequences. *Psychology of Aesthetics, Creativity, and the Arts*, *8*, 62–70. doi:10.1037/a0034898.

(2016). The Dynamics of Creative Self Concept: Changes and Reciprocal Relations between Creative Self-Efficacy and Creative Personal Identity. *Creativity Research Journal*, *28*, 99–104. doi:10.1080/10400419.2016.1125254.

Karwowski, M., Royston, R. P., and Reiter-Palmon, R. (2019). Exploring Creative Mindsets: Variable and person-centered approaches. *Psychology of Aesthetics, Creativity, and the Arts*, *13*, 36–43. doi:10.1037/aca0000170.

Keller, R. T. (2001). Cross-Functional Project Groups in Research and New Product Development: Diversity, Communications, Job Stress, and Outcomes. *Academy of Management*, *44*, 547–555. doi:10.2307/3069369.

Kessel, M., Kratzer, J., and Schultz, C. (2012). Psychological Safety, Knowledge Sharing, and Creative Performance in Healthcare Teams. *Creativity and Innovation Management, 21,* 147–157. doi:10.1111/j.1467-8691.2012.00635.x.

Klein, K. J., Conn, A. B., and Sorra, J. S. (2001). Implementing Computerized Technology: An Organizational Analysis. *Journal of Applied Psychology, 86,* 811–824. doi:10.1037/0021-9010.86.5.811.

Kozlowski, S. J., and Bell, B. S. (2008). Team Learning, Development, and Adaptation. In V. I. Sessa, M. London, V. I. Sessa, M. London (Eds.), *Work Group Learning: Understanding, Improving and Assessing How Groups Learn in Organizations* (pp. 15–44). New York: Taylor and Francis Group/ Lawrence Erlbaum Associates.

Lewis, M. W. (2000). Exploring Paradox: Toward a More Comprehensive Guide. *Academy of Management Review, 25,* 760–776. doi:10.2307/259204.

Li, C., Lin, C., Tien, Y., and Chen, C. (2017). A Multilevel Model of Team Cultural Diversity and Creativity: The Role of Climate for Inclusion. *The Journal of Creative Behavior, 51,* 163–179. doi:10.1002/jocb.93.

Li, J. (1997). Creativity in Horizontal and Vertical Domains. *Creativity Research Journal, 10,* 107–132. doi:10.1207/s15326934crj1002and3_3.

Litchfield, R. C., Fan, J., and Brown, V. R. (2011). Directing Idea Generation Using Brainstorming with Specific Novelty Goals. *Motivation and Emotion, 35,* 135–143. doi:10.1007/s11031-011-9203-3.

Malakate, A., Andriopoulos, C., and Gotsi, M. (2007). Assessing Job Candidates' Creativity: Propositions and Future Research Directions. *Creativity and Innovation Management, 16,* 307–316. doi:10.1111/j.1467-8691.2007.00437.x.

Malik, M. A. R., and Butt, A. N. (2017). Rewards and Creativity: Past, Present, and Future. *Applied Psychology, 66,* 290–325. doi:10.1111/apps.12080.

Malik, M. A. R., Butt, A. N., and Choi, J. N. (2015). Rewards and Employee Creative Performance: Moderating Effects of Creative Self-Efficacy, Reward Importance, and Locus of Control. *Journal of Organizational Behavior, 36,* 59–74. doi:10.1002/job.1943.

Makel, M. C. (2009). "The Malleability of Implicit Beliefs of Creativity and Creative Production." Unpublished doctoral dissertation, Indiana University, Bloomington, Indiana.

Mandal, A., Thomas, H., and Antunes, D. (2009). Dynamic Linkages between Mental Models, Resource Constraints and Differential Performance: A Resource-Based Analysis. *Journal of Strategy and Management, 3,* 217–239. doi:10.1108/17554250910982471.

Marlow, S. L., Lacerenza, C. N., Woods, A. L., and Salas, E. (in press). Training Creativity in Teams. In R. Reiter-Palmon (Ed.), *Team Creativity and Innovation.* New York: Oxford University Press.

Mathieu, J., Maynard, M. T., Rapp, T., and Gilson, L. (2008). Team Effectiveness 1997–2007: A Review of Recent Advancements and a Glimpse into the Future. *Journal of Management, 34* (3), 410–476. doi:10.1177/0149206308316061.

McLeod, P., Lobel, S., Cox, T. (1996). Ethnic Diversity and Creativity in Small Groups. *Small Group Research, 2,* 248–264. doi:10.1177/1046496496272003.

Medeiros, K. E., Partlow, P. J., and Mumford, M. D. (2014). Not Too Much, Not Too Little: The Influence of Constraints on Creative Problem Solving. *Psychology of Aesthetics, Creativity, and the Arts, 8,* 198–210. doi:10.1037/a0036210.

Mehta, R., and Zhu, M. (2016). Creating When You Have Less: The Impact of Resource Scarcity on Product Use Creativity. *Journal of Consumer Research, 42,* 767–782. doi:10.1093/jcr/ucv051.

Milliken, F. J., Bartel, C., and Kurtzberg, T. (2003). Diversity and Creativity in Work Groups: A Dynamic Perspective on the Affective and Cognitive Processes That Link Diversity and

Performance. In P. B. Paulus and B. Nijstad (Eds.), *Group Creativity* (pp. 32–62). New York: Oxford University Press.

Miron, E., Erez, M., and Naveh, E. (2004). Do Personal Characteristics and Cultural Values That Promote Innovation, Quality, and Efficiency Compete or Complement Each Other? *Journal of Organizational Behavior*, *25*(2), 175–199. doi:10.1002/job.237.

Mitchell, K., and Reiter-Palmon, R. (in press). Creative Leadership: How Problem Solving, Decision Making, and Organizational Context Influence Leadership Creativity. In J. Kaufman (Ed.), *The Cambridge Handbook of Creativity across Domains*. Cambridge: Cambridge University Press.

Mobley, M. I., Doares, L. M., and Mumford, M. D. (1992). Process Analytic Models of Creative Capacities: Evidence for the Combination and Reorganization Process. *Creativity Research Journal*, *5*(2), 125–155. doi:10.1080/10400419209534428.

Montouri, A. (1992). Two Books on Creativity. *Creativity Research Journal*, *5*, 199–203.

Mueller, J. S., and Kamdar, D. (2011). Why Seeking Help from Teammates Is a Blessing and a Curse: A Theory of Help Seeking and Individual Creativity in Team Contexts. *Journal of Applied Psychology*, *96*, 263–276. doi:10.1037/a0021574.

Mumford, M. D. (1986). Leadership in the Organizational Context: A Conceptual Approach and Its Applications. *Journal of Applied Social Psychology*, *16*, 508–531. doi:10.1111/j.1559-1816.1986.tb01156.x.

Mumford, M. D., and Gustafson, S. B. (1988). Creativity Syndrome: Integration, Application, and Innovation. *Psychological Bulletin*, *103*, 27–43. doi:10.1037/0033-2909.103.1.27.

Mumford, M. D., and Hunter, S. T. (2005). Innovation in Organizations: A Multi-Level Perspective on Creativity. In F. Dansereau, F. J. Yammarino (Eds.), *Multi-Level Issues in Strategy and Methods*. (pp. 9–73). New York: Emerald Group Publishing Limited.

Mumford, M. D., Hunter, S. T., and Byrne, C. L. (2009). What Is the Fundamental? The Role of Cognition in Creativity and Innovation. *Industrial and Organizational Psychology: Perspectives on Science and Practice*, *2*(3), 353–356. doi:10.1111/j.1754-9434.2009.01158.x.

Mumford, M. D., Hunter, S. T., Eubanks, D. L., Bedell, K. E., and Murphy, S. T. (2007). Developing Leaders for Creative Efforts: A Domain-Based Approach to Leadership Development. *Human Resource Management Review*, *17*, 402–417. doi:10.1016/j.hrmr.2007.08.002.

Mumford, M. D., Lonergan, D. C., and Scott, G. (2002). Evaluating Creative Ideas: Processes, Standards, and Context. *Inquiry: Critical Thinking across the Disciplines*, *22*, 21–30. doi:10.5840/inquiryctnews20022213.

Mumford, M. D., Robledo, I. C., and Hester, K. S. (2011). Creativity, Innovation and Leadership: Models and Findings. In A. Bryman, D. Collison, K. Grint, B. Jackson, and M. Uhl-Bien (Eds.), *The SAGE Handbook of Leadership* (pp. 405–421). Washington, DC: SAGE Publications.

Mumford, M. D., Scott, G. M., Gaddis, B., and Strange, J. M. (2002). Leading Creative People: Orchestrating Expertise and Relationships. *Leadership Quarterly*, *13*, 705–750. doi:10.1016/S1048-9843(02)00158-3.

Mumford, M. D., Supinski, E. P., Baughman, W. A., Costanza, D. P., and Threlfall, K. V. (1997). Process-Based Measures of Creative Problem-Solving Skills: V. Overall Prediction. *Creativity Research Journal*, *10*, 73–85. doi:10.1207/s15326934crj1001_8.

Nitin, N., and Gulati, R. (1996). Is Slack Good or Bad for Innovation? *The Academy of Management Journal*, *39*, 1245–1264. doi:10.2307/256998.

Ohly, S., and Fritz, C. (2010). Work Characteristics, Challenge Appraisal, Creativity, and Proactive Behavior: A Multi-Level Study. *Journal of Organizational Behavior*, *31*, 543–565. doi:10.1002/job.633.

O'Reilly, C., Williams, K., and Barsade, S. (1997). Group Demography and Innovation: Does Diversity Help? In E. Mannix and M. Neale (Eds.), *Research in the Management of Groups and Teams.* Greenwich: JAI Press.

Paletz, S. B. F., Peng, K., Erez, M., and Maslach, C. (2004). Ethnic Composition and Its Differential Impact on Group Processes in Diverse Teams. *Small Group Research, 35*, 128–157. doi:10.1177/1046496403258793.

Patterson, F., and Zibarras, L. D. (2017). Selecting for Creativity and Innovation Potential: Implications for Practice in Healthcare Education. *Advances in Health Sciences Education, 22* (2)1–12. doi:10.1007/s10459-016-9731-4.

Paulus, P. B., and Brown, V. R. (2003). Enhancing Ideational Creativity in Groups: Lessons from Research on Brainstorming. In P. B. Paulus, and B. A. Nijstad (Eds.), *Group Creativity: Innovation through Collaboration* (pp. 110–136). New York: Oxford University Press.

Paulus, P. B., Nakui, T., Putman, V. L., and Brown, V. R. (2006). Effects of Task Instructions and Brief Breaks on Brainstorming. *Group Dynamics: Theory, Research, and Practice, 10*(3), 206–219. doi:10.1037/1089-2699.10.3.206.

Peterson, D. R., Barrett, J. D., Hester, K. S., Robledo, I. C., Hougen, D. F., Day, E. A., and Mumford, M. D. (2013). Teaching People to Manage Constraints: Effects on Creative Problem-Solving. *Creativity Research Journal, 25*(3), 335–347. doi:10.1080/10400419.2013.813809.

Pfeffer, J., and Salancik, G. R. (2003). *The External Control of Organizations: A Resource Dependence Perspective.* Stanford: Stanford University Press.

Pirola-Merlo, A., and Mann, L. (2004). The Relationship between Individual Creativity and Team Creativity: Aggregating across People and Time. *Journal of Organizational Behavior, 25*, 235–257. doi:10.1002/job.240.

Polyhart, R. E., Schneider, B., and Schmitt, N. (2006). *Staffing Organizations: Contemporary Practice and Theory*, 3rd ed. Mahwah: Lawrence Erlbaum Associates Publishers.

Rasulzada, F., and Dackert, I. (2009). Organizational Creativity and Innovation in Relation to Psychological Well-Being and Organizational Factors. *Creativity Research Journal, 21*(2–3), 191–198. doi:10.1080/10400410902855283

Redmond, R. R., Mumford, M. D., and Teach, R. (1993). Putting Creativity to Work: Effects of Leader Behavior on Subordinate Creativity. *Organizational Behavior and Human Decision Processes, 55*, 120–151. doi:10.1006/obhd.1993.1027.

Reiter-Palmon, R. (2018). Creative Cognition at the Individual and Team Level: What Happens before and after Idea Generation. In R. Sternberg and J. Kaufman (Eds.), *The Nature of Human Creativity* (pp. 184–208). Cambridge: Cambridge University Press.

Reiter-Palmon, R., de Vreede, T., and de Vreede, G. J. (2013). Leading Creative Interdisciplinary Teams: Challenges and Solutions. In S. Hemlin, C. M. Allwood, B. Martin, and M. D. Mumford (Eds.), *Creativity and Leadership in Science, Technology and Innovation* (pp. 240–267). New York: Routledge.

Reiter-Palmon, R., Herman, A. E., and Yammarino, F. J. (2007). Creativity and Cognitive Processes: Multi-Level Linkages between Individual and Team Cognition. *Research in Multi-Level Issues, 7*, 203–267. doi:10.1016/S1475-9144(07)00009-4.

Reiter-Palmon, R., and Illies, J. J. (2004). Leadership and Creativity: Understanding Leadership from a Creative Problem-Solving Perspective. *The Leadership Quarterly, 15*, 55–77. doi:10.1016/j.leaqua.2003.12.005.

Reiter-Palmon, R., Mumford, M. D., and Threlfall, K. V. (1998). Solving Everyday Problems Creatively: The Role of Problem Construction and Personality Type. *Creativity Research Journal, 11*(3), 187–197. doi:10.1207/s15326934crj1103_1

Reiter-Palmon, R., and Royston, R.P. (2017). Leading for Creativity: How Leaders Manage Creative Teams. In M. D. Mumford and S. Hemlin (Eds.), *Handbook of Research on Leadership and Creativity* (pp. 159–184). Northampton: Edward Elgar Publishing.

Reiter-Palmon, R., Wigert, B., and de Vreede, T. (2011). Team Creativity and Innovation: The Effect of Team Composition, Social Processes and Cognition. In *Handbook of Organizational Creativity* (pp. 295–326). London: Academic Press.

Richter, A. W., Hirst, G., van Knippenberg, D., and Baer, M. (2012). Creative Self-Efficacy and Individual Creativity in Team Contexts: Cross-Level Interactions with Team Informational Resources. *Journal of Applied Psychology, 97*, 1282–1290. doi:10.1037/a0029359.

Royston, R. P., and Reiter-Palmon, R. (2016). "Predicting Creative Performance: Creative Mindsets vs. Creative Self-Efficacy." Mining Mindsets, Symposium conducted at the meeting of American Psychological Association, Denver, Colorado, J. Katz-Buonincontro (Chair).

Rosen, M. A., Bedwell, W. L., Wildman, J. Fritzsche, B., Salas, E., and Burke, C. S. (2011). Managing Adaptive Performance in Teams: Guiding Principles and Behavioral Markers for Measurement. *Human Resource Management Review, 21*, 107–122.

Runco, M. A. (2004). Creativity. *Annual Review of Psychology, 55*, 657–687.

Salas, E., Sims, D. E., and Burke, C. S. (2005). Is There a "Big Five" in Teamwork? *Small Group Research, 36*, 555–599. doi:10.1177/1046496405277134.

Schein, E. H. (2010). *Organizational Culture and Leadership*, 5th ed. San Francisco: John Wiley and Sons.

Schneider, B., Breif, A., and Guzzo, R. (1996). Creating a Climate and Culture for Organizational Change. *Organizational Dynamics, 24*, 6–9.

Scopelliti, I., Cillo, P., Busacca, B., and Mazursky, D. (2014). How Do Financial Constraints Affect Creativity? *The Journal of Product Innovation Management, 31*, 880–893. doi:10.1111/jpim.12129.

Scott, S. G., and Bruce, R. A. (1994). Determinants of Innovative Behavior: A Path Model of Individual Innovation in the Workplace. *The Academy on Management Journal, 37*, 580–607. doi:10.2307/256701.

Scott, G. M., Leritz, L. E., and Mumford, M. D. (2004). The Effectiveness of Creativity Training: A Meta-Analysis. *Creativity Research Journal, 16*, 361–388.

Silvia, P. (2008). Another Look at Creativity and Intelligence: Exploring Higher-Order Models and Probable Confounds. *Personality and Individual Differences, 44*, 1012–1021. doi:10.1016/j.paid.2007.10.027.

Silvia, P. J., Kaufman, J. C., Reiter-Palmon, R., and Wigert, B. (2011). Cantankerous Creativity: Honesty-Humility, Agreeableness, and the HEXACO Structure of Creative Achievement. *Personality and Individual Differences, 51*, 687–689. doi:10.1016/j.paid.2011.06.011.

Silzer, R., and Church, A. H. (2009). The Pearls and Perils of Identifying Potential. *Industrial and Organizational Psychology: Perspectives on Science and Practice, 2*, 377–412. doi:10.1111/j.1754-9434.2009.01163.x.

SIOP (2003). *Principles for the Validation and Use of Personnel Selection Procedures*, 4th ed. College Park: SIOP.

Shalley, C. E., Gilson, L. L., and Blum, T. C. (2000). Matching Creativity Requirements and the Work Environment: Effects on Satisfaction and Intentions to Leave. *Academy of Management Journal, 43*(2), 215–223. doi:10.2307/1556378.

Shalley, C. E., Zhou, J., and Oldham, G. R. (2004). The Effects of Personal and Contextual Characteristics on Creativity: Where Should We Go from Here? *Journal of Management, 30*, 933–958. doi:10.1016/j.jm.2004.06.007.

Smith, W. K. (2014). Dynamic Decision Making: A Model of Senior Leaders Managing Strategic Paradoxes. *Academy of Management Journal, 57*, 1592–1623. doi:10.5465/amj.2011.0932.

Smith, W. K., and Lewis, M. W. (2011). Toward a Theory of Paradox: A Dynamic Equilibrium Model of Organizing. *Academy of Management Review, 36*, 381–403. doi:10.5465/AMR.2011.59330958.

Sonenshein, S. (2014). How Organizations Foster the Creative Use of Resources. *Academy of Management Journal, 57*, 814–848. doi:10.5465/10.5465/amj.2012.0048.

Sternberg, R. J. (1997). *Successful Intelligence*. New York: Plume.

Sternberg, R. J., and Lubart, T. I. (1999). The Concept of Creativity: Prospects and Paradigms. In R. J. Sternberg (Ed.), *The Cambridge Handbook of Creativity* (pp. 3–16). Cambridge: Cambridge University Press.

Sy, T., and Reiter-Palmon, R. (2015). "Follower-Leader Identity Integration." Unpublished paper.

Tierney, P., and Farmer, S. M. (2002). Creative Self-Efficacy: Its Potential Antecedents and Relationship to Creative Performance. *The Academy of Management Journal, 45*, 1137–1148. doi:10.2307/3069429.

(2004). The Pygmalion Process and Employee Creativity. *Journal of Management, 30*(3), 413–432. doi:10.1016/j.jm.2002.12.001.

(2011). Creative Self-Efficacy Development and Creative Performance over Time. *Journal of Applied Psychology, 96*, 277–293. doi:10.1037/a0020952.

Vincent, A. S., Decker, B. P., and Mumford, M. D. (2002). Divergent Thinking, Intelligence, and Expertise: A Test of Alternative Models. *Creativity Research Journal, 14*, 163–178. doi:10.1207/S15326934CRJ1402_4.

Wang, D., and Hong, Y. (2010). "Work Support and Team Creativity: The Mediating Effect of Team Psychological Safety." Paper published at 17th Industrial Engineering and Engineering Management Conference. Xiamen, China. doi:10.1109/ICIEEM.2010.5645894.

Weiss, M., Hoegl, M., and Gibbert, M. (2011). Making Virtue of Necessity: The Role of Team Climate for Innovation in Resource-Constrained Innovation Projects. *The Journal of Product Innovation Management, 28*, 196–207. doi:10.1111/j.1540-5885.2011.00870.x.

West, M. A. (2002). Sparkling Fountains or Stagnant Ponds: An Integrative Model of Creativity and Innovation Implementation in Work groups. *Applied Psychology, 51*, 355–387. doi:10.1111/1464-0597.00951.

West, M. A., Hirst, G., Richter, A., and Shipton, H. (2004). Twelve Steps to Heaven: Successfully Managing Change through Developing Innovative Teams. *European Journal of Work and Organizational Psychology, 13*, 269–299. doi:10.1080/13594320444000092.

Woodman, R. W., Sawyer, J. E., and Griffin, R. W. (1993). Toward a Theory of Organizational Creativity. *Academy of Management Review, 18*, 293–321. doi:10.5465/AMR.1993.3997517.

Zachner, H., Robinson, A. J., and Rosing, K. (2014). Ambidextrous Leadership and Employees' Self-Reported Innovative Performance: The Role of Exploration and Exploitation Behaviors. *The Journal of Creative Behavior*. doi:10.1002/jocb.66.

Zachner, H., and Rosing, K. (2015). Ambidextrous Leadership and Team Innovation. *Leadership and Organization Development Journal, 36*, 54–68. doi:10.1108/LODJ-11-2012-0141.

Zhang, W., Zhang, Q., and Song, M. (2015). How Do Individual-Level Factors Affect the Creative Solution Formation Process of Teams? *Creativity and Innovation Management, 24*(3), 508–524. doi:10.1111/caim.12127.

14   Enhancing Creativity

ROBERT J. STERNBERG

INTRODUCTION

Creativity involves the generation of ideas that are novel, surprising, and compelling (Kaufman and Sternberg, 2010, 2019). Creative people are not only intellectually capable of coming up with such ideas; they are also people who have a creative attitude toward life (Sternberg, 2017) and approach problems insightfully (Davidson and Sternberg, 2003). They also are motivated to solve problems in a creative way (Dai and Sternberg, 2004; Hennessey, 2019). Although average levels of creativity may vary from one time or place to another (e.g., Niu and Sternberg, 2003; Baas, 2019; Ivcevic and Hoffmann, 2019; Lubart, Glǎveanu et al., 2019), a major variable in creativity is simply a mindset toward thinking in novel, surprising, and compelling ways – and this mindset can be taught.

How can people enhance their **creativity**? In this chapter, I consider responses to this question. First, I review some of the major programs for enhancing creative thinking. Then I describe some techniques for enhancing creative thinking that are consistent with a variety of theories of creativity. Next, I describe prompts for teaching and assessing creativity. Then I describe some barriers to enhancing creativity and how they can be overcome. Finally, I draw conclusions.

Programs for Enhancing Creativity

Brainstorming

One of the earliest systematic attempts to develop creative thinking was a group-based method called **brainstorming** (Osborn, 1953, 1963), which involves giving free rein to the imagination and not criticizing ideas that are presented. Brainstorming is typically used in groups where members can bounce ideas off each other. Group members are encouraged to let their imaginations run wild, to say whatever comes to mind, to feel free to explore truly novel ideas, and not to criticize each other. The idea is that people in a group will build off each other and come up with solutions that none would have come up with individually, or if people criticized each other.

This chapter is based upon and modified from Sternberg, R. J. (2019). Enhancing People's Creativity. In J. C. Kaufman and R. J. Sternberg (Eds.), *The Cambridge Handbook of Creativity*, 2nd ed. (pp. 88–103). New York: Cambridge University Press.

In the Creative Problem Solving program (Parnes, 1981; Isaksen and Treffinger, 1985; Treffinger, McEwen, and Witting, 1989), there are three stages of brainstorming: understanding the problem, generating ideas, and planning for action. Understanding the problem itself involves three substages: mess finding, data finding, and problem finding.

Brainstorming and related techniques can work (Meadow, Parnes, and Reese, 1959; Parnes and Meadow, 1963; Reiter-Palmon, Mitchell, and Royston, 2019), at least in some circumstances. But brainstorming is limited in certain ways. First, although it can be used by individuals, it primarily is targeted at groups. When used by an individual, the idea would be to hold back on criticizing one's own ideas. Second, if an idea is bad, it may be better to say so right away rather than to wait, especially when the stakes of the decision to be made are high. Waiting until later may be too late, or "later" may never happen at all. Third, brainstorming is primarily a search device, not an evaluative device (Nickerson, 1999). So, if multiple plausible alternatives are generated, there is all the more need for an evaluative phase to decide which idea is best. Fourth, the technique is rather non-specific. It amounts to little more than telling people to "be creative" and to let the ideas flow forth. It would be better, at the very least, to have one or more techniques that are more specific and more easily usable.

CoRT

CoRT stands for Cognitive Research Trust, an organization that was founded and also run by Edward de Bono, a Maltese physician, scholar, and educator. The CoRT program is designed to teach people to think better, not only creatively, but also critically (www .edwarddebonofoundation.com).

The goal of CoRT is to produce individuals who can think for themselves (de Bono, 1973) both creatively and critically. CoRT comprises six units. Each unit in turn comprises multiple lessons. There are a total of sixty lessons in all. CoRT 1, Breadth, is designed to help individuals broaden their perception – to see things they may not have seen before. CoRT 2, Organisation, shows individuals ways of organizing and systematizing their thinking. CoRT 3, Interaction, is about evidence – how to argue for a point and what kinds of evidence to present. CoRT 4 is devoted specifically to creativity. It is designed to help students break out of familiar concepts and to see things in new ways. CoRT 5, Information and Feeling, deals with our assessing what information we have, what information we need, how we can get that information, and the values and feelings we can apply to that information. CoRT 6, Action, covers how visual symbols can be used to direct thinking and how thinking can be translated from mere thought into action.

DeBono (2015) has suggested lateral thinking as a way to be creative. Lateral thinking is essentially departing from the linear (vertical) mode of thinking, which is to take a concept and then make the usual associations to it. In particular, in **lateral thinking**, one departs from the usual associations and tries to see a concept in a new way and to make unusual associations with the concept.

De Bono has suggested several thinking "tools" that people can use to help them think laterally. Here are a few examples.

The first is *random entry idea generation.* The idea here is first to think of an object or concept at random, say from a dictionary. Then try to find an association with the problem with which one is dealing. For example, suppose one is trying to decide whether to buy a car or continue to use public transport. Now one comes upon the word "red." One might think about, on the positive side, what it would be like to have a red car, or on the negative side, of all the red lights one would have to face if one drove a car. Or if one came across the word "tangible," one might think of the car as a tangible asset or as a possession one actually could touch.

A second tool is *provocation.* The idea of a provocation is, first, to think of a false, impossible, or ridiculous statement about a problem one is dealing with then ask whether somehow that provocation, despite its being false, might be useful in solving one's problem. Techniques for provocation include wishful thinking about, exaggeration of, reversal of, and distortion of reality.

A third tool is *movement,* or focusing on how to move from one mental place in creative problem solving to another. The idea here might be to focus on either positive or negative aspects of a potential solution, or to focus on differences, or to try to generate a general principle that might apply to the problem. The goal is to keep one moving in one's mental search for a solution to a problem.

A fourth tool is *challenge.* Here, one challenges obvious practices, such as that one drives with a steering wheel or that one eats with utensils. In fact, not all moving vehicles use steering wheels and not everyone eats with utensils. The idea is to challenge conventional ways of thinking.

A fifth tool is the *concept fan.* This tool involves thinking more broadly about a problem than one initially does. For example, one might sketch out a problem, draw a circle around it, and then draw lines radiating out with as many diverse and offbeat solutions as one can think of.

A sixth tool is *disproving.* First, consider anything that people consider obvious. Then show why it is wrong.

De Bono (1999) further suggested that one can arrive at more creative and better solutions to problems by donning **six thinking hats**, or six different ways of thinking about problems, for example, objectively versus emotionally versus cautiously. Either one person can alternately don the hats, or better, different individuals working as a group to solve a problem can don the hats in a group discussion. The six thinking hats include

- white hat: thinking that is objective, neutral, and as unbiased as possible; it is concerned with facts, not with speculations or imaginings.
- red hat: thinking that is emotional and heavily value-laden; it is concerned with how a problem or a possible solution affects oneself and others affectively.
- black hat: thinking that is cautious and careful and that considers the possible problems with a potential solution; it involves playing the devil's advocate to any possible solution to a problem.

- yellow hat: thinking that is positive, upbeat, and optimistic; it is sunny and bright and looking at the best possibilities that can emerge from a potential solution.
- green hat: thinking that is associated with creativity and expanding one's range of ideas; it is green in the sense of the greenness of growing plants.
- blue hat: thinking that is cool and unemotional; the blue hat often can serve as an organizing basis for the other hats.

Synectics

Synectics was proposed by George Prince and William Gordon, who were management consultants (see Gordon, 1961, 1966, 1981). According to Gordon, synectics involves three basic principles. First, creative thinking is learnable – it can be taught. Second, creativity in both the arts and in the sciences depends on the same fundamental processes of thinking. Third, individual and group processes in creativity are largely analogous to each other.

Synectics is a program that emphasizes the importance of unconscious thought, emotion, and the irrational in creativity. Often, creative ideas come about when one lets go of traditional and safe assumptions. Emotional responses to problems that at first can seem irrational may turn out to have kernels of useful ideas that later can be fashioned into viable solutions.

Springboarding in synectics is a way of starting out in the solution of a creative problem where people bounce ideas off each other without being critical. It builds on brainstorming and then goes on to fashion useful ideas and criticize them as necessary. It emphasizes the roles of imagery, analogy, metaphor, and emotion in generating creative ideas.

Productive Thinking Program

The Productive Thinking Program (Covington et al., 1974) is a general program for developing thinking skills with a special emphasis on creativity. The program comprises fifteen booklets, aimed at children in the fifth and sixth grades of school. Results for the program have been mixed (Mansfield, Bussé, and Krepelka, 1978). The program is not widely used today.

Specific Techniques for Teaching Creative Thinking

There are a number of specific techniques that can be used to teach for creativity. These techniques fit with varied models of creativity (see Sternberg and Williams, 1996, 2001; Sternberg, Grigorenko, and Jarvin, 2009; Sternberg, 2018a; Kaufman and Sternberg, 2019). However, the techniques described here derive directly from the idea of creativity as an attitude toward life – as a seeking out for opportunities to think of solutions to problems that are novel, surprising, and compelling (Sternberg, 2003).

Defying Past Thinking

Many creative thinkers **defy the crowd** by asking how what everyone else believes may be wrong (Sternberg and Lubart, 1995). To think creatively, one needs further to be willing to **defy oneself**, meaning that one is willing to challenge and ultimately to let go of one's past ideas or beliefs in order to think in novel and useful ways. Finally, one must be willing to **defy the Zeitgeist**, meaning that one is willing to identify, question, and, if necessary, reject common cultural beliefs that one may not even recognize one has (Sternberg, 2018a, 2018b).

Redefining Problems

Redefining a problem requires a shift in perspective whereby one perceives an old problem in an entirely different way. Over a lifetime, people always have problems that they just don't see how to solve. They are stuck, as though they are in a box. Redefining a problem means, in essence, getting oneself out of the box. This process can be seen as the synthetic part of creative thinking. It is crucial to what de Bono (1973) has called "lateral thinking," as described earlier. It involves seeing problems in a more effective way (Kaufman, 2018).

Teachers and parents alike can and should encourage students to define and then to redefine problems for themselves. Such a practice would be in contrast to business as usual – doing the definition and redefinition for the students. Teachers and parents can facilitate creativity by encouraging children to define and redefine *their own* personal problems (Renzulli, 2018). Adults can facilitate creative thinking by asking young people to choose their own topics for papers, projects, or presentations. Really, all individuals – children and adults alike – should choose their own ways of solving problems. Sometimes, the individuals will have to choose again if they discover that their original choice was mistaken. It is always fine to make mistakes, just so long as one learns from them.

Adults cannot always offer young people choices (e.g., of whether to take an examination). But offering choices to young people is the only way for the students to learn how to choose problems and methods of solution for themselves. Granting young people latitude in making choices helps them to develop both taste and good judgment. These elements are vital for creativity in people of all ages.

Somewhere along the line, everyone makes a mistake in choosing a project or in the procedures they select to complete the project. We need to keep in mind that an essential part of creativity is the analytic part, including learning to identify mistakes. Thus, we all need at times the opportunity to redefine our choices as necessary. Such redefinitions are essential parts of the creative process.

Challenging Assumptions

Sometimes it is not until some years later that society fully recognizes the limitations or possibly the errors of its assumptions and embraces the thoughts of the creative individual who defies the crowd (Simonton, 2019). The impetus of those creative individuals who question assumptions allows for cultural, technological, and other forms of advancement.

Teachers can model questioning assumptions by showing their students that what the students assume they know, for sure, they often actually do not know. Of course, students should not question every assumption they make. There are situations when it is worthwhile to question and try to reshape the environment, but there also are situations to adapt to it. Some creative individuals question so many things, and so often, that others eventually dismiss them. Everyone, even the most creative individuals, must learn which assumptions are worth challenging and which battles are worth the trouble. We need to learn to pick our battles wisely.

Mentors can aid students to further this talent for questioning assumptions by making questioning a part of their daily exchange with the students (Sternberg, 1987). It is far more important for students to figure out what questions to ask – and how to ask those questions – than to learn the answers to the questions. This is sometimes called "problem identification" (Reiter-Palmon and Robinson, 2009). Adults should not perpetuate the view that their primary role is to teach students a fixed set of facts. In most sciences, at least, what are believed to be "facts" often turn out not to be. Instead, teachers should help students to comprehend that what matters more than having facts is using those facts for good ends.

Society makes a pedagogical mistake when it emphasizes obtaining the so-called right answer. Instead, the emphasis should be on asking the "right" question, or at least, a good question (Sternberg, 1994; Csikszentmihalyi, 2013). The so-called good student is viewed as the one who rapidly provides the right answers to questions teachers ask. On this view, the expert in a given field unfortunately becomes an extension of the so-called expert student – the one who knows and can quickly spit back a lot of information. As John Dewey (1997) believed, how one thinks about issues often is more important and consequential in life than exactly what one thinks. For example, there is no one solution to the problem of global climate change. What matters is whether and how one thinks about achieving a solution. Schools should teach students how to ask important questions (questions that are worth answering and that are interesting) and reduce their emphasis on rote learning of facts. And they need to reorient their emphases in diverse domains, not just in the arts (Gardner, 2011), to emphasize creativity. Contemporary creativity research embraces a wide variety of distinct domains, from science to engineering to business to architectural design to the arts to athletics, all of which are ripe for creative investigation.

Selling Creative Ideas

We all would like to assume that our sparklingly innovative, fresh, and original ideas will sell themselves to anyone who wants to listen. But life experience teaches us that they do not sell themselves. Rather, creative ideas usually are viewed with suspicion, skepticism, and distrust (Sternberg and Lubart, 1995). Moreover, those who propose such creative ideas may be viewed as problematic individuals. Most people are comfortable with, and set in the ways that, they already think about things. They usually have a vested interest in their current perspectives on things. They try to justify beliefs, no matter how inadequate those beliefs may be. As a result, it can be extremely challenging to dislodge people from their current perspectives and ways of thinking.

At some point, we all must learn how to convince other people of the value of our original ideas (Sternberg, 1985). This persuading other people of our ideas is an important part of the practical element of creative thinking. When students or scholars present the results of a scientific project, for example, they need to show not only what they found but also show why the project makes an important contribution. Just as students need to learn to defend their ideas, so do teachers. Teachers may find themselves needing to justify their ideas about, and practices in, teaching, whether to their principal or some other supervisor. Thus, everyone needs to think about how to explain and justify their creative ideas to others.

Generating Ideas

Creative people utilize a **legislative style of thinking** (see Sternberg, 1997; Sternberg and Grigorenko, 2001): They like to come up with new ideas and to think in new ways. The environment for coming up with new ideas should be constructively, not destructively critical (see Beghetto, 2010). Students need to learn to recognize that some ideas are better than others. Today, that knowledge is especially important because the internet and social media have so blurred the line between truth and falsehood. Teachers and students should work together in identifying and encouraging creative new ideas. When ideas do not seem to be of much value, teachers should not merely criticize the ideas and leave it at that. Young people should contribute their thoughts on the limitations of novel ideas – sometimes older people don't see the value of an idea that may be obvious to younger people. Students also should receive praise for generating new ideas, regardless of whether some of the ideas seem at the time silly or unrelated to what was expected.

Knowledge As a Double-Edged Sword

Of course, one cannot think creatively in the absence of knowledge. One cannot go beyond the current state of knowledge if one is unaware of what that state is. Often, students have ideas that are creative, but only with respect to themselves. Sometimes, students' ideas are not viewed as creative with respect to the current state of a given field because others previously have had the same ideas. Individuals with a more substantial knowledge base can show creativity in ways that others who are still acquiring the basic knowledge of the field cannot yet do.

Knowledge is not always helpful to creativity, however. People with an expert level of knowledge can display tunnel vision, a narrowed field of thinking, and just plain entrenchment (Adelson, 1984; Frensch and Sternberg, 1989). In other words, experts can become trapped in a particular old way of thinking. They may become unable or unwilling to go beyond that way of thinking. The greatest risk occurs when people believe they know all there is to know. They then are unlikely ever to show truly meaningful creativity again.

The upshot is that teachers or any experts can learn as much from students as the students can learn from their teachers. On the one hand, teachers possess knowledge students lack; on the other hand, students often have a kind of mental flexibility that teachers lack – precisely because the students do not have the knowledge that their teachers have. The students are not stuck because they do not know enough to be stuck. Teachers can enhance their own creativity by learning from their students, just as the students learn from the teachers.

In most societies, those who are more senior, and thus who are more likely to be convinced of the truth of their ideas, land in positions of power and authority. Yet those senior people often are at risk for being less creative than the younger ones if they are too convinced of the rightness of their ideas. Leaders need to seek new ideas, not get stuck in old ones.

Identifying and Overcoming Obstacles

Buying low and selling high requires an individual to defy the crowd – to think independently. Individuals who defy the crowd – who think creatively – virtually inevitably confront resistance. The question is not whether they will confront obstacles – they will. Being creative is tantamount to confronting obstacles. Rather, the question is whether the creative individual has the courage to persevere in the face of obstacles, sometimes, severe ones (Simonton, 1994, 1997, 2004, 2009).

Why is it that so many individuals begin doing creative work, only to disappear from view later in their career? In some cases, the answer is that, at some point, they decide that their creative efforts are not worth the pushback. These efforts are not worth the punishments they encounter. In other cases, of course, people simply run out of ideas and do not take the steps they need to replenish their mental wellspring of ideas, such as trying working on something totally new and different. Seriously creative thinkers must be willing to pay a short-term cost because they realize that they may be able to make a positive difference over the longer term. But it may be a long time before the value of an individual's creative ideas is both seen and fully appreciated (Sternberg and Lubart, 1995). And that value may never be recognized during the individual's lifetime.

Parents and teachers can help students to prepare for rejection experiences by telling young people about obstacles that they, as adults, have faced. They also can point out that famous people have faced obstacles while trying to express their creativity; otherwise, students may come to believe that they alone are confronted by obstacles. Teachers will want to include accounts of colleagues who were not supportive, about students who received bad grades for their creative ideas, and about unwelcoming responses to ideas they may have considered to be among their very best ideas. Students need to learn about the large number of creative individuals whose ideas initially were rejected. Students also need to learn how to mitigate their concerns regarding what other people think is valuable. Creative people of any age always encounter others who think that their work is not valuable. That said, it often is challenging for students to reduce their reliance on the views of their peers.

When students or others try to surmount an obstacle, they should be rewarded for the attempt. It really does not matter whether or not they were successful. Having an entire class of students reflect on ways to tackle a particular challenge can start the class members thinking: What strategies can they employ to confront and ultimately surmount the obstacles that will face them in their lives? Some obstacles are inside themselves, such as self-sabotage or performance anxiety. Other obstacles are external to themselves, such as the negative opinions of others regarding their actions. Whether the obstacles are internal or external, to be creative, individuals must surmount the obstacles that inevitably will confront them.

Encouraging Prudent Risk-Taking

When creative people take on and resist the crowd, they incur risks, much as do people who are good investors and buy low and sell high. Some investments ultimately just do not work out. Furthermore, taking on the crowd typically results in one's experiencing the crowd's wrath. Nevertheless, creative individuals are willing to incur sensible risks and to produce ideas and products that others eventually may admire and regard as setting new trends. But of course, in taking risks, creative individuals have to be ready to fail. Moreover, they probably will fail multiple times.

A teacher should stress the importance of prudent risk-taking. To assist students in learning to take prudent risks, adults can encourage the students to take some prudent risks by giving them choices of activities rather than by pre-specifying the activities.

Almost every significant discovery or invention involved some degree of risk. Computers, televisions, video streaming, cell phones – almost every invention we use initially entailed risk. But if no one were willing to take the risk, none of the products would be available to us.

Relatively few students are eager to take risks in the setting of the school. Students learn early on that risk-taking can be costly. What schools seem most to value are perfect test scores reflecting that students have done exactly what they were told to do. Such work receives praise and opens up expanded future possibilities. Teachers may inadvertently send a message to students to "play things safe" when they ask questions with a limited set of allowable answers. In sum, teachers must not only encourage prudent risk-taking but also reward it in a highly visible way.

Tolerating Ambiguity

People often like to see things in black and white. On this view, things simply are either good or bad. For example, people often like to perceive a country as an ally or as an enemy. Or they perceive a colleague as a friend or foe. The challenge is that there usually are a lot of middle grounds in creative enterprises (Sternberg and Lubart, 1995). Scientists often need to do experiments and then, in a subsequent research project, modify them to make them work better. Artists often draw and redraw, design and redesign. All creative individuals need to learn to tolerate ambiguity and the uncertainty that results from it as they develop and refine their ideas (Zenasni, Besancon, and Lubart, 2008).

Creative ideas typically develop slowly and sometimes fitfully and even painfully over time. The idea-development stage of the creative process is often uncomfortable. Lacking time or the willingness to tolerate ambiguity, some creators first may reach a nonoptimal solution for whatever creative task they set out for themselves. When students have a near-miss topic for a paper or project, it is tempting for teachers and students alike to accept the near miss as good enough. But to support student creativity, teachers should encourage students to extend the period of time during which their ideas do not quite come together. This, in turn, requires students to start projects early rather than waiting until the last minute. Students must learn that ambiguity and discomfort are inevitable parts of living any kind of creative life. In the end, students will benefit from the development of their tolerance of ambiguity by generating better ideas.

Self-Efficacy

Creative people often come to a moment at which they feel as if no one believes in them or their work. (I reach this point fairly regularly, feeling that no one cares about, values, or in the least appreciates what I am doing.) Because creative and especially highly creative work often receives a frosty reception, at least initially, it is essential that creative individuals show **self-efficacy**, a belief in the value of their enterprise and in their ability to keep doing meaningful work (Bandura, 1997). Of course, there is no one for whom it can be said that every idea he or she has is a good idea. Rather, creative individuals have to believe that, in the long run, they have the skills and perseverance to make a positive difference, even if, in the short run, they sometimes cannot reach the solutions they look for.

The main limitation on what creative people can accomplish is what they think they are capable of accomplishing. All individuals are potential creators who could experience the joy that results from creating something new. But first, the individuals must believe in themselves and their potential (Bandura, 1997; Beghetto, 2006; Jaussi, Randel, and Dionne, 2007).

Finding What One Truly Loves to Do

To do optimal creative performance, individuals need to discover what excites them. Teachers (and parents!) need to keep in mind that what excites a student may not be what excites the teacher or parent. Individuals who truly excel in creative pursuits almost always are genuinely excited and even passionate about what they are doing.

Helping students discover what they truly enjoy doing is often a difficult and frustrating job. But it is the only way to pave a path for students to have a creative future.

Teachers inevitably meet students who are pursuing a particular career path not because that path represents what they want to do with their lives, but rather, because the path represents what their parents or some other authority figures expect or even require them to do. Although the students ultimately may do satisfactory work in that field, they are very unlikely to do their most creative work (Sternberg and Lubart, 1995; Amabile, 1996; Hennessey, 2019).

Delaying Gratification

Part of living creatively means that one is able to work on projects or tasks for long periods of time without some kind of reward – intrinsic, extrinsic, or a combination of both. Individuals need to learn, however, that rewards often are not immediate and that there can be substantial benefits to delaying gratification (Mischel, Shoda, and Rodriguez, 1989; Mischel, 2015). Unfortunately, in the short term, people who do creative work are often ignored or even penalized for doing it, which makes delay of gratification a key to creative enterprise.

The short-term focus of the majority of assignments given in schools does little or nothing to teach students how to delay gratification. Longer-term projects are clearly better in achieving this goal. But it is challenging for teachers to assign projects to be done at home if the teachers are not confident of the students' receiving parental involvement and support. Often, parents are busy or unavailable, and such support is not forthcoming.

An Environment That Fosters Creativity

Teachers, parents, and employers should provide an environment that nurtures creativity. The most compelling way to nurture creativity is to *role model creativity*. People best develop creativity not when they merely are told to be creative, but rather when they are shown how to be creative (Amabile, 1996; Amabile and Kramer, 2011). The teachers we remember best from our school days often are not those who were the best lecturers, but rather, those who best role modeled creative thinking.

Teachers and parents also can enhance creativity in students by encouraging the students to *cross-fertilize their thinking* across various disciplines (Sternberg and Williams, 2001). The traditional environment in the school, at least past the elementary-school level, often has separate teachers, classrooms, and classmates for each particular subject. Students may conclude that learning occurs in discrete compartments – the mathematics box, the language-arts box, the history box, the arts box, and the science box. Creative ideas and insights, however, often arise from the integration of material across diverse subject-matter areas.

Teaching students to cross-fertilize in their thinking and learning draws on the students' individual skills and interests, regardless of the particular subject matter at hand. If students are having difficulty in understanding mathematics, for example, teachers might ask the students to create mathematical test questions related to their personal special interests. For example, teachers might ask the baseball fan to devise geometry problems related to the most effective way to run the bases in baseball. The cross-fertilization of contexts may promote creative ideas because the student likes the topic (in this case, baseball). Working with an enjoyable topic also may lessen some of the anxiety arising from learning the geometry. Cross-fertilization can help motivate students who connect with subjects that are taught with concrete examples.

One way in which teachers can facilitate cross-fertilization in the classroom is by challenging students each to identify their individual academic strengths and weaknesses. Teachers then can challenge students to generate project ideas in an area of weakness based on ideas taken from an area of greater strength. For example, teachers can show students how they can transfer their interest in natural science to social studies by analyzing political trends in support of scientific research through federal agencies such as the US National Science Foundation or the US National Institutes of Health.

Students also need *time to think creatively*. People in many societies today are in a rush. They eat on the run and hurry from one class or appointment or meeting to the next. They value speed. Indeed, one way to communicate that someone is smart is to say that the person is *quick*. The emphasis is on speed. In the same way, many standardized tests comprise large numbers of multiple-choice problems that students need to answer during a very brief period of time. These problems, of course, involve little or, usually, no creativity at all.

Most creative insights, unlike solutions to test problems, do not come to us in a hurry. Creators need time to understand a problem, figure out how to solve it, and then generate a solution that satisfies them. Students need time to be creative. So does everyone else. If teachers or standardized testers pack too many questions into their tests or give their students more homework than the students reasonably can complete within the time they have, the teachers are not giving the students the time they need to think creatively.

Teachers further should both *instruct and assess for creativity*. Basically, it does not work to ask students to think creatively and then assess them only for factual recall or analytical thinking.

Teachers also must *reward creativity* in their students. It is one thing for teachers to talk about the need to be creative and another actually to reward creativity when students show it. Students expect teachers and other authority figures to require things to be done in a certain way. Surprise them!

Teachers also must *allow students to make mistakes and learn from them*. Buying low and selling high in the world of ideas always carries with it a certain risk. When all is said and done, many ideas never catch on simply because they are bad ideas. Creators need to make their mistakes to reach the ideas that are not only novel, but also compelling.

Although being creative usually involves making mistakes along the creative path, schools and the tests given in them tend often to be relatively unforgiving of mistakes. For example, teachers may mark errors on schoolwork with a large red X. When a student gives the wrong answer, some teachers criticize the student for not having understood or perhaps not even having read the material, whether these critiques are true or not. Classmates may then snicker. Through repeated experiences of this kind, students may learn that it is not acceptable to make mistakes. They then become afraid to risk the kind of independent and the sometimes-flawed thinking that ultimately leads to creativity and to making the world a better place.

When students make mistakes, teachers should challenge the students to reflect on and find value in their mistakes. Often, mistaken or ill-formed ideas contain within them the seeds of good ideas. Teachers in Japan often recognize this fact. In Japan, teachers often devote significant class time challenging students to analyze and learn from their mistakes in mathematical thinking. Enabling students to understand and explore mistakes can provide the students with an opportunity to learn and to grow.

A further aspect of teaching students to think creatively is to teach them *to take responsibility for both their successes and their failures.* Students who focus on blaming others, or even themselves, for their mistakes lose opportunities to learn because they are more concerned with assigning blame than with learning.

Teachers also should *encourage creative collaboration* (Sawyer, 2003, 2017). Creative performance sometimes is thought of as a solitary pursuit. We may imagine an artist painting in a solitary workshop, a scientist pondering in a lab, a writer slaving away alone in a studio, or a musician unendingly practicing in a small stuffy music-practice room. In reality, we mostly work in groups, whether we wish to or not. Collaboration can and often does produce creative work.

Students further should learn how *to imagine things from diverse viewpoints.* An essential aspect of maximizing the gains of collaborative creative work is to imagine oneself placed in other people's shoes. People can broaden their perspectives by imagining the world as others see it (Sternberg, 2010a).

Teachers also should help students recognize the importance of person-environment fit. Creativity always is judged with respect to a particular environment. What products are judged as creative results from an interaction between a person and the environment in which the person functions. The product that is viewed as creative in one time or place may be viewed as nothing special or even as pedestrian in another.

By developing an awareness of the need for person-environment fit, teachers can help prepare their students for selecting environments that are conducive to their achieving personally meaningful creative success, encourage students to develop this same awareness, evaluate their environments, and to select and match with environments in which people appreciate their skills.

In conclusion, creativity is in large part a decision – a set of attitudes toward life – that teachers and parents can encourage in students or in themselves. Students can learn through assessment (Brown, Roediger, and McDaniel, 2014), but are they learning? For the students to learn to be creative, the assessments must encourage the students to think creatively (Runco, 2013; Runco and Acar, 2019).

Prompts for Developing Creativity in Students

In this section, I first present some prompts to help develop creative thinking.

Students are creative when they (a) create, (b) discover, (c) invent, (d) imagine if ..., (e) predict, or (f) suppose that ... (Sternberg and Lubart, 1995; Sternberg and Williams, 1996;

Sternberg and Grigorenko, 2007; Sternberg, Jarvin, and Grigorenko, 2009, 2011). Consider some examples of instructional activities that help student develop their skills in creative thinking.

(a) Create an alternative ending to a novel you recently have read or a movie you recently have seen that presents a different way in which things might have come out for the main characters. (Literature)
(b) Write a dialogue between an American tourist from New York in Madrid and a Spanish woman he encounters on the street. (Spanish)
(c) Discover a mathematical formula that will help to solve all of the following mathematical word problems. (Mathematics)
(d) Imagine if the government of the United States keeps changing and advancing over the course of the next thirty years in more or less the same way it has been changing in recent times. What do you believe the government of the United States will be like in thirty years? (Government/Political Science)
(e) Suppose that you were to add a new musical instrument to a symphony orchestra. What might that instrument look like and sound like, and why? (Music)

Barriers to the Development of Creativity

There are many obstacles to teaching for creativity. Beghetto (2010, 2019) described some of the barriers that interfere with the development of creativity in classrooms (as well as in other places). These include (a) convergent teaching practices, (b) suppression of creative expression, (c) pressures on teachers to teach in conventional ways, (c) accountability mandates, and (d) "either-or" thinking, whereby teachers think that if they teach for creativity, they are not teaching students to learn the material. Beghetto also points out flaws in teachers' thinking about creativity. First, they may confuse originality with creativity, believing that any novel idea is creative. Second, they may have a "Big-C" bias, believing that creativity is what people such as Albert Einstein or Frida Kahlo do, not what students in a classroom can do. Third, they may have a "product bias," believing that creativity must result in a tangible product. These biases make it hard for them to teach effectively for creative thinking.

I believe the largest barrier to teaching for creativity is quite simple: Teachers do not know how to do it and have no incentive to learn. They have not learned how to teach for creativity in their training, and the standardized tests given to students on the basis of which the teachers, not just the students, will be evaluated place no emphasis on creativity. If we want teachers to teach for creativity, we have to remove the barriers. We could start by teaching teachers how to teach for creativity. Then we could encourage rather than discourage creativity on standardized tests.

Finally, it is important to temper creativity with **wisdom**, which is the use of one's knowledge and skills to attain a common good over the long- as well as the short-term.

Creativity can be used for good ends or bad (Cropley et al., 2010; Gascon and Kaufman, 2010; Sternberg, 2010b). Creativity in itself is morally and ethically neutral. It can be an enormous force for good, but it also can be a force for evil. It is up to teachers to ensure that when they teach for creativity, they teach it in such a way that it will become a force for good rather than for evil.

CONCLUSION

This chapter discusses how people can enhance their creativity. It opens with a discussion of what creativity is and why it is important. Then the chapter discusses some programs for teaching creative thinking, such as the CoRT program and Synectics. Then the chapter discusses specific techniques for enhancing creativity, such as developing willingness to defy the crowd, defy oneself, and defy the Zeitgeist. Creative people have to be willing to redefine problems, or see those problems in new ways, and to tolerate ambiguity, or to realize that solutions to creative problems often do not come quickly and can be shrouded in mystery before they finally become apparent. Then I discuss prompts that can be used for developing creativity. Finally, I discuss some barriers to enhancing creativity, such as the use of standardized tests that often do not measure and may actively discourage creativity. I also discuss how to overcome these barriers.

My Research Contribution

My colleagues and I have questioned whether conventional standardized tests that are used for admission to undergraduate and graduate programs, including programs in the natural and social sciences, adequately measure the skills that are actually involved in scientific thinking, or whether they measure instead skills that at best are only marginally relevant in some way (Sternberg, Todhunter, and Sternberg, 2017; Sternberg and Sternberg, 2018; Sternberg, Wong, and Sternberg, 2019). To this end, we developed tests that measure what we and others believe to be the skills actually involved in scientific thinking, in particular, hypothesis generation, experiment generation, and drawing conclusions.

In our series of studies, we presented students with scientific-reasoning problems that emphasized the need to think creatively, particularly, in generating alternative hypotheses and generating experiments. In the former test, participants were presented with a hypothetical situation and a hypothesis about why that situation occurred as it did. The students then had to generate alternative hypotheses as to why it might have come out in the way it did. In the latter test, participants were told that a particular student wanted to test a scientific hypothesis but did not know how. The participants were asked to design an experiment to test the hypothesis. In a third test, students were presented with an experiment and a conclusion; they were asked whether the conclusion was scientifically defensible and why or why not. In one study, participants also

(cont.)

saw professors teach some lessons, and the participants had to state what was wrong with the way the lessons were being taught.

The results were consistent across studies. Our tests of scientific reasoning correlated well with each other and, statistically, formed a factor. Standardized tests also correlated with each other and, statistically, formed a factor, or unified source of individual differences. But the scientific-reasoning tests showed only mixed and sometimes negative correlations with the standardized tests. In other words, the standardized tests were measuring reasoning skills other than those involved in scientific reasoning.

The research is important, we believe, both in terms of who is admitted to various kinds of programs but also in terms of enhancing creativity. Generating hypotheses, generating experiments, and drawing conclusions are all *learned skills*. Schools should be teaching these skills in addition just to scientific knowledge so that students are in a better position later to become able scientists themselves, should they so choose.

Critical/Creative Thinking Questions

1. What kinds of steps could you take now to improve your own creativity?
2. Do standardized tests in any way encourage or discourage creativity? If so, how?
3. What are some of the main obstacles to creative thinking?
4. Should developing creativity be taught as a separate course (e.g., CoRT) or infused directly into already existing instruction in classrooms?
5. In what ways does creativity reflect an attitude toward one's life and one's work rather than merely some kind of inborn ability?

GLOSSARY

brainstorming: A technique that involves giving free rein to the imagination and not criticizing ideas so as to encourage people to think divergently without fear of criticism.

creativity: Involves the generation of ideas that are novel, surprising, and compelling.

defy the crowd: Asking how what everyone else believes may be wrong.

defy oneself: Be willing to challenge and ultimately to let go of one's past ideas or beliefs in order to think in novel and useful ways.

defy the Zeitgeist: Be willing to identify, question and, if necessary, reject common-cultural beliefs that one may not even recognize one has and others have as well.

lateral thinking: Thinking about problems in new and unusual ways by making unusual associations between concepts.

legislative style of thinking: Liking to come up with new ideas.

redefining a problem: Requires a shift in perspective whereby one perceives an old problem in an entirely different way.

self-efficacy: A belief in the value of their enterprise and in their ability to keep doing meaningful work.

six thinking hats: Six different ways of thinking about problems, for example, objectively versus emotionally versus cautiously.

synectics: Emphasizes the importance of unconscious thought, emotion, and the irrational in creativity.

wisdom: The use of one's knowledge and skills to attain a common good over the long- as well as the short-term.

REFERENCES

Adelson, B. (1984). When Novices Surpass Experts: The Difficulty of a Task May Increase with Expertise. *Journal of Experimental Psychology: Learning, Memory, and Cognition, 10*(3) 483–495.

Amabile, T. (1996). *Creativity in Context: Update to the Social psychology of Creativity*. Boulder: Westview.

Amabile, T., and Kramer, S. (2011). *The Progress Principle: Using Small Wins to Ignite Joy, Engagement and Creativity at Work*. Cambridge, MA: Harvard Business Review Press.

Baas, M. (2019). In the Mood for Creativity. In J. C. Kaufman and R. J. Sternberg (Eds.), *The Cambridge Handbook of Creativity*, 2nd ed. (pp. 257–272).

Bandura, A. (1997). *Self-Efficacy: The Exercise of Control*. New York: Worth.

Beghetto, R. A. (2006). Creative Self-Efficacy: Correlates in Middle and Secondary Students. *Creativity Research Journal, 18*, 447–457.

  (2010). Creativity in the Classroom. In J. C. Kaufman and R. J. Sternberg (Eds.), *The Cambridge Handbook of Creativity* (pp. 447–463). New York: Cambridge University Press.

  (2019). Creativity in Classrooms. In J. C. Kaufman and R. J. Sternberg (Eds.), *The Cambridge Handbook of Creativity*, 2nd ed. (pp. 587–606). New York: Cambridge University Press.

Brown, P. C., Roediger, H. L. III, and McDaniel, M. A. (2014). *Make It Stick: The Science of Successful Learning*. Cambridge, MA: Belknap.

Covington, M. V., Crutchfield, R. S., Davies, L., and Olton, R. M. (1974). *The Productive Thinking Program: A Course in Learning to Think*. Columbus: Merrill.

Cropley, D. H., Cropley, A. J., Kaufman, J. C., and Runco, M. A. (Eds.), *The Dark Side of Creativity*. New York: Cambridge University Press.

Csikszentmihalyi, M. (2013). *Creativity: Flow and the Psychology of Discovery and Invention*. New York: Harper Perennial.

Dai, D. Y., and Sternberg, R. J. (Eds.). (2004). *Motivation, Emotion, and Cognition: Integrative Perspectives on Intellectual Functioning and Development*. Mahwah: Lawrence Erlbaum Associates.

Davidson, J. E., and Sternberg, R. J. (Eds.). (2003). *The Psychology of Problem Solving*. New York: Cambridge University Press.

DeBono, E. (1973). *CoRT thinking*. Blanford: Direct Educational Services.

  (1999) *Six Thinking Hats*. New York: Back Bay Books.

Dewey, J. (1997). *Experience and Education*. New York: Free Press.

Frensch, P. A., and Sternberg, R. J. (1989). Expertise and Intelligent Thinking: When Is It Worse to Know Better? In R. J. Sternberg (Ed.), *Advances in the Psychology of Human Intelligence*, vol. 5 (pp. 157–188). Hillsdale: Lawrence Erlbaum Associates.

Gardner, H. (1983). *Frames of Mind: The Theory of Multiple Intelligences*. New York: Basic.
(2011). *Creating Minds*. New York: Basic Books.

Gascon, L. D., and Kaufman, J. C. (2010). Both Sides of the Coin?: Personality, Deviance and Creative Behavior. In D. H. Cropley, A. J. Cropley, J. C. Kaufman, and M. A. Runco (Eds.), *The Dark Side of Creativity* (pp. 235–254). New York: Cambridge University Press.

Gordon, W. J. J. (1961). *Synectics: The Development of Creative Capacity*. New York: Harper and Row.
(1966). *The Metaphorical Way of Learning and Knowing*. Cambridge, MA: Porpoise Books.
(1981). *The New Art of the Possible: The Basic Course in Synectics*. Cambridge, MA: Porpoise Books.

Hennessey, B. A. (2019). Motivation and Creativity. In J. C. Kaufman and R. J. Sternberg (Eds.), *The Cambridge Handbook of Creativity*, 2nd ed. (pp. 374–395). New York: Cambridge University Press.

Isaksen, S. G., and Treffinger, D. J. (1985). *Creative Problem Solving: The Basic Course*. Buffalo: Bearly.

Ivcevic, Z., and Hoffmann, J. (2019). Emotions and Creativity: From Process to Person and Product. In J. C. Kaufman and R. J. Sternberg (Eds.), *The Cambridge Handbook of Creativity*, 2nd ed. (pp. 273–295). New York: Cambridge University Press.

Jaussi, K. S., Randel, A. E., and Dionne, S. D. (2007). I Am, I Think I Can, and I Do: The Role of Personal Identity, Self-Efficacy, and Cross-Application of Experiences in Creativity at Work. *Creativity Research Journal*, *19*, 247–258.

Kaufman, J. C. (2018). What Creativity Can Be, and What Creativity Can Do. In R. J. Sternberg and J. C. Kaufman (Eds.), *The Nature of Human Creativity* (pp. 125–134). New York: Cambridge University Press.

Kaufman, J. C., and Sternberg, R. J. (Eds.) (2010). *The Cambridge Handbook of Creativity*. New York: Cambridge University Press.
(2019). *The Cambridge Handbook of Creativity*, 2nd ed. New York: Cambridge University Press.

Lubart, T. I., Glaveanu, V. P., De Vries, H., Camargo, A., and Storme, M. (2019). Cultural Perspectives on Creativity. In J. C. Kaufman and R. J. Sternberg (Eds.), *The Cambridge Handbook of Creativity*, 2nd ed. (pp. 421–447). New York: Cambridge University Press.

Lubart, T. I., and Sternberg, R. J. (1995). An Investment Approach to Creativity: Theory and Data. In S. M. Smith, T. B. Ward, and R. A. Finke (Eds.), *The Creative Cognition Approach* (pp. 269–302). Cambridge, MA: MIT Press.

Mansfield, R. S., Bussé, T. V., and Krepelka, E. J. (1978). *The Psychology of Creativity and Discovery*. Chicago: Nelson-Hall.

Meadow, A., Parnes, S. J., and Reese, H. (1959). Influence of Brainstorming Instruction and Problem Sequence on a Creative Problem Solving Test. *Journal of Applied Psychology*, *43*, 413–416.

Mischel, W. (2015). *The Marshmallow Test: Why Self-Control Is the Engine of Success*. New York: Back Bay Books.

Mischel, W., Shoda, Y., and Rodriguez, M. L. (1989). Delay of Gratification in Children. *Science*, *244*, 933–938.

Nickerson, R. S. (1999). Enhancing Creativity. In R. J. Sternberg (Ed.), *Handbook of Creativity* (pp. 392–430). New York: Cambridge University Press.

Niu, W. and Sternberg, R. J. (2002). Contemporary Studies on the Concept of Creativity: The East and the West. *Journal of Creative Behavior*, *36*, 269–288.

O'Hara, L. A., and Sternberg, R. J. (2000–2001). It Doesn't Hurt to Ask: Effects of Instructions to Be Creative, Practical, or Analytical on Essay-Writing Performance and Their Interaction with Students' Thinking Styles. *Creativity Research Journal*, *13*(2), 197–210.

Osborn, A. (1953). *Applied Imagination*. New York: Scribner's.

(1963). *Applied Imagination: Principles and Procedures of Creative Thinking*. New York: Scribner's.

Parnes, S. J. (1981). *Magic of Your Mind*. Buffalo: Bearly.

Parnes, S. J., and Meadow, A. (1963). Development of Individual Creative Talent. In C. W. Taylor and F. Barron (Eds.), *Scientific Creativity: Its Recognition and Development* (pp. 311–320). New York: Wiley.

Reiter-Palmon, R., Mitchell, K. S., and Royston, R. (2019). Improving Creativity in Organizational Settings. In J. C. Kaufman and R. J. Sternberg (Eds.), *The Cambridge Handbook of Creativity* (pp. 515–545). New York: Cambridge University Press.

Reiter-Palmon, R., and Robinson, E. J. (2009). Problem Identification and Construction: What Do We Know, What Is the Future? *Psychology of Aesthetics, Creativity, and the Arts*, *3*, 43–47.

Renzulli, J. S. (2018). The Malleability of Creativity: A Career in Helping Students Discover and Nurture their Creativity. In R. J. Sternberg and J. C. Kaufman (Eds.), *The Nature of Human Creativity* (pp. 209–223). New York: Cambridge University Press.

Runco, M. A. (2013). *Divergent Thinking and Creative Potential*. New York: Hampton Press.

Runco, M. A., and Acar, S. (2019). Divergent Thinking. In J. C. Kaufman and R. J. Sternberg (Eds.), *The Cambridge Handbook of Creativity*, 2nd. ed. (pp. 224–254). New York: Cambridge University Press.

Sawyer, R. K. (2003). *Group Creativity: Music, Theater, Collaboration*. New York: Psychology Press.

(2017). *Group Genius: The Creative Power of Collaboration*. New York: Basic Books.

Simonton, D. K. (1994). *Greatness: Who Makes History and Why*. New York: Guilford.

(1997). Creative Productivity: A Predictive and Explanatory Model of Career Trajectories and Landmarks. *Psychological Review*, *104*, 66–89.

(1999a). *Origins of Genius: Darwinian Perspectives on Creativity*. New York: Oxford University Press.

(1999b). Talent and Its Development: An Emergenic and Epigenetic Model. *Psychological Review*, *106*, 435–457.

(2004). *Creativity in Science: Chance, Logic, Genius, and Zeitgeist*. New York: Cambridge University Press.

(2009). *Genius 101*. New York: Springer.

(2019). Creativity's Role in Society. In J. C. Kaufman and R. J. Sternberg (Eds.), *The Cambridge Handbook of Creativity*, 2nd ed. (pp. 462–480). New York: Cambridge University Press.

Sternberg, R. J. (1985). Teaching Critical Thinking, Part 1: Are We Making Critical Mistakes? *Phi Delta Kappan*, *67*, 194–198.

(1987). Questioning and Intelligence. *Questioning Exchange*, *1*, 11–14.

(1994). Answering Questions and Questioning Answers. *Phi Delta Kappan*, *76*(2), 136–138.

(1997). *Thinking Styles*. New York: Cambridge University Press.

(2003). The Development of Creativity As a Decision-Making Process. In R. K. Sawyer, V. John-Steiner, S. Moran, R. J. Sternberg, D. H. Feldman, J. Nakamura, and M. Csikszentmihalyi, (Eds.), *Creativity and Development* (pp. 91–138). New York: Oxford University Press.

(2010a). *College Admissions for the 21st century*. Cambridge, MA: Harvard University Press.

(2010b). The Dark Side of Creativity and How to Combat It. In D. H. Cropley, A. J. Cropley, J. C. Kaufman, and M. A. Runco (Eds.), *The Dark Side of Creativity* (pp. 316–328). New York: Cambridge University Press.

(2017). Creativity, Intelligence, and Culture. In V. P. Glăveanu (Ed.), *Palgrave Handbook of Creativity and Culture* (pp. 77–99). London: Palgrave.

(2018a). The Triangle of Creativity. In R. J. Sternberg and J. C. Kaufman (Eds.), *The Nature of Human Creativity* (pp. 318–334). New York: Cambridge University Press.

(2018b). A Triangular Theory of Creativity. *Psychology of Aesthetics, Creativity, and the Arts, 12*, 50–67.

Sternberg, R. J., and Grigorenko, E. L. (2001). A Capsule History of Theory and Research on Styles. In R. J. Sternberg, and L. F. Zhang (Eds.), *Perspectives on Thinking, Learning and Cognitive Styles* (pp. 1–21). Mahwah: Lawrence Erlbaum Associates.

(2007). *Teaching for Successful Intelligence*, 2nd ed. Thousand Oaks: Corwin Press

Sternberg, R. J., Jarvin, L., and Grigorenko, E. L. (2009). *Teaching for Wisdom, Intelligence, Creativity, and Success*. Thousand Oaks: Corwin.

(2011). *Explorations of the Nature of Giftedness*. New York: Cambridge University Press.

Sternberg, R. J., and Lubart, T. I. (1995). *Defying the Crowd: Cultivating Creativity in a Culture of Conformity*. New York: Free Press.

Sternberg, R. J., and Sternberg, K. (2017). Measuring Scientific Reasoning for Graduate Admissions in Psychology and Related Disciplines. *Journal of Intelligence*. www.mdpi.com/2079-3200/5/3/29/pdf.

Sternberg, R. J., Sternberg, K., and Todhunter, R. J. E. (2017). Measuring Reasoning about Teaching for Graduate Admissions in Psychology and Related Disciplines. *Journal of Intelligence*. www.mdpi.com/2079-3200/5/4/34/pdf.

Sternberg, R. J., and Williams, W. M. (1996). *How to Develop Student Creativity*. Alexandria: Association for Supervision and Curriculum Development.

(2001). Teaching for Creativity: Two Dozen Tips. In R. D. Small, and A. P. Thomas (Eds.), *Plain Talk about Education* (pp. 153–165). Covington: Center for Development and Learning.

Sternberg, R. J., Wong, C. H., and Sternberg, K. (2019). The Relation of Tests of Scientific Reasoning to Each Other and to Tests of Fluid Intelligence. *Journal of Intelligence, 7*(3), 20. doi.org/10.3390/jintelligence7030020.

Treffinger, D. J., McEwen, P., and Wittig, C. (1989). *Using Creative Problem Solving in Inventing*. Honeoye: Center for Creative Learning.

Zenasni, F., Besançon, M., and Lubart, T. (2008). Creativity and Tolerance of Ambiguity: An Empirical Study. *Journal of Creative Behavior, 42*, 61–73.

Index